www.wadsworth.com

wadsworth.com is the World Wide Web site for Wadsworth and is your direct source to dozens of online resources.

At *wadsworth.com* you can find out about supplements, demonstration software, and student resources. You can also send email to many of our authors and preview new publications and exciting new technologies.

wadsworth.com
Changing the way the world learns®

✳

Women, Prison, & Crime

Women, Prison, & Crime

SECOND EDITION

JOYCELYN M. POLLOCK
Southwest Texas State University

Australia • Canada • Mexico • Singapore • Spain • United Kingdom • United States

WADSWORTH

THOMSON LEARNING™

Executive Editor, Criminal Justice: Sabra Horne
Development Editor: Terri Edwards
Assistant Editor: Dawn Mesa
Editorial Assistant: Lee McCracken
Marketing Manager: Jennifer Somerville
Marketing Assistant: Neena Chandra
Project Manager: Sandra Craig

Print/Media Buyer: Christopher Burnham
Permissions Editor: Robert Kauser
Production and Composition: Buuji, Inc.
Copy Editor: Linda Ireland
Cover Designer: Laurie Anderson
Cover Image: © PhotoDisc 2001
Printer: Webcom, Ltd.

Printed in Canada
1 2 3 4 5 6 7 05 04 03 02 01

Excepts on the following pages are from Barbara Owen's *"In the Mix": Struggle and Survival in a Women's Prison*: 48, 69, 71, 72, 73, 109, 130, 138, 140, 143. Copyright permission was granted by State University of Albany Press. All rights reserved.

Wadsworth Thomson Learning
10 Davis Drive
Belmont, CA 94002-3098
USA

For more information about our products, contact us:
Thomson Learning Academic Resource Center
1-800-423-0563
http://www.wadsworth.com

International Headquarters
Thomson Learning
International Division
290 Harbor Drive, 2nd Floor
Stamford, CT 06902-7477
USA

UK/Europe/Middle East/South Africa
Thomson Learning
Berkshire House
168-173 High Holborn
London WC1V 7AA
United Kingdom

Asia
Thomson Learning
60 Albert Street, #15-01
Albert Complex
Singapore 189969

Canada
Nelson Thomson Learning
1120 Birchmount Road
Toronto, Ontario M1K 5G4
Canada

To Eric and Gregory

Contents

Foreword

As editor of the *Wadsworth Series on Contemporary Issues in Crime and Justice,* I am delighted to announce the publication of the second edition of Joycelyn Pollock's *Women, Prison, and Crime.* The *Contemporary Issues* series is devoted to furthering our understanding of important issues in crime and justice by providing an in-depth treatment of topics that are neglected or insufficiently discussed in today's textbooks. *Women, Prison, and Crime* is an excellent example of the kind of work the series was designed to foster.

It is common knowledge that the criminal justice system has been growing for over two decades. Most people also know that women make up a small minority of felony offenders—about 20 percent of felons, and about 9 percent of prisoners. What is not well known is that for more than a decade, the growth rate of female offenders has been higher than that of male offenders. And among victims, women are more numerous than they are among offenders: about 40 percent of the victims of violent crime are women.

This is an important book for two reasons. First, it deals with a topic of growing importance—the incarcerated woman. While women make up a minority of prisoners, for years their numbers have been growing at a faster rate than those for men, to the extent that most states now have significant difficulty expanding their correctional capacity fast enough to handle the growth. Second, this book pulls together a myriad of studies to provide the single, most comprehensive treatment of the problem of women in confinement that is now available.

It is a cliche to say that men and women are different, whether we are saying this about everyday men and women or those who are confined. Like all cliches, this one both misleads yet holds truth. Among those who are confined, men and women differ in important respects, but they also have much in common. Sorting out the differences and understanding what makes the separate study of female prisoners a worthwhile project is a vital objective of this book. At the same time, knowing how prison policy affects the prospects of both men and women, regardless of gender, builds our understanding of the results, mostly failures, of our approach to treating the confined. This, too, is an aim of Professor Pollock's text.

The irony is that female prisoners have suffered from *both* sides of the comparison to men. For many years, women were thought of as "the gentler sex," and this stereotype tended to excuse all manner of neglect of the female prisoner's needs as an average adult who sought social and personal fortune, instead pigeonholing her into feminine gender roles. This was one of the reasons why a number of critics called for correctional systems to treat men and women equally, what became a call for parity. But the move for equal treatment of female prisoners has not always been good for women, because when programming was cut back nationally for men in favor of harsher prison regimes, the same trend began to appear for women—a kind of a parity of pain.

Thus, we face a conundrum: To deal with female offenders with regard for their human needs, we must provide services and programs especially suitable to their needs, but to treat them fairly, we must subject them to a program of correctional services that is neither appreciably less than nor more than that provided to men. How do we solve this dilemma?

This book shows the way. It begins with a careful analysis of the failures of the past, so that we may understand the challenges for the present. It then shows why the problem of difference versus parity is in some ways a false dichotomy, because women who go to prison have different criminal etiology and thus different correctional needs. This "reality of difference," as Professor Pollock puts it, calls for correctional programming that is sensitive to the needs of female inmates, many of which are quite different from the kinds of needs that dominate a male prison population, but some of which are no different. This introduces a rich discussion of critical correctional issues in the design and administration of correctional programming for female prisoners.

The story does not stop there, as Professor Pollock ably shows. In separate chapters on the legal, cultural, and administrative issues in women's prisons, she demonstrates that the range of issues encountered in the study of confined women is broad and complex. A chapter on comparative studies of incarceration of women in other countries equally serves to show that questions about the incarceration of women do not end at our country's borders.

This book is more than a study of women in confinement. It is, in fact, a forceful argument for a compelling new vision of what is possible, if we decide we want to treat women behind bars with fairness and dignity. It will change preconceptions about the world of women in correctional settings.

That is why I am so pleased to announce this new edition, and welcome its renewal in the *Wadsworth Series on Contemporary Issues in Crime and Justice*. This book illustrates so well the kind of work we are trying to make available. *Women, Prison, and Crime* is a significant work, and some of you who read it will be called to accept its challenge for a more fair, more just correctional system for women. This, I am sure, will be the book's most valuable legacy— the future actions of those who have learned from its pages.

Todd R. Clear
New York City
May 2001

Preface

Since the first edition of this book was published in 1990, there has been a tremendous increase in the number of published articles and books about women in prison. All are remarkably similar in their descriptions of the women found in prison, the histories of these women and their problems and needs. This book provides no surprising or groundbreaking "new" facts regarding women in prison. The stories are depressingly similar and frustratingly the same; every study, survey, and expert recites the same litany of problems. Women in prison are more likely than either men in prison or men or women in the general population to have been victims of sexual and physical abuse as children and adults. They are likely to use drugs and have their lives and their children's lives ruined by drugs. They are likely to have families marked by alcoholism, addiction, and criminality. They have few skills and even less education. Their outlook and potential are not positive.

Despite the common knowledge among academics and practitioners that women in prison are neither dangerous nor even very criminal, there has been little change in the nation's appetite for incarceration. In fact, numbers increase so rapidly that published "facts" are outdated before they even reach final publication. In this text I wrote that the number of women incarcerated was about 85,000, which was true in 1998, the date of the published figures available at the time. The most recent news release from the Bureau of Justice Statistics (*BJS News Release*, May 1, 2001) states that at mid-year in 2000, 92,688 women were incarcerated in state and federal prisons. The increase was 3.6 percent over 1999 figures. This percentage increase is quite small compared to the average 8.1 percent increase that was typical throughout the 1990s. Maybe we are finally realizing that incarcerating every drug offender and property criminal is not an effective or cost-efficient solution to the problems of drugs and crime in this society.

With the almost decade-long trend of decreasing crime rates, and a relatively healthy economy, we have the opportunity and ability to rethink the "crime problem" and solutions to it. We need to take a hard look at our pattern of using prison sentences instead of community alternatives, imposing increasing sentence lengths, and passing draconian "habitual sentence" laws for repeat offenders. We may find that people respond better to drug treatment in the community than to a prison sentence—that they are less likely to continue comitting crimes when their economic, social, and psychological environments change. We may find that a dollar spent on helping the child of a prison inmate reaps benefits far in excess of the dollars spent on prisons and correctional officers. Solutions to the problems of violence in the home, drug addiction, economic desperation, and poor parenting are neither simple nor quick.

We know that the best crime prevention occurs in early childhood. It is with children that we have the best chance of effective intervention, and it is toward children that we should allocate and commit scarce resources. Each child, however, is a product of parents. We have to help both men and women become better parents; otherwise, we will reap the consequences.

ACKNOWLEDGMENTS

Every author has many people to thank, and I am no exception, though I hesitate to present a list because inevitably I will forget someone very important who should have been included. I thank the anonymous reviewers of the first edition, as well as the number of people throughout the years who have commented on and/or criticized the book. I thank Linda Ireland, the copyeditor, and the numerous people who have been involved in transforming the manuscript into this book. Sabra Horne, the general editor at ITP, deserves recognition as the taskmaster without whom many fewer books in criminal justice would exist. (Students might prefer not to thank her for that!)

I also thank my community of colleagues. They have shaped my thinking on these topics and provided me with not only food for thought, but also facts, data, and research findings. Although this list is by no means complete, I thank Barbara Owen, Barbara Bloom, Meda Chesney-Lind, Dorothy Mc-Clellan, Merry Morash, Angela Browne, Pat Carlen, Russ Immarigeon, Alida Merlo, and Nicole Rafter. I also have benefited greatly and learned from practitioners in the field, such as Sterling O'Ran in California, Elaine Lord in New York, and Ellen Halbert in Texas. My experience has shown that many caring and committed individuals have tried, and are still trying, to live up to the promise and philosophy of the field of "corrections." I hope they never give up.

Joycelyn M. Pollock
May 2001

1

Introduction
to Women's Prisons:
Differences
and Disparities

The first sentence of the 1990 edition of this book read: "Three basic facts characterize women's institutions. First, they are smaller than most prisons for males. Second, there are fewer of them. Third, they are different from prisons for males" (Pollock-Byrne, 1990: 1). Ten years later, these statements are still true; however, it must be added that the average women's prison has grown larger—much larger in some states, with some women's prisons housing over 1,000 women. Second, while there are still fewer prisons for women than for men, building has been proceeding at an unprecedented rate. The percentage increase of incarceration of women has surpassed that of men for over 10 years now, and this increase has caught many correctional systems by surprise. Finally, while women's prisons are still "different," the trend in the last decade has been to make them the same. *Parity* has been defined as *uniformity*, and that has become the mantra for the administration of women's prisons, and especially of staff who have been trained in or are coming from prisons for men, or who transfer back and forth between prisons for women and men. The positive and negative effects of this trend will be discussed in the following chapters.

This chapter examines the tremendous increases that have occurred across the country in the number of women sentenced to state and federal prisons. Possible reasons for the increased number of women in prison are explored, and the number and range of women's prisons across the country are briefly examined. Finally, the research on female prisoners is reviewed, and the questions left unanswered from the 1990 edition of this text are explored.

INCREASING NUMBERS, INCREASING CONTROVERSY

In the past we have incarcerated women reluctantly, hesitantly, and with no very clear mandate for what to do with them once they are incarcerated. Chapman (1980) described the rate of imprisonment as peaking in 1931–1935, during the Depression, and in 1961–1963, when the country underwent an economic recession. The low numbers of the early 1970s continued to rise unabated until fairly recently. As we enter the new century, some jurisdictions have begun to show a slight decrease in their rate of increase.

The percentage of women in prison is still miniscule compared to the large numbers of men behind bars; however, there has been a dramatic increase in the number of women involved at every stage of the criminal justice process. Near the end of the 1990s, women made up 20 percent of all arrests, a little over 10 percent of all jail inmates, just under 21 percent of community correction clients, and just over 6 percent of prison inmates (about 85,000). About one in every 113 men and one in every 1,754 women were sentenced prisoners under the jurisdiction of state or federal authorities (Camp and Camp, 1997: 1).

In 1988, the Bureau of Justice Statistics (BJS) reported that the number of women in prisons had increased at a faster rate than men every year since 1981 (BJS, 1989). That trend continued through the 1990s. The percentage increase, for instance, between 1976 (with 11,000 women imprisoned) and 1986 (with 26,000) was 138 percent (for men it was 94 percent) (BJS, 1989). The percentage increase in the number of women sent to prison between 1990 (with 44,065) and 1998 (with 84,427) was 92 percent (compared to 67 percent for men). States with the largest average yearly percentage increases included North Dakota at 16.7 percent, Montana at 15.9 percent, West

Virginia at 13.6 percent, and New Hampshire at 12.9 percent. The smallest percentage increases were reported by New York at 3.8 percent, Vermont at 2.8 percent, and Michigan at 2.5 percent; the District of Columbia's population actually went down (−2.9 percent) (Beck and Mumola, 1999). During 1998, the number of female prisoners rose by 6.5 percent (compared to 4.7 percent for men) (BJS, 1999a; Beck and Mumola, 1999). Women are receiving longer sentences than in years past; the number of women with sentences of over 20 years doubled between 1983 and 1993 (Ryan and McCabe, 1997: 30). (See Table 1.1.)

In 1990, state and federal prisons housed 44,065 women; today that number exceeds 85,000. Incarceration rates vary across states, however. The states with the lowest incarceration rates (i.e., Maine and Vermont at 9 per 100,000 people) evidently use imprisonment in a very different way from the jurisdictions with the highest incarceration rates (i.e., District of Columbia at 173 per 100,000) (BJS, 1999a; Beck and Mumola, 1999: 10) (see Table 1.2).

The increase in the number of incarcerated women does not appear to be directly related to an increase in criminality or arrests. Chapman (1980) pointed out that in 1970, 45 percent of convicted female murderers were sent to prison, whereas in 1975, 73 percent were sent; in 1970, only 25 percent of women convicted of robbery were sent to prison, whereas in 1975, 61 percent were sent; and only 15 percent of women convicted of writing worthless checks were sent to prison in 1970, but in 1975, 33 percent were incarcerated. Simon and Landis (1991) found that 54 percent of all women convicted of felonies in 1978 went to prison, but 79 percent of women convicted of felonies were sent to prison in 1987. Raeder also noted that probation is used less often as a sentencing option than in the past; in 1971, about 66 percent of women sentenced for federal crimes were given probation, while in 1991, only 28 percent of federally sentenced women received probation (1993b: 927).

The decision to incarcerate became even more prevalent during the 1990s (see Table 1.3). In fact, total arrests for women between 1987 and 1996 increased by 31.4 percent, but the incarceration rate for this same time period increased by 159 percent (Chesney-Lind, 1998: 67).

Table 1.1 Trend in Incarceration Rate/per 100,000

Year	All Women	White Women	Black Women
1990	31	19	117
1992	33	20	136
1994	45	26	169
1996	51	30	185
1998	57	34	212[a]

[a]Projections.

SOURCE: Bureau of Justice Statistics, 1999, *Special Report: Women Offenders* (Washington, D.C.: U.S. Department of Justice), p. 10.

Table 1.2 Female Inmate Populations, 1998

Jurisdiction	Actual Number	Rate per 100,000
States (total)	75,241	51
Federal	9,186	5
Total	84,427	57
States with at least 1,000 women prisoners:		
Alabama	1,525	64
Arizona	1,780	66
California	11,694	67
Colorado	1,070	53
Connecticut	1,357	43
Florida	3,526	45
Georgia	2,474	61
Illinois	2,646	43
Indiana	1,198	39
Kentucky	1,046	51
Louisiana	2,126	94
Maryland	1,140	39
Michigan	2,052	41
Mississippi	1,213	77
Missouri	1,880	67
New Jersey	1,653	39
New York	3,651	38
North Carolina	1,932	35
Ohio	2,912	50
Oklahoma	2,091	122
Pennsylvania	1,517	24
South Carolina	1,412	63
Texas	10,343	102
Virginia	1,806	47
Washington	1,018	35
Wisconsin	1,169	42

SOURCE: Bureau of Justice Statistics, 1999, *Special Report: Women Offenders* (Washington, D.C.: U.S. Department of Justice), p. 9.

Although the actual number of women in prison has always been relatively small, the actual numbers are no longer small. In 1988, 30,834 women were incarcerated in state or federal prisons, and in 1999 that number exploded to over 84,000. In fact, there are now over 951,900 women under some form of correctional custody (BJS, 1999a; Beck and Mumola, 1999). Of course, even this number is dwarfed by the over one million men who are incarcerated; women still account for only a little more than 6 percent of the total state and federal prisoner population (BJS, 1989, 1999a).

Table 1.3 Percent Increase of Incarceration and Arrest Rates

	1980–1989[a]		1986–1990[b]		1989–1998[c]	
	ARRESTS/PRISON POP.		ARRESTS/PRISON POP.		ARRESTS/PRISON POP.	
Female	65.5	230	29.3	76.9	27.5	91.6
Male	32.1	120.5	19.5	46.2	2.3	66.8

SOURCES: [a]Chesney-Lind, M., 1991, "Patriarchy, Prisons and Jails: A Critical Look at Trends in Women's Incarceration," *The Prison Journal* 71, 1: 56; [b]Chesney-Lind, M., 1995, "Rethinking Women's Imprisonment: A Critical Examination of Trends in Female Incarceration," in B. Price and N. Sokoloff (eds.), *The Criminal Justice System and Women Offenders, Victims, and Workers,* 2d ed. (New York: McGraw-Hill), p. 108; [c]Beck, A., and C. Mumola, 1999, *Bureau of Justice Statistics Bulletin: Prisoners in 1998,* Washington, D.C.: U.S. Department of Justice; *Uniform Crime Reports, 1999* (Washington, D.C.: U.S. Department of Justice), p. 217.

A Different Criminal?

From all accounts, this increase in incarceration is not in response to a different, more violent female criminal. Chesney-Lind (1991, 1995, 1998) and others[1] discuss the reasons for the increased incarceration rate for women, attributing it, at least partially, to a backlash of gender equality. Owen and Bloom (1995b), as well as the other authors cited, write that harsher sentencing (especially toward drug crimes), determinate sentencing systems, and a fervor to treat women "equally" accounts for the increased numbers. Another factor in the increased numbers of women sent to prison seems to be an increased tendency to revoke parole or probation, usually for failed drug tests (Chesney-Lind, 1995: 112).

It seems clear that women are not being sent to prison because they pose a greater risk to the public or commit significantly more violent crimes than in years past. The typical female criminal continues to commit largely property crime and/or drug offenses.

The War on Drugs

The dramatic rise in women's imprisonment has been attributed most often to the criminal justice system's response to drug use and abuse. By all accounts, female offenders who end up in prison are more likely to use drugs than male offenders, use more drugs than male offenders, are more likely to report drugs as a problem in their lives, and are increasingly more likely to be sentenced to prison for a drug conviction.

Asseo (1999), Gilliard and Beck (1997), and Mauer, Potler, and Wolf (2000) report on a study by the "Sentencing Project" in which the sentencing trends of New York, California, and Minnesota were examined in the years 1986 through 1996. The study found that in these states, the number of women in prison for drugs increased tenfold from 1986 to 1996. Drug crimes accounted for half of all new imprisonments; for men, drug crimes accounted for about one third of the increase in the same 10 years. The rate of incarceration varied by state, however. Drug offenses accounted for 91 percent of the increase in the number of women imprisoned in New York, 55 percent in California, and 26 percent in Minnesota.

In New York in 1996, twice as many women were being incarcerated for drug crimes as in 1986; further, in 1986, one out of 20 women arrested were sentenced to prison, but by 1995, that ratio had increased to one in 7 (Mauer, Potler, and Wolf, 2000: 21). During the period 1986 to 1995, total arrests of women increased by 15 percent, but drug arrests rose by 61 percent. In fact, drug convictions accounted for 82 percent of the increase in women's convictions in 1986–1995. A further breakdown of drug-related prison commitments showed that 77 percent of Hispanic women, 59 percent of African-American women, and 34 percent of white women were incarcerated for drug crimes (Mauer, Potler, and Wolf, 2000: 22).

The study found that in California, less of the arrest figure increase was attributed to drugs than in New York. Researchers also found, however, that the incarceration rate rose 10 times faster than the arrest rate for drug offenses in California during the time period studied (Mauer, Potler, and Wolf, 2000: 30).

Minnesota presented yet a different picture. Drug offenses comprised a much smaller portion of court and prison populations. Drug offenses accounted for 10 percent of the rise in women's arrests and 26 percent of the increase in prison terms (Mauer, Potler, and Wolf, 2000: 31). Thus, the pattern of drug sentencing varies widely from state to state. It is important to explore what factors lead to these differences.

One thing is clear. These women are not drug "kingpins." For the most part, they are low-level users and dealers, and often their foray into the drug world is intertwined with an intimate relationship (Huling, 1995; Raeder, 1993a & b). The women who are incarcerated for drug offenses include women like Sylvia Foster, age 34, sentenced to 24 years' imprisonment (despite it being her first offense) for facilitating the drug-dealing activities of her boyfriend, and Angela Thompson, age 17, who received 15 years to life for selling two ounces of cocaine for an uncle who was her legal guardian. She served 10 years before public pressure resulted in a grant of clemency (Amnesty International, 1999: 20).

Nowhere is the impact of drug sentencing felt more strongly than in the federal system (see Table 1.4). Because of the increasing "federalization" of drug crimes, the jump in the number of female inmates has been dramatic. Most of the increase is attributed to the determinate nature of federal sentencing (Raeder, 1993a & b). United States Sentencing Guidelines do not allow sex, or even single parenthood, to be used in the determination of a sentence. This "gender-neutral" sentencing ignores the fact that women are often involved in drug networks because of an intimate relationship with either a husband, family member, or lover. While they may be aware of, benefit from, and perhaps participate in a minor way in the drug enterprise, they typically are not as actively involved as their male codefendants. More importantly, for women to avoid such criminal entanglement would mean terminating a marital or intimate relationship; this is a much different choice than other

Table 1.4   Federal Female Inmates

CRIME	1984 NUMBER/PERCENTAGE OF TOTAL	1995 NUMBER/PERCENTAGE OF TOTAL
Drug	496 (28%)	4,460 (66%)
Robbery	204 (11.5%)	256 (3.8)
Property	NA	388 (5.7%)
Violent	78 (4.4%)	53 (.8%)
Firearms	132 (7.5%)	202 (3%)
White collar	373 (21%)	187 (2.8%)
Extortion	7 (.4%)	870 (13%)

SOURCE: Fleisher, M., R. Rison, and D. Helman, 1997. "Female Inmates: A Growing Constituency in the Federal Bureau of Prisons," *Corrections Management Quarterly* 1, 4: 28–35, p. 30.

codefendants, such as business partners, face, especially if there are children involved (Raeder, 1993b: 907).

Although studies show that women receive lower sentences on average in the guideline range, these studies do not control for factors such as employment, first offense status, and other important variables. After completing a comprehensive examination of the federal sentencing guidelines and their effect on women, Raeder concluded that they are not "gender neutral" at all and impact unfairly on women. She remarked that: "By robbing single mothers of the chance to have judges sentence them based on narratives which fully portray the contexts of their lives, the Guidelines often needlessly disrupt the lives of their children" (Raeder, 1993b: 915).

Appellate decisions are mixed regarding trial courts' sentencing decisions based on single parenthood, but there is a trend to consider such a circumstance as "not extraordinary" and, therefore, not deserving of a downward adjustment of a sentence. While it is true that a woman acting as a single parent and sole custodian of one or more children is not extraordinary in a statistical sense, statistically it is extraordinary for a criminal defendant (most of whom are male) to be the sole custodial parent. Another issue is whether being a "bad" parent should result in an upward adjustment of sentencing. Raeder found that there was only one case in which a father was sentenced more harshly because he had introduced his adult children to drug dealing. In all other cases, the parent sentenced more harshly for "bad parenting" was the mother (Raeder, 1993b: 968).

Thus, women are more likely to be sentenced to prison than ever before, and very often the incarceration is a result of their drug use and abuse, either directly or because a woman commits property crime to fund her drug habit. The huge numbers of women (as well as men) sentenced to prison during the 1980s and 1990s spurred a "prison boom" that fueled the rise of the corrections "industry." Scores of private corporations and contractors now vie for the correctional dollar, and several private correctional companies trade their stock on the New York Stock Exchange. Although the dollar amount for women is miniscule compared to the amount of money expended nationally to incarcerate men, building continues across the country. Danner (1998) is one of many who point out how the War on Drugs and this country's punitive sentencing practices have hurt women, not only by placing more of them in prison, but also by siphoning public resources away from health and social programs into prison construction and maintenance.

WOMEN'S PRISONS ACROSS
THE UNITED STATES

Women's prisons range from Bedford Hills' turn-of-the-century brick buildings, situated in affluent Westchester County, New York, to the collegelike "campus" of Purdy Treatment Center for Women, surrounded by towering trees and overlooking picturesque Gig Harbor in Washington state. Some states built their first separate prison for women as recently as the 1970s; however, these same states are now frantically adding on to existing facilities or building new prisons. Several states still send their female prisoners to other states for confinement. However, this phenomenon used to exist because the state did not have a separate institution for women; today it exists because there are more women being sent to the state women's prisons than there are beds available.

Rierden (1997) describes the Connecticut women's prison in Niantic as facing such severe overcrowding in past years that the gymnasium was converted into a dormitory and "sani-cans" were brought in for hygiene needs. Newly arriving women were housed in a prison for men as an emergency measure. Lord (1995) describes Bedford Hills in New York as facing similar increases and subsequent difficulties in housing all the incoming women. Such stories were repeated throughout the country during the 1990s. Even small states like Vermont are dealing with large increases, and considering sending women inmates out of state. However, corrections officials report that they are not seeing more violent female offenders, and that offenders are basically the same as in the past. What is different is public and judicial attitude and treatment of them. Harsher sentencing has resulted in prison terms for property offenders, many of whom have serious substance abuse problems (Ring, 1999).

A Brief Description of Prisons and Prisoners

The history of women's prisons, described more fully in the next chapter, indicates that the treatment of women has always been different from that of men. Until the 1800s, men and women were incarcerated together and women were preyed upon and exploited by male prisoners and guards. When women were separated from male prisoners and housed in separate wings or buildings, they were only marginally more secure. They often were still exploited by male guards and suffered from neglect because of their small numbers and the perception that they were unredeemable. In the later part of the 19th century, northeastern states began building separate institutions for women. Some of these new facilities were built in response to a reformatory ideal and sought to make over the female inmate into a "lady." Those who ran the reformatories only accepted inmates thought to be susceptible to their influence; and those who were not sent to reformatories served their time in poorly supervised, dirty, miserable rooms or wings in penitentiaries for men (Feinman, 1983, 1986; Freedman, 1974, 1981; Rafter, 1985, 1990).

Today, some women's institutions still carry the legacy of their reformatory past. Consequently, institutions for women may very well "feel" different. That is, the architecture may follow a "cottage" style, the signs of security are more subtle, and the interactions between staff and inmates appear to be more informal and personal than what occurs in prisons for men. However, the trend today is to build facilities that can and do house men and women interchangeably. Increasingly, staff, too, are "interchangeable" and are transferred back and forth between facilities for men and women. The differences between prisons for men and women are still present to some degree, but staff training, administrative policies, and "unisex" architecture all combine to minimize and de-emphasize any differences between the two population groups. Of course, the model of the "unisex" prison is a male model. Women have always been the stepchild of the corrections system; in the past, grudging accommodations were made because women were perceived to be "different," and today the pressure is on administrators of women's units to accommodate to the (male) system standard.

Except for a few states like Texas and California, most states have only one or two institutions for women. This means that, whether housed in cottages or a Gothic castle, all custody grades and all variety of offenders are housed together. Security is set at the highest level for everyone, based on the 15 percent or so who need it. Newly arriving women are housed separately until they can be classified into custody rank and given housing, job, and program assignments, but the options are often quite meager. The experience of entering prison will be described in more detail in Chapter Four.

Descriptions of women's institutions have portrayed them as being found in "pastoral areas," with well-kept buildings and few signs of strict security (see, for instance, Baunach, 1977). These institutions typically are described as less violent than male institutions, with "softer" indicia of security. However, women complain of oppressive supervision and staff attempts to "play with their minds" (see, for instance, Burkhardt, 1973; Dobash, Dobash, and Gutteridge, 1986; Pollock, 1986; Watterson, 1973/1996). Women have had fewer vocational and treatment programs offered to them, although this fact has been increasingly challenged in the court. Training programs continue to be sex-stereotyped to some degree. Although most institutions for women have programs in cosmetology, office skills, and food service, few have nontraditional programs that can help a woman achieve economic self-sufficiency upon release. This is true despite the fact that female prisoners have children, and most will be the primary economic providers for these children upon release. (These issues will be discussed in more detail in Chapters Four and Five.)

Race and Background Characteristics Women's prisons are like prisons for men in one way; they both house a disproportionate number of minorities and poor. In 1982, the population of women's prisons was 50 percent African American, although African Americans comprised only 11 percent of the total population in this country; 9 percent Hispanic, when Hispanics were only 5 percent of the total population; and 3 percent Native American, although this group comprised only four-tenths of one percent of the total population (Flowers, 1987: 150). In 1999, 48 percent of women in prison were African American, 15 percent were Hispanic, and 4 percent were "other" (BJS, 1999c; Greenfield and Snell, 1999). After analyzing sentencing patterns, Bush-Baskette (1995) concluded that the War on Drugs has been a "war" against African-American women who are disproportionately impacted.

Like men, women in prison are likely to come from impoverished back-grounds. Very often, the female prisoner is a single mother (divorced, separated, or never married). Often women in prison come from dysfunctional and impoverished backgrounds and believe that the future holds nothing for them; criminal activity is a choice partially explained by desperation (Carlen, 1988; Chesney-Lind 1997). The latest figures report that 44 percent of women in prison do not have a high school diploma (BJS, 1999c; Greenfield and Snell, 1999). Needs assessment surveys illustrate that the women have had poor work histories and have few job skills (Fletcher, Shaver, and Moon, 1993; Owen and Bloom, 1995a & b; Pollock, Williams, and Schroeder, 1996).

In the 1980s, prison admittees were most often sent for property crimes (51 percent), and only about 10–11 percent of entering felons were incarcerated for violent crimes (Crawford, 1988a & b). More recently, the breakdown of those entering U.S. prisons was as follows: 28 percent were sentenced for violent crime; 27 percent were sentenced for property crimes; 34 percent were sentenced for drug offenses; and 11 percent were sentenced for public order offenses (BJS, 1999c; Greenfield and Snell, 1999).[2]

Women Under Sentence of Death

Some women serve their time in prison under a sentence of death. The unique aspects of living under a sentence of death are seldom discussed in relation to female offenders because there are so few of them (although see Coontz, 1983, and Morgan, 2000). However their numbers are increasing.

Baker (1999: 60) found that from 1632 to 1997, only 357 women were executed in the United States. Of these, 39 percent were white, 58.6 percent African American, 1.5 percent Native American, and .9 percent Latinos (the others' race or ethnic origin was not known). Most were executed for murder, but other crimes included witchcraft (26), arson, and slave revolt. The South Atlantic states were the most frequent site of executions. Baker argues that women were more likely to be executed in times when women were challenging power structures, such as during slave revolts. Today, 44 women are serving time under a sentence of death. States with one woman on death row are: Arizona, Idaho, Mississippi, Missouri, Nevada, and New Jersey. Illinois and

Tennessee each have two women on death row; Alabama, North Carolina, and Oklahoma each have three; Pennsylvania has four; Florida has six; Texas has seven; and California has eight. Thirty of these women are white, and 14 are African American (BJS, 1999c; Greenfield and Snell, 1999: 11).

While the nation and world watched in 1997, Texas executed Karla Faye Tucker, a woman who epitomized many of the themes we will discuss in this book. Her brutal, horrific crime seems to belie the principle that women are less violent than men, and seems completely incomprehensible. However, examining her background—physical and sexual abuse as a child, early entry into prostitution, drug addiction at an early age, and extremely dysfunctional relationships with men—helps us to understand how it happened. At the time she murdered a robbery victim, she was highly intoxicated on a combination of drugs and, in fact, had been on a drug binge for days. In prison, she appeared to represent the possibilities of rehabilitation. She became a devout Christian, provided support and nurturance for other women on death row, and exhibited no bitterness or anger regarding her impending death. Decades after the crime occurred, and despite the pleas of clemency from groups and individuals worldwide, including the Vatican, she was executed.

RESEARCH AND THE FEMALE OFFENDER

Because of their small numbers, women in prison have received little attention from correctional policy makers and the research community. For instance, the study of crime by the President's Commission on Law Enforcement and Administration of Justice in the 1960s contained no information on female criminals or prisoners. It was not until the 1970s that any comprehensive descriptive studies were published, including those of Glick and Neto (1977) and the Government Accounting Office (GAO; 1979). In 1977 Glick and Neto published a comprehensive examination of programs and services in women's prisons and also provided a demographic profile of the incarcerated female offender. They included 16 state prisons, 46 county jails, and 36 community-based programs in a total of 14 states in their survey. In all, 1,607 women were surveyed.

Until the late 1970s and early 1980s, few articles explored the issues of female offenders or prisons for women (although see Baunach and Murton, 1973; Rasche, 1975). In 1978, Chapman (1980) surveyed a number of different women's prisons and community programs and presented summary data on their policies and available programs. In the 1980s a few national surveys were conducted. The National Institute of Corrections published a "state-of-the-art" analysis of programs in adult female institutions in 1984 (Ryan, 1984). A few other studies also appeared (see Hunter, 1984). Crawford (1988a & b), under the auspices of the American Correctional Association, surveyed 71 facilities for women and girls. This study provided a wealth of information on female prisoners and the prisons that housed them and was used liberally throughout the 1990 edition of this text.

In the 1990s information on women's prisons expanded dramatically. The American Correctional Association (1990, 1993) published statistical summaries of the female offender. The most current statistical information on women in prison comes from the Bureau of Justice Statistics. For instance, the BJS (1994b) informed us that women in prison (compared to men in prison):

- Were less likely to have been employed at time of arrest
- Were more likely to be serving time for a drug offense
- Were less likely to have been sentenced for a violent crime
- Were more likely (if having committed a violent crime) to have victimized a relative
- Had shorter criminal records
- Received shorter maximum sentences
- Used more drugs
- Were more likely to have committed crime while under the influence of drugs or alcohol
- Were more likely to have been physically or sexually abused (Women are more than three times as likely to report abuse as a child and six times as likely to report physical abuse as an adult as compared with men.)

A 1999 BJS report (Greenfield and Snell, 1999) provided a broad array of demographic and other information that will be used throughout this text. For instance, this report stated that women comprised 51.6 percent of population over 10 years old in the United States. Their percentage of any criminal justice population, however, was much smaller, as can be seen in the accompanying table (see Table 1.5). The report also informed us that:

- The per capita arrest rate of juvenile women was twice that of adult women.
- The number of female defendants has grown at twice the rate of males.
- There are 1.3 million children of mothers under some form of correctional supervision.
- Six in 10 women reported physical or sexual abuse in the past; over one third were abused by an intimate, and 25 percent reported abuse by a family member.

More detailed "needs assessments" of women in prison have been done in California (Owen and Bloom, 1995a & b), Oklahoma (Fletcher, Shaver, and Moon, 1993), and Texas (Pollock, Williams, and Schroeder, 1996). These needs assessments provide more detailed information than the national surveys and flesh out the picture of prior abuse, economic marginalization, dysfunctional relationships, and the stress of being responsible for children. Finally, there have been a few national studies of prison programs for women that have surveyed what is available and made recommendations for effective programming

Table 1.5 Women's Contribution to Criminal Populations

Population	Women's Percent of Total
Violent offenders	14
All arrestees	22
Felony defendants	16
Correctional population	16
Prison inmates	6
Jail inmates	11
Probation	21
Parole	12

NOTE: 85 percent of women under correctional supervision are on probation or parole.

SOURCE: Bureau of Justice Statistics, 1999, *Special Report: Women Offenders* (Washington, D.C.: U.S. Department of Justice), p. 9.

(Morash and Bynum, 1995; Morash, Haar, and Rucker, 1994; Wellisch, Prendergast, and Anglin, 1996).[3]

Researchers interested in the internal world of the prison have been almost exclusively concerned with prisons for men. This field has a rich and extensive tradition, starting in the 1940s and 1950s with works by Clemmer (1940) and Sykes (1958) on the prisoner subculture, and continuing through the 1970s and 1980s with descriptions of the prison experience by Toch (1975, 1977), Jacobs (1977), and Johnson (1987/1999). Other writers have chosen to document other aspects of prison life, such as victimization (Bowker, 1980), staff (Crouch, 1980), racial issues (Carroll, 1974; Davidson, 1974), and philosophical issues of imprisonment (Hawkins, 1976). However, few of these writers have chosen to explore the world of female prisoners. Exceptions include Bowker (1979, 1981) and Fox (1975, 1982, 1992).

The literature on women's prisons has a separate and much truncated history that began almost 30 years after research began in prisons for men. Apart from a single history and description published in 1931 (Lekkerkerker, 1931), Giallombardo (1966) and Ward and Kassebaum (1965) pioneered the line of works describing women's prisons. These initial works were followed several years later by other studies that further explored female prison homosexuality (Propper, 1976, 1981, 1982) and looked at other aspects of the female prisoner subculture (Heffernan, 1972; Mitchell, 1975). Freedman (1981), Feinman (1983), and Rafter (1985, 1990), provided us with seminal works on the history of women's prisons. Journalistic accounts of prisons contributed to the literature by adding the voices of prisoners and staff (Burkhardt, 1973; Chandler, 1973; Flynn, 1963; Watterson 1973/1996).

Since the first edition of this book was published in 1990, many other sources have appeared, usually in the form of survey reports. Unfortunately, the richly detailed studies of prisoner subcultures done in earlier years seem to be a thing of the past; however, a few researchers continue to use phenomenological methods. Owen (1998), Girshick (1999), and Rierden (1997) have utilized phenomenological research to open the door to life in the women's prison. Eaton (1993) offers expanded interviews with several female offenders in Great Britain covering their experiences in prison as well as reentry to society.

Other books cover counseling issues relative to female offenders and/or women in prison (Harden and Hill, 1998; Pollock, 1998; Zaplin, 1998a). More general books on the female offender also shed light on issues in women's prisons (Belknap, 1996/2000; Chesney-Lind, 1997; Pollock, 1999a). Faith's (1993b) exhaustive study on women's prisons and the treatment of women by the criminal justice system provides information on both the United States and the Canadian systems. Cook and Davies (1999) provide an international perspective in their book of readings. Carlen has provided a number of excellent reports on British prisons (1983, 1985, 1988, 1990), and more recently (1994) she has questioned whether women's prisons (and prisoners) should be studied separately from prisons for men, concluding that writers and researchers should be looking more generally at the punishment power of prisons and the prison's place in society—for men and women.

In addition to academic research and statistical profiles, a number of recent investigations of women's prisons have been conducted with an eye to policy change. A Government Accounting Office study, commissioned by Eleanor Holmes Norton, a legislator from the District of Columbia, looked at the federal system, as well as the prison systems in California and Texas (Santana, 2000; also see GAO, 2000). The study, conducted in 1999 and released in 2000, found that mandatory minimum and repeat offender provisions have had the unintended effect of sharply increasing female incarceration (even though women's crimes are nonviolent). Other findings included the following:

- While the number of female inmates has increased, drug treatment programs have been reduced.
- Females have higher rates of HIV infection and mental illness.
- Racial disparities are even more pronounced for women than for men (black women are eight times as likely as white women to be incarcerated).
- There is a serious problem of sexual misconduct among guards. (Santana, 2000)

Amnesty International (1999) published a report condemning the treatment of female prisoners in the United States and describing such treatment as constituting human rights violations and violating international treaties against torture. The most extreme criticisms in the Amnesty International report were directed at health care, the policy of separating mothers and babies after birth, and the seemingly increasing incidence of sexual assaults by male correctional officers. It was also reported that poor opportunities for treatment existed for women. Using a 1997 National Institute of Corrections survey, Amnesty International reported that only 27 departments indicated they had substance abuse programs developed specifically for women; only 19 departments had domestic violence programs developed specifically for women; only 9 departments offered programs for victims of sexual assault; and only 9 departments provided special programs to address women's health education (Amnesty International, 1999: 35).

The Amnesty International report also condemned the practice of shackling women during labor and birth or other medical procedures regardless of their history of violence or escape. This policy still exists in some states despite medical personnel's opinion that shackles pose a medical risk; for instance, if a woman in childbirth needs to be moved to caesarian delivery immediately, even a five-second delay can result in brain damage to the infant (1999: 62). Another concern was inadequate medical care, especially gynecological care. There have been widespread allegations, lawsuits, and investigations of inadequacy involving such issues as lack of prenatal care and lack of treatment following miscarriages.

The 1999 report also condemned the use of a "four-point restraint chair" in which women are shackled to immobilize them. The chair has been implicated in serious injuries and humiliation when misused. Reports included situations where inmates were forced to urinate on themselves, officers taunted immobilized inmates, and other abuse. For instance, in a report from a Sacramento County jail, a woman was stripped naked and left in a chair for eight and one-half hours in full view of male and female officers and civilian workers. Finally, Amnesty International condemned the use of super-max units for those women who were incarcerated for property crimes and disciplined for minor infractions. Many women housed in such units have histories of mental illness (1999: 70, 74, 90).[4]

CONCLUSION: UNANSWERED QUESTIONS

In 1990 many questions regarding the women's prison were still unanswered. Questions left unanswered included:

- What methods do women use to distribute contraband goods?
- What forms of leadership exist among women?
- What sanctions are imposed against those who violate the norms, and what is the general adherence to an inmate code by the female population?
- What subcultural groupings exist in different types of prisons?
- What is the level of drug and alcohol abuse in prison?
- What forms and levels of aggressiveness and violence are displayed in prisons for women?
- What is the nature and effect of the interaction between staff and inmates?

The authors cited in this chapter have provided a great deal of information that helps to address these questions, and their work will be used in the chapters that follow.

The following questions were also asked in 1990:

- Did the increase in women's incarceration parallel an increase in female crime, or did it result from a change in sentencing practices?

- Were prison sentences needed for these women, or were community placements more efficacious and appropriate?

- Were programs for women improving in number and quality, and were they serving the needs of women prisoners who must support themselves and their children upon release?

- Was the litigation that focused on equal protection serving the best interests of female prisoners, or did it endanger the few beneficial aspects of the different philosophy that seems uniquely to characterize the prison for women?

We now can begin to address these issues, given that greater attention has been given to female offenders during the last 10 years.

The increasing and long overdue interest in female prisoners has no doubt been influenced by the rapid escalation in their numbers, including the numbers of female juvenile offenders. The rate of incarceration of young women in detention facilities has increased as dramatically as the rates for adult women. Juvenile women's facilities will not be covered in this text; however, other excellent sources are available (see, for instance, Chesney-Lind, 1982, 1988; Chesney-Lind and Shelden, 1998).

Unfortunately, the available information leads to an inescapable conclusion: Women prisoners face overwhelming problems, and incarceration is usually not the best answer for them or for society. Unless there are extensive resources and excellent aftercare, incarceration merely provides a hiatus from their lives of the street. Dysfunctional backgrounds, early motherhood, poor job skills, and a lack of positive role models all contribute to women's subsequent poor coping choices, including the choice to use drugs or commit other crimes. Incarcerated women are largely drug and minor property offenders and pose little risk to the public. They very often have been victims of sexual and physical abuse, and they abuse drugs to self-medicate; in fact, all studies indicate that women are greater users of drugs than male offenders. Often, however, they become criminally active through a relationship with a male offender, and play a very peripheral role in drug and other criminal networks. They have medical problems from their lifestyle choices; for instance, female prisoners are more likely to be HIV positive than male prisoners. They are likely to have minor children, and probably will regain custody upon release. As stated, they have few job skills and a poor or nonexistent job history.

Despite these facts, programs for women lag behind those for men; for example, there are fewer drug programs available to female offenders than to male offenders. Many states have extremely minimal parenting programs that do not provide settings conducive to maintaining the bond between a mother and child. What is even more troubling is that because there are fewer women's facilities, women are likely to be even further away from their children and family than are many male offenders. Few states provide a forum to address victimization issues, and thus the cycle continues: drug use to self-medicate and cope with past trauma, dysfunctional relationships as a result of and as part of the drug lifestyle, and continued or recurring criminal activity and drug use (as well as revictimization).

Bernat (1995) and many others (see, for instance, Chesney-Lind, 1997; Daly, 1989c, 1994; Heidensohn, 1985; Pollock, 1998) point out that women live different lives from men and from each other because of the intersections of gender, culture, race, and class. What this means is that women do crime differently, for different reasons. Women have economic realities and other pressures that are different from those of men. Elaine Lord (1995), one of the most progressive and innovative superintendents in the United States, explains that women and men are not identical—in the way they commit crime, or the way they "do time": "Men and women are different, even in terms of the crimes they commit, their roles, their risks of being violent, their victims, their risks of recidivism" (1995: 265). Further, she explains, "Men concentrate on 'doing their own time,' relying on their feelings of inner strength and their ability to withstand outside pressures to get themselves through their time in prison. Women, on the other hand, remain interwoven into the lives of their significant others, primarily their children and their own mothers . . ." (1995: 266). Susan Cranford, from her experience as a progressive and innovative warden of a women's prison, also urges recognition of the differences between female and male prisoners—in their need to communicate, and in their need to "connect" (Cranford and Williams, 1998: 131).

The basic point that should not be overlooked is that prison is a poor solution to the problems of drug use and crime, and to the myriad of social and health problems of the incarcerated women. For the cost of each new prison cell, many social programs could be created to meet the needs of women and their children in the community—preferably before women make the choice to commit criminal acts (Lord, 1995: 267). What is needed is a mandate for change: change in our sentencing laws that adopt a purely punitive approach to drug abuse, and change in our policies and priorities that provide little support for women and children in the community and few treatment programs for those addicted to drugs, but do find the money to build new prisons at the cost of $150,000 to $200,000 per bed (Chesney-Lind, 1995: 114).

One example of skewed priorities is provided by Hirsch (2000) in her description of the impact that a recent federal law has had on struggling women. The Personal Responsibility and Work Opportunity Reconciliation Act of 1996 includes a federal ban on welfare benefits to women who have any felony drug conviction. This act prohibits states from providing these women with food stamps or housing assistance for their lifetime. Note that this ban extends only to drug crimes, not to convictions for murder or other violent crimes, no matter how heinous. Hirsch found that women affected by this ban may have been convicted of selling as little as $10 worth of crack and may have been first offenders. Some states have chosen to opt out of the ban (27 states), but others, such as Pennsylvania, have not. The women Hirsch interviewed often started using drugs at an early age as a partial coping response to sexual and physical abuse in their homes. The ban makes it difficult or impossible for them to regain custody of their children upon their release, so the conviction and prison sentence, in effect, take their children away from them forever.

Another example of a federal law that has had an impact on women in prison is the Adoption and Safe Families Act of 1997, which mandates that a child who is under state care for 15 of the past 22 months must be released for adoption, unless certain specified exceptions apply. This law makes it much easier for child protective services to permanently take away an incarcerated woman's children, against her will, without any showing that she was a bad mother before her imprisonment.

Finally, there must be a change in our perception of women in prison as evil or dangerous. Although certainly some women in prison have committed violent acts and others have entrenched criminal lifestyles, the majority of women in prison have struggled against overwhelming odds to survive with some measure of humor, self-esteem, and ability to love. Their choices have not been good ones, but given many of their life histories and the alternatives available to them, they are certainly understandable. Further, given the right setting, these women usually show a great propensity for and enthusiasm toward change.

NOTES

1. See, for instance, Acoca and Austin 1996; Bloom, Chesney-Lind, and Owen, 1994; Bloom, Immarigeon, and Owen, 1995; DeConstanzo & Scholes, 1988; Morton, 1998; Owen and Bloom, 1995a & b; Pollock-Byrne, 1992; Pollock, 1998, 1999a; Rafter, 1992; Ryan & McCabe, 1997; Steffensmeier, Kramer, and Streifel, 1993.

2. Note that when the prison population is broken down into crimes of conviction, violent crime comprises a higher percentage than the percentages of prison admittees. This is because violent criminals receive much longer sentences, and consequently, their numbers are higher in prison population statistics.

3. Also see Wellisch et. al, 1994; Wellisch, Anglin, and Prendergast, 1993.

4. This report has been met with criticism by correctional administrators in this country. Primarily, they argue that the methods employed do not provide an objective view of the prevalence of the problems detailed.

SUGGESTED READINGS

Belknap, J. 1996/2000. *The Invisible Woman: Gender, Crime and Justice.* Belmont, CA: Wadsworth.

Carlen, P. 1990. *Alternatives to Incarceration.* Philadelphia: Open University Press.

Chesney-Lind, M. 1997. *The Female Offender: Girls, Women and Crime.* Thousand Oaks, CA: Sage.

Faith, K. 1993. *Unruly Women: The Politics of Confinement and Resistance.* Vancouver, Canada: Press Gang Publishers.

Lord, E. 1995. "A Prison Superintendent's Perspective on Women in Prison." *Prison Journal* 75, 2: 257–269.

2

History of Women's Prisons: The Legacy of Difference

The history of women's institutions reflects the history of women. Deviant women have been treated differently not only by their more law-abiding sisters but also by their male counterparts. Female offenders have been a class of people perceived as not wholly feminine, but definitely not masculine either. Dobash, Dobash, and Gutteridge wrote, "From the very beginning, women in prison were treated differently from men, considered more morally depraved and corrupt and in need of special, closer forms of control and confinement" (1986: 1). Some have described these women as "lost," and indeed in both physical surroundings and attitudes toward their redemption, female prisoners have been either brutalized or ignored for the greater part of history.

This chapter relies extensively on two major works of history. Estelle Freedman (1974, 1981) published an extensive exploration of the reformatory movement in the late 1800s and early 1900s, which proposed an environment designed to help deviant women become "ladies" in the model of their female administrators and advocates. Nicole Rafter (1985) provided a more complete picture of the historical treatment of women, showing that only a small proportion of women were ever "treated" in reformatories, while the vast majority continued to spend sentences in harsh penitentiaries or the plantation-style prison farms of the South and West.

Although primarily concerned with prisons for women in Great Britain, Dobash, Dobash, and Gutteridge (1986: 1) offered the following summary of women's treatment in the United States:

> In the first decades of nineteenth century America, women were predominantly confined in separate wings of prisons for men, usually provided with poorer living conditions and sometimes subjected to physical and sexual abuse by male warders. By the end of the century, wider social and ideological forces produced strong pressures to change the conditions of confinement for these women. Reformatories for women emerged in the context of growing concern for the regulation of youth, public morals and domestic training. The American reformatory movement was the answer to the neglect and repression experienced by women. Reformatories were not built in every state. They spread primarily in the north and northeast. These institutions were the epitome of progressive ideals. According to their creators women would be diagnosed and assessed by a group of professionals who would then be able to apply the best individualized treatment.

EARLY PUNISHMENTS AND PLACES
OF CONFINEMENT

Early English law made it very clear that women and men were different and possessed different rights under the law. For instance, some behavior, such as adultery, was not considered criminal or was punished much less severely when committed by men. For other crimes, however, women may have been punished less often or less severely than men who committed the identical activity (Dobash et al., 1986: 17). The social order was a male hierarchy, and behaviors that threatened this social order were defined as criminal and punished severely. For instance, women who were too vocal, too critical of men, or promiscuous were punished. Men who let their wives dominate them or who allowed themselves to be "cuckolded" were also punished.[1]

Women who violated the social order were subject to the ducking stool or more serious punishments. For instance, Dobash, Dobash, and Gutteridge (1986: 19) describe the "branks":

The branks was an iron cage placed over the head, and most examples incorporated a spike or pointed wheel that was inserted into the offender's mouth in order to "pin the tongue and silence the noisiest brawler." This spiked cage was intended to punish women adjudged quarrelsome or not under the proper control of their husbands.

Thus, women were firmly under the control of men and their behavior judged against a model of femininity that included submissiveness. First fathers, and then husbands, had almost complete legal control over their daughters and wives. Punishment could be imposed whenever the wife or daughter was considered disobedient or unchaste.

Wives had some legal recourse against brutal or improvident husbands, but very little. If a woman was married to a drunk who did not give her money to buy food, there was little she could do to provide for herself and her children. Consequently, many of the women committed to prisons or bridewells[2] in the 1700s and 1800s were there for theft or begging. Others turned to prostitution, the only other way women could earn money. Female criminals, when sentenced to bridewells, often received substantially longer sentences than men (Fox, 1984: 16).

Women did not escape their "female duties" by incarceration. Women in poorhouses and bridewells were expected to do the cooking and cleaning, spinning and sewing required for the institution (Dobash et al., 1986: 24–25). Some incarcerated women were sexually exploited. Women in bridewells in England found that prostitution was one of the few ways to better their living conditions in the prison (Fox, 1984: 16). The following quotation describes what awaited women who were transported to Australia in the early 1800s:

> In 1812, the Committee on Transportation observed that women were ". . . indiscriminately given to such of the inhabitants as demanded them, and were in general received rather as prostitutes than as servants. . . ." The British Government transported women for the purpose of preventing unrest among the free and convict male population by providing convict women as sexual commodities. (Dobash et al., 1986: 33)

Feinman described the early treatment of women in the United States as basically egalitarian during the colonial period because women's labor was valued equally to that of men's, and thus women were considered equal partners to men. Both men and women were likely subjected to physical punishments and treated similarly by the courts (Feinman, 1983: 12). However, with increasing urbanization and industrialization after the American Revolution, women's labor was less essential and the cult of "true womanhood" developed in the East. Women were expected to be "pure, submissive, and pious" and expected to confine their activities to the home. Those who did not fit this mold were considered in some ways more deviant than criminal men, since they went against a natural order (Feinman, 1983: 13).

Freedman (1974) explains that the cult of "true womanhood" created a model of female virtue that was hard to live up to. According to this theme, women provided the moral boundaries of society and controlled social disorder. Thus, the female deviant, whether a prostitute, vagrant, murderess, or thief, "threatened social order doubly, both by sinning and by removing the moral constraints on men." Further, society "justified harsher treatment of female criminals by the argument that female convicts were more depraved than men since, having been born pure, they had fallen further than had their male counterparts in crime" (Freedman, 1974: 78).[3]

Descriptions of early places of confinement for women indicate that there was little regard for the safety or health of female prisoners. Before classification of the sexes in Europe and the United States, men and women were housed together in large rooms where the strong preyed upon the weak and each individual's life was made bearable only by the resources received from his or her family or what could be acquired by begging, bartering, or stealing from other prisoners. After the separation of the sexes, women's lives in prison were only marginally better.

Freedman describes early institutions for women as overcrowded and filthy. In the 1820s, a Philadelphia jail had 7 women in a cellar with only two blankets among them; and in Albany, a jail placed 15 women in one room (Freedman, 1974: 78). Freedman also describes the New York City Tombs jail as having 42 cells to hold 70 women in 1838 (Freedman, 1981: 16). Women were found only in jails because prisons were built solely for male prisoners at that time (Strickland, 1976: 40). In 1825, separate quarters for women were built at a Baltimore prison, and in 1835 officials at Ossining State Penitentiary (Sing Sing) built a separate unit for women (Strickland, 1976: 40).

Feinman described Sing Sing Penitentiary in 1843 as a place where mothers and other women were housed in a room 18 feet square and where the "hot, crowded, and unsanitary conditions during the summer led to the death of one baby" (Feinman, 1983: 15). Further, floggings and harsh physical punishments led to miscarriages and even death (Feinman, 1983: 15). Women were subject to forced prostitution by male warders (Freedman, 1981: 17). Freedman reports that a young male prisoner in Indiana State Prison at Jeffersonville revealed that younger female prisoners were "subjected to the worst of debasement at the hands of prison officials and guards," while the older ones were "obliged to do the work of all." In that prison, the warden established concubinage, and there were "sadistic beatings," "rape," and "illegitimate births" (Freedman, 1981: 60). This terrible treatment was rationalized by a belief that the women were beyond any redemption or reformation.

More often than not, women were simply left alone in the wing or building that comprised the women's portion of the institution. Rafter writes that female prisoners experienced lower levels of surveillance, discipline, and care. For instance, women held in Auburn Prison in 1825 were housed in an attic and visited only once a day when a steward came to deliver food and remove waste (Rafter, 1985: 6).

Before the mid–1800s, the use of imprisonment for female criminals was very limited. In 1831 an average of only one in 12 prisoners was female, and in 1850 women comprised only 3.6 percent of the incarcerated in 34 states (Freedman, 1981: 11). Shortly after 1840, however, the number of female prisoners began to rise. Indeed, in 1864, females represented 37.2 percent of all commitments to prisons and jails in Massachusetts (Freedman, 1981: 13). By the end of the 19th century, nearly every state had some place to confine women criminals; however, women's quarters were usually within the walls of male prisons, and the few that were in separate buildings were typically supervised by the male warden (Rafter, 1983, 1985: xxi).

Early Reformers

In the late 19th century, the perception of female criminals changed somewhat: They began to be seen as not so much evil as misguided. It was believed that the female deviant was influenced by poverty and a poor home environment, and her descent into depravity was attributed more often than not to an evil man (Freedman, 1974: 84). With this change in perception came a number of reformers who sought to improve the prison conditions of women.

Elizabeth Fry in England and several reformers in the United States advocated not only separate housing but also female supervision of women in prison. Women were marginally protected from male inmates in their separate quarters, but the possibility of exploitation from male warders still existed as long as female prisoners were administratively and physically located in institutions for men.

Dobash, Dobash, and Gutteridge (1986) wrote that Elizabeth Fry was the first penal reformer to devote her attention solely to the plight of imprisoned women. Fry visited Newgate in 1813 and was "shocked and sickened" by the "blaspheming, fighting, dram-drinking, half naked women" found there. In her words: "All I tell thee is a faint picture of reality; the filth, the closeness of the rooms, the furious manner and expressions of the women towards each other, and the abandoned wickedness, which everything bespoke, are quite indescribable" (Dobash et al., 1986: 43). Fry went on to visit northern jails and bridewells and wrote and spoke on the terrible conditions she found there. Her book, *Observations on the Siting, Superintendence and Government of Female Prisoners,* published in 1825, advocated work, training, religion, routine, manners, and continuous surveillance for female prisoners.

Further, Fry proposed that female prisoners should be supervised by women, not men. "Since female felons were of 'light and abandoned character' it was impossible and unreasonable to 'place them under the care of men . . .' because it 'seldom fails to be injurious to both parties' " (Dobash et al., 1986: 51). Elizabeth Fry advocated female warders for three reasons: first, they would prevent sexual abuse by male guards; second, they would set moral examples of "true womanhood" for their female charges; and third, they could provide a sympathetic ear for female inmates (Freedman, 1974: 79). Primarily through her efforts, a separate system for female inmates developed in England long before the United States undertook the same reforms.

> By mid-century, the British had created unique and austere institutions that usually provided secure, sanitary conditions for prisoners. . . . In contrast to the United States where women were held in cramped, unsanitary gaols and often subjected to sexual assaults by warders, it seems that women in British prisons had been granted a fair degree of security and protection by this time. (Dobash et al., 1986: 61)

In the United States, reformers such as Dorothea Dix, Mary Wister, Sarah Doremus, and Abby Hopper Gibbons advocated female warders in the 1820s. In 1845, Doremus and Gibbons established a Ladies Association within the New York Prison Association, which became autonomous several years later as the Women's Prison Association of New York. This organization opened the Isaac Hopper Home for released women (Freedman, 1974: 80).

Private institutions for female deviants were created when public agencies were recalcitrant. In 1825, a House of Refuge was established in New York City. In 1833 the Magdalen Home for wayward women was created to inculcate virtue through education, religious instruction, and work. The House of Shelter was opened in Indiana in 1869; the Home for the Friendless in New York City hired a female manager in 1870; and homes for women opened in Dedham, Springfield, Richmond, and other cities in the 1870s and 1890s. These homes—serving homeless women and prostitutes—emphasized religion, education, discipline, reading, and sewing (Freedman, 1981: 52, 55).

The goal of the reformers, however, was to establish separate state penal institutions for women prisoners, run by women and with the purpose of instilling feminine values in the female residents. The reformers felt that only women could be successful in pursuing this goal. The female reformers encountered strong resistance to the notion of a female institution run by women. Primary among the reasons such an idea was so abhorrent to those in charge was that the place for women was considered to be in the home, not in public service. Moreover, women were seen as incapable of controlling female prisoners; the institution run by women would lack a normal, family atmosphere if men were excluded; and women's institutions would reduce male dominance in society and destroy femininity (Freedman, 1974: 86).

Gradually the resistance to female administration of prisons for women gave way, and women were hired to run the separate buildings or wings that housed women offenders. In 1822, Maryland became the first state to hire a female jail keeper (Freedman, 1974: 80). In 1827, Connecticut hired a woman to oversee the female department of the state prison. In 1828, a separate building for women was built at Ossining, New York (euphemistically called Mt. Pleasant) (Rafter, 1985: 17). In 1830, Maine and Ohio also opened separate buildings for women prisoners (Freedman, 1974: 80).

Elizabeth Farnham, appointed in 1844 as matron of Mt. Pleasant, was strongly influenced by Elizabeth Fry. She made many changes in the institutional surroundings, designed to "feminize" the women prisoners there. For instance, she allowed female prisoners to decorate their rooms with curtains and flowers. She brought in a piano and instituted educational classes and readings. Her tenure lasted only two years, however, because of harsh critics who objected to her "atheism" and lack of discipline (Feinman, 1983: 17; Freedman, 1981: 46).

The women who championed the cause of female prisoners could not be described as advocates of women's rights. Rather, they believed that women had a special and unique ability to help their "fallen sisters" achieve the chastity and moral virtue that all women should possess. Freedman (1981: 34) explained the difference between these reformers and suffragists; while suffragists believed women should be involved in politics and the public sphere, reformers believed in the unique moral virtue of women and maintained an apolitical stance.

> Like temperance advocates, social purity leaders, and settlement house founders, the postwar prison reformers believed in women's separate sphere and superior morality. Even as they entered the public sphere and gained valuable skills by building separate women's organizations, social feminists continued to argue that women had unique, feminine virtues that should be embodied in social policy. (Freedman, 1981: 39)

THE REFORMATORY ERA AND WOMEN

By the late 1800s, female reformers were finally successful in their quest to establish separate female institutions run by women. The advocates of separate correctional facilities for women were able to include their goals in the 1870s Prison Congress, a national meeting of correctional specialists and reformers. During this important meeting, it was agreed that women and juveniles should be separated from male offenders. Further, the attendees recognized the value of employing female professionals, and the need for adequate facilities and programs (Morton, 1998: 5).

In the 1870s, separate institutions in Indiana and Massachusetts were built and female staff were hired. In 1881, the New York House of Refuge for female misdemeanants was created, and in 1900, Bedford Hills was built (Freedman, 1974: 80). Houses of Refuge were designed for young women (as young as 12 or 15) who had been convicted of minor crimes, such as "petit larceny, habitual drunkenness, or being a common prostitute, of frequenting disorderly houses or houses of prostitution or of any misdemeanor," and who were "not insane or mentally or physically incapable of being substantially benefited" by the discipline found there (Lekkerkerker, 1931: 102).

Four factors contributed to the women's prison movement: first, an apparent increase in female criminality during the 1860s, composed primarily of convictions for prostitution and abortion associated with the Civil War;

second, educated women's Civil War social service experience; third, the development of the charities organization movement and of a prison reform movement that emphasized the investigation of criminality and the reformatory ideal; and fourth, an embryonic feminist analysis of women's place in U.S. society (Freedman, 1974: 82).

Ironically, the first completely separate institution for women run by women did not follow the reformatory ideal. In 1873, the Female Prison and Reformatory Institution for Girls and Women was opened in Indiana. Here, the reformatory concept was only partially followed. The institution received only felons; it did not originally use indeterminate sentencing; it made no attempt to reform through education; and its architecture did not follow the cottage system (Rafter, 1985: 33). In fact, the first prisons for women in Indiana and Massachusetts were described as castlelike—"grim, dark, 'bastille-like' structure[s]" (Freedman, 1981: 70). However, the women in Indiana did have separate rooms and wore gingham dresses instead of prison uniforms (Lekkerkerker, 1931: 99).

The Massachusetts prison, opened after a long delay, had 300 individual cells and two 50-bed dormitories. Run by a female manager with an entirely female staff, this institution, like others, was ultimately under the authority of a male. In many of these institutions, top administrators were men because of the belief that only men could solve the management problems and make decisions regarding the management of women. Other men held staff positions to take care of such things as construction and mechanical needs (Freedman, 1981: 71).

It was also a struggle to retain female supervisors once they were in place. For instance, Freedman wrote that Clara Barton reluctantly agreed to be superintendent of Framingham for nine months in order to prevent the governor from appointing a man in 1882 (Freedman, 1981: 74). Low pay, uncomfortable living conditions, and questionable status made qualified women difficult to find and keep (Freedman, 1981: 75).

Male reformers of the late 1800s who advocated reformatories for males agreed that women would be useful in the care and treatment of female prisoners. Zebulon Brockway, for instance, advocated using women to supervise women because of their "sisterly care, counsel and sympathy"; he advocated the use of "family life, where they shall receive intellectual, moral, domestic, and industrial training, under the influence, example and sympathy of refined and virtuous women" (Rafter, 1985: 26). Brockway had himself dealt with female prisoners in a House of Shelter at the Detroit House of Correction during the period from 1865 to 1869, and there he had developed his idea that prisoners should be able to earn limited freedoms through good behavior. He later implemented his ideas with male prisoners at Elmira Reformatory (Strickland, 1976: 41).

Later institutions more strictly followed the ideals of the reformers. These institutions followed a pattern similar to the private homes and shelters described earlier. Institutions like the Hudson House of Refuge, which opened in New York in 1887, were built on the cottage system, were staffed almost entirely by women, and followed a "domestic" routine. In 1893, Albion Training School for Girls was opened and followed the Hudson model, and then in 1901, Bedford Hills was opened (Freedman, 1981: 57). Although primarily for misdemeanants, these facilities also accepted some felony offenders (Strickland, 1976: 47).

Lekkerkerker viewed the female reformatories as entirely different from reformatories for men and unique in the world (Lekkerkerker, 1931: 4). Part of the reason for their difference was the vague line drawn between crime and sexual immorality. According to Lekkerkerker, women's deviance took place primarily in the sexual area, and thus the institution used to control females, the reformatory, was concerned with the women's morality rather than their criminality (Lekkerkerker, 1931: 9).

Freedman described the early reformatories as "benevolent matriarchies" that offered a homelike atmosphere free "from the contaminating influences of men" (Freedman, 1974: 88). Training consisted of household work, including sewing, knitting, cooking, washing and ironing clothes, gardening, and farming. So, for instance, the Massachusetts Reformatory Prison for Women at Framingham, built in 1877, had private rooms, each with its own "iron bedsteads and white linen" (Freedman, 1981: 68).

The early administrators of these institutions were often the same reformers who had struggled so hard to create them. These women believed they had a moral duty to improve the lives of their female charges. The early group of advocates had a kind of religious fervor and felt kinship with their fallen sisters (Rafter, 1985: 66). As these women retired, they were replaced by "professional administrators." These women were less zealous than their forerunners. Freedman writes that women entering prison reformatories as paid administrators after the early years did not share the missionary spirit that had motivated the founders (Freedman, 1981: 109). These later women, who had experience in education and settlement houses, had different reasons for entering prison work. Fewer had a religious "mission"; and those who had training in social work, law, medicine, and the social sciences approached prisoners as subjects or clients (Freedman, 1981: 110). Rafter (1985: 66) wrote that some were patronizing and showed condescension and contempt for their charges.

Those given reformatory terms were carefully chosen. The women who found themselves in reformatories were young, relatively unhardened, guilty of misdemeanors, or victims of difficult circumstances. Most were under the age of 25, white, and native-born. Two-thirds were married at some time but were widowed, divorced, or separated. Most had no prior convictions and their crimes were minor: more than half had been incarcerated for drunkenness and prostitution (Freedman, 1981: 78–79). Rafter wrote that some of the women sent to Albion were there not for prostitution but because "exasperated mothers or embarrassed husbands" charged them with sexual misconduct (1985: 117). It is instructive to note that these "new" penal institutions were being used to control female behavior in much the same way as bridewells had been used in earlier times. In short, prisoners were usually young moral offenders with short sentences (Freedman, 1981: 82).

Life in the Reformatory

Lekkerkerker (1931: 410–411) described the daily routine in early institutions as follows:

> The inmates get up at six-thirty or seven o'clock in the morning, except those having kitchen or farm service who frequently have to rise earlier. Usually each inmate fixes her own room either before or immediately after breakfast. After this, the women go to their respective departments for work or instruction. For the rest of the day different systems prevail. In some institutions one half of the population goes to work in the morning and to classes in the afternoon, while the other half follows the reverse order; in other institutions classes are spread over the whole day and the work is made more or less subservient to the classwork; in others the women work all day while classes and further activities, if any, are held in the evenings. . . . Usually, the women cease working for about an hour at noon time for dinner, and finish their work or classes at about five o'clock in the afternoon. Recreation is provided in some institutions for half an hour after dinner, in others no free time is provided during the day except a little time before or after meals or between the periods to enable the girls to go from one building or department to another. . . . After supper, which is about five or half past five, there may be various activities, such as sports and gymnastics, cottage or community entertainments, singing or bible-classes, lectures, self-government meetings, etc., or the inmates may simply stay "at home" to mend their clothing, to read, do fancy-work, play games, or converse with each other. . . . At nine-thirty or ten o'clock the lights are usually turned off.

The institutions offered domestic training and very little else. Academic classes were underfunded, industrial training was opposed by civilian industry, and only a small number of women could get jobs in skilled trades (Freedman, 1981: 90). Many women were trained in the "domestic sciences." In Massachusetts, an indenture law was passed in 1879, and 1,500 women went into service in family homes (Freedman, 1981: 92). Rafter wrote: "Albion provided trained, inexpensive household help. It was the institution's policy 'to place our girls in the home of a woman who will take a motherly interest in them'"(1985: 163). One-quarter of the prisoners were paroled directly to live-in domestic positions. In fact, parole revocation usually occurred because of sexual misconduct or "sauciness" to employers (Rafter, 1985: 125).

Some institutions, however, had an expanded view of domesticity. At Bedford Hills, the women did outdoor work, such as gardening, slaughtering pigs, and draining a swamp (Freedman, 1981: 134). Women there also "poured concrete sidewalks, laid floors for new buildings, painted cottages, graded the grounds, filled washouts, put up fences, planted trees and began a farm" (Strickland, 1976: 47). Clinton Farms, in New Jersey, also took a nontraditional view of women's work and included an early form of inmate self-government (Freedman, 1981: 137). Most institutions emphasized a feminine ideal, however, and women were rewarded for maintaining ladylike decorum and cleanliness with privileges such as prettier uniforms (Rafter, 1985: 39).

In Niantic, Connecticut, the women's reformatory, built in 1918, was set in the woods with farmland and a stocked lake. In the 1930s, Lekkerkerker (1931: 121) described "The Farm" at Niantic in the following way:

> The Farm certainly has charms: the buildings, scattered wide apart, form an attractive whole with the romantic lake, the wood and thicket, the rolling hills and green pasture, which offer the women abundant opportunity for healthy outdoor sports, such as hiking, swimming, fishing, sleighing and skating in winter, picking berries, chopping wood, etc. which, in fact, is often done by them.

Niantic started with four farmhouses that were renovated as cottages for about 29 "troubled, diseased and defective" women. The farm became almost self-sufficient; by the late 1930s, inmates were selling the surplus food grown there. Niantic, like several prisons in the early to mid-1900s, had a prison nursery. Only after WWII did overcrowding require a curtailment of the farm activities and closing down the prison nursery (Rierden, 1997: 48).

Overall, the interaction between female staff and female prisoners was one of mutual dependency. Freedman wrote that the prisoners transferred their dependency needs to the female staff members. The staff became surrogate mothers to their female dependents. The staff, in turn, needed the prisoners because they were the only appropriate outlet for the female professionals' training and energy (Freedman, 1981: 105).

The life of a matron was a difficult one. She was expected to live at the institution and, in some institutions, to eat with the prisoners during all meals. She had only a day off each week with vacation days determined by how many years she had worked for the institution. Twelve-hour shifts were not uncommon (Lekkerkerker, 1931: 279–280). Rafter (1985: 75) wrote:

> Meager salaries, long hours, and unpleasant working conditions undermined the morale of staff members. According to a report of the late 1920s, at Marysville matrons worked twelve-hour shifts with only two days off each month. Some lived in rooms designed for inmates, and both they and the superintendent received salaries that were "disgracefully low."

Primary complaints centered on inadequate resources, overcrowding, and lack of programs (Rafter, 1985: 77). Lekkerkerker described the prisons that existed in the 1930s as varied in staff size. Bedford Hills had a ratio of one staff person to 3 inmates, whereas the Ohio reformatory had a ratio of one to 14. Staff filled both custodial and educational roles; there were sewing instructors and farm supervisors as well as matrons (Lekkerkerker, 1931: 255). Lekkerkerker bemoaned the fact that the matron's low pay and absence of responsibility were insufficient to attract the quality of staff thought desirable for the position (1931: 265).

Women incarcerated in the early reformatories were not serious criminals and did not often pose a security risk for the staff, but those that did found that punishment in a women's reformatory might be the same as in any other prison. Lekkerkerker's descriptions of the discipline used in early prisons and reformatories indicate that the power of persuasion was used more than force. Sympathy and emotion usually were used to appeal to women inmates, rather than either rationality or force (1931: 424–425). However, harsher punishments did exist, including forfeiture of wages, distinctive dress, cutting the hair close to the scalp, and solitary confinement (1931: 427).

"Dungeons," rooms with no ventilation or light, were available for those who attacked officers, destroyed property, or threatened safety (Freedman, 1981: 99). Some serious disturbances did occur in 1888 in Framingham, Massachusetts, and in 1899 in Hudson, New York (Freedman, 1981: 100). These disturbances may have been caused by inefficient security and overcrowding. A more prevalent problem, according to early discipline reports, might have been homosexuality between the races. Because of this "unnatural attraction," staff wanted to segregate African-American women in Bedford Hills and other institutions (Freedman, 1981: 140). Female staff could be as prone to abusive treatment of prisoners as their male counterparts. A scandal at Bedford Hills in 1915 involved the use of physically abusive punishments. Eventually, some of these problems led to riots, such as those at Bedford Hills in the 1920s (Rafter, 1985: 77–79).

The Custodial Institution

Rafter's (1985) historical study explained that women's prisons evolved into two distinct types: the reformatory and the custodial institution. Although the reformatory model is most often viewed as the model of early institutions for women, it should be noted that more women served time in "custodial" prisons than in reformatories. Whether these women were confined in wings or separate buildings on the grounds of men's prisons or housed in a separate facility, the policies and administration of the facilities followed a traditional, punitive, and custodial approach. The custodial model, with minimal adherence to any of the reformatory concepts, was followed most often in new construction after 1930.

Women in custodial institutions were older than those in reformatories. Rafter reported that half the women at custody institutions were between the ages of 31 and 50, whereas reformatory (Albion) women were between the ages of 15 and 30 (1985: 126). Reformatory women were also disproportionately white; African Americans were almost entirely excluded. Albion, for instance, was 97 percent white. This exclusion of African-American women occurred despite the fact that African Americans composed a disproportionate share of prison commitments. In New York, African Americans comprised 12.5 percent of the commitments in 1831; this figure had risen to 40 percent by 1934 (Rafter, 1985: 132). Tennessee had even higher figures. Between 1860 and 1887, African Americans comprised 70 percent of the women incarcerated;

in 1900 they comprised 90 percent. The figure declined to 65 percent by 1926-1934 (Rafter, 1985: 132). The African Americans who were placed in reformatories were segregated into separate cottages (Rafter, 1985: 37).

In other regions of the country, such as the West and the South, only makeshift arrangements were available for female prisoners long into the 1900s. The prison farms popular in the South were thought to be extremely inappropriate places for women. Consequently, the female felon was dealt with by alternative methods, unless she was an extremely serious offender or an African American. If she met either of those criteria, she may have ended up on the prison farm and been expected to do less arduous physical work, such as gardening or housework in the home of the superintendent (Rafter, 1985: 88).

In the South, inmates were often "leased out" to private farmers for labor. Women were not wanted by private lessees because they were not considered economically productive. Consequently, the state kept them with the old and sick men (Rafter, 1985: 151). In 1910, all women prisoners in Texas were transferred to a central state farm called Goree. There, African-American women worked in the field and white women worked at sewing and in the garden. This institution was in a dilapidated condition, and all 60 inmates, except for the few white women there, were housed in one building (Rafter, 1985: 89).

Research in the Reformatory

One of the interesting aspects of some early reformatories was the presence of female social scientists who gathered information and conducted experiments on the inmates. Female professionals who studied female prisoners were outcasts from the male professions of medicine and science (Freedman, 1981: 121). Some institutions, like Bedford Hills, became centers of research on female criminality. These female researchers pointed out factors in crime causation, such as poor family life and temptation, years ahead of their "discovery" by male criminologists; yet this earlier work was largely ignored by the field of criminology.

Katharine B. Davis was one such early physician and superintendent who conducted research with female delinquents (Freedman, 1981: 116). In 1910, she obtained a grant for psychological testing of feebleminded mental defectives and established the Bureau of Social Hygiene at Bedford Hills. These women were isolated on the reformatory grounds and studied by female researchers (Rafter, 1985: 69). The thrust of this testing and research was eugenics. Women were thought to be the breeders of future classes of criminals; evidently, the goal of the research was to test for defectiveness and then prevent those found to be defective from having children.

Frances Kellor was another American researcher who measured and tested physical qualities of female prisoners and compared them to a "normal sample." She found that very few of Caesare Lombroso's[4] findings could be replicated. In her comparisons, nativity proved to be a strong intervening factor, as did the social environment from which the criminal women came. Kellor wisely attributed many of the criminal sample's lower scores in smell, hearing, pain, fatigue, and memory to poor physical health brought on by poor living conditions. Kellor found that workhouse women had even lower scores than penitentiary women on all physical tests and were more likely to come from backgrounds of poverty (1900a & b).

Kellor, as well as others who studied women in prison in the late 1800s and early 1900s, believed that the women's life experiences and generally deprived backgrounds had much to do with their entry into criminality. For instance, Kellor wrote that many female criminals came from the ranks of domestic service. She found several explanations for this fact: proportionally, many women were employed in domestic service; inadequate salaries spurred women to steal; workers engaged in domestic service were typically unskilled and unable to do anything else; domestic service was an easy route to prostitution; and employment bureaus were often procurement places for prostitution (Kellor, 1900a: 676).

Jean Weidensall studied female prisoners and conducted research at Bedford Hills in the early 1900s. She compared reformatory inmates to working women and schoolgirls using a variety of tests that measured intelligence, skill, and mechanical ability. She also collected comparisons on height, weight, strength of grip, and visual acuity. The reformatory inmates generally did worse on all tests. Criminal women were found to be "dull," meaning they had lower intelligence and mechanical scores than the average general population. They also were found to be easily frustrated, emotionally unstable, suspicious, and unthinking. Obviously, some of these observations must be understood in light of the times. Women were held to a strict standard of conduct, and criminal women's conduct did not fit into the ladylike mold. The female researchers were also a product of their time, and they no doubt were influenced by stereotypes of women that held that women were, or should be, more docile, compliant, and "nicer" than men. Weidensall believed there were several types of female criminals. Some, she wrote, were intelligent but too lazy to work, some were truly criminal, and some were just so unintelligent that they drifted into crime. She believed the latter type could be guided by moral training (Weidensall, 1916).

The Laboratory of Social Hygiene at Bedford Hills, the site of Weidensall's research, was funded by outside grants. This laboratory was housed in a separate building on the grounds of the prison; Weidensall was both the director of the laboratory and superintendent of the prison. One account of an experiment undertaken with "intractable and trouble-making" inmates at Bedford is interesting in its use of "innovative" methods for dealing with prisoners. Spaulding (1923) noted how a number of these prisoners were identified and moved to isolated patient cottages on the grounds of Bedford Hills. These "psychopathic" prisoners were then encouraged to create a type of self-government. Spaulding wrote that the research was not a success; the prisoners wore down the staff by the frequency and seriousness of their outbursts. Soon the self-government attempt was abandoned and institutional discipline reinstated, including wet packs and isolation.

Another group of female researchers collected large amounts of information from female prisoners in the State Prison for Women at Auburn, New York, the New York County Penitentiary, the New York City Workhouse, and the New York Magdalen Home. They collected case studies from many female prisoners and compared histories. Two general causal factors were identified: poor economic background, with its resulting impoverished home environment, and inferior mental ability. They found that almost half the women studied had "defective strains" within their families, such as alcoholism, feeblemindedness, neuroticism, or sexual irregularities (Fernald, Hayes, and Dawley, 1920). This identification of genetic strains paralleled earlier research on families of male criminals, such as the research by Dugdale (1895), and reflected a Darwinian influence in criminology.

Hahn (1979; later known as Rafter) called these studies "cacogenic," explaining that they identified the woman as a breeder of criminals and elevated her to the status of "social menace." According to Rafter/Hahn, researchers such as Dugdale believed harlotry was hereditary and that the bad woman was inevitably the mother of children who would grow up to be criminals and degenerates. The old imagery of the bad woman thus underwent considerable modification and embellishment in the Social Darwinist family studies. These studies showed her promiscuity to be a matter far more serious than mere personal immorality: the loose woman became a prolific breeder of harlots and a criminal type in her own right (Hahn, 1979: 8). Zedner (1991) also discussed how control shifted from controlling the criminality of women to controlling the sexuality/procreation of women. Images of genetic defectiveness replaced visions of evil women, but women still needed to be locked up.

Freedman found that there were two competing theories of female criminality during the early 1900s (1981: 40). The social determinism implicit in the family studies and studies conducted at the Laboratory for Social Hygiene at Bedford Hills encouraged such policies as sterilization and the incarceration of women for long periods of time in reformatories and penitentiaries (Hahn, 1979: 15). Another train of thought was slightly more feminist and pointed out the "bad influence" of men in the women's histories. However, this approach refused to view women as more than hapless victims of males; these researchers were either unwilling or unable to see women as individuals in their own right. Freedman wrote, "The economic explanation predominated in women's rights movement literature; it constituted a minor theme for prison reformers, who launched their major attack on the sexual victimization of women by men" (1981: 41).

Thus, women's criminality was explained by either biological or social causes. Some women were still thought to be born criminal, either because of defective strains they inherited (and could pass on to their children) or because of mental defectiveness or stupidity, which created a propensity to commit crime. Social causes involved the environment in which women were raised. If a woman had poor parental models, or if she was corrupted by an evil man, then she was only weak and not inherently defective. Such a woman could be saved.

In a very real sense, the reformatory was used as a method for restraining defective women from getting pregnant and producing children who would be criminal, defective, or both. Even into the mid-1930s, the Gluecks (1934) believed that some of the women should be kept indeterminately or sterilized in order to prevent them from reproducing. Promiscuous urges also would decline with age, thus allowing the release of older offenders. Those without biologically caused degeneracy could be retrained, and their delinquency could be prevented by education and social work.

Certainly concern about reproduction may have been the reason for the longer sentences given for relatively trivial crimes committed by women considered promiscuous (Rafter, 1985: 54). Albion inmates served an average term of 33.8 months compared to 28 months for those incarcerated in Ohio's custodial institution, despite the fact that Ohio's inmates were probably there for much more serious crimes whereas Albion's inmates were all misdemeanants (Rafter, 1985: 121). It is also possible that reformatories were considered such a good idea that many courts decided to keep women in them for longer terms. Some legislatures granted courts more discretion in sentencing women, and longer sentences were available for women (Freedman, 1981: 129).

Those researchers who emphasized the social factors in female crime causation believed that training and moral uplifting offered the best chance of rehabilitation. As a man may have caused the woman offender's downfall, a good man could be her salvation (Healy and Bronner, 1926). Consequently, theories regarding crime and treatment solutions were oriented to isolating and teaching her better moral habits in the hope that she could attract a suitable marriage partner. Women in prison were taught domestic skills to prepare them for this goal. The fact that these women would probably need to support themselves as they had before prison and needed skills to do so was ignored.

THE END OF THE REFORMATORY ERA

The women's reformatory movement gathered momentum slowly. From its inception about 1870 to the century's close, it produced only four institutions. But this was a period of germination during which reformers experimented, venturing ever further from traditional concepts of the prison as they evolved their own model. . . . Between 1900 and 1935, seventeen states opened women's reformatories. . . . By 1935, the women's reformatory movement had exhausted itself. (Rafter, 1985: xxiii)

Reasons given for the demise of the reformatory ideal include the increasing disinterest with prostitution as a national issue and the gradual exit of the zealous reformers described previously. The Depression also hastened the end of interest in reformatories (Rafter, 1985: xxiii). By the 1930s, the population of reformatories had changed in response to increasing numbers of female criminals. Felons were sent to women's reformatories because states started closing custodial units (Rafter, 1985: 81). For instance, in 1933 a portion of the custodial unit for women at Auburn Prison in New York was closed and the women were transferred to Bedford Hills (Strickland, 1976: 48). For all practical purposes, the transfer of these women ended the reformatory experiment at Bedford Hills; the emphasis after this time was on custodial issues.

Women's prisons were first built as separate institutions in states in and outside the Northeast through the early and mid-1900s—indeed, even into the 1970s. (See Table 2.1.) Those institutions built after 1930 were built and operated primarily under a modified custodial model. Women's prisons tended to continue to follow the same vague ideals that defined women as different and institutions for women as a place to prepare them for womanhood. At least we assume they did; little was actually written detailing the methods or goals of these institutions. We see no attention directed to women's prisons between the time Lekkerkerker did her study in the early 1930s and the mid-1960s, when Ward and Kassebaum (1965), Giallombardo (1966), and Strickland (1976) looked again at the women's prison.

Morton (1998) describes this time period as one where many women served their time in wings of male units. These women may have been punished by being locked alone in abandoned buildings and/or having their heads shaved. Women were housed in facilities with no heat, light, or water; and they had to use latrines and shower areas with no privacy screens in full view of male officers. Some were locked in rooms with no lights or ventilation, and so small it was impossible for them to stand up. Many served their sentence with absolutely no programs available to better themselves.

Overlooked sources useful in discovering what was occurring in women's prisons between 1930 and the 1970s are the biographies and histories of early superintendents. For instance, the career of Edna Mahan, superintendent of Clinton Farms (New Jersey's Reformatory for Women) from 1928 to 1968, almost completely overlaps the period of time in question. Hawkes (1998) describes Mahan as one of the most powerful and successful women of the 20th century.

Edna Mahan began her term as superintendent when she was only 28 and served for 40 years, dying of colon cancer at the age of 68. Her career bridged the reformatory era and the "rehabilitative" era of the 1970s. She attempted, and was successful at, many innovations at Clinton Farm. For instance, she promoted and utilized "student government," perhaps allowing it to prosper more completely than at any other institution (Hawkes, 1998: 9). Mahan also was an advocate for the children of women; Clinton Farm had a nursery from 1916–1975. Mahan hired pediatric nurses, held baby hygiene classes, and coordinated with other state agencies to arrange for community plans (Hawkes, 1998: 12). Until 1949, infants up to 2 years old could stay with their mothers. This practice stopped only after WWII because of overcrowding and concerns that it was not healthy for the baby (Hawkes, 1998: 14). In the 1960s, increasing numbers of younger, disturbed, assaultive, and addicted inmates entered the prison (Hawkes, 1998: 18). Overcrowding,

Table 2.1 State and Federal Correctional Institutions for Women, 1873–1975

State	Title at Opening	Date
Indiana	Woman's Prison	1873
Massachusetts	Reformatory Prison for Women	1877
New York	House of Refuge for Women, Hudson	1887
New York	House of Refuge for Women, Albion	1893
New York	Reformatory Prison for Women, Bedford Hills	1902
New Jersey	State Reformatory for Women	1913
Maine	Reformatory for Women	1916
Ohio	Reformatory for Women	1916
Kansas	Industrial Farm for Women	1917
Michigan	Training School for Women	1917
Connecticut	Farm for Women	1918
Iowa	Women's Reformatory	1918
Arkansas	Farm for Women	1920
California	Industrial Farm for Women	1920
Minnesota	Reformatory for Women	1920
Nebraska	State Reformatory for Women	1920
Pennsylvania	State Industrial Home for Women	1920
Wisconsin	Industrial Home for Women	1921
United States	Industrial Institution for Women (Alderson)	1927
Delaware	Correctional Institution for Women	1929
Connecticut	Correctional Instutution for Women	1930
Illinois	State Reformatory for Women	1930
Virginia	State Industrial Farm for Women	1932
North Carolina	Correctional Center for Women	1934
California	Correctional Institution for Women	1936
Kentucky	Correctional Institution for Women	1938
South Carolina	Harbison Correctional Institution for Women	1938
Maryland	Correctional Institution for Women	1940
Alabama	Julia Tutwiler Prison for Women	1942
West Virginia	State Prison for Women	1948
Georgia	Rehabilitation Center for Women	1957
Missouri	State Correctional Center for Women	1960
Louisiana	Correctional Institution for Women	1961
Ohio	Women's Correctional Institution	1963
Nevada	Women's Correctional Center	1964
Oregon	Women's Correctional Center	1965
Tennessee	Prison for Women	1966
Colorado	Women's Correctional Institute	1968
Washington	Purdy Treatment Center for Women	1970
Oklahoma	Women's Treatment Facility	1973
South Carolina	Women's Correctional Center	1973

SOURCE: Estelle Freedman, *Their Sister's Keepers* (Ann Arbor: University of Michigan Press, 1981), pp. 144–145.

reaching crisis proportions, eliminated many of the innovations and "bucolic" living that characterized Clinton Farm in the early part of the century.

Morton (1998) writes of Martha Wheeler, superintendent of Ohio Reformatory for women from 1958–1974. In describing Wheeler's career, Morton notes that Wheeler, like other superintendents, advanced innovations and programs for women, but also had a maternalistic and patronizing attitude toward female inmates. Women were called and treated as "girls." Policies were adopted following a belief system that women were "special" and needed special care and special resources. Since the system was, by and large, run by men, for men, these early superintendents were constantly frustrated by the lack of resources allotted to female inmates.

CONCLUSION: THE LEGACY
OF DIFFERENCE

Freedman concluded that early reformatories did accomplish good things: they prevented sexual abuse, allowed freedom from exploitation of labor, and provided services for women such as nurseries that were possible only in centralized prisons. However, problems did remain, and some were actually created by the reformatory. Women's needs were still unmet, overcrowding and classification were still problems, and the reformatory ideal created a legacy of differential care based on stereotypes of what women were like and what they needed. This legacy lingers, exemplified in sexual stereotypes in work and vocational training programs and treatment of women prisoners as "children" (Freedman, 1981: 152).

Rafter concluded that the custodial institutions present a truer picture of female prisoners in the early years, since most women were sent to these institutions. Only a small portion of women ended up in the "nicer" reformatories; most served their sentences in grim custodial institutions or prison farms in the South. Only young, white misdemeanants escaped these conditions.

Prisons for women have inherited the legacy of the reformatory ideal. Although two specific types of institutions for women emerged, the custody institution and the reformatory, the ideas surrounding them merged together, and the institutions that were built after 1930 followed vague ideals that mixed both types. It becomes clear that the history of women's prisons has shaped contemporary prisons. Further, the conceptions that influenced early institutions—that women are different from men, that they need "feminizing" and domestic training, and that they are not so much criminal as sexually immoral—are still very prevalent today.

NOTES

1. Men, for example, might be subjected to a "cuckold's court" or forced to ride backward on a donkey for allowing their wives to cuckold or dominate them. They might also provoke community sanction for overstepping the bounds of appropriate patriarchal domination, when, for example, they beat their wives to excess. It was only when a man grossly overstepped the bounds of appropriate chastisement, however—for example, by mutilating or nearly killing his wife—that he might be sanctioned by the community through the performance of a misrule or a charivari (Dobash et al., 1986: 18).

2. Bridewells were early places of confinement that were usually used for vagrants, debtors, and petty criminals.

3. For an example of this type of thinking, see Adams, 1914.

4. An Italian doctor, called the "father of criminology" for pioneering positivist methodology in the study of crime in the mid to late 1800s, Lombroso compared samples of criminals to "normal" men and women and concluded that criminals were less evolved and had atavistic features, such as heavy musculature and excessive hairiness, that showed their primitiveness. Eventually he identified other types besides the "born criminal," such as the opportunistic criminal and the passionate criminal. He also developed a theory regarding female criminals; specifically, that they were less evolved and that they also could be identified by their physical attributes.

SUGGESTED READINGS

Dobash, R., R. Dobash, and S. Gutteridge. 1986. *The Imprisonment of Women*. New York: Basil Blackwell.

Feinman, C. 1983. "An Historical Overview of the Treatment of Incarcerated Women: Myths and Realities of Rehabilitation." *The Prison Journal* 63, 2: 12–16.

Freedman, E. 1974. "Their Sister's Keepers: A Historical Perspective of Female Correctional Institutions in the U.S." *Feminist Studies* 2: 77–95.

Lekkerkerker, E. 1931. *Reformatories for Women in the U.S.* Gronigen, Netherlands: J.B. Wolters.

Rafter, N. 1985. *Partial Justice: State Prisons and Their Inmates, 1800–1935*. Boston: Northeastern Press.

3

Who Are the Women in Prison?

Do women commit less crime than men, as evidenced by official statistics and self-reports? If so, why? Are women committing crime more often today than in the past? If so, why? What types of crimes do women commit? Are women becoming more violent? What are the characteristics of women in prison? What differences exist between female and male prisoners? These are the topics explored in this chapter.

FEMALE CRIMINALITY

One of the most potent correlates of crime is sex. That is, if one were to guess the first demographic characteristic of an offender, the first guess should be that the offender is a man. For most crimes, and especially for violent crime, men are much more likely to be arrested, convicted, and sentenced to prison than are women. Why this is so is subject to a variety of explanations.

One argument is that crime statistics indicating that men are more criminally inclined than women are simply wrong. There has been a persistent belief that the numbers presented in official statistics do not represent the true statistics on female crime (for instance, see Pollak, 1950). The premise is that the male system of criminal justice protects and excuses women from their actions and punishments. This argument has been coined the "chivalry hypothesis." Many attempts have been made to discover whether this belief is myth or reality. Much of the differential sentencing of men and women can be attributed to factors other than sex, for example, to differences in criminal history, participation level in the crime, single parenthood, economic dependency, or relative seriousness/loss of the crime (even within crime categories) (Daly, 1989c, 1994; Kruttschnitt and Green, 1984; Steffensmeier, 1980, 1983; Steffensmeier and Steffensmeier, 1980; Tjaden and Tjaden, 1981).

After reviewing all the studies in the area, however, it appears that "chivalry" has probably had a moderate but real influence historically (Pollock, 1999a). In other words, some women, for some offenses, may have benefited from a type of chivalry. Certain studies, for instance, found that women who were economically dependent, were mothers, and were not the primary participant in the crime were more likely to receive lenient sentences (Farrington and Morris, 1983; Kruttschnitt, 1982). On the other hand, research also indicates that other women, those typically perceived as less deserving and/or perceived as less "feminine," did not benefit from any chivalry of the system (Wilbanks, 1986). Also, in more recent years, whatever chivalry might have existed in the system has been eliminated or drastically reduced to negligible effects due to determinate sentencing and a "get tough" approach (Pollock, 1999a; Raeder, 1993b).[1]

Chesney-Lind (1982, 1988, 1997; also see Chesney-Lind and Sheldon, 1998) points out that female delinquents have always received differential treatment, but in a negative way. Even if adult women may be less likely to receive prison sentences, female juveniles are (or at least were) more likely to receive institutionalization than their male counterparts. They were also more likely to be drawn into the juvenile justice system because of status offenses such as incorrigibility rather than delinquent offenses, despite the fact that self-reports show that boys and girls are fairly similar in the commission of their delinquencies. The reasons for this may be found in the prevalent beliefs regarding the female delinquent; for instance, that she is more psychologically disturbed than the male delinquent or that her home life is more dysfunctional.

Today, adult women's criminal activities continue to be largely in the areas of crime long associated with women—larceny (primarily shoplifting) and forgery (use of checks and credit cards). Like men's crimes, some women's crimes have shown a decline in the last several years. As reported in the 1990 edition of this text, between 1978 and 1987, some women's crimes showed large percentage increases (*Uniform Crime Reports,* 1988):

   Embezzlement (135.2 percent increase)

   Curfew/loitering laws (130.9 percent increase)

   Other assaults (80.8 percent increase)

   Offenses against family and children (82.4 percent increase)

   Liquor laws (85.4 percent increase)

These large percentage increases, however, translated into fairly small real numbers for women as compared to men. For instance, whereas the 80.8 percent increase in arrests of women for "other assaults" translated to 40,194 arrests, a 67.8 percent increase of males translated to 203,310. Thus, the "explosion" that supposedly took place in female crime meant little in terms of real numbers.

During the next decade (1988 through 1997), women's increases in some crime categories were more modest, while others showed even greater increases (*Uniform Crime Reports,* 1998):

   Embezzlement (48.9 percent increase)

   Curfew/loitering laws (233.6 percent increase)

   Other assaults (111.5 percent increase)

   Offenses against family and children (188.6 percent increase)

   Liquor laws (19.6 percent increase)

The index crimes showed general increases (except for murder), but the rate of increase varied across crime categories (*Uniform Crime Reports,* 1998):

   Murder and nonnegligent manslaughter (28.6 percent decrease)

   Forcible rape (2 percent increase)

   Robbery (27.5 percent increase)

   Aggravated assault (88.1 percent increase)

   Burglary (9.4 percent increase)

   Larceny/theft (9.6 percent increase)

   Motor vehicle theft (22.5 percent increase)

   Arson (9.2 percent increase)

See Table 3.1.

Interestingly, the *Uniform Crime Reports* of 1999, which compare the percentage change of arrest rates of men and women for the decade 1990–1999, show a very different picture. Both men and women show overall percentage decreases in all index crimes, except for one—women show a 48 percent increase in aggravated assault (*Uniform Crime Reports,* 1999: 217).

Table 3.1 Women's Involvement in Crime by Category

	PERCENT OF TOTAL ARRESTS	
Crime	1988	1998
Murder and nonnegligent manslaughter	12.5%	11%
Forcible rape	1.2%	1%
Robbery	8.1%	10%
Aggravated assault	13.3%	20%
Burglary	7.9%	13%
Larceny/theft	31.1%	35%
Motor vehicle theft	9.7%	16%
Arson	13.7%	15%
Other assaults	15.1%	22%
Forgery and counterfeiting	34.4%	39%
Fraud	43.5%	46%
Embezzlement	38.1%	49%
Stolen property	11.6%	16%
Prostitution	64.8%	58%
Drug abuse violations	14.9%	18%
Offenses against family and children	17.4%	22%
(Other crime categories excluded)		

SOURCE:*Uniform Crime Reports, 1988* (Washington, D.C.: U.S. Department of Justice); *Uniform Crime Reports, 1998* (Washington, D.C.: U.S. Department of Justice). Same information also found in Bureau of Justice Statistics, 1999, *Special Report: Women Offenders* (Washington, D.C.: U.S. Department of Justice), p. 5.

Even with increased participation in some crime categories, women continue to represent a fairly small proportion of the criminal offender population. For instance, 22 percent of all arrestees are women; and only 14 percent of all those arrested for violent offenses are women (BJS, 1999c; Greenfield and Snell, 1999). The number of convicted women is smaller still—women represent only 16 percent of all convicted felony defendants. However, their participation varies tremendously by type of crime. Although only about 8 percent of all convicted violent felons in state courts are women, women represent 23 percent of all those convicted of property offenses, 17 percent of all those convicted of drug offenses, and 41 percent of all those convicted of forgery, fraud, and embezzlement offenses (BJS, 1999c; Greenfield and Snell, 1999: 5).

Violent Crime

Despite a popular belief that women are becoming more violent, women continue to be underrepresented in violent crime rates. The Bureau of Justice Statistics (BJS 1999c; Greenfield and Snell, 1999: 2) reports that men's per capita violent crime rate is seven times that of women. Further, most women (three out of four) who are arrested for a violent crime have committed simple assault. Other characteristics include the following:

- Women most often victimize other women (three out of four victims are women).

- About 62 percent of female perpetrators had a prior relationship with the victim (compared to 36 percent of male perpetrators).

- Women contributed to about half of all child murders; they were more likely to kill infants than older children.

- A little over a quarter (28 percent) of violent female offenders are juveniles.

- About 40 percent of female violent offenders were under the influence of alcohol or drugs.

- About 60 percent of female murder offenders are African American. (BJS, 1999c; Greenfield and Snell, 1999)

Uniform Crime Report figures show that between 1990 and 1999, violent crime arrests of men declined by 15 percent, but increased for women by 37 percent. However, looking at the index crimes, one sees that the increase is completely attributable to an increase in aggravated assault. Increases in domestic violence arrests as a result of mandatory arrest policies have been proposed as an explanation for this increase. Also, it is very misleading to use percentage increase figures for women's violent crime because of the extremely small base numbers.

In 1998 women represented 2 percent of those convicted of sexual assault, 7 percent of those convicted of robbery, 11 percent of those convicted of aggravated assault, and 18 percent of those convicted of simple assault. The murder rate for women was 1.3 per 100,000 (for men it was 11.5 per 100,000). The murder rate for women has been declining since 1980, and the per capita rate for women committing murder is the lowest it has been since 1976 (BJS, 1999c; Greenfield and Snell, 1999: 2–7).

Earlier studies of women's crime patterns also reported small percentages of women convicted and incarcerated for violent crimes (DeConstanzo and Valente, 1984; Goetting and Howsen, 1983). Crawford, for instance, reported that 37 percent of the women in her prison sample were in prison for violent crimes—murder, rape, robbery, aggravated assault, arson, other assaults, and weapons (1988b: 8). Today, about 28 percent of imprisoned women were sent there for violent crimes (BJS, 1999c; Greenfield and Snell, 1999: 6). The lower percentages of women in prison for violent crimes today are partly explained by the decreasing arrest rates for violent crimes, and partly by the large numbers of women sent to prison for drug and property crimes.[2]

Spousal Homicide. A number of researchers have reported on the issues concerning women who are in prison for killing abusive husbands (Browne, 1987; Ewing, 1987; Mann, 1984, 1988; also see Blount, Kuhns, and Silverman, 1993). Ewing, for instance, reports on samples where from 40 percent to 78 percent of women who killed their husbands or boyfriends had been abused (1987: 23). In the late 1980s, an average of 11 percent of adult incarcerated women were in prison for domestic violence (Crawford, 1988b: 8).

The woman who has been battered and psychologically abused by her husband or boyfriend for a period of time may see no way out of her pain and danger other than to kill him. When she does, the same criminal justice agencies that were unwilling or unable to protect her are now ready to prosecute. Many of these women, historically and today, serve long prison sentences for their actions. Ewing reports that of the 100 battered women he surveyed, 12 received life sentences and 17 more received sentences in excess of 10 years (Ewing, 1987: 42). Although some celebrated cases have resulted in acquittals due to the defense based on the "battered woman syndrome," many others have resulted in years of imprisonment for women convicted of murder or manslaughter.

There has been mixed acceptance of the self-defense argument based on the "battered woman syndrome." Some courts are unwilling to allow jurors to hear expert witness testimony explaining the psychological state of the woman who suffers over a long period of time. Absent that evidence, jurors find it hard to understand why the woman does not just leave the abusive husband or seek outside help. In many cases, of course, there is substantial evidence that women have tried to leave, have sought help, and have suffered increased violence and threats because of their attempts. Browne (1987) found that battered women who killed their abusers, as compared to battered women who did not kill, more often had husbands who used drugs and alcohol and were more frequently intoxicated. The men had also used more threats and had exhibited assaultive behavior more often; the men had been more likely to threaten not only the woman but her children or other family members as well; many of them had abused the children; and the abuse of their wives was more likely to include sexual abuse (Browne, 1987: 182).

Mann (1988, 1993) offered a cautionary note in her study; she found that not all women who kill their boyfriends or spouses fit the battered woman syndrome. Mann analyzed 145 cases of homicide where the victim had been sexually intimate with the offender and found that the relationship was most often common law; the offender and victim were most often nonwhite; and alcohol or drugs were more likely to be a factor than in nondomestic killings. Although 58.9 percent of the women claimed self-defense as a motivation for the killing, Mann observed that the circumstances of the killing did not seem to warrant such a justification in many cases. Also, 30 percent of the women had records of previous arrests for violent crimes, including assault, battery, and weapons charges (Mann, 1988: 45). Thirty-seven percent of the women charged with domestic killings received prison sentences, and the average sentence was 10 years (1988: 47). Mann concluded that in many cases, because of premeditation, previous criminal histories, and use of alcohol or drugs by both victim and offender, the battered woman syndrome may not be warranted.

In more recent years, the number of women who kill a spouse or intimate has decreased. A Bureau of Justice Statistics study shows that from 1977 to 1995, the rate of male intimates killed by female partners declined by two-thirds, from 1.5 to .5 per 100,000. The rate of female intimates killed by male partners declined also, but not by much (from 1.6 to 1.3 per 100,000) (BJS,

1994a). Speculation is that more easily obtained divorces and the presence of battered women's shelters have provided options for women in abusive situations. The fact that the rate of men who kill their female partners has not shown such a significant decrease lends support to the theory that a proportion of spousal or intimate homicides on the part of women were a product of self-defense.

Property Crime

As stated before, women's contribution to crime is largely in the "female" crimes of larceny, forgery, and embezzlement. Percentage increases paint a troubling picture of increases in female criminality. For instance, between 1990 and 1996, the number of men convicted of property felonies dropped about 2 percent while convicted female defendants increased 44 percent (BJS, 1999c; Greenfield and Snell, 1999: 7). However, the *Uniform Crime Report* comparison of 1990 to 1999 arrests shows that male arrests decreased 30 percent and female arrests also decreased, although not as much (13 percent) (*Uniform Crime Reports,* 1999: 217). There is no doubt that females are now more likely than ever before to participate in property crime. As noted, their arrest rate is almost equal to that of men in forgery, embezzlement, and larceny.

However, one must be cautious when interpreting such statistics. Daly's (1989b, 1994) research indicates, for instance, that although women and men may be convicted of the same charge, for example, embezzling, their crimes tend to be very different. Women's crimes tend to involve small amounts of money, and the women gain access through low-level jobs, for example, as cashiers.

Drug Crime

In the late 1980s, Crawford (1988a: 20) reported that about one-third of incarcerated women used heroin and about half used cocaine. More than 20 percent of the women were incarcerated for drug offenses, and 25 percent of the women said they committed the crime they were sentenced for to get money to buy drugs (Crawford, 1988a: 32). These numbers seem small when compared to today's figures. This section will present women's arrest patterns for drug crimes, while a later section will discuss drug use patterns and the relationship between drug use and prior victimization. In Chapter 5, treatment issues regarding drug use and abuse will be discussed.

According to a Bureau of Justice Statistics (1994b) report, over 30 percent of female prisoners' crimes of conviction were drug offenses (compared to 20.7 percent of male prisoners).

Women were more likely than men to have been under the influence of drugs at the time of offense (36 percent compared to 31 percent); they were also more likely to have committed an offense to get money to buy drugs (one in four compared to one in six). Finally, according to the BJS report, women with drug histories were twice as likely to have committed robbery, burglary, larceny, and fraud as those who were not on drugs.

It should be noted that sentencing figures do not necessarily indicate greater drug use among women, only that they are more likely to be arrested and sentenced to prison. Raeder points out that 20 years ago, nearly two-thirds of the women convicted of federal felonies (the majority of which would be drug crimes) were granted probation, but in 1991 only 28 percent of women were given probation. Average sentences increased from 27 months in 1984 to 67 months in 1990 (Raeder, 1993a: 31–32). As mentioned in a previous chapter, Raeder believes that gender-neutral sentencing under federal guidelines is unfair for women because family responsibilities are not ordinarily considered "extraordinary" and, therefore, are not taken into account during sentencing. Since ordinarily women are not major dealers and do not play a big role in drug offenses, they have no bargaining tools and therefore get sentences similar to the sentences of those who are much more involved but who have information to trade (Raeder, 1993a & b).

Huling (1991, 1995) details the plight of some arrested drug couriers in New York. These women often knew nothing about the operation, yet received incredibly harsh sentences, including life imprisonment. They typically came from Columbia or African nations and were coerced or bribed into making the trip. In Huling's study, most of the women (96 percent) had no criminal record, yet received the 15 years to life mandatory term as mandated by New York's harsh sentencing statutes.

Crime Pattern Changes Over Time

One can draw either rosy or gloomy conclusions after reviewing women's offense patterns. The figures have shown huge increases in criminal activity as measured by percentage increases; for instance, since 1990, the number of female defendants convicted of felonies in state courts has increased at more than twice the rate of increase for male defendants (BJS, 1999c; Greenfield and Snell, 1999: 6). However, women's actual contributions to the total crime index continue to be relatively small, except in certain crime categories, and in the last decade, the numbers show percentage decreases in all index crimes except aggravated assault.

Although juveniles will not be covered in this text, it should be noted that this group of women also show greater increases in arrests than males. From 1990 to 1999, there was a 40 percent increase in violent crime arrests of female juveniles and a 3 percent increase in property crime arrests—compared to an 11 percent decline in violent crime arrests and a 30 percent decline in property crime arrests of male juveniles (*Uniform Crime Reports,* 1998: 215). Again, however, the problem of low base numbers calls into question the efficacy of percentage increase figures. Female juveniles' proportion of all arrests grew from 21 percent to 24 percent between 1989 and 1993—hardly a dramatic increase (Poe-Yamagata and Butts, 1996).

Female Criminals—In Their Own Words

Several sources offer brief glimpses into the lives of women criminals (Carlen, 1985; Mann, 1984; Worrall, 1990). These vignettes indicate that women in prison are there sometimes for extremely brutal crimes and sometimes for behavior that seems hardly criminal and often sad.

Women's stories of crime emphasize men and money. Many women participate with their husbands or boyfriends in various illegal activities up to and including murder; at times the husband or boyfriend is the target of homicide by the woman or the reason she kills a suspected rival. However, women are often active criminals by themselves or in conjunction with other women, especially in prostitution, shoplifting, and even some types of robbery.

Women who commit crimes such as robbery at times resort to violence when the victim attempts to resist. Violence may be more common when the victim is male, since he may be tempted to offer resistance: "I put the knife up to his throat and took the money, but as I was coming out of the shop he started to fight me, and three old women coming past the shop went next door and rang the old bill" (called the police) (Carlen, 1988: 20).

An element of excitement is also mentioned by many women who try to explain why they could not stay out of trouble. For these women, trouble started early, often beginning as teenage pranks that only later developed into serious crime. Carlen wrote that four major factors are correlated with women's criminality: poverty, being in foster or state care as a child or teenager, drugs, and the quest for excitement (1988: 12). Owen (1998: 56) recorded the explanations of some female prisoners, including the following:

> I am just wild. I have always been wild . . . it is just something in me. . . . I have been gang-banging hard since I was ten. I started hanging around with my older brothers and sisters in the hood. . . . I was raised on the streets. My family is pretty damn good, but I grew up in the hood. My parents both worked and they were too busy worrying about my older brothers and sisters.

In the stories told to Owen (1998: 61), the fast life, or "la vida loca"—meaning excitement, hustle, drugs, and money—was a constant theme.

EXPLANATIONS FOR FEMALE CRIMINALITY

Any explanation of female criminality should explain the "gender gap" between men and women, but also should explain why women seem to have increased their criminal activities in the last 30 years. There are a number of theories available that attempt to answer these questions.

Women's Liberation/Opportunity Theory

One of the most persistent explanations of why women have increased their participation in crime is that "women's liberation" opened the door for illegitimate as well as legitimate occupations for women. Adler (1975) and Simon (1975; also see Simon and Landis, 1991) are the two most cited proponents of this theory, and also the two most heavily criticized. Basically, the problem with the theory that equal opportunity has affected female crime is that women experienced their greatest gains in those crime categories traditionally associated with women, that is, petty larceny (shoplifting), forgery (bad checks and credit card fraud), and embezzlement (petty theft by cashiers) (Steffensmeier, 1980; Steffensmeier and Steffensmeier, 1980; Weishet, 1984). Thus, increased opportunity has apparently not increased women's criminality in crime categories traditionally associated with men. When one uses percentage of total figures, rather than percentage increase figures, it is clear that women's contribution to violent crime has remained virtually unchanged for decades.

Criminal women have not changed their criminal activity patterns, nor do they seem to be especially "liberated." Both adult and juvenile female offenders show very little evidence of "liberated" attitudes or egalitarian views of sex roles (Campbell, Mackenzie, and Robinson, 1987; Giordana and Cernkovich, 1979).[3] More current findings also indicate that women in prison express idealistic and traditional views of sex roles; the most common fantasy includes a "Prince Charming" and a future as a housewife with a husband to provide for the woman (Owen, 1998: 12; also see Chesney-Lind and Rodriquez, 1983; Girshick, 1999).

Further, the theory that equal sex roles leads to greater criminality among women cannot be proven on an international basis. Countries where women possess more equality in social and economic spheres do not show an increase of violent crime by women (Bowker, 1981).[4]

Social/Cultural Explanations

The most accepted explanation for the gender differential in crime is that women and men are socialized differently and these socialization differences influence the crime choices of men and women. This theory presumes that men and women are largely equal in their propensity to commit crime; however, they are raised differently and held to different standards of behavior. Hoffman-Bustamante (1973) and others point out, for instance, that the socialization of boys includes skills and opportunities that are conducive to delinquent choices (e.g., mechanical abilities, guns, and cars all have delinquent applications), whereas girls' socialization does not.

This theory is similar and, in fact, inherent in the opportunity theory described earlier. Variations of this theory depend on whether one presumes that women are being socialized differently today or not. Evidence exists for both versions. Although more boys and girls seem to have some exposure to guns, more girls have cars, and some evidence indicates that girls do not receive the same supervision as in past decades; there are still important differences in socialization patterns. Crime rates do not clearly support either proposition, that is, that socialization patterns immunize girls from criminal choices or that changes in socialization have facilitated more criminal choices by women.

Economic Marginalization

Chapman (1980) postulated almost the reverse of the liberation theory in her economic explanation of female crime. Because women, especially single women with children, have become a growing percentage of the poor in this society, Chapman predicted that the numbers of women committing property crimes would increase. This increase would be due, however, not to liberation but to need. Further, she predicted that women's crime would continue to be sex-specific, involving forgery, welfare fraud, and shoplifting. In fact, Chapman's predictions of 20 years ago have been extremely accurate. Women have increased their participation rates in the very categories she predicted.

Another study that partly supported this concept found that women's recidivism rates were negatively correlated with the receipt of unemployment checks or employment, indicating an economic motivation for crime (Jurik, 1983). A British study also supported a correlation between economic distress and crime for women (Box and Hale, 1983). Steffensmeier (1983; also see Steffensmeier, Kramer, and Streifel, 1993) also supports the economic marginalization theory.

Biological Explanations

Historically, and even to some extent today, women have been seen as more defective than male offenders, and biological or psychobiological theories (Cowie, Cowie, and Slater, 1968; Thomas, 1937) to explain female criminality have been utilized, such as the premenstrual syndrome defense (Dalton, 1964). Social control over women has been influenced and continues to be influenced by women's reproductive capabilities.[5]

Although biological theories are vociferously criticized, since the most potent crime correlate is sex, criminal choice probably is influenced in some way by biology. Today's biological theories look to brain chemistry, hormonal differences, learning patterns, and moral definitions of men and women to propose why men and women participate differentially in violent crime (see Fishbein, 1992; Pollock, 1999a).[6]

Biological theories point out that learning disabilities, ADD/hyperactivity, and early conduct disorder are all correlated with sex (all these characteristics are much more common among boys). These characteristics are also associated with delinquency. Certain brain chemicals are implicated in these characteristics and others, such as impulsivity, and the levels of such chemicals are determined by sex. Although the relationship is extremely attenuated and affected by environmental factors, such as socialization and structural opportunities and resources, there seems clear evidence that biology plays some role in one's propensity toward violent, impulsive crime.[7]

The Intersection of Race and Gender

It is extremely important to include race in any discussion of gender and crime choice. One's identity as an African-American, Hispanic, or white woman in this society influences every aspect of life. Too often we forget to note that race may be more important than, or at least as important as, gender in determining one's life choices. It also may affect system response. Bloom and Chesney-Lind (2000: 196) review a number of studies examining the effect of race and find that race tends to correlate with increased sentence length. Minority women are differentially impacted by long drug sentences—so much so that many call the "War on Drugs" a de facto war on African Americans, and especially African-American women.

Race also may be a factor in criminal choice; that is, different causal factors may be influenced by race. Hill and Crawford (1990) have shown, for instance, that for white women, social-psychological issues (e.g., family disorganization) seem to be more influential to crime causation than for African-American women. African-American women's crime choices seem to be more influenced by structural factors (economic marginalization). Although more work needs to be done in the area of the intersecting and overlapping effects of race and gender, attempting to explain women's crime choices without considering the issue of race would be a mistake.

Two other attempts to consider the factor of race are Miller's (1986) and Richie's (1996) investigations of the crime paths of African-American women. Miller concluded that African-American women were more likely than white or Latina women to enter crime through domestic networks (e.g., family members), while the other two groups were more likely to enter crime because of running away or drug use.

Richie (1996) identified a number of different pathways by which African-American women entered into crime. Being involved with an abusive and criminal partner led to crimes either with him or against him. Other groups engaged in sex work and other crimes for economic reasons. Richie describes the limited choices of poor African-American women as gender entrapment. These women are not rebels against societal values, but rather victims of it. In Richie's words, women of color in the correctional system have experienced untold and unknown physical assaults, emotional degradation, marginalization, and overt racism that has created a "web of despair" around them. Despite this, many show resolve and resistance—they are survivors. Arnold (1994) also discusses the role of early victimization of African-American women in their subsequent dislocation from family and other institutions of society.

Lujan (1995) is one of the few researchers who has reported on other minority groups, in her case, Native-American women. Like African

Americans, Native-American women are disproportionately represented in prison. In 1988, almost half of the women in South Dakota's prisons were American Indian, yet they comprised only 7 percent of the state's population. In Alaska, about one-third of the prison population were Indian; and in Montana in 1991, 23 percent were American Indian (Lujan, 1995: 22).

Native-American women's lives are marked by alcohol and despair. Some statistics indicate that over 70 percent of crimes committed by American Indians are alcohol related (Lujan, 1995: 23). According to Lujan, American Indian women are more likely to die from motor vehicle accidents, homicide, and alcoholism than other women, and those under 45 also have higher rates of suicide (1995: 25). Lujan, like those who write of the experiences of African Americans, states that the interaction between ethnicity and criminal justice includes racist stereotyping, labeling, paternalism, cultural differences, internal colonialism, and "unresolved historical grief of violence and genocide" (1995: 25). In part because of their small numbers, the experiences of Native-American and Hispanic women in the criminal justice system have not been understood or explored by researchers.

Feminist Criminology

Feminist writers have contributed a great deal to the understanding and analysis of how criminology has systematically ignored or stereotyped criminal women (see Naffine, 1996). Sexism, according to Price and Sokoloff, comprises the "socially organized cultural beliefs, practices and institutions that result in systematic male superiority and male domination over women as a group" (1982: xiii). Early theories used stereotypes to explain female criminals, and traditional criminology ignored women. In fact, we are still attempting to construct a unified theory that can account for both male and female behavior (see Pollock, 1999a).

Smart (1976, 1979, 1989, 1995), Crites (1976), Klein (1973), and Pollock (1978) focused on the early theories of criminality, exposing the stereotypes and methodological inconsistencies between the study of male and female criminals. Later, Leonard (1982), Heidensohn (1985), Morris (1987), and Naffine (1987) critiqued the traditional theories and their weaknesses. There is disagreement over what exactly feminist criminology comprises. For instance, some would call Adler (1975) a feminist criminologist, and some would not. There is no disagreement, however, on the basic principles of feminist analysis: first, that females have been largely invisible or marginal in theories of crime; and second, that when women are studied, "special" theories, often stereotypical and distorted, are used to explain their behavior (Heidensohn, 1985: 146; also see Simpson, 1989).

Unfortunately feminist criminology has not offered any comprehensive theory to supplant those it has criticized. The attempts have either emphasized women's domination and their control in and by domestic structures of society (Heidensohn, 1985: 161–178), emphasized economic factors and the women's greater poverty (Carlen, 1988), or only offered "suggestions" toward the construction of a theory (Naffine, 1987). The first alternative seems not too different from earlier theories such as control theory and Hoffman-Bustamante's (1973) opportunity theory. The second suffers from the same criticism that all economic theories must face; namely, the correlation between poverty rates and crime rates is not very clear and convincing. Further, there is no attempt in these theories to specifically explain the differential in violent crime relative to the differential in property crime.

One contribution of feminist analysis has been to make linkages between female victims and female criminals. For instance, using a phenomenological approach, we have discovered that many female criminals have been victims in their past—victims of sexual and physical abuse as children and adults. Women are often victimized by an economic system that undervalues women's labor and makes it impossible for them to support themselves if they have small children to care for. These issues, although relevant for all women, impact the female criminal and must be addressed for a full understanding of how women end up in prison.

A PROFILE OF THE FEMALE PRISONER

In 1998 there were about 952,000 women under some form of correctional supervision (about one percent of all adult women in the United States). About 15 percent of those were in prison (about 85,000 in state and federal prisons) (BJS, 1999c; Greenfield and Snell, 1999: 6).

One must be careful to differentiate between a profile of a female prisoner and a profile of a female offender (or prison admittee). For instance, the percentage of women in prison for violent crime is not a reflection of their representation in arrest or conviction rates because violent offenders serve longer sentences; therefore, their numbers are higher in prison population breakdowns than they are in arrest breakdowns. Likewise, the state's inclination to send drug offenders to jail will affect the percentage of all other offenders in a prison population breakdown; if we send more drug offenders to prison, the percentage of violent offenders will go down but that will not mean any change has occurred in the number of women sent to prison for violent offenses. Table 3.2 illustrates the offenses of women in jails, prisons, and federal prisons. Drug offenses account for the largest percentage of women in prison.

The typical female prisoner has changed little over the years (see Table 3.3). Women in prison are increasingly members of minority groups; they are more likely to be older than in previous years; and they continue to be undereducated and underemployed or unemployed before incarceration. They are more likely to be married than in years past. Most women in prison are mothers of young children. They are increasingly in prison for drug crimes and admit to having drug problems.

Compared to men in prison, women in prison tend to be slightly older, slightly more educated, and more likely to be unemployed prior to

Table 3.2 Offenses of Women in Prison and Jail (Percentages)—1998 (Compared to 1983)

Crime	Jail	Prison	Federal Prison	1983[a]
Violent	12	28	7	49
Homicide	1	11	1	
Property	34	27	12	39
Larceny	15	9	1	
Fraud	12	10	10	
Drug	30	34	72	11
Public Order	24	11	8	3
DUI	7	2	0	
Number of Women	27,900	75,200	9,200	

[a]Figures from A. Goetting and R. Howsen, 1983, "Women in Prison: A Profile," *The Prison Journal* 63, 2: 27–46.

SOURCE: Bureau of Justice Statistics, 1999, *Special Report: Women Offenders* (Washington, D.C.: U.S. Department of Justice), p. 6.

Table 3.3 Demographic Profile of Women in Prison

Race	1986 (%)	1998 (%)
White	40	33
Black	46	48
Hispanic	12	15
Other	2.5	4
Age		
24 or less	23	12
25–34	50	43
35–44	19	34
45–54	6	9
55 and older	2	2
Marital Status		
Married	20	17
Widowed	7	6
Separated	11	10
Divorced	21	20
Never married	42	47
Education		
8th grade or less	17	7
Some high school	40	37
High school graduate/GED	28	39
Some college or more	15	17

SOURCE: BJS/Greenfield and Snell, 1999, *Special Report: Women Offenders.* (Washington, D.C.: U.S. Department of Justice), p. 7; BJS/Greenfield and Minor-Harper, 1991, *Special Report: Women in Prison* (Washington, D.C.: U.S. Department of Justice), p. 10.

incarceration (60 percent compared to 40 percent for men in prison) (BJS, 1999c; Greenfield and Snell, 1999). They are more likely than men to have been the primary caregivers of their children. They are also more likely than men to admit to drug problems, although men are more likely to report problems with alcohol. The profile of women in prison is roughly similar whether one utilizes large national samples or smaller state samples (see, for instance, Chesney-Lind and Rodriquez, 1983; Fletcher et al., 1993; Owen and Bloom, 1995a & b; Pollock et al., 1996).

Criminal History and Recidivism

In the past, women tended not to have extensive criminal backgrounds, especially compared to those of men. In one study of the New York prison population, it was found that whereas only 11 percent of male prisoners had no prior records, 28 percent of female prisoners had no prior criminal history. Women were also less likely to recidivate. It was found that only 12 percent of the female offenders were returned to the Department of Correctional Services for the State of New York within five years, while 36 percent of the male offenders released were returned within that time (McDonald and Grossman, 1981). It must be noted, however, that a federal study found no differences in the recidivism rates of men and women as measured within risk categories (Hoffman, 1982).

In the 1980s, women were more likely to be admitted to prison as adults rather than as youthful offenders and were less likely than men to have been admitted while on some form of conditional release or escape status. A little more than half (54.55 percent) of female prisoners reported having been on probation at least once, whereas 65.55 percent of the men had experienced at least one probation sentence. Only 22.25 percent of women served a probation sentence as juveniles, whereas 41.19 percent of men had juvenile probation records (Goetting and Howsen, 1983: 36).

In the 1990s, almost two-thirds (71 percent) of female prisoners had served a prior sentence of probation or incarceration. About 20 percent of those had served a sentence as a juvenile (BJS, 1994b; Snell, 1994). In a recent BJS report, 65 percent of women (compared to 77 percent of men) had prior convictions; 19 percent of women (compared to 38 percent of men) had juvenile histories; 33 percent of women (compared to 43 percent of men) had more than three convictions; and one in three women (compared to one in five men) had been on probation at time of conviction (BJS, 1999c; Greenfield and Snell, 1999: 7, 9).

Thus it appears that women are more likely to have criminal histories today than in the past, although they still are less likely than men to recidivate. A recent Bureau of Justice Statistics report indicated that in a follow-up of women released in 1983, it was found that 52 percent of women were rearrested and 33 percent were returned to prison (BJS, 1999c; Greenfield and Snell, 1999; also see Jones and Sims, 1997).

Family Background

One of the most consistent findings in research on female prisoners is that they tend to come from dysfunctional families. There has been consistent evidence that women in prison may come from more dysfunctional backgrounds than men in prison. Velimesis (1981) reviewed the literature and found that previous studies suggested that female inmates are more likely than male inmates to come from families marked by alcoholism, drug addiction, mental illness, erratic use of authority, and desertion. Another study showed that of one sample of men and women, women were more likely to come from broken homes and had greater difficulties in their interpersonal relationships with family and peers. In addition, 24 percent of the female sample, compared to 12 percent of the male sample, had been treated for mental problems (Panton, 1974: 333).

More recent findings support the notion that female prisoners may come from more disordered backgrounds than men. For instance, women are twice as likely as men in prison to have grown up in single parent household. Also, one-third of women, compared to one-fourth of men, reported that their guardians had abused drugs (BJS 1994b; Snell, 1994). Owen (1998) details the early family life of some of her interviewees. Her findings are consistent with many others (see Rosenbaum, 1989, 1993) that female inmates' childhoods were often marked by "maternal passivity, cruelty, absence and neglect" (Owen, 1998: 49).

Losing family members to death seems to be a theme that comes up consistently in research that utilizes interviews with female prisoners. Women experience this type of loss often; they lose their relatives to sickness and fatal violence (Owen, 1998: 126). Deaths of friends and family members are common and seem more frequent than those experienced in the general population (Rierden, 1997: 120; also see Pollock, 1998).

Another way to lose family members, however, is abandonment, and that happens fairly frequently in the lives of female prisoners as well. Women in prison often had one or both parents abandon them to other relatives or the state. Many recite sad childhoods of constantly trying to gain the affection of a physically or emotionally absent parent: "Even though my father smoked weed and drank alcohol and shot and stabbed people I still loved him. I thought that he would love me more for being just like him. I was wrong. He didn't care" (Bedell, 1997: 29).

Criminal Histories of Family Members Crawford's (1988a & b) study reported that almost half of the women in prison surveyed (48.4 percent) had other family members incarcerated. Girshick (1999), in her sample of female prisoners, found that 73 percent had a family member who had been arrested, and 63 percent had a family member who had been incarcerated, usually a brother and/or father. Owen (1998: 51) also reports that many women had family members in prison, usually a father or brother. About 60 percent in a previous study by Owen reported incarceration of a family member (Owen and Bloom, 1995a & b). Other studies also find that women are very likely to have family members either in prison or having served prison terms, and that they are more likely to have family members with criminal backgrounds than are male inmates (Fletcher et al., 1993; Pollock et al., 1996).

> I have five brothers. Three of them was in the penitentiary. . . . One was on robbery, two was on drugs and my baby brother still going to school. He's 17. And I have a baby sister and she has two husbands that have been killed in the last 2 months since I've been locked up. . . . They took her children, she's an addict also. (Pollock et al., 1996)

Intimate Relationships Welle and Falkin (2000) review research on women's romantic and crime partners. They discuss the situation where a woman will be charged and receive a harsher sentence as a result of noncooperation with prosecutors because she is being threatened by a crime partner/lover. Imprisonment or enforced drug treatment sometimes is a haven and a way to separate oneself from the relationship. In treatment groups, women critically examine their romanticization of drug use, their relationships, and their criminal choices (Welle and Falkin, 2000: 52). Those who were involved with more powerful drug dealer partners evidently are treated differently by the system; they are "policed" more (and often threatened with long prison terms in order to gain information or as leverage against a male partner). Farr (2000a) also discusses how women were "policed" by romantic partners and family members. That is, their lives were controlled by others, and the criminal justice system is just another form of the control they experience. Some of the women were accomplices to planned crimes that escalated to serious assault or murder (2000a: 56).

Sexual or Physical Abuse

Studies consistently show that a substantial percentage of incarcerated women have been abused, both sexually and physically, as children (Gilfus, 1988, 1992; Owen and Bloom, 1995a & b; Sargent, Marcos-Mendosa, and Ho Yu, 1993). For instance, Chesney-Lind and Rodriquez (1983) reported that half the women sampled had been raped as children, and 63 percent had been sexually abused. Crawford (1988a & b) reported that over half (53 percent) of the women in her sample reported being physically abused, either as a child (35 percent) or by a husband or boyfriend (49 percent). They had also experienced sexual abuse (35.6 percent). More than 60 percent of the abused women had been sexually abused before the age of 15 (Crawford, 1988a: 12-21).

A study conducted by the Oregon Department of Corrections (1993) found that the incidence of physical and sexual abuse of women inmates was considerably higher than in the general population. In a study of Oregon female prisoners, 45 percent reported physical abuse, 66 percent reported sexual abuse, and 37 percent reported both before 18. Other studies also found high percentages of women in prison have suffered abuse (Fletcher et al., 1993;

Owen and Bloom, 1995a & b; Pollock et al., 1996). Blount, Kuhns, and Silverman (1993: 425) had this to say:

> To conclude that incarcerated women suffer physical abuse to a greater extent than other women would seem the grandest of understatements. This rate is many times that of women in the general population—conservatively 6 to 10 times as great.

The effects of childhood abuse are long-standing and probably play a role in criminal choices. Rosen (1998) reports that the effects of childhood sexual abuse can include anger and hostility toward others, distrust of authority and adults as juveniles, alienation from others, a negative self-view, substance abuse (self-medication), emotional volitility (either an overreacting or numb approach to life), inappropriate use of sex and sexuality, and distant or dysfunctional family relationships. Others also document the effects of childhood sex abuse on drug use and dysfunctional and risky sexual behavior (Mullings, Marquart, and Brewer, 2000).

A Bureau of Justice Statistics (1994a) study reported that victims of abuse were more likely to be in prison for violent offense than others (42 percent versus 25 percent). Widom (1989, 1996), in a national study of abuse or sexual molestation and criminality, found a correlation between type of crime and prior abuse. A recent Bureau of Justice Statistics report explored this issue. Some of the findings were that:

- Women in prison were more likely than the general population to have experienced abuse (6–14 percent of male offenders and 23–37 percent of female offenders report abuse compared to the general population figures: 5–8 percent of males and 12–17 percent of females).

- Male prisoners are more likely to report abuse only as children; women reported abuse as children and adults.

- The abuse of men was by family members; the abuse of women was by family members and intimates.

- Abuse is associated with foster care, parental abuse of drugs or alcohol, and/or criminal history.

- Abused prisoners are more likely to be serving sentences for violent crimes.

- The use of drugs and alcohol is higher among those who have been abused. (BJS, 1999b; Harlow, 1999)

See Tables 3.4, 3.5, and 3.6.

Surveys consistently replicate the finding that large numbers of imprisoned women lived through sexual abuse and exploitation, often when they were very young. No numbers, however, can possibly relay the experience or the effects of such an experience on one's psyche. Bedell's (1997: 28) interview with a woman offers a small insight into what such a childhood must have been like.

Table 3.4 History of Physical or Sexual Abuse

	Probation (%)	Jail (%)	Prisons (%)
Physically or Sexually Abused	41	48	57
Before age 18	16	21	12
After age 18	13	11	20
Both	13	16	25
Abused			
Physically	15	10	18
Sexually	7	10	11
Both	18	27	28

SOURCE: Bureau of Justice Statistics, 1999, *Special Report: Women Offenders.* (Washington, D.C.: U.S. Department of Justice), p. 8.

Table 3.5 Prior Abuse of Prisoners by Sex

		PERCENT EXPERIENCED ABUSE BEFORE SENTENCE			
		ABUSED		ABUSED BEFORE 18	
	Total	Male	Female	Male	Female
Abused					
State prison	18.7	16.1	57.2	14.4	36.7
Federal prison	9.5	7.2	39.2	5.0	23.0
Jail	16.4	12.9	47.6	11.9	36.6
Probationers	15.7	9.3	40.4	8.8	28.2
Physically Abused					
State prison	15.4	13.4	46.5	11.9	25.4
Federal prison	7.9	6.0	32.3	5.0	14.7
Jail	13.3	10.7	37.3	–	–
Probationers	12.8	7.4	33.5	–	–
Sexually Abused					
State prison	7.9	5.8	39.0	5.0	25.5
Federal prison	3.7	2.2	22.8	1.9	14.5
Jail	8.8	5.6	37.2	–	–
Probationers	8.4	4.1	25.2	–	–

SOURCE: Bureau of Justice Statistics, 1999, *Selected Findings: Prior Abuse Reported by Inmates and Probationers* (Washington, D.C.: U.S. Department of Justice).

When I was eight or nine my mother's boyfriend molested me. I was afraid to say anything. He did it again and I told my mother; they got in a fight and she killed him with a knife. When she went away to prison, nobody talked to me. They acted like it was my fault. It was my fault, I should have stayed silent. I started to drink when I was eleven. A boy

Table 3.6 Comparison of Studies

	PHYSICAL ABUSE		SEXUAL ABUSE	
	(under 18)	(as adult)	(under 18)	(as adult)
Owen and Bloom (1995)	29%	59%	31%	22%
Fletcher et al. (1993)	37%	69%	40%	55%
Pollock (1996)	31%	60%	31%	35%
Gilfus (1992)	(When combined, 88% of sample had experienced at least one type of abuse.)			
Oregon (1993)	37%	45%	37%	66%

SOURCE: Owen, B., and B. Bloom, 1995, "Profiling Women Prisoners: Findings from National Surveys and a California Sample," *The Prison Journal* 75, 2: 165–185; Fletcher, B., et al., 1993, *Women Prisoners: A Forgotten Population* (Westport, CT: Praeger); Pollock, J., et al., 1996, *The Needs of Texas Women Prisoners—Final Report* (Unpublished report); Gilfus, M., 1992, "From Victims to Survivors to Offenders: Women's Routes of Entry and Immersion into Street Crime," *Women and Criminal Justice* 4, 1: 63–88; Oregon Department of Corrections, 1993, *Childhood Abuse and the Female Inmate: A Study of Teenage History of Women in Oregon Prisons* (Salem, OR: Oregon Department of Corrections, Information Services Division).

raped me on the roof when we were drinking. I was too afraid to tell anyone, even when I became pregnant. Everyone was shocked when I gave birth at thirteen years old.

Drug Use and Abuse

As discussed in the first chapter and in the earlier section on drug crimes, women's drug use and the system's punitive response have dramatically affected women's prison populations. There are ever-increasing numbers of women sentenced to prison for drug crimes; they admit to drug problems; and there are not enough treatment slots for those who need them.

A study of drug use and criminality among imprisoned women (Bount et al., 1991) reviewed the literature and found that women in prison were heavier users of drugs than men in prison, and that women's drug-related crimes included property crime and minor roles in violent crime. This study also found that in a prison population, substance abusers were more likely to be Caucasian, come from broken homes, and have worse employment histories than non–substance abusers. Substance abuse was also related to age at first arrest (younger), number of prior arrests, and number of prior incarcerations. Problem users were more likely to have family members incarcerated, more likely to be under the influence at the time of the crime, and more likely to have committed the crime for money to buy drugs.

The most recent figures indicate that about half of women in prison had been regularly using drugs or alcohol; and 40 percent of women compared to 32 percent of men had been under the influence of drugs at the time of offense. Women evidently are more likely than men to abuse drugs, while men are more likely to abuse alcohol (BJS, 1999c; Greenfield and Snell, 1999: 8). According to this same report, 60 percent of women said they used drugs in the month before the offense, 50 percent were daily users, 40 percent were under the influence at the time of offense, and nearly one in three committed an offense to get money for drugs. Women also were more likely to have been through treatment programs (56 percent compared to 41 percent) (BJS, 1999c; Greenfield and Snell, 1999: 9).

In Owen and Bloom's (1995a & b) study, almost three fourths of their sample of incarcerated women reported drinking alcohol before the age of 18; 11 percent reported drinking before age 10; 59 percent reported drug use before age 18; and 15 percent began using drugs at age 12 or 13. Other needs assessments also show that women in prison are extremely likely to be heavy users of drugs and that their drug use started very early. Another consistent finding was that drug use was often introduced to them by family members (Fletcher et al., 1993; Owen and Bloom, 1995a & b; Pollock et al., 1996).

A review of past literature offered by Anglin and Hser (1987) indicates that drug addiction for women seems to be correlated mostly with three types of crimes: prostitution, reselling narcotics or assisting male drug dealers, and property crimes such as larceny. Studies previously reported that between 40 and 70 percent of female drug users supported their habit through prostitution. However, female addicts also report participation in a relatively wide range of other criminal activity (Anglin and Hser, 1987: 361).

In fact, Anglin and Hser (1987), in a study with 328 white and Chicana methadone maintenance clients, found that the female addicts did use prostitution but did not depend on it and committed other types of crimes (primarily burglary, theft, and forgery) to support their habits. Anglos favored theft, and Chicanas favored burglary and theft. One-third of the Anglo and 49 percent of the Chicana women were first arrested before becoming addicted; however, these first arrests were often for such things as curfew violations, incorrigibility, trespassing, and vandalism. Arrests became more common and frequent after addiction, and crime commission was correlated with high drug use. Participation in treatment programs and low drug use were correlated with lower rates of crime. The authors compared these findings to studies of male addicts and concluded that women are slightly more likely than men to have never been arrested; women (except Chicanas) are less likely than men to have extensive arrest records before addiction; for both men and women robbery seems to occur only at high levels of drug use; and women differ greatly from men in the level and type of criminal activity (Anglin and Hser, 1987: 392–393).

Farrell (2000) reviewed the literature on criminality and drug use among women. He found that women tended to be lower-level dealers or accomplices (also see Inciardi, 1993). While they do resort to crimes in pursuit of drugs, they usually do not commit violent crimes. In his study, he found that they often come from abusive backgrounds, have chaotic and dangerous lifestyles, and use drugs as a coping mechanism. Drugs are part of the relationship network of women; they are part of the lifestyle women share with intimate partners or with their nuclear family members. Pettiway (1987: 761) also found that being married or living with a criminal boyfriend or husband was one of the most important factors in drug-crime partnerships for women.

There seems to be some evidence that women's motivations for drug use might be different from men's. For instance, Covington's (1985) study of female heroin addicts indicated that social disorganization was more causally significant for female than for male addicts. Needs assessments also indicate that women use drugs to "self-medicate" (see Pollock, 1998, 1999a). That is, drugs are used to forget prior victimization or current dysfunctional and abusive relationships.

Personalized accounts (see, e.g., Carlen, 1988: 24) also illustrate how predominant drugs and alcohol are in the lives of women criminals.

> I started using marijuana at age of eight, with my sisters and my cousin. I started drinking about that time too. Then I started cocaine binges. I started running away when I was eleven. It seems like I have always been in trouble. My family was having trouble when I ran away at eleven. I was angry and always fighting. (Owen, 1998: 46)

Drug use also seems to be correlated with other dysfunctional behaviors, such as risky sexual behaviors. Several studies have tracked a correlation between drug use and sexual choices (such as multiple partners, no condoms, and sex with drug injectors) that increase the risk of AIDS (Cotton-Oldenburg et al., 1999; Mullings, Marquart, and Brewer, 2000).

Self-Esteem and Other Characteristics

This section will summarize a few other studies that have examined various characteristics of women in prison. Some studies compare men and women; others look only at samples of imprisoned women. Some studies attempt to validate commonly held perceptions, such as the belief that female inmates have lower self-esteem than nonincarcerated women. Others use personality tests to develop profiles of female prisoners. Some find that women in prison are statistically different from women outside on one or several indices; others find that women in prison represent their sex fairly accurately.

Self-Esteem One long-standing belief is that women in prison have very poor concepts of self. Tittle (1973) reported that women experienced lowered self-esteem during a prison term, although their self-esteem increased as they neared release. Hannum, Borgen, and Anderson (1978), using a sample of 57 female inmates, found that self-concept improved after a time in prison. No correlation was found between age and self-concept, but those with higher educational levels had lower self-concepts (Hannum et al., 1978: 276). Widom (1979) reported no difference in a prison group and a control group of women on measures of self-concept, masculinity, or personal autonomy. The only difference between the groups was that the nonoffender group scored higher on the femininity scale—"feminine" being defined as affectionate, loyal, sympathetic, sensitive to needs of others, understanding, and compassionate (Widom, 1979: 371).

Officers and treatment professionals report that female inmates express low self-esteem in their interactions. As one professional observed:

Women tended not to feel successful with anything. They didn't feel successful as wives—they didn't feel successful as lovers—they didn't feel successful as mothers—they didn't feel successful as daughters, whereas men felt a lot more success, relatively speaking, I found, than women did. Men could say I was a good carpenter or I did this well or I screwed more women than anybody else on the block or again anything from sex to sports to whatever, although the men didn't have much going for them either. . . . Women were always zero in their own eyes. In fact, they even showed this by self mutilation. (Pollock, 1981)

A study by Culbertson and Fortune (1986) reviewed the earlier research and concluded that much of the methodology was flawed; for instance, some studies used stereotyped descriptions of the women's role. Culbertson and Fortune used the Tennessee Self Concept scale with a sample of 182 women in the Dwight Correctional Facility. The women were classified into role types: butch, femme, or dependent; and the cool, the life, or the square. The authors found that low self-concept varied with education and social role. Those who had higher educational levels had a higher self-concept. Those who played a self-perceived "butch" role had a higher self-concept. Those who had low "femme" scores had a lower self-concept (Culbertson and Fortune, 1986: 44–48). These findings indicate that self-esteem is related to self-identity; and any strong identity, as either "butch" or "femme" in this case, may improve self-concept.

Fletcher et al. (1993) found that self-esteem was related to health, locus of control, and level of education (higher levels resulted in lower self-esteem). Childhood victimization and use of drugs or alcohol were associated with lower self-esteem. From their stories of childhood, it would be incredible, indeed, if women could emerge unscathed and with self-esteem intact. Many chronicle extreme emotional abuse from parents.

I was told I was stupid. I was told I was fat. I was told I was ugly. Just a lot of things. My dad—I think that's his favorite word—we're all stupid. We were never physically abused. I guess the mental and emotional abuse is worse. . . . (Pollock et al., 1996)

Values A few studies have examined the different values of men and women in prison. Kay (1969) found that in a sample of 258 women and 335 men in prison, women showed significantly more negative attitudes toward law and legal institutions than did men, as measured on a survey instrument. There was no significant difference between the two groups on a "moral value scale." Erez (1988) also conducted a comparison of female and male prisoners in their attitudes and values toward law and criminal justice. She found that women had higher prosocial values regarding law but were more negative toward specific actors in the system.

In another study examining values, Cochrane (1971) found that women in prison had a more "masculine" value system than a female control group did. The female prisoners valued such things as an exciting life, freedom, independence, and intellectualism. The female prisoners rated freedom more highly than even male prisoners. Although it is obviously sexist to label these values as "masculine," it is interesting to note the differences in the priorities of men and women. It may be that this study reflects the prevalent view that women do "harder time" than men, since women's responses indicate that freedom is very important to them.

CONCLUSION

This chapter has demonstrated that women's crimes have increased dramatically in the last decade in traditionally "female" offenses, but women's participation in violent crime has remained stable at around 10 percent of the total. Whether drug use is increasing, decreasing, or remaining stable is hard to tell, but we do know that drug users are now very likely to be sentenced to some correctional supervision and, increasingly, prison. There is no doubt that drugs and other crimes are related, and there are large numbers of women (and men) in prison who could benefit from drug treatment (and are not getting it).

Today, we have more or less discredited the notion that female "liberation" has had any effect on female crime. The most comprehensive theories of female criminality include socialization, opportunity, and economic factors; each has different implications for treatment. As mentioned in the first chapter, the rate of imprisonment of women is going up, contributing to overcrowding. This increase may be reflective of a general increase in severity of sentencing, an effect of determinate sentencing, or an effect of the faulty perception that female criminality, and especially violent criminality, has tremendously increased, which may have influenced judicial sentencing.

Women in prison are not necessarily representative of the women who commit crime. They are more likely to be members of a minority group and poor, and more likely to have had problems with drugs or alcohol. They also are more likely to have been single, not taking care of their children at the time of sentencing, or both. They often have committed violent crimes or have been parties to violent crimes. Very often, however, their victims have been family members and, for some, husbands who have abused them.

Adelberg and Currie (1993) describe female prisoners' lives as marked by neglect, molestation by family members, relationships with men who demean and abuse them, a fruitless search for love, imprisoned by poverty, with a negative self image, and relationships that they cannot escape. They conclude, "[T]he struggle by women to attain love, that is, love defined in a man's world, and on men's terms, compromises women's chances to live their own lives, and to live in a state of well-being" (Adelberg and Currie, 1993: 144).

In study after study, the profile of female prisoners is the same. An Oregon study of female prisoners concludes:

> This survey presents a picture of women inmates characterized by low achievement, early delinquency and high experience of abuse. The women have generally low education levels, worked at unskilled jobs as teenagers, and a high percentage used alcohol and drugs as teenager. A third grew up without their natural father in the family, and a third had some experience in foster care or living with caretakers other than her parents. Families of origin tended to be large (average 5.6 children). Two-thirds of the women ran away from home at least once while growing up, and half were arrested at least once. Two-thirds had parents or siblings who had been arrested (Oregon Department of Corrections, 1993: 9).

Owen (1998: 11) writes: "The offense profile also suggests that women tend to commit survival crimes to earn money, feed a drug-dependent life, and escape brutalizing physical conditions and relationship."

This chapter has painted a comprehensive portrait of the women who are sentenced to prison; it is consistent with both pictures painted in the previous paragraph. There are no surprises in any surveys or needs assessments anymore. We know the sad plight of many prisoners' lives before prison. In the next chapter, we will follow them into the prison to understand what they experience there.

NOTES

1. At least one research effort has postulated that the treatment of women in the criminal justice system has to do with the sex ratio of males to females in society. According to South and Messner (1986), the sex ratio influences not only women's victimization rates but also their treatment as offenders in the system. When men outnumber women, the female is highly valued, crimes against women such as rape are harshly punished, and the traditional domestic role is emphasized. The female offender is protected from the system and treated more leniently, and her rate of offending is also less. When there are more women in a society, they are not as highly valued; consequently, violence directed against them is only moderately punished, and the female offender is treated harshly by the system. Although this theory is interesting, it seems highly speculative.

2. Those researchers who infer that women are becoming more violent use small samples of violent crimes (see Sommers and Baskin, 1992).

3. But also see Cullen, 1979; Kruttschnitt and Dornfield, 1993.

4. But also see Simon and Landis, 1991.

5. For instance, the criminalization of fetal alcohol or drug endangerment, use of contraceptives as part of the conditions of probation or parole, and state response toward pregnancy in prison (Welch 1997).

6. One current test of a biological theory shows how biology, socialization, and system response intersect in complicated ways. Fishbein (2000) questioned whether there was a biological reason for why there seemed to be a

disproportionate number of lesbian and women with masculine appearances in a detention center, and whether they were more likely to be responsible for violent crime. To her credit and unlike previous researchers, the author, a noted researcher in biological explanations of criminality, carefully noted sociological hypotheses as well, e.g., that women turned to female partners because of childhood sexual abuse, that sexual preference was induced by the same-sex environment of the prison, or that the system somehow treated women who displayed masculine traits or lesbian choices differently. The research concluded that these women were no more likely to commit violent crime, but they were more likely to receive, and did receive, longer prison sentences for their crimes.

Other findings by Fishbein (2000) were that lesbian women did report higher averages for assaultiveness; this seemed to be explained by the fact that they also experienced more abuse as children (2000: 76). Lesbians were more likely to exhibit hypermasculine traits and a dislike for men, and were jailed more often and for longer periods of time than heterosexual women (2000: 78). Farr (2000b) reinforced this finding in her study that indicated homosexual women convicted of murder and serving time on death row were treated more harshly by the media, engendered less public sympathy, and were less likely to receive lenient treatment by the formal criminal justice system.

7. There is a great deal of controversial research in this area that cannot be covered here; for a review, see Pollock, 1999a.

SUGGESTED READINGS

Chesney-Lind, M. 1997. *The Female Offender: Girls, Women, and Crime.* Thousand Oaks, CA: Sage.

Fletcher, B., L. Shaver, and D. Moon. 1993. *Women Prisoners: A Forgotten Population.* Westport, CT: Praeger.

Owen, B., and B. Bloom. 1995. *Profiling the Needs of California's Female Prisoners: A Needs Assessment.* Washington, D.C.: National Institute of Corrections.

Pollock, J. 1998. *Counseling Women in Prison.* San Francisco, CA: Sage.

Pollock, J. 1999. *Criminal Women.* Cincinnati, OH: Anderson Publishing Company.

4

Entering Prison
and Adjustment

This chapter chronicles the rise in the number of women's prisons and introduces the reader to the prison world. The experience of entering and adjusting to prison is explored in this chapter; the issues involved in rehabilitative and vocational programs for women have been reserved for Chapter 5. Thus, this chapter discusses such issues as health care, rules and punishments, and cocorrectional institutions. Also, a few observations are offered on the differences between prisons for women and men.

A BUILDING BOOM
OF WOMEN'S PRISONS

In the 1930s, many states did not have separate women's prisons. Women were housed in county jails or in separate wings of male institutions, or they were transferred to other states. Between 1930 and 1966, a number of states built small institutions to house women offenders. These institutions typically used the cottage model or a modified cottage model. Strickland (1976) described women's institutions in the 1960s as typically small and patterned after the cottage model. Her findings included the following:

- Two-thirds had populations of less than 200.
- Most of the prisons had less than 150 staff (14 employed fewer than 50).
- Many of the prisons were located in the northeast and north central region of the country.
- Inmates ranged in age from 16 to 65.
- Living units were often cottages (13 institutions).
- The majority of institutions used simple classification techniques to assign inmates. (Strickland, 1976: 237–240)

Strickland also described the women's institutions in terms of their orientation or management philosophy. Of those she surveyed, 17.85 percent were termed "custodial," 32.15 percent were termed "custody-oriented," 17.85 percent were "mixed," 14.3 percent were considered "treatment-oriented," and 17.85 percent were deemed "treatment institutions" (Strickland, 1976: 206). This distribution was interesting, since the general belief was that women's institutions were more treatment-oriented than institutions for men. Women's institutions had been described as "softer" or "nicer" and as having fewer formal and custodial aspects. According to Strickland, however, a larger number of institutions for women fell closer to the custody than to the treatment end of the continuum. The variables she used for her determination included the ratio of treatment staff to inmates and meeting frequency. This observation was supported by later researchers, such as Burkhardt (1973) and Taylor (1982), who also described the women's institution as having many rules and strict policies governing every aspect of the inmate's life. (This topic is discussed in more detail later in this chapter in the section entitled "Rules and Punishments.")

Schweber (1984) reported that in 1971 there were two federal institutions for women, and only 34 states had completely separate institutions for women. All other states housed women in prisons for men or in county jails, or else they contracted with other states to take the few women deemed deserving of a prison term. By 1985, only two reporting states still did not have institutions for females. New Hampshire left female inmates in county jails or sent them to Massachusetts or federal facilities, and West Virginia sent its female prisoners to Alderson, a federal prison for women (Ryan, 1984: 13). In the 1980s,

34 women's prisons were built, by 1990 there were 71 women's prisons in the country, but only five years later there were 105 (Chesney-Lind, 1998: 66). In the 1990s, the number of women's prisons escalated in a building boom that is still continuing. (See Table 4.1.)

The first chapter of this text chronicled the massive increase in the incarceration rate for women. It is not necessary to revisit those numbers, except to note that what has occurred in some states is that an increase in women sent to prison resulted in overcrowding, which led to building new prisons, which then seemed to encourage even higher numbers of women sent to prison. Some advocates worry that promoting programs for women in prison sometimes leads to the result that more women are sent to prison "for help," when their problems would be much better addressed in the community.

ENTERING THE PRISON

Entering prison is a frightening experience. Even women who have long criminal histories, including several probation terms, report that their first trip to prison gave rise to fears of homosexual rape, guard brutality, and loss of friends and family. Upon entry, a woman is fingerprinted and photographed, stripped, searched, and given prison clothing. Reception may include a medical exam, a psychiatric exam, and educational testing. Often this is done in groups so women may be forced to stand naked in lines waiting for prison issue clothing. Prison orientation indoctrinates women to the extensive rules and regulations of the prison and what is expected of them. Most women describe this experience as stressful, frightening, and dehumanizing (DeGroot, 1998; Girshick, 1999; Owen, 1998).

In many prisons, newcomers are placed in administrative segregation until they have been classified and/or until beds are available. This means that they are housed in a special wing and have extremely limited movement, with no access to yard privileges, programs, or the central mess hall. Often women stay in administrative segregation for a long period of time until beds open up in general population. They may await the transfer with dread or relief, depending upon whether they are returning prisoners or "fish" who fear general population.

The women that Owen (1998) interviewed in California viewed entry to prison as better or worse than jail, depending on where they spent time in jail. Those coming from Los Angeles believed that, compared to jail, prison was better, less violent, with more compassionate officers (Owen, 1998: 66). Those coming from smaller cities, however, believed that prison was worse (Owen, 1998: 67):

> I remember it was scary. We were driving on the way up there. Everybody was talking and laughing, cracking jokes about going to prison. They were all happy because maybe they had been there before, and I am sitting in the back of the bus, nineteen years old, wondering, "Why are they so

Table 4.1 Number of Women Prisoners by State

Under 100	100–500	500–1,000
North Dakota	West Virginia	Oregon
Vermont	South Dakota	Iowa
Maine	Alaska	Tennessee
Montana	Idaho	Colorado
	Rhode Island	Washington
	Delaware	Kentucky
	Kansas	Wisconsin
		Massachusetts
1,000–1,500	**1,500–2,000**	**2,000–2,500**
Maryland	Missouri	Illinois
Connecticut	Michigan	
Indiana	North Carolina	
Mississippi		
Virginia		
South Carolina		
Oklahoma		
Alabama		
Pennsylvania		
2,500–3,000	**3,000–3,500**	**3,500–4,000**
Ohio	Florida	New York
Over 10,000		
California		
Texas		

SOURCE: Pollock, J., 1999, *A National Survey of Parenting Programs in Women's Prisons,* Unpublished monograph available from the author.

happy that they are going to prison?" . . . They told me about the homo-sexuals, the lesbians. Since I am young and new, they were going to take what they wanted, which was me. I was like, nah, they don't do that. . . . And (they told me) they fight, and use shanks, which is homemade knives, and three or four different girls can jump you.

The process of entry involves a dehumanizing sequence of shedding one's outer identity and becoming a "number," with prison clothes, prison rule-books, and prison toiletries (at least until one can gain back some measure of comfort by buying personal items in the commissary). For women who are not used to it, the procedures can be quite frightening and alienating.

Being processed was like an assembly line. Each person had a job to do. You go in there, you weren't a person anymore, you weren't human any-more, they could care less. About forty-two of us came in together. They threw us all in the same room, and we, four of us, shower together, it was awful. We were in orange jump suits, with no underwear. For some girls it was that time of the month. One girl had to keep a pad on with a jump suit with no panties on. That's just the way it was. And they don't care. (Owen, 1998: 77)

During the first days of a prison sentence, the inmate is indoctrinated into the prison world; prison rules are explained, procedures are described, and program opportunities are explained. Classification is also conducted, although the type and purpose of classification vary quite a bit from state to state.

Classification

Most women's prisons in the country are designated medium/maximum security prisons. One of the biggest differences between facilities for men and women is the absence of custody-graded institutions for women. Typically only one or two facilities are available for women in the state. Consequently, the single facility must house the whole range of security grades. Men, on the other hand, are sent to a prison that matches the risk they present. Minimum-security prisons exist for those male prisoners who pose little risk; medium- and maximum-security institutions are for those who pose a more serious risk. There are even "maxi-maxi" prisons in some states for exceptionally violent or escape-prone inmates. Because there are still fewer facilities for women, custody grade has little meaning. In reality, most women, regardless of the risk they present, are subject to medium- and maximum-security measures because of the few who need them (Brennan, 1998; Nesbitt, 1992). Owen (1998: 64), for instance, found that more than 75 percent of the women in the California prison system are classified at the two lowest classification levels (compared to 58 percent of men). But many of these women serve time in facilities with maximum-security classification measures.

"Administrative classification" refers to the determination of risk (escape or violence to self or others). "Treatment classification" refers to an assessment of needs (medical, educational, rehabilitative). Administrative classification systems that utilize risk-factor scores have almost always been developed with and for men, and may not be useful for a female inmate population.[1] Crawford found that only 22 percent of female facilities used a classification system designed especially for women (1988b: 15). Later, Wellisch, Prendergast, and Aglin (1996: 34) found that only 25 percent of reporting institutions used a classification system designed specifically for women.

Burke and Adams (1991) found that classification systems that were developed for men tend to overclassify women, meaning that they indicate women deserve higher custody levels than is probably necessary. The reason is that the systems do not differentiate between types of (or motivations for) violent crime. Since women's violent crimes tend to be personal, it is entirely possible that they do not ordinarily pose a violence risk to others in the prison. Farr (2000a) also points out that many factors that predict risk in men are invalid predictors of risk in women, and argues that the current systems in place lead to excessive use of overrides (ignoring classification instruments findings).

In their national survey, Morash and Bynum (1995) found that 39 states used the same instrument for classifying women and men, 7 states made adaptations for women, and 3 states had an independent system. Some authors present the argument that not having a gender-specific classification system may be problematic legally as well as programmatically (Farr, 2000a). Because women in general pose little risk (e.g., escape, assault to inmate or officer), some argue that classification systems for women should focus much more comprehensively on needs, including such factors as drug use, mental illness, prior victimization, special medical needs, and occupational deficiencies. In today's climate of "sameness," it is unlikely that we will see a rapid rise in the use of gender-specific classification systems.

Adjusting to Prison

After classification, the woman enters the general population. She will live in either a dormitory or a cell shared by one to three other women (in most state systems). Learning to live with other inmates is difficult. Many women continue to be frightened.

> I am still fearful of the inmates here. I am especially scared at shower time. These women are rough in line. I am always scared that you can lose your place in line. Naturally, you let them go in front of you if they are bigger than you. I have to learn to stand up for myself and not let people walk on me. (Owen, 1998: 83)

Women learn to get along by following prison etiquette; they do not ask about others' crimes, and they accommodate others' needs for privacy. There are also ways to make prison life more comfortable, for instance, finding one or several other inmates to share food and goods with, and avoiding "trouble" by staying out of the yard (Owen 1998: 93). Although all prisons have some type of formal classification, there is the informal distribution of jobs and slots as well. Owen (1998: 96) discusses those women who have "juice," meaning they have the power to get assignments or goods (usually because of access or relationships with staff). Some women "pass down" coveted assignments to friends when they leave.

Adjusting to prison includes deciding how much one wants to participate in "programming"—either work or school, or some combination. Women who feel as if they have "real" jobs appreciate the feeling of doing work and being of value. Programs are felt to be important, but many women opt for jobs so they can earn money (Owen, 1998: 99). Depending on the prison, women may work in the field, with farm animals, in large industrial laundries, on yard crews, doing maintenance tasks, at clerical duties, in jobs set up by private corporations on the prison grounds, or in a myriad of other activities. Programs, which will be described in the next chapter, are also varied; some prisons have a large number of them, while some have only a few.

One of the hardest things for women to adapt to in prison is being treated like a child. Clark (1995), an inmate at Bedford Hills, discusses the "infantilization" of prisoners. She notes the hypocrisy of a system that makes women dependent, but tells them they need to be responsible; that calls women girls, but expects them to act like adults; that forces them to become passive and dependent, and then expects them to take on all the problems of living immediately upon release.

Owen (1998: 72) noted how adjustment to prison is different, depending on what type of criminal the woman represents. Inmates with long sentences remarked on how hard it was to live with "short-timers." These women often held fairly conventional beliefs and values; perhaps they had killed an abuser and ended up in prison because of it. According to the inmates in Owen's study, "short-timers" do not care about punishment; they have gotten in trouble all their lives, and they are hard to live with.

In fact, one of the most difficult elements of adjustment for all women in prison is adjusting to other women, especially since many women in prison are not the easiest individuals to live with. One woman described a night in punitive segregation as follows:

What bothers me most back here is these stinking-ass women. They come to the door and they do some of the stupidest shit. Like last night they woke me up at 2:30 and I stayed woke from 2:30 to 4:00 listening to them cuss an officer. I mean the officer wasn't bothering them or anything. So what was the purpose? (Owen 1998: 116)

Eventually each woman learns to adjust, gets a job, enters some type of program, and settles in to the prison world.

THE PRISON WORLD

The typical prison is divided into housing units (either dormitory, cell, or some combination); an adjoining yard or recreation area; an education building (sometimes including a gymnasium, sometimes not); an infirmary or hospital; an administrative segregation unit and special housing or punitive segregation unit; industry buildings (perhaps, although many women's prisons have no industry); perhaps a laundry; and an administrative building housing counselors and other administrative staff. Movement throughout the prison is typically restricted so that a woman either moves within a group or is issued a "pass." Being somewhere other than where she is supposed to be or has permission to be is a serious offense.

A prisoner's day starts at 6:00 A.M., or earlier if she is on kitchen duty, and typically ends at 10:00 P.M. with lights out. After breakfast the women are sent to their various assignments: school, training, or work. Relatively few women stay in the living units during the morning or afternoon hours unless they are on "daylock," in which a woman is locked in her cell all day as punishment, or they have a medical excuse for staying in. The women come back at 11:30 or 12:00 for "count" and lunch and then are sent to their afternoon assignments. Dinner is relatively early, sometimes as early as 4:30, in order for kitchen staff to have the meal cooked, served, and cleaned up by a reasonable hour. Evening hours are spent either in recreation (the prison yard or dayroom) or in some type of program (college class, group therapy, art class, community meeting, AA meeting, charity work).

Count is taken periodically during the day, usually before breakfast, before lunch, after dinner, and sometime in the evening. If there is a discrepancy in the figures, women are kept in their cells until the numbers can be reconciled. They may wait for hours if the error cannot be found. The noon count is the most problematic, and an error or a missing inmate may mean afternoon classes are postponed or canceled, visitors are kept waiting, and women who need to go to the medical unit must wait.

Food in prison is uniformly criticized as bland, starchy, and unappetizing. Some women, if they have the means, ignore the mess hall meals altogether and use food bought in the commissary. Jean Harris (1988) describes how she practically lived on cereal, shunning the food and company of the mess hall. In Bedford Hills, where Harris was serving time, women had access to stoves in the living units. Groups of women shared supplies and cooked dinners in these small kitchens. This luxury is not available in many prisons, however, and is a remnant of the cottage days of Bedford when women were expected to need the domesticity of home. Inmates in other prisons may cook in their living units, but they resort to using homemade implements such as "stingers," which are electrical devices that will heat water.

Burkhardt (1973) provided a journalistic account of women's prisons in the early 1970s that emphasized the psychological effects of imprisonment and the infantilization of adult female prisoners by the correctional staff. She visited 21 jails and prisons for women and conducted formal and informal interviews with more than 400 women. She painted a bleak picture of institutional life: staff patronized and taunted the women offenders, and the inmates spent prison time in useless pursuits, often turning to one another in homosexual relationships that served as a cushion against the anomic life of the prison. She pointed out that many of the programs offered to help women prepare for release, such as cosmetology, were outdated and sex-stereotyped.

More recent descriptions of women's prisons describe a place that is, in some ways, similar and, in some ways, different from the women's prison of the 1970s and earlier. Today's prisons are perhaps less obviously managed under the influence of traditional stereotypes of women, but these stereotypes still exist in officers' informal beliefs and treatment of women. The ravages of drugs on women's lives are apparent—many women have lost one or several children to the state because of drug use, and many continue to pursue drugs even while inside the prison. There is more pressure to make the women's prison like the men's, so rules and policies have changed and certain "special" privileges women may have received in the past no longer exist (special visitation, cooking or clothes washing on the living units, and greater freedom of movement).

Visitation and Recreation

Visitation Visiting is a necessary and important tool to continue family ties and aid in reintegration. Unfortunately, many women's prisons are far removed from the urban areas from which most prisoners come and where their families live. Visiting poses problems for the families of female prisoners even more than for the families of male prisoners. Because there are fewer women's prisons in any particular state, the female prisoner is likely to be further removed from her family than is the male prisoner. This problem is especially acute in the federal system, which has only a few institutions for women scattered across the country. Despite traveling difficulties, prisons often allow for no flexibility in visiting times; visiting may be restricted to specific hours during the day and may be limited to a couple of days a month. This discourages families who may have to travel hundreds of miles to see the incarcerated woman.

Despite these problems, in some studies, women reported more frequent outside communication with family members than did men. Of females, 46.07 percent received at least monthly visits from family, whereas only 41.12 percent of males received monthly visits; and 73.08 percent of women had telephone contact monthly, whereas only 54.31 percent of men had monthly contact (Goetting and Howsen, 1983: 41).

Prison officials remark that visitation rooms in women's prisons are mostly filled with family members (typically mothers and sisters) and children; visitation rooms in men's prisons are usually filled with wives and girlfriends. There is a general tendency for women in prison not to have continued support from the men in their lives; they either are not married or have been abandoned by husbands and boyfriends. Children are certainly present in the visiting rooms of men's prisons, but they are more predominant in prisons for women. In the next chapter, we will discuss more fully the issues regarding the children of women in prison.

Recreation Recreation is also an important component of any institution's offerings, and women's institutions tend to offer less of it than comparable institutions for men. One writer observed that the most common recreational facilities available for women were television and board games (Mann, 1984: 215). There is a belief that men are in greater need of recreational outlets, and consequently a men's prison may have basketball courts, weight-lifting equipment, and a range of supplies for handicrafts. Women tend to be less enthusiastic about physical sports, such as softball, when they are offered; therefore, authorities justify the lack of such programs by the apparent disinterest on the part of female inmates. It is not clear, however, that women would not be interested in other types of physical activity, such as swimming, aerobics, or gymnastics, if these were offered to them.

Women may become involved in any number of charitable activities. In women's prisons across the country, female inmates may be engaged in taping books for the blind, sewing teddy bears and dolls for distribution by police officers to traumatized children at crime scenes, knitting blankets for the poor, even beginning the training of Seeing Eye dogs. Women who engage in these activities do so during evening recreation hours, and although some may be involved because they believe it will speed their release, probably the majority participate in these activities because of a genuine interest in helping others.

According to one study, more incarcerated women than men spend the better part of their day in some form of work assignment, classes, or training; women spend significantly fewer hours walking, exercising, and playing sports (Goetting and Howsen, 1983: 39). Their leisure time is often spent watching television or playing card games and board games. The events that brighten the day are few. Women look forward to the commissary where they can buy candy, soda, and luxury items (sometimes these are not so much luxuries as necessities—for instance, a gentler shampoo than prison issue). Some women spend as much time as they can in their cells, removed from other prisoners by their own choice. Other women are involved in the social organization of the prison and gather around them a group of "family" who provides needed items and social support.

Health Care

Health care for women has been the focus of several lawsuits filed by female prisoners. Typically, women are in greater need of medical services for reasons having to do with the needs of women versus men in general, as well as the special needs of female offenders. Women in general are more likely than men to seek health care, and the same rule applies in prison; requests for medical care by female prisoners far exceed those by men in prison.

There is no question that women in prison suffer from a range of health problems, some very serious (Epp, 1996; Faiver and Rieger, 1998; Fogel, 1991, 1995; Ross and Lawrence, 1998a & b). Imprisoned women may have gynecological problems, be pregnant, suffer from sexually transmitted diseases, or have a host of other problems related to their generally unhealthy lifestyle and the poor health care they probably received while on the street. Many women are addicts and suffer from the medical problems associated with that addiction. Fogel (1995) reported on the experiences of a sample of pregnant women in prison. She found that most had no partner, 87 percent had a pregnancy within the two years before incarceration, and many had habits or conditions that were health threatening (i.e., smoking, 57 percent; drug use, 27 percent; alcohol use, 15 percent; symptoms of clinical depression, 80 percent; and clinical anxiety, 50 percent) (1995: 177).

Ross and Lawrence (1998b: 177) contend, after studying health care in New York, that women show higher rates of AIDS and tuberculosis (TB), depression, and anxiety disorders than do men in prison. Further, mental health problems often go untreated (Fogel and Martin, 1992; Moss, 1996; Ross and Lawrence, 1998a & b). Ross and Lawrence (1998a & b) found that the most common medical problems of prisoners included asthma, diabetes, HIV/AIDS, TB, hypertension, unintended/interrupted/lost pregnancy, dysmenorrhea, chlamydia infection, papillomavirus (HPV) infection, herpes simplex II infection, cystic and myomatic conditions, chronic pelvic inflammatory disease, anxiety, neurosis, and depression. Women in prison are reported to have greater risk than the general population for cervical cancer, substance abuse, suicide, sexually transmitted disease, HIV, and gynecological problems (Brewer et al., 1998; Morris and Wilkinson, 1995).

While the reality may be that most women receive better health care in prison than they would have on the outside, there is no doubt that some egregious situations have existed in the past and probably still exist in some institutions. For instance, there have been reports of women who received no care during pregnancy, were misdiagnosed, or did not receive medical care for diagnosed illnesses. Others have had prescribed pills withheld as punishment, and there also have been reports that drugs, especially tranquilizers, are used excessively to control the population (Mann, 1984: 212).

Women's prisons, unlike men's, typically do not have the numbers to justify a staffed hospital on the prison grounds. Consequently, although a doctor is on call and there are scheduled examination periods, emergency cases and women with serious medical problems are taken to hospitals outside the prison. The time involved in arranging and transporting may pose a potential danger to the inmate-patient. Belknap's (1991) small study of 100 inmates in one prison reinforced other sources, reports documenting the difficulties women have in attempting to access health care and treatment for drug addiction.

Todaro v. Ward[2] was a 1977 case challenging health care delivery at Bedford Hills in New York. The prisoners' complaints, which included the charge that no physician was on permanent duty at the institution, were upheld by the court. The complaint also included the fact that women had to be bussed out of the institution to a local hospital for many types of medical problems, which resulted in delays and possible further risk. Other court cases have been won in California and other states. For instance, Ross and Lawrence (1998b: 187) discuss a court settlement between county jail inmates and Santa Rita County in California that resulted in a new facility and comprehensive pre- and antenatal care with a multidisciplinary medical team.

However, even when inmates win a court case, compliance tends to be slow and not completely ideal. Courts typically allow prison administrators a great deal of flexibility in the time and manner in which they comply with court mandates. If no monitor is appointed to oversee compliance, another court case may be necessary to bring violations to the court's attention.

Barry (1991, 1996), a prisoner rights' attorney who has been active in many of these court cases, describes horrible cases of medical neglect, but reserves her harshest criticism for cases involving the treatment of pregnant women (1989). Barry describes the treatment of pregnant women in prison as misogynistic, citing cases of women having to give birth when their legs were shackled together (the twin babies died); having to give birth in a prison hallway assisted only by an untrained correctional officer because labor started the night before and the woman was told she would have to wait until the clinic opened in the morning to give birth; having a miscarriage because of being forced to clean floors with a heavy buffer while eight months' pregnant;

miscarrying in a prison clinic and being told it was better for the baby to be dead than to be born; and finally, a case where a five months' pregnant woman experiencing bleeding and cramping was diagnosed by the prison doctor (an orthopedist) as having a vaginal infection and given Flagyl, a drug that should never be used by pregnant women because it causes premature labor—it did, and the baby died.

Ryan reported over 15 years ago that 42 of the 45 responding institutions in his survey provided medical care through intake screening and health appraisal, yearly checkups, gynecological and obstetrical service, and 24-hour emergency service (1984: xi, 19). Ryan reported that medical services for women offenders had roughly doubled in the period between the Glick and Neto (1977) study and his own study in 1983 (Ryan, 1984: 20). Yet there seems to be a gulf between official statements regarding health care services and women's allegations of neglect. Barry (1996), for instance, cites numerous problems related to women's health care, including:

- Nonmedical staff being used as "gatekeepers" and deciding whether or not the woman will see a doctor, despite several court rulings that screening should be conducted by medical personnel

- Women being unable to get a second medical opinion even over very serious health issues

- Lack of training of nonmedical staff who often have to perform emergency services such as childbirth delivery

- Attitudes of medical and nonmedical staff toward imprisoned women, assuming they are lying and refusing help to those in critical need, leading at times to death

- Lack of needed treatment for such conditions as cancer, asthma, cardiac problems, burns, pancreatitis, and other life-threatening illnesses

Acoca (1998) reported on a National Council on Crime and Delinquency study of health care for women prisoners in 1996. The study found that the majority of women were experiencing one or more health and/or mental health disorders. In a sample of 151 female inmates, 61 percent currently required medical treatment for one or more problems; 45 percent required mental health treatment. The report indicated that access to health care was very limited. Problematic issues included: no follow-up; overmedication with psychotropic drugs; lack of prenatal care; poor transportation and procedures for delivery; shackling; no help to dry up milk, leading to postpartum depression and breast infections; problems with language barriers between medical staff and inmates; and no care for dying inmates. Ross and Lawrence (1998a & b) reported that health care routinely available to male inmates (i.e., geriatric services, renal dialysis, and reconstructive surgery) was either nonexistent or difficult to acquire for women. Acoca (1998) reported on the increasing trend in prisons to have prisoners pay for health care, arguing that this practice discourages those who need it most. Even though the cost is nominal, women's income in prison is also nominal or nonexistent.

A growing problem in all prisons is the presence and spread of the HIV virus and AIDS. Acoca (1998) reported that, nationally, about 3.5 percent of the female prison population tested positive for the virus (compared to 2.2 percent of men). From 1991 to 1995, the number of male HIV-infected prisoners increased 28 percent while the number of women increased by 88 percent (BJS, 1997a: 6). Some facilities have much higher percentages than others (Ross and Lawrence, 1998a: 51).

Ross and Lawrence (1998b: 183) reported that the percentage of female admittees testing positive for HIV was about 10 percent in New York, 7 percent in Texas, 15 percent in Maryland, and 6 percent in North Carolina. In all these states, the percentages for women were higher than those for men. Barry (1996) cited a New York study that found 19 percent of female and 17 percent of male prisoners to be HIV positive.[3]

Vigilante et al. (1999) also discussed the greater prevalence of AIDS among imprisoned women, speculating that the reasons may be because women in prison are likely to be heavy drug users, be involved with drug users, and/or have been involved in sex work. Acoca (1998), however, has pointed out that tuberculosis and sexually transmitted diseases (such as hepatitis B and C) may eventually pose even bigger problems than AIDS. In one California study, 54 percent of incoming female prisoners tested positive for hepatitis C (Acoca, 1998: 53). Some health care professionals warn that hepatitis will be "bigger" than the AIDS problem. Rates of tuberculosis in 1991 were higher for female inmates in New York than for men (Ross and Lawrence, 1998b: 125).

Mental Health Services It is well accepted that there is a great need for mental health care in prisons. The mental health problems of vulnerable women are often exacerbated by the stressful nature of prison (Fogel, 1993; Fogel and Martin, 1992). Ross and Lawrence (1998b: 181), as well as others, report that manic and depressive states are probably underdiagnosed in prison. Girshick (1999) reported many of the women in her sample suffered from depression and bipolar disorder. Reasons for their high rates of depression included physical abuse and separation from families.

Acoca (1998) estimates that 25 percent to 60 percent of the prison population may have mental health problems. Unfortunately many go untreated because of poor screening, diagnosis, and follow-up services. Critics observe that untrained staff misinterpret psychotic breakdowns as willful misbehavior and punish the inmates rather than refer them to mental health services.

Deinstitutionalization of the mentally ill probably has contributed to the number of women in prison with mental problems (Ross and Lawrence, 1998b: 181). Women perhaps are more likely than men to admit to problems and desire mental health services. However, the mental health services that exist in women's prisons seem to be inadequate, and in some cases, extremely inadequate. Female prisoners, like male prisoners, complain that psychiatrists and psychologists often have restricted hours and that, for many of them, English is a second language, so they are hard to understand. Typically, the inmate does not feel comfortable or able to identify with mental health professionals. A large part of treatment has been reported to be the administering of psychotropic drugs (Velimesis, 1981: 130). Psychologists may be used to classify inmates rather than to provide psychotherapy. In this area of medical services, court cases and complaints have led to an increase in the available services. Ryan reported that psychological and psychiatric services doubled between 1977 and 1983 (1984: 28). Yet, problems remain.

Some observers have noted that there is a tendency to characterize women's (as opposed to men's) problems as psychiatric. This tendency may influence the estimates of the percentage of women in prison with mental health problems. This expectation or assumption also may be somehow projected to women, leading to their believing that they have "problems." It is important to keep this in mind when discussing the need for mental health service in order to avoid the stereotype that women automatically need these services more than male inmates. Considering, however, that greater percentages of female (as compared to male) inmates have histories of childhood abuse and drug problems, and come from families with dysfunction (i.e., alcoholism, criminality, etc.), it is also possible that the estimates of mental health problems of female inmates are not merely evidence of stereotyping women's issues as "all in their minds."

Rules and Punishments

The impression one receives on entering a women's institution is that it might be a pleasant, albeit restricted, place to spend some time. Grounds are typically attractive, and rooms may be decorated in homey ways. Upon further examination, however, one discovers that the institutions typically operate by means of dozens of serious and trivial rules governing behavior. Women may not be allowed freedom of movement except in groups and with passes. They may have their letters from or to home read and censored. They may be forced to go eat in the cafeteria whether they want to or not. Officers constantly check passes and interrogate women accused of being out of place. Several observers agree that the rules in women's prisons may be more strict and cover more petty details than those in prisons for men (Mann, 1984: 209; also see McClellan, 1994a & b). One explanation for this disparity may be that women's institutions do not have the same physical security present in male facilities; thus, in the absence of guns, towers, and stone walls, prison security is based on minute rules of behavior that govern the movement and interactions of the female prisoners.

The most obvious fact of life in women's prisons is that women are dependent on the officers for practically every daily necessity. Women may have to ask for personal items such as tampons or napkins from the officer in the living unit, and the number issued per day may be regulated. Although commissaries provide the "luxuries" of life, they are relatively expensive, and the inmate must have either some sort of prison work or a financial source on the outside to pay for things like candy and cigarettes. Further, she is limited in the number of items she may buy and the amount of money she can spend each month. Women in segregation must ask for everything, including toilet paper and razor blades. They are dependent on the officers to bring them what they need, including food. If the officer is busy or irritated, the food on the cart may sit undistributed until it is cold. To ask another adult for permission to do such mundane things as use the kitchen facilities or go to the bathroom is demeaning and humiliating. Women in prison may adapt by adopting an abrasive and hostile attitude toward the experience; thus, a request may be phrased as a demand, often capped with an obscenity for good measure. This tactic only results in making the situation worse, however, since the officer may then ignore the woman, demand that she rephrase the request, or write her up for insolence.

Strickland's (1976) study of women's institutions contained the observation that a basic list of rules for female prisoners included strictures regarding personal cleanliness, what type of clothing could be worn, and what items were considered contraband, which included "immoral" magazines and dice; and prohibitions against exchanging presents, bartering, offensive language, gambling, and disorderly conduct, including sexual conduct (Strickland, 1976: 114). Female inmates seem to be more strictly controlled than male inmates in personal areas such as dress and living-unit activities. Female staff tend to take a maternal approach to their charges and demand that the women brush their hair or take better care of their appearance—concerns that are likely rarely expressed in an institution for men.

Punishments Strickland described included confinement; loss of movie, recreation, store, or visitation privileges; loss of good time; and loss of smoking and letter-writing privileges (Strickland, 1976: 239). These punishments are roughly the same today. Fewer women receive serious punishments, such as loss of good time and segregation; this difference is related to the lack of serious infractions (e.g., drug violations, weapons) in women's facilities. Women tend to be involved frequently in minor personal altercations, contraband other than drugs, and insubordination. For these infractions, daylock or some type of privilege deprivation is common. Those women who do commit a serious infraction may well find themselves in segregation, the "prison within a prison." As Burkhardt (1973) described them, segregation units fully illustrate the extent of the women's powerlessness in the face of state control:

> These cells are drearily the same in every jail I've visited—windowless and bare. Some have one thin, dirty and bloodstained mattress on the floor. Some have no mattress. Some jails provide blankets for the women confined, some do not. In some quarters, women locked in solitary are allowed to wear prison shift—in others they are allowed to wear only their underwear or are stripped naked. Toilets are most often flushed from the outside, and women complain that on occasion sadistic matrons play games with flushing the toilets—either flushing them repeatedly until they overflow or not flushing them at all for a day or more at a time. (Burkhardt, 1973: 148)

A fairly consistent history of findings documents the greater rate of rule-breaking of women in prison, as compared with men. Lindquist (1980), for instance, found that women committed an average of 4.38 offenses in prison, compared to 2.61 by men. Usually women received less serious punishments for their infractions (Lindquist, 1980: 307). About 33 percent of the men's violations involved fighting or assaults, while 23.8 percent of the women's violations were for fighting or assaults (Lindquist, 1980: 310). Another study by Selksky (1980) found that the ratio for Bedford Hills Women's Prison in New York was one assault per 24.8 inmates, whereas at Great Meadow, a prison comparable in size but housing men, the ratio was one assault per 27.7 inmates. Studies in other institutions have made similar findings. McKerracher, Street, and Segal (1966) found that women in a forensic unit of a British mental hospital also exhibited more aggressive acting-out behavior than did male patients. They found that women committed more aggressive acts toward others, property, and themselves. They were also more likely to commit noisy disturbances and exhibit psychiatric symptoms. Others have replicated this finding; professionals have reported more incidences of self-mutilation, more aggressive rule-breaking, and more psychiatric disturbances among female prisoners than male prisoners. These reports, however, may be influenced by a perception that female inmates will react more emotionally and cause more trouble than male inmates; the reporting may reflect the expectation (Heidensohn, 1985: 74; also see Mandaraka-Sheppard, 1986a & b).[4]

Officers have offered a possible explanation for the greater number of recorded assaults by women inmates:

> Women tend to showboat, men don't. Like even here if a girl was going to fight, quite often she'd wait until she got in the messhall so that all the girls were around, not just three or four girls on her unit. Where men will, at least from what little I've observed here and what I know the male officers have said, they'll tend to get you later, on the side of the building and that way nobody gets hurt—I mean not have to go to lock. We've had a couple instances here where a guy has shown up with a black eye and we ask and they give you some bull story about tripping down the stairs and yet after it all comes out eventually you hear that somebody met him out behind the gym or something and cleaned his clock.
>
> With females you get yelling spats that some people think are regular barroom brawls—you know, a little yelling back and forth that gets out frustration as far as I'm concerned. (Pollock, 1981)

The woman who is most often disciplined seems to fit the profile of those offenders most prone to prisonization and the inmate subculture. Faily and Roundtree (1979; also see Failey, Roundtree, and Miller, 1980) found that the women most likely to commit violations were African-American, in their late twenties, incarcerated for manslaughter or narcotics, from urban areas, single, with no children. They had sentences of six to ten years and often were sentenced without parole (Faily and Roundtree, 1979: 82–83; also see Roundtree, Mohan, and Mahaffey, 1980). Some of these characteristics (African-American, urban, and convicted for a violent crime) are shared by male prison assaulters. Mandaraka–Sheppard (1986) found that women who committed prison infractions were more likely to be young, single, and without children. They were not distinguished by race, type of offense, criminal record, or length of sentence. Her findings were very similar to those of Pollock; officers observed women as acting out emotionally and spontaneously, but rarely with lethal violence (Pollock, 1986: 107). Mandaraka–Sheppard also pointed out that institutional factors seem to lead to violence, including severe methods of punishment, no incentives for good behavior, variations in the quality of inmate–staff relations, and the age and experience of the staff (1986: 199).

While older theories regarding women's rule-breaking point to personality differences between men and women, and even biological explanations (i.e., menstruation),[5] current theory looks to staff expectations and differential responses. Staff in women's prisons may tolerate much less in the way of acting-out behavior before they issue disciplinary tickets. There also may be more rules in women's institutions. It is also possible that much of men's rule-breaking is covert and not subject to discovery. Assaults, drug dealing, and the black market are hidden; rarely do officers have evidence to discipline such behaviors. McClellan (1994a & b) provides excellent data from Texas prisons, for instance, that shows that women were more subject to petty rule enforcement and received harsher punishments compared to men. Thus, official data indicated that women were more frequent rule violators, consistent with the studies cited previously, but the type of rules violated were likely to involve such misbehaviors as "not cleaning your plate" or "talking in the pill line." This indicates that any interpretation of infraction rates (like crime rates) must take into account the fact that the numbers represent a dynamic between the actor and the reporter, and it is important to understand the relative contribution of each to get a better sense of reality.

COCORRECTIONAL FACILITIES

In 1971, Ft. Worth, a cocorrectional facility for federal inmates, was opened. Thus we came full circle from the date in 1873, almost 100 years earlier, when female reformers were finally successful in establishing a separate female facility. Schweber reported that approximately 61 percent of adult women were housed in cocorrectional facilities in 1984 (Schweber, 1984: 5). Crawford reported that 27 percent of the facilities for women in her survey were cocorrectional (1988b: 10). Although the cocorrectional institutions of today bear no resemblance to those of the past, there are still disadvantages as well as advantages to housing male and female inmates together.

> The observable effects on inmates of a sexually integrated prison, which in many ways is a microcosm of society, appear to provide a more humane environment, albeit one in which women often assume a subservient position. Inmates and staff at coed facilities frequently comment

that women humanize the prison atmosphere; that all inmates care more about their appearance, and sloppiness or bad language is unusual; that coed women are "softer," more ladylike, and they assume traditional helping/dependency roles; and that homosexuality and violence among men is drastically reduced (Schweber, 1984: 6).

As Schweber points out, however, there are real trade-offs between single-sex institutions and cocorrectional facilities. While women and men may enjoy the more normal environment of both sexes housed together with some interaction, more often than not the situation creates more control and security precautions for at least one of the sexes. It also appears that women less often take advantage of program opportunities in a cocorrectional prison and that they may be less likely to take leadership roles or to express themselves in a positive, assertive manner. Staff also may be more restricted in a cocorrectional facility, and female staff may have fewer opportunities for advancement.

In 1984, Ryan reported that six states had cocorrectional facilities (Ryan, 1984: x). He also reported that of the 48 facilities that reported vocational education, 31 percent of them had cocorrectional vocational programs. These programs may bus the inmates to a nearby prison or have the program in the women's facility (Ryan, 1984: 17). Some studies have been done on the differences in activities between the two groups of inmates. Wilson (1980) discovered that more women than men appeared to be involved in academic pursuits (66.7 percent, compared to 57.7 percent). More men than women, however, set a goal of a college degree (21.2 percent, compared to 1.3 percent). Men and women were about equal in their requests for vocational education (73.1 percent to 74.4 percent). However, as might be expected, there were gender differences in program requests. Both sexes preferred programs traditionally associated with their own gender (Wilson, 1980).

Just because a facility is cocorrectional does not necessarily mean that male and female inmates are able to interact. Crawford indicates that some cocorrectional facilities do not allow recreation, leisure activities, eating, or working together (1988b: 10). Often this means that women are the ones who suffer from increased restrictions on their movement.

An exhaustive look at cocorrectional facilities is beyond the scope of this text; however, the interested reader may find several good sources that document the success of cocorrectional facilities and their stated goals. Smykla and Williams (1996) reviewed all available sources on cocorrections covering the period of 1970–1990. They found that there were 9 cocorrectional programs in 1979 and 52 in 1994 (noting, however, that the institutions were not the same ones; 41 opened and closed within this time span). These reviewers found that, almost without exception, evaluators viewed cocorrections as not benefiting female offenders, and, in fact, providing negative experiences for them. Serving time with men evidently reinforces traditional sex stereotypes, since women tend to concentrate on relationships and not self-improvement, and recreate dysfunctional relationships similar to those that got them into trouble on the outside. Sex ratios in cocorrectional prisons tend to disadvantage women—there are usually more men than women, so programming is targeted to men and greater restrictions are placed on women's movements.

DIFFERENCES BETWEEN WOMEN'S AND MEN'S PRISONS

Women's institutions in the past have looked different from institutions for men. The inmates may have lived in closed rooms rather than open cells or dormitories. They may have been allowed to have curtains and bedspreads and to decorate their cells with pictures of children and handiwork. Women have been more likely to be allowed to wear their own clothing, at least in the living units. They may have had more access to personal items from the commissary, such as cosmetics and shampoo. Some prisons have had cooking facilities on the floors or washers and dryers. Uniforms, if provided, may have been available in more variety than in men's institutions—for example, in different colors or combinations. Some differences were less favorable to women. Taylor (1982) found that in a comparison of Chino (for men) and Frontera (for women):

- Women's education was more humiliating because adult education materials were not used.
- Fewer external school learning centers were available for women.
- A higher percentage of women were enrolled in vocational programs, but they had fewer programs from which to choose.
- No apprenticeship programs were available to female inmates.
- Women had less opportunity to be paid for prison work.
- Only one industry, sewing, was available for women, whereas men had six.
- Women were, in general, further from their homes.
- Women had fewer visitors than men.
- Rules for visiting were stricter for female inmates.
- Men had easier access to telephones.
- There were more volunteer programs at the men's institutions.
- Men had more limitations on their personal property.
- Known homosexuals were segregated at the institution for men but allowed in the general population at the women's institution.
- All men were given a battery of psychological tests, but this was done only for selected women. (Taylor, 1982: 238–242)

These findings must be interpreted with caution. They were based on a comparison of only two prisons and should not be presumed to be representative across the country. Also, the findings are quite dated, and today's prisons may bear no resemblance to Chino and Frontera in the late 1970s. However, observers still contend that women are treated differently and often receive fewer services than male inmates.

Although differences between men's and women's prisons may still exist in architecture and physical appearance, the trend has been to minimize and eliminate these differences. Private corrections firms build "cookie-cutter" prisons that are marketed interchangeably for men, women, and even juvenile offenders. There is a philosophy and policy among many state corrections departments that women's units should be "brought into line" with the male model of corrections. Sometimes this has had humorous results. In one newly opened private prison that housed both male and female inmates, the women's side, although exactly the same as the men's structurally, looked completely different. The walls were painted an attractive deep mauve, and there were murals and flowers painted on the walls. Carpet remnants were scattered in the dayrooms, and posters with positive and/or religious messages dotted the bulletin boards. There was definitely a different atmosphere because of these minor adjustments. Several years later, the walls were back to institutional greenish gray, the murals were gone, and the inspirational messages were replaced with prison rules, just as on the men's side. When the changes were questioned, the response was that it was decided that prisons should not be "pink."

It is unlikely that one could mistake even the most progressive women's institution for anything but a prison. Officers are in uniform, and rules and regulations govern everything from showers to letters. Women are frequently prohibited from visiting in one another's rooms or exchanging clothing. Although the atmosphere may seem almost jovial at times in the living units, it is also sometimes punctuated with physical altercations between angry inmates or the cries and screams of women who "go off," reacting to imprisonment with violent self-destructiveness or madness.

Sex Differences in Prisons

One of the more interesting subjects of study is the analysis of sex differences between incarcerated men and women. Many of the findings discussed here lead to hypotheses regarding behavioral differences between men and women, particularly in prison. Unfortunately several problems prevent such studies from being more than merely suggestive. The major problem is the difficulty of getting comparable samples. The small number of imprisoned women leads to studies that compare a small number of women with a large number of men or that compare women to a sample in one male facility that is not representative of the total imprisoned population. Ages and offense histories may not be comparable. If one is comparing men and women in a coed prison, the comparability of the sample is the issue. If one is comparing men and women in single-sex institutions, comparability of institutions is a problem. Any measurements of prison behavior are suspect because of different measuring tendencies; for instance, findings that compare male and female inmates' infractions are suspect because there may be a greater, or lesser, tendency to report infractions in a prison for women.

Another problem in the studies that purport to show sex differences is the contamination of popular stereotypes. This is especially true for articles written in the past; for example, a description of women in a training school stated: "It is common knowledge, for instance, that women become upset if another female wears the same style dress" (Catalino, 1972: 122). A discussion of two women aiding a runaway boy included the remark: "It seems doubtful the girls would have done the same thing for another girl, whereas boys have performed similar 'services' for other boys" (Catalino, 1972: 125). Finally, in describing a reaction to a sick girl, the author stated: "Despite the facade of genuine empathy with the sick girl, an appearance of superficiality was evident. Male relationships appear to be based on firmer fidelities. . . ." (Catalino, 1972: 126). These examples of subjective interpretations are rare in the descriptions of women inmates today but were very common not long ago; they are examples of the difficulty of separating popular stereotypes from "general knowledge."

Pollock (1986) examined correctional officers' perceptions of sex differences and found that both male and female officers perceived inmates as reflecting sex differences commonly ascribed to males and females in society. For instance, they described female inmates as emotional and manipulative and males as cool and aloof. They also reported that women were more difficult to supervise, primarily because they were less respectful of officers' authority and more argumentative. Although one must be careful in accepting perceptions at face value, the consistency in responses of people who work with men and women in custody and in their descriptions of differences lends some support to the idea that women may exhibit different behaviors from men in the prison environment. The source of these differences may be sex differences, socialization, or different treatment by officers; probably it is a mixture of all three.

One of the differences noted between male and female inmates by those who work with them is the greater emotionality of women. This difference is no doubt partly cultural and partly stereotypical. Basically, the emotionality of women as described by officers can be broken into three constructs: expressiveness, attachment, and mood swings (Pollock, 1984). Expressiveness relates to the tendency to spontaneously and openly display emotions. Whether it is sadness, anger, happiness, love, or any other emotion, female inmates are observed to be more open in their display.

> Men hold emotion in. It comes out aggressively or they're aloof. Women are tearful and crying.
>
> First time I ever had an inmate cry on my shoulders I was here two days. I never thought that would happen in a jail.
>
> Women can hug and show expression to each other but the public doesn't accept men hugging and showing affection to men (Pollock, 1981).

Another related component of emotionality is attachment. Attachment is a tendency to become involved with other people. Female inmates are observed to care more for one another, even though some researchers report that this caring seems superficial or transitory. Attachments may be stronger love attachments or the tendency of female inmates to be concerned with one another's problems.

> One of the females in the group may be having an emotional problem, may be having a physical problem, a family problem that's got her all upset and all her friends would congregate around her to give her sympathy and console her, to give her direction, to give her moral support, whatever. . . .
>
> Men will take their problems to their cell, close the door and read a book, whatever, but a woman will take theirs out and share it, display it, let everybody see what was bothering them (Pollock, 1981).

The final component of emotionality is the greater variability in moods observable among many female inmates. Although this variability may simply be another measurement of openness, many officers and treatment professionals do report that female inmates tend to undergo extreme mood swings with drastic behavioral consequences. Further, these mood swings may or may not be related to external events. Finally, the mood swings may be relatively rapid, so that a woman can show various moods even during one particular day.

> Men seem to be more stable than women. One woman can be at a high one day and the next day she can be very low and the men generally you get one man and he's generally that way most of the time unless something comes up, you know, to push him over the edge, but generally they're the same way the whole time you know them. The women go up and down (Pollock, 1984: 87).

As mentioned earlier, perceptions such as those in the previous examples derive from both the actions of the female inmates as well as the expectations and projections of the officers. However, the prevalence of the comments and the consistency in which they continue to be made year after year seem to lend some legitimacy to the officers' perceptions that there are differences. Whether these differences are truly sex differences or are elicited from the different supervision styles in prisons for men and women is a difficult research question and one that has not, as yet, been answered.

CONCLUSION

This chapter illustrated in general terms what prisons for women are like today. Obviously, one cannot be completely accurate when describing prisons across the country. Generalities reduce accuracy. While some prisons are cottages, others are of the warehouse variety. Some may have more liberal policies and procedures than those that have been described. Some may not allow the amenities that make women's prison life more comfortable physically, if not psychologically. Even in the area of programs offered to women inmates, dramatic differences appear. Whereas some prisons offer none, others offer more than a dozen. Some prisons have continued with the traditional sex-typed programs, while others have been remarkably innovative. Some newer prisons are virtually indistinguishable from men's prisons; others retain remnants of the legacy of the early reformatories.

Despite these differences, some general principles can be gleaned from this broad look at institutions across the country. Although litigation, increased attention, and more professional training of officers may have lessened the paternalism described in women's prisons of the 1960s and 1970s, the atmosphere and treatment of inmates by staff are still different in women's and men's institutions. Arguably less harsh physical surroundings and treatment are used to control female inmates, but the psychological control seems much more pervasive—resulting in an institution that looks nice but within which the incarcerated women feel that staff attempt to control every aspect of their lives. They are confused because, on the one hand, they receive signals that indicate they should be grateful for the opportunities and pleasant aspects of the institution ("They have nothing to complain about"), yet on the other hand they are constantly besieged by signals that tell them they are children or incompetent adults who need to be told what to do. This situation results in an institution remarkably similar to a high school with rowdy students. Staff spend a great deal of time concerned with such behavior as walking and talking loudly and rough horseplay, because there are relatively few serious infractions like drug dealing or homicide to worry about.

It is a strange place. It is a place where women inmates may pleasantly and animatedly discuss hairstyles with women officers, then a short while later swear bitterly at the same officers for refusing to allow them some special privilege. It is a place where women 40 years old are called "girls" and mothers are treated like children. It is a place where a new officer can be the target of a vicious game played by inmates, who subject her to taunts about her ignorance, her body, and her personal life as she attempts to understand her duties and deal with the new job. If she is reduced to tears, the inmates may never forget her weakness and will constantly intimidate her until she requests a position with less contact or quits. It is also a place where an inmate will spend countless hours by the bedside of a dying AIDS patient, bathing her, comforting her, and helping her come to terms with impending death.

The women's prison is not as violent as the prison for men, but it still possesses an undercurrent of fear. There are the "stud broads" who control others by sheer force of personality and occasional violence. There are instances of officers, with full riot gear, subduing female inmates who might be breaking up a cell or attacking other inmates or officers, either because of intentional hostility or undirected anger borne of frustration and hopelessness. There are instances of male officers sneaking into cells at night to extort sex from a powerless woman. Women who enter prison must adjust. Many who manage to survive and get something out of the prison experience do so because of programs offered. These programs will be the topic in the next chapter.

NOTES

1. Although Shaffer et al. (1983) discuss the application of the Megargee classification system (using MMPI scores) with a female sample with some success.

2. 431 F. Supp. 1129 (S.D.N.Y. 1977), *aff'd,* 565 F.2d 48 (2d Cir. 1977).

3. It is not clear why Barry's and Ross and Lawrence's figures are so different; it could be that Barry's figures include jail inmates.

4. Goetting and Howsen (1983: 37) provides the only contrary finding. In their study, nearly 41 percent of women had been guilty of breaking prison rules during incarceration, but 47.74 percent of men had; men also obtained more serious punishments, such as solitary confinement, loss of good time, or transfer.

5. Ellis and Austin (1971) conducted a study and concluded that there was a correlation between violent acts by women and menstruation, since about half of the incidents reported occurred within 8 days of a 28-day cycle. Since the study utilized self-reports and officer observations for incidents of violence, however, it is questionable whether the results mean anything. Climent et al. (1977) also proposed a psychobiological explanation for women's violence.

SUGGESTED READINGS

Burkhardt, K. 1973. *Women in Prison.* Garden City, NJ: Doubleday.

Girshick, L. 1999. *No Safe Haven: Stories of Women in Prison.* Boston, MA: Northeastern University Press.

Morton, J. 1998. *Complex Challenges, Collaborative Solutions: Programming for Adult and Juvenile Female Offenders.*

Lanham, MD: American Correctional Association.

Owen, B. 1998. *"In the Mix": Struggle and Survival in a Women's Prison.* Albany, NY: State University of Albany Press.

Rierdan, A. 1997. *The Farm: Life Inside a Women's Prison.* Amherst, MA: University of Massachusetts Press.

5

Gender-Responsive Programming: The Reality of Difference

I n the previous chapter, a woman's entry into prison was described. Part of the entry process is deciding what combination of programs and work activities will occupy her time. This chapter looks more closely at the programs available in prisons. We concentrate on two areas in particular: drug programs and parenting programs.

PROGRAMS

Activities for women in prison fall into four major categories. The first category includes those activities necessary for the maintenance of the institution—activities such as clerical work in administration, food service for inmates and staff, and general cleaning and maintenance work around the grounds. The second category is education. As is true of men in prison, the majority of women prisoners need remedial education, although some are ready for college programs. The third category is vocational training; ordinarily in prisons for women, most of these programs prepare women for traditionally female types of employment, such as food service and office skills. The fourth category of activities includes those activities designed to rehabilitate the prisoner through personal growth or individual change; for example, group therapy, eclectic therapy models, or Alcoholics Anonymous.

Most women in prison do something during the day. Fox (1984) reported that in 1972, 20 percent of the women in Bedford Hills held full-time work or program assignments and another 40 percent held part-time assignments. In a Texas survey, larger numbers of women said they participated in some type of program: about 60 percent of women said they attended education classes; 36 percent attended drug or alcohol counseling programs; and 26 percent participated in vocational training programs (Pollock et al., 1996). These figures may be high. Gabel and Johnston (1995) reviewed a number of other studies and concluded that less than 20 percent of women were involved in any parenting program, less than 10 percent were involved in drug treatment, about 10 percent received psychological counseling, and less than 6 percent were engaged in any vocational training. However, some women in prison are either working or in an educational or rehabilitative program from early morning until late at night. Other female inmates prefer to do as little as possible in prison, spending their free time in the yard, dayroom, or cell.

Female inmates are used to perform needed services and jobs in the prison community. Almost all (95 percent) facilities require women to perform some maintenance or institutional work assignments (Crawford, 1988b: 23). Ordinarily the pay is almost nonexistent: the U.S. average in the late 1980s was $1.66 per hour (Crawford, 1988b: 23). Pay for such work is not appreciably different today. Prison industry may provide some skills and work experience for the female inmate. About half (53 percent) of Ryan's responding institutions had some type of industry (1984: xi).

Work assignments are typically menial and often are performed over and over again for the mere purpose of keeping the women busy. For instance, floors may be scrubbed every day or sometimes twice a day. The laundry employs many women and is considered by most to be the worst of assignments because of the heat, the physical toil of the work, and the potential for danger from the chemicals and boiling water available for aggressors. In some states, the women's institution houses the laundry for the whole system, and large truckloads of institutional laundry, filled with prison uniforms, sheets, and towels come and go every day. Female inmates also are employed to do clerical tasks in the administration building; at times, if they prove capable, they may be given quite a lot of responsibility. Much of any prison's daily maintenance, in fact, is performed by the inmates who live there. This is true for men's as well as women's prisons. There has been a tendency in women's institutions to employ more outsiders to perform typically "masculine" tasks, such as lawn care, electrical and plumbing work, and construction or renovation tasks. Some prison administrators, however, use female inmates for these tasks, supervised by a civilian foreman.

Some women, like some men, refuse to work for the prison, maintaining the view that the prison sentence itself is their punishment; they argue that they will not help the state in their own imprisonment. Other women appreciate the opportunity to do something useful during the day. The more esteem the job entails, the more pride women take in doing it, so that those who work in the administration building are more satisfied with their job than those who work in the laundry.

A few prisons have established partnerships with outside companies so that the company brings in the raw materials or tools necessary to do a task and employs women as workers. In these partnerships, women earn free-world wages. Their income is taken away except for a small allowance and used to pay back the state for room and board, child support, and to establish a nest egg for the woman for release. Such partnerships include manufacturing companies (e.g., grinding lens for eyeglasses) and service industries (800 reservation or order operators, or data entry).

Education and Vocational Training

Educational Programs Chapman (1980) discussed the great need for education. She found that 60 percent of the female inmates were high-school dropouts. Similarly, Crawford found that only 33 percent of inmates in her sample had completed high school (1988b: 26). Today, about 40 percent of women in prison have graduated from high school or obtained a general equivalency diploma (GED) (BJS, 1999c; Greenfield and Snell, 1999: 7). It should be noted that high-school graduation does not necessarily mean that the woman reads at a 12th-grade or even a 10th-grade level. This is important because reading level is relevant to entry in vocational programs.

In 1975, 83 percent of women's prisons offered educational and reading programs (Chapman, 1980: 103). In 1984, 83 percent of the respondents in one national survey covering 45 states had GED programs, and 83 percent had adult basic education programs. College programs were present in 72 percent of the institutions (Ryan, 1984: x). In a 1985 survey, all but one of the institutions offered educational programs (Weishet, 1985).

Adult basic education (ABE) was present in most of the institutions surveyed in Ryan's (1984) study in the mid-1980s. This type of education comprises basic literacy and living skills. Ryan reported that the hours women spent in ABE courses ranged from 2 to 35 hours per week; the average was 15, and the mode was 20 (Ryan, 1984: 15). In Crawford's sample, 35 percent of the institutions required women to participate in ABE programs (1988b: 26). The GED programs are designed to give the women the equivalent of a high-school diploma. Ryan reported that most institutions had GED programs, but 27 percent of them had fewer than 10 women enrolled. New York, on the other hand, reported 175 women enrolled in its GED preparatory course. The average enrollment across the country was 26 (Ryan, 1984: 15). The mean number of hours spent in these programs was 15 hours per week; the mode was 20 and 30 hours.

Crawford reported that 17.5 percent of the facilities in her survey required GED participation for those women who needed it (1988b: 26). Three states had programs that led to high-school diplomas instead of GED certificates— Texas, Maine, and Washington (Ryan, 1984: 15). Fewer institutions had college programs. Ryan (1984) reported that only 72 percent of the responding facilities had college programs for female inmates. Enrollments ranged from 0 in Maine to 198 in Texas (1984: 18). Most of these programs were offered at the institution, but a few were community programs.

Crawford found that about half of the facilities reported women being paid for classroom attendance (1988b: 26). Payment is important, because when women are forced to choose between an institutional job that pays at least some amount of money and education that does not, they often have to choose the assignment that results in money, especially those women who have no family or whose families are too poor to provide packages from home or money to put into their institutional accounts. The candy, shampoo, and food-stuffs obtained in the commissary often provide the only treats in the woman's day; and some of the products are necessary—for instance, products for women whose skin is too sensitive for institutional soap or products designed for black women's hair and skin not available in institutional supplies.

More recent findings indicate that almost all institutions continue to have ABE or GED classes, but there are not substantially more college programs than there were in the 1980s. Part of the reason for this might be that PELL grants (federally funded student loans) have been made unavailable to prisoners, and therefore, college classes have to be funded by some other means, reducing the number of inmates who can take advantage of them. Some colleges that were offering courses in prisons in the 1980s are no longer doing so today.

Vocational Programs Moyer (1984) described prison vocational programs in the early 1980s as primarily falling into stereotyped areas, such as cosmetology, food service, laundry, nurse's aide training, housekeeping, sewing, garment manufacturing, clerical work, and IBM keypunch. Most institutions, in the past as well as today, have not had the resources or interest to offer a broad range of programs for women. Specialized and nontraditional programs are rare. Many programs do not have the capacity to serve large numbers of imprisoned women, and consequently popular programs have long waiting lists.

Zaitzow (1998: 165) lists the reasons that vocational programs are lacking in women's prisons as:

- They are not cost-effective.
- Women pose less of a threat to society; therefore, high-cost programs are unwarranted.
- There is a low rate of participation.
- Women's prisons are inaccessible.
- Women are still regarded primarily as wives and mothers.

In the last 20 years, however, both the number and variety of vocational programs have increased. In the mid-1980s, Ryan (1984) reported that 83 percent of facilities responding to his survey had at least one vocational education program. The number of programs varied, ranging from one to thirteen (Ryan, 1984: xi, 17). Texas, California, Georgia, Nevada, Oklahoma, and Pennsylvania offered the most programs (twelve to thirteen each) (Ryan, 1984: 17). A few years later, Crawford (1988b) reported that 90.2 percent of the facilities responding to her survey had some type of vocational program. Further, she reported that 57.5 percent of those facilities paid the women for their vocational training assignment (Crawford, 1988b: 25).

Weishet (1985) reported an association between the size of the institution and the number of programs it offered. Weishet's study also found an increase in the number of nontraditional programs. In 1973, none of the prisons surveyed had nontraditional programs; in 1979, four had started such programs; and in 1985, fifteen had nontraditional programs. Today, there are more programs, but there are not enough program slots for the huge increase of prisoners. (See Table 5.1.)

One continuing problem seems to be underutilization of some programs, or programs "on paper" that do not translate to real opportunities for women. More research needs to be done to uncover why some programs are not being utilized. It may be that the qualifications for program entry are too difficult or have disadvantages attached to them that outweigh the advantages. For instance, many vocational programs, especially in the clerical area, require at least a 9th- or 10th-grade reading level. Many inmates may not meet this entry qualification.

The smallest enrollments seem to be found in nontraditional programs. Women in prison may be more committed to traditional feminine roles than their middle-class sisters when it comes to choosing vocational programs. Institutions that have opened nontraditional programs have found they need to do public relations work and "consciousness-raising" to get female inmates interested. For instance, in one state prison, a heavy equipment course was offered to women that would train them for high-paying jobs outside prison, but the women's perception of the program was that it was a "leftover" program from a men's prison and another indication that prison administrators did not understand their needs. Actually getting a job in a traditionally male area of employment is another hurdle. If vocational programs in prison have no job placement component, it is entirely possible that the expensive training may be wasted upon release.

Table 5.1 Vocational Programs

Program	Number of Institutions Offering	
	$n = 36$ (Weishet)	$n = 58$ (Ryan)
Sewing	30 (83%)	31 (53%)
Food services	28 (78%)	15 (36%)
Secretarial	31 (86%)	26 (45%)
Education	35 (97%)	51 (83%)
College	28 (78%)	40 (72%)
Basic skills	32 (88%)	48 (83%)
Domestic	20 (56%)	n/a
Cosmetology	16 (44%)	15 (36%)[a]
Auto repair	8 (22%)	11 (27%)[a]
Welding	9 (25%)	11 (27%)[a]
Carpentry	15 (42%)	10 (24%)
Computer	21 (58%)	8 (20%)
Electrical	15 (42%)	9 (22%)
Plumbing	12 (33%)	2 (5%)

[a]Data was reported by state: $n = 41$.

SOURCE: Ryan (1984); Weishet (1985).

One nontraditional program for women is Wider Opportunities for Women (WOW). A private program operating primarily in northeastern prisons (Washington, D.C., and New York), it combines nontraditional jobs with self-assertion training to help women learn to be independent (Kestenbaum, 1977). This program and others like it promote nontraditional careers in such areas as carpentry, welding, electrical work, and so on. The primary reason these occupations are touted is that they are far more lucrative than traditional women's work. The WOW program places women in construction jobs and helps with day-care and housing.

Ryan reported that courses with the largest enrollments included business education, cosmetology, nurse's aide training, home economics, cooking, and food service (1984: 17). Chapman (1980) reported that of the prisons surveyed in her study, the offerings included upholstery, drapery making, ADP keypunch, welding, marine electrical, auto mechanics, clerical, college, cosmetology, and cleaning services. Today one is likely to see computer repair and programming courses in prisons, as well as a wide range of other types of programs, at least in some state systems.

Part of the reason for the increase in the number and variety of vocational programs has been litigation that challenged the lack of programs under an equal opportunity argument. Cases such as *Glover v. Johnson*,[1] which will be discussed more fully in a later chapter, helped encourage prison administrations to institute new programs for women. Although such challenges typically object to the number of programs available, criticism is also directed at the nature of such programs.

Treatment Programs

Treatment-oriented programs help female prisoners to experience personal growth or to acquire other introspective or social skills. Weishet (1985), in his survey of women's prisons, found that almost all prisons offer some sort of treatment programs. All surveyed offered alcohol programs, drug programs, and mental health programs. Thirty-three of 36 surveyed offered parenting classes; 25 of the 36 offered personal etiquette classes, with no explanation of what was taught in such a class; and 34 of the 36 offered health programs.

Treatment programs may range from group therapy to art therapy. Programs may be contracted out to private service providers, run by prison staff, or run by the inmates themselves. The most common treatment programs in prison are for drug addiction; drug programs are covered separately in a later section of this chapter. Other types of programs emphasize anger management, personal growth, goal setting, and communication. Many prisons offer general "life skills" programs that offer a little bit of everything in a 6- to 24-week course format. Other programs employ therapeutic communities or utilize behavior modification.

Therapeutic communities emphasize inmate participation, open communication, and shared decision making in an isolated tier or living unit. Inmates attend "group" at least once a day and sometimes twice a day. In these groups, discussion centers around such issues as personal responsibility and goal setting. Incidents that occur in the living unit are dealt with and used as part of the learning process. Some programs in women's prisons may be therapeutic communities in name only, practicing none of the elements crucial to the theory behind the therapy.

Behavior modification employs the use of rewards to shape behavior. The most common form of behavior modification programs in prison is the token economy, where prisoners earn greater liberties by exemplary behavior. Aversive conditioning also has been used, employing electric shocks or other painful stimuli. Behavior modification may be less effective with female offenders than with male offenders. In one study reported on by Ross and Fabiano, female delinquents who were participating in a behavior modification program increased their rate of self-mutilation, vandalism, escape attempts, and assault (1986: 18).

Negy, Woods, and Carlson (1997) discussed the correlation between a female inmate's coping skills and prison adjustment and concluded that programs that help women develop and adopt better ways of coping with stress would help them in prison and upon release. Zang et al. (1998) described a comprehensive life skills program offered in Michigan. The program was organized to meet the identified needs of female inmates, specifically, their need for job skills, and personal growth related to the following characteristics: reduced locus of control, a sense of fatalism, overly accommodating to others, weak social networks, avoidance of problem solving, use of money as a means to impress people, and lack of long-range planning skills. The phases of the program were as follows:

1. Assessment: involves psychological, education, medical testing, comprehensive look at life history, criminal history, and current needs.

2. Institute: curriculum includes self-efficacy, problem solving, stress management, anger management, communication, employability skills, negotiation, money and time management, family and community living.

3. Individualized reintegration plan: focus is on what she is going to do while in prison to prepare for release, along with periodic updating and review of plan.

4. Return to community: advocacy involves pairing a released offender with an advocate who meets with her three times each week and provides linkage to support services.

Vigilante et al. (1999) described an HIV/prison prevention program for high-risk offenders (intravenous drug use, commercial sex work, or history of prison recidivism). A physician and social worker assist each woman in developing an individual discharge plan and work with her, along with a peer counselor, after release. A preliminary evaluation comparing a group of program graduates to a semi-matched sample[2] concluded that significantly fewer of the program group recidivated, compared to the matched sample at three months (5 percent versus 18.5 percent) and at twelve months (33 percent versus 45 percent).[3]

Sultan and Long (1988; also see Sultan et al., 1984) described a program for violent female offenders who had been victims of sexual and physical abuse. After participating in a 16-week group therapy treatment program that utilized the psychodidactic-support model (sharing information in a therapeutic way), the participants reported higher self-esteem, greater personal control, reduced alienation, and increased trust in others.

Childhood Victimization As stated in the previous chapter, a disproportional number of female inmates (compared to the general population and also compared to a male inmate sample) have been either sexually or physically victimized as children. Reviewing all the studies in this area leads to the conclusion that at least a third, and probably a much higher percentage, of the women's prisoner population has experienced childhood abuse of some kind.

This history leads to a number of adult consequences. Victimization as a child may lead a woman to seek a relationship, any relationship, rather than be alone; unwanted as a child and told she is undesirable, the girl grows up to accept whatever abuse a man gives her as long as he stays (Bedell, 1997). Some empirical support for this premise is available. For instance, Mullings, Marquart, and Brewer (2000) found that a history of sexual abuse in childhood was associated with increased sexual risk-taking behaviors in adulthood as well as pursuing "marginal" living situations (living with different men, chaotic lifestyle).

Childhood abuse also may create a greater sensitivity to the authority of male officers. For instance, Heney and Kristiansen (1998) noted first that about 50 percent of Canadian female prisoners had been subject to sexual abuse, and then pointed out how these women were retraumatized in prison by incidences of pat downs, strip searches, verbal abuse, and other interactions with male officers that emphasized their powerlessness. Heney and Kristiansen speculated that at least some of the "acting out" in prisons for women is due to feelings of power-lessness: "One might speculate that the more survivors feel helpless, the more they will try to control their immediate reality, and thereby preserve their psy-chic survival" (1998: 33).

In a later chapter, we will discuss the problem of sexual harassment and exploitation by male officers. Those who argue that it is not always the inmate who is the victim in a situation involving a sexual relationship with an officer, point out that sometimes female inmates "seduce" or "entice" officers into sex-ual relationships. The notion that a grown, trained professional in a position of power over others can be induced to engage in an activity that is against prison policy and, in some states, against the law, is a weak argument. It also over-looks the dynamics of what is occurring.

Women in prison have been defined by their sexuality all their lives—espe-cially those who have been the victims of incest. To respond to men in a sexual manner has become a self-defense mechanism for them and a mode of interact-ing that is reinforced by male officers who sexualize the prison environment in their references and treatment of women. "Hey, you lookin GOOD today!" is a comment by a male officer that is heard in many prisons across the country where men guard women. Men may be innocently attempting to make the female inmate feel good; the meaning of the statement, however, is that her worth, her identity, her whole being is defined by men, and for men. That is how she has been raised, and that is her reality. Is it any wonder, then, that some women respond to male officers by using their sexuality? Far from being free agents, they are probably merely living out the relationship they had with their father or other male relatives who held power over them.

Powerlessness also leads to other anomalous situations, such as the use of humor as a reaction to fear and distress. Some observe that women freely engage in sexual repartee with male officers, and their ribald humor seems to contradict other statements that they find male officers' sexualization of super-vision offensive; however, it may be that humor is a nervous and inappropri-ate reaction of the powerless.

Two examples of the presence of humor will be presented. First, in an inci-dent in Kingston Prison for Women that will be discussed more fully in a later chapter, prisoners in segregation who were disruptive were stripped naked by a male special force team from a neighboring prison for men. Each woman was in an isolation cell in segregation. One by one, the team burst into each woman's cell, and held her down and stripped her naked. The shackled woman was then left standing naked with a small paper half-gown covering a small portion of her body while the cell was stripped clean. The other women could only hear screams and the sounds of the struggle. As each incident occurred, women would cry out to find out what was happening; after a time, women who had been stripped called out to other women not to fight. The last several women offered to come out of their cells voluntarily but were overpowered and stripped the same way. During the course of this incident, women, either in their cells or standing naked while their cells were being stripped, engaged in nervous laughter and sexual jokes. There was no question that this was a very frightening and traumatizing experience, yet later the joking was brought up as "proof" that they were not affected by the presence of male officers in such a use of force (Arbour, 1996).

It was clear, however, to sensitive observers, that the joking was a reaction to the traumatization. Women in our culture smile when they are angry, and sometimes laugh (nervously) when they are afraid. Their socialization is such that they must seek training to learn to say no and to overcome socialization to be "nice" in occupations such as law enforcement so that people believe them when they give orders.

Another example presents somewhat similar circumstances: Elizabeth Morgan, a "middle-class" woman imprisoned in Riker's Island, described an incident where a woman was the victim of a gang rape by other women (Morgan, 1999). Everyone was laughing, including the victim, although she was clearly terrified, until Morgan stopped the incident. Why the victim in such a circumstance was laughing can be understood only through an explanation of a lifetime of sexual victimization and powerlessness that is reinforced by the prison experience.

Evaluation of Treatment Programs

Gendreau (1996: 120–125) cited several principles that are associated with effective programs:

- Services that are intensive and behavioral in nature
- Behavioral programs that address the criminogenic needs of high-risk offenders
- Programs in which contingencies and behavioral strategies are enforced in a firm but fair manner
- Relationships between therapists and offenders that are interpersonally responsive and constructive
- Program structure and activities that promote prosocial behavior
- Relapse prevention strategies provided in the community to the extent possible
- Advocacy and brokering services between offenders and the community that are attempted whenever community agencies offer appropriate services

Palmer (1995) identified staff characteristics, staff and client interaction, and setting as the most important elements in a successful program and indicated that these characteristics may be more influential than the modality of the particular program. However, these and most other evaluation studies either have not utilized a female sample or have included women as such a small portion of the sample that it would be dangerous to project the findings to a female population. Thus, we simply do not know which treatment programs work best with women or whether certain treatment programs are received differently by men and women.

A rare exception is Austin, Bloom, and Donahue's (1992) study that surveyed community-based programs for women. This study concluded that the most promising programs were those that "combined supervision and services to address the specialized needs of female offenders in highly structured, safe environments where accountability is stressed" (1992: 21). "Promising" programs were those that used an "empowerment" model that allowed and expected women to gain some level of independence and responsibility over their own needs.

As stated in an earlier chapter, the rate of recidivism among women seems to be increasing. Reasons for recidivism typically involve a constellation of economic and personal factors. Morris and Wilkinson (1995) interviewed 200 women in England during the early phase of their sentence, at prerelease, and after release (three to five months later). They found that:

- Many reported drinking or drug use.
- Many reported unemployment, and that it contributed to the crime.
- Postprison plans for supervision did not meet the women's needs.
- Those who reoffended had poor living conditions and were not managing financially.

Results of evaluations show that most programs have limited influence on participants (Ross and Fabiano, 1986). Zaitzow (1998: 170) reviewed the studies of effectiveness and concluded that the elements of effective programs include:

- Inspired and dedicated leaders
- A sense of purpose and mission to offenders
- A unified treatment team
- Participants with decision-making power
- A development of skills
- Uniqueness
- Adequate community networks
- No alienating formal decision makers

Koons et al. (1997) surveyed correctional professionals to discover what was perceived to be the most effective programs or program elements with female offenders. Their findings indicated that there was some agreement on what administrators felt were elements of successful programming, and these included:

- The use of a comprehensive approach
- A continuum of care

- Individualized and structured programming
- Emphasis on skill development (parenting, life skills, job skills)
- Addresses individual needs
- Caring staff members
- Staff members who are ex-addicts or ex-offenders and are women
- Separation from the general population
- Partnerships with outside services
- Adequate money and resources
- "Homey" environment (1997: 523–525).

As part of the same research study, Morash and Bynum (1995) found that correctional administrators reported the need for more programming in areas of vocational education, work skills, family development, substance abuse, domestic violence, physical and sexual abuse, and aftercare, especially with housing.

It is clear that treatment programs are essential, and that there are not enough of them to accommodate all women who desire to better themselves while in prison. One of the interesting aspects of evaluating treatment programs is that women report highly positive attitudes toward all types of treatment; in fact, their only complaint seems to be that there are not enough of them (Pollock et al., 1996). In study after study, quotations are recorded that indicate that not only treatment, but even prison, is considered by women to be a positive intervention in their lives. Owen (1998: 188), for instance, recorded an inmate who said, "[Prison is] the best thing that ever happened to me. I know I would be dead if I hadn't been sent here. It has made me stop and think about what I was doing to myself and my kids"; "In prison I found out who I was"; and "I probably would have been dead if I had not come to prison." Kendall (1994b: 2) obtained almost exactly the same remarks, as well as these: "I think when I was on the street I wasn't really free at all, but now I feel like I'm becoming truly free." Again and again, women indicate they are ready to change and prison has the potential to be a place where they can overcome life's problems and learn to make better choices.

DRUGS: A SOLUTION
BECOMES A PROBLEM

As mentioned in the last chapter, one of the most consistent findings regarding female offenders is that drug use seems to be more strongly correlated with their criminality than it does for men. Yang (1990) and Biron et al. (1995) are a few of the many researchers who have noted the growing numbers of addicts in the correctional system, the smaller number of treatment programs for women, women's greater likelihood (as compared to male offenders) of being addicted or having abuse problems, and the unique needs of female drug abusers (i.e. they seem to have more medical problems, greater mental health needs, fewer vocational skills, and unique issues related to children).

Drug Use Forecasting (DUF) reports show that female arrestees are more likely to be under the influence of drugs at the time of the offense and at the time of arrest, and women in prison self-report heavier drug use and admit to drug problems more often than do men in prison (Blount et al., 1991). In fact, DUF numbers indicate that half, and in some cities up to three-fourths, of arrested women test positive for drugs (Prendergast, Wellisch, and Falkin, 1995). Girshick (1999) and several others who have talked to women in prison have found that many describe their lives as having been ruined by drugs, and despite seeing the devastation of drug addiction of their parents, have begun the cycle again with their own children. Drug abusers are at risk for: dehydration, weight loss, digestive disorders, skin problems, dental problems, gynecological and venereal infections, tuberculosis, hepatitis B, hypertension, seizures, respiratory arrest, and cardiac failure (Prendergast, Wellisch, and Falkin, 1997: 319).

> I woke up in this abandoned house, and shooting gallery, where addicts go and shoot drugs. I hadn't taken a bath in about 3 days. My body hygiene was bad. I had destroyed my face from using cocaine. . . . I had abscesses on my body . . . And I just got tired. . . . I didn't want to live that way anymore. (Pollock, 1998, p. 81)

Thus, it is imperative that female offenders in prison have access to effective drug treatment programs. Whether or not they do have such access is subject to debate. Covington (1998b), for instance, reported that although 60 percent of the women in California's prisons were there for crimes related to drugs, only about 3 percent had access to drug or alcohol programs. Furthermore, treatment programs in prison are commonly drug education classes, Alcoholics Anonymous and/or Narcotics Anonymous, or some hybrid modeled after these 12-step modalities. Many women's treatment programs are simply patterned after programs that were developed for men (such as those that use some form of "attack therapy").

Before one can help female drug abusers, however, it is important to understand the sequence of drug use and abuse, and the motivations for it. There is much more literature available on male drug users than on female drug users; however, there have been a few studies that provide relevant information. Rosenbaum (1981) characterized women's drug abuse as the end of a gradual reduction of opportunities—that is, drug-using people were their only friends, they had no legitimate employment, their children had been taken away, and survival became completely centered around drugs.

Female addicts evidently are different from male addicts in a number of ways. One national study found that female drug-abusing offenders:

- Started at an early age
- Had physical and mental problems
- Were unemployed or underemployed

- Lacked skills or education
- Had psychosocial problems (prior victimization)
- Came from families with addiciton, mental illness, and/or suicide
- Were single parents, without supportive family or social networks
- Had family members in the criminal justice system (Wellisch, Prendergast, & Aglin, 1996: 29–32)[4]

One consistent finding is that female drug-abusing prisoners were more likely than non–drug abusers to have been victimized in the past. For instance, in one study it was found that 46 percent of drug abusers had been raped, and 28–44 percent had been victims of incest (Prendergast, Wellisch, and Falkin, 1997: 320). They also are most likely to come from families with dysfunctions like mental illness, criminality, alcoholism, and violence. A continuing theme of the research—both survey and phenomenological—is that the motivation for drug use may be different for male and female offenders: women tend to use drugs more often to "self-medicate," men more often for experiential rewards (thrill). For instance, Lord (1995: 262) writes: "Drug use becomes a way to numb pain, to take oneself out of a painful and hopeless world. The drug use, in and of itself, is not the problem that needs to be addressed but is only a symptom—of feelings that must be kept in check to ensure survival."

Thus, for women, drugs are used as a "solution" to life's problems—to blunt the pain of past or current victimization, to bolster feelings of self-worth, to help bond with a male or female partner, or to reduce the stress of single parenthood. Obviously, the solution becomes a bigger problem and leads to choices that ultimately result in prison.

Evaluations of Drug Treatment Programs

Farrell (2000), in a small ($n = 79$) study of program participants, found involvement in a therapeutic community helped to prevent relapse for alcohol but not so much for other drugs (at least not significantly, although the trend was in the right direction). In fact, there was virtually no difference in recidivism between the two groups (about 39 percent). The therapeutic community did not seem to have much effect in helping women create supportive networks outside; there were no significant differences in their number of moves or in the presence of family and friends. Participation in a therapeutic community did not seem to influence their likelihood of caring for children or of going to work or school, nor did it appreciably reduce feelings of isolation. It seemed that there were only a few factors related to reduced recidivism. These were degree of contact with a significant person, having responsibility for children, and identification with their community (Farrell, 2000: 40).

On the other hand, Inciardi (1996) reported on a successful drug treatment program for women inmates in Delaware that used the therapeutic community approach. Results indicated that program participants were much less likely than a comparison group to use drugs after release (35 percent compared to 70 percent) and to be rearrested (18 percent compared to 38 percent). As with treatment programs for male offenders, the evaluation of programs tends to result in mixed findings.[5]

Wellisch, Prendergast, and Aglin (1996) conducted a survey of the needs of drug-abusing women offenders, as well as a nationwide survey of community-based treatment programs.[6] After reviewing 165 community-based programs, they concluded that there were widespread inadequacies in treatment delivery and that women-only programs seemed to offer more special services. Most programs offered case management, relapse prevention, HIV/AIDS education, counseling, and 12-step meetings. Few programs made accommodations for children, although women-only programs were more likely to meet women's special needs (1996: 34). The authors noted that the "most promising programs were intended to broaden clients' responses and enhance their coping and decision-making skills, rather than operate from a deficit model. . . . [M]ost effective approaches link emotional support with practical skill development and deal specifically with women's issues, including alcohol/drug dependence." The authors' general findings (including both community-based and institutional programs) were as follows:

- More treatment programs are available than in the past but still do not meet need.

- Many programs do not address multiple problems of women offenders.

- Treatment is limited in intensity and duration.

- Services offered for women are found mostly in women-only programs.

- A continuum of support is needed.

- More family services are needed, including treatment programs for women with small children. (Wellisch, Prendergast, and Anglin, 1994)

Reed (1987: 151) found that "Women oriented drug dependence treatment services are defined as those that (a) address women's treatment needs; (b) reduce barriers to recovery from drug dependence that are more likely to occur for women; (c) are delivered in a context that is compatible with women's styles and orientations and is safe from exploitation; and (d) take into account women's roles, socialization and relative status within the larger culture." One of the most important findings of this literature is that because motivations for drug use, and motivations to change, may be different between men and women, it is imperative to develop women-centered treatment programs rather than simply pick up a treatment program designed for men and transplant it into the women's prison. Women respond less well to attack therapy and better to nurturance; their motivation to change is largely found within their guilt toward their children and others; and their vulnerabilities toward recidivating tend to be found in their low self-worth and inability to cope with stress. These issues must be addressed in any treatment program.

INMATES AS MOTHERS

One of the most important differences between incarcerated men and women is the predominance of children in the lives of female prisoners (Bloom and Steinhart, 1993; Catan, 1992; Dressel and Barnhill, 1994; Fox, 1992; Gabel and Johnston, 1995).[7] Many researchers have documented the pervasive presence of children in the women's prison. Children are either physically present (in visiting rooms or other programs at the prison), or their presence is felt in the increased social and legal problems they create. Women prisoners also experience depression and guilt because of their children, which may have behavioral manifestations (Baunach, 1985b; Kiser, 1991).

Owen's (1998: 121) phenomenological study of women in prison reinforces older studies that detailed the predominance of children in the prison world of women. Sharing stories, cells decorated with pictures, the prevalence of knitting and handcrafts for or by children, and the effects of stress concerning child-care arrangements all form part of the culture of the women's prison. Another key element in this culture is the excessive scorn and hate directed at those convicted of child abuse and/or murder. Some observers believe that part of the reason child abusers are so hated comes from the guilt and anxiety women feel regarding their own mothering capabilities.

Fogel and Martin (1992) compared the mental health of mothers and non-mothers in a prison in North Carolina. They found that the anxiety of mothers was a little lower than nonmothers at entry, but remained elevated six months later while nonmothers' scores went down. No significant interaction was found between depression and being a mother; both groups showed very high levels. Almost 70 percent of the mothers reported that at least one child was having significant problems because of the incarceration.

Separation from children is considered to be one of the worst aspects of prison for women. Imprisoning the woman is much more likely to break up the family unit than the incarceration of the man. Imprisoned men may have wives who work or receive support and preserve the family so it is relatively intact upon their release. An imprisoned woman may not have had a stable family life to begin with, and even if she does have a husband, he is unlikely to keep custody of the children, and often will desert her during her prison term.

Koban (1983) compared a sample of female prisoners in Kentucky to male prisoners and their children. Findings included the fact that women were more likely to have children than men (76 percent, as compared to 56 percent) and were more likely to have lived with them prior to prison (65 percent compared to 47 percent). Men's children were more likely to be living with their mother, while women's children were more likely to be living with other family members (90 percent of fathers, but only 25 percent of mothers, said their children were living with the other parent). Of women's children: one-third lived with the father, one-third with a grandparent, and one-third with friends, relatives, or foster placements (Koban, 1983: 174). Women whose children were in foster placements experienced fear and frustration because the arrangements allowed only limited contact and fostered ignorance of what was happening in the children's lives. Only 31 percent of the men but 58 percent of the women still retained legal custody (Koban, 1983: 175). While 72 percent of the women expected to be consulted over decision making related to the child, only 52 percent of the men expressed this view (Koban, 1983: 177).

Current findings are consistent with these older studies. The only difference is the dramatic increase in the numbers of children affected by a mother's imprisonment. As indicated in Table 5.2, almost a quarter of a million children have a mother in prison or jail. Of course the number of children with a father in prison or jail is much higher (about 1.1 million), but as previously noted, the impact on children is less because fathers were less likely to have lived with their children before imprisonment (44 percent of fathers compared to 64 percent of mothers), and children of imprisoned fathers almost always continue to live in the same preprison setting with their mothers (about 90 percent), as opposed to the children of imprisoned mothers whose lives are often disrupted, not once, but many times during the imprisonment period (BJS, 1991; Enos, 1998; Greenfield and Minor-Harper, 1991; Johnston, 1995c, 1997a & b; Pollock, 1999b).

It should be noted that not all women in prison are mothers or mothers of small children; it would be stereotypical and inaccurate to portray women in prison with the single theme or issue of motherhood.[8] However, accepting the fact that a portion of imprisoned women do not need and do not want parenting programs, and have their own unique needs and desires unrelated to parenting, it must be recognized that the issue of children is one of the most overriding concerns of women in prison and policy makers.

The Need for Parenting Programs

The majority of women in prison expect to live with their children after imprisonment (Bloom, 1993; Immarigeon, 1994). In Baunach's study, 89 percent of the women reported that they expected to regain custody and live with their children; only 20 percent indicated they did not expect to have difficulties in reestablishing a relationship (1979: 44). Many women feared that their children would reject them or not respect them. Others feared the economic problems they would face with housing and support (Baunach, 1979: 45). Today, about the same percentage of female inmates, if not more, expect to be reunited with children. Thus, it is imperative that during the time they are in prison, these women maintain their bonds with their children and, if needed, improve their parenting abilities.

Who Cares for the Children? As stated earlier, most children of incarcerated women are cared for by relatives, usually the maternal grandmother. One of the earliest studies on the children of women in prison was conducted during the early 1960s in California. Questionnaires were distributed to female inmates, and 26 percent were identified as mothers. This percentage was very low, and it may not have been representative of inmate mothers in general. Findings indicated that 50 percent of the children were placed with relatives

Table 5.2 Children of Women Under Correctional Supervision

	Total	Women with Minor Children	Number of Minor Children
Total	869,600	615,500	1,300,800
Probation	721,400	516,200	1,067,200
Jail	63,800	44,700	105,300
State prison	75,200	49,200	117,100
Federal prison	9,200	5,400	11,200

SOURCE: Bureau of Justice Statistics, 1999, *Special Report: Women Offenders*. Washington, D.C.: U.S. Department of Justice, p. 7.

other than the father, 24 percent went to the father, and 26 percent were placed in foster homes. More white children were placed in foster homes than African-American children, who were more likely to be placed with family members. The study also showed minimal contact between the agencies responsible for the children and the incarcerated mother, and it advocated better communication (Zalba, 1964).

A comprehensive study conducted with samples from Kentucky and Washington found that the majority of the 190 women surveyed were mothers (70.4 percent), and they each had an average of 2.2 children (Baunach, 1979: 19). Crawford (1988a: 9) reported that 80 percent of imprisoned women were mothers. In Baunach's sample, 82 percent of the children were living with relatives of the mother; 36 percent with the mother's parents; 25 percent with other relatives; and 20 percent with the father of the child. Other reports reinforce these findings. Only half of the women in Baunach's study still had legal custody of their children (1979: 33). About three-fourths of the children had been living with the mother before her incarceration, and 62 percent had never been separated from the mother before her incarceration. During incarceration, fewer than half visited the mother regularly; the reason most frequently given was the inconvenience and difficulty of getting to the prison (Baunach, 1979: 32). Baunach also found that African Americans were more likely to have relatives caring for the children, and the children of whites were more likely to be found in foster care or cared for by nonrelatives (1979: 29).

Bloom (1988a) reports that only 10 percent of the fathers in her study had custody of children. Crawford's 1988 study shows that family members continue to take care of the children of incarcerated women (68.3 percent). Only 10.6 percent of the women reported that a spouse or boyfriend was taking care of their children (Crawford, 1988a: 10). Similarly, more recent figures indicate that the most common placement is with relatives (BJS 1991; Greenfield and Minor-Harper, 1991; Pollock, 1999b).

Pollock (1999b) found that only a few states keep records concerning placement of children. However, of those states, the most common placement recorded was with grandparents (Idaho, 85 percent; Indiana, 75 percent; Mississippi, 85 percent; Pennsylvania, 34 percent). The father rarely had custody; the highest percentage was reported by Maine at 28 percent, and the lowest was reported by Mississippi at 3 percent.

One of the most troubling findings regarding the placement of children is that they often move, sometimes several times, during the mother's imprisonment. This lack of stability and frequent change of primary caregivers is noted by child development experts as quite detrimental to the child's psychological health and well-being.

Reasons for the moves usually involve such issues as illness or old age on the part of the caregiver, or the fact that the caregiver may also become embroiled in the criminal justice system and require other relatives to care for all the children under her care. Sometimes there is conflict with the incarcerated mother. It is very difficult for the mother in prison to let the caregiver make decisions regarding her child. Often there is constant conflict and arguments concerning the child so that the caregiver, in frustration, sends the child to live with another relative (see Gaudin, 1984). For whatever reason, the lives of these children are very unsettled; the children are often passed around from family member to family member and treated as an economic burden. We know that this negatively affects the child's ability to trust, to feel loved and secure, and to concentrate on such things as learning.

Pregnancy in Prison Roughly 10 percent of this nation's female prison population is pregnant at any given time. Many of these women will give birth during their prison term. Researchers document the fact that prenatal care is often sadly lacking in women's institutions, and women have difficulty meeting the nutritional requirements of pregnancy (Mann, 1984: 228; also see Schupak, 1986). If a woman is addicted at the time of her incarceration, forced withdrawal may injure the fetus or even cause a miscarriage. The institution's practice of waiting until the woman is in labor before transporting her to the hospital increases the risk of birth complications. The quick return to prison after birth, usually within a day or two, and the separation from the baby in most cases is extremely traumatic and perhaps harmful to both mother and baby. These issues have been the source of court cases challenging prison practices and will be covered again in a later chapter dealing with legal issues involving women prisoners.

Owen (1998: 102) discussed the experience of giving birth in prison with some of the women she interviewed:

> When you return from the hospital, everyone here is pretty nice to you. All of us know this feeling because the majority of us have children. My roommates were supportive. They talk to me when I need it so I won't feel too hurt about leaving my son. . . .

The experience of having to find alternative placement for a newborn is obviously distressing, but other issues make the experience even worse: there is a pervasive fear of state control and permanent loss of custody; there are often health issues involved with a variety of birth problems present; there is anxiety over turning the baby over to a family that may have been abusive or neglect-ful; and there may be the realization that because of a long sentence, the woman may never truly be a "mother" to her child.

Effects of Incarceration on Children The effects of separation on the child can be severe, although we do not have good current research in this area. For instance, most studies simply ask the imprisoned woman or her caregiver whether or not they have observed problems with the children (see Fritsch and Burkhead, 1982; Hungerford, 1993). Obviously a much more accurate study would chronicle learning dips, developmental delays, and other objective cri-teria of trauma. Further, few studies are able to separate the effects of the mother's imprisonment from other negative influences in the child's life, such as poverty, dysfunctional family settings, and other environmental factors (see Johnston, 1995d; Kempfner, 1995).

Baunach's study, for instance, found that 38 percent of the mothers reported no problems and another 13 percent said they were unaware of any problems. The rest said children experienced physical, emotional, or psycho-logical and academic problems, including hypertension, aggressive behavior, withdrawal, and trouble in school (Baunach, 1979: 31). McGowan and Blumenthal (1976, 1978) reported that children, especially infants and children of preschool age, responded with constant crying, little response to stimula-tion, little effort to crawl, and incidents of self-punishment. School-age chil-dren showed difficulty with social relationships.

Stanton reported that the separation itself may not be connected with psy-chological problems and juvenile delinquency as much as the disruption in the child's life (1980: 7–9). She looked at the effects of separation on children and found that a high percentage showed short-term behaviorial symptoms, such as expressions of sadness, withdrawal, and a drop in school performance. Antisocial behavior continued in a small number of children; children also experienced feelings of shame and demoralization (Stanton, 1980: 10). She found that more than half of the jailed sample's children displayed poor class-room behavior and created disciplinary problems at school, compared to 22 percent of a probation sample's children. There was a significant difference in academic standing as well. Jailed mothers' children were more likely to be below average academically: 70 percent were below average, compared to only 17 percent of the probationers' children. Only 4 percent of the jailed sample's children were in the top third of their class, compared to 33 percent of the pro-bationers' children (Stanton, 1980: 92). Other factors may be influencing these statistics, but it seems likely that incarceration, especially of the mother, affects the children in a negative manner.

More sophisticated studies of the effects of incarceration point out that it is difficult to separate the effects of incarceration from other traumatic events that are also occurring in the child's life. It must be remembered that often these children are at high risk for delinquency and other problems because of the dysfunctional and disordered lifestyles they experience, even before the mother's incarceration (Johnston, 1995d).

Issues and Concerns Many mothers in prison have lost custody of their children or will lose custody during, and partially because of, their imprisonment. Although usually imprisonment alone is not enough to negate parental rights, it can be used as one factor to deprive the woman of her legal custody. Further, a recent federal law regarding adoption mandates that a child may be available for adoption after one year if there has been no contact with the biological parents.[9]

Obviously, if the mother is in prison, she will not be able to appear at a hearing concerning the child's welfare and defend herself, especially if she has not been notified. Legal help is often nonexistent, and consequently no one is there to represent the woman's interests. Obviously the woman's preprison behavior may have included behaviors that would give rise to a motion by the state to take the children, such as drunkenness, abandonment, or abuse. Communication with child welfare workers is often conflictual and difficult, many times necessitating that prison counselors spend an inordinate amount of time fielding calls and mediating between the woman and the child welfare office (see Beckerman, 1989, 1994).

Many women in prison have complicated caregiver relationships with their children. While their children may have been and continue to be very important to them, others may have been the day-to-day caregiver. One study found that although the mother often lived with children prior to her incarceration, she also believed that the primary responsibility for child care often belonged to relatives, especially her own mother (Henriques, 1982). In the extended family structures often associated with African-American families, it is not uncommon for children to be cared for by grandmothers or aunts. When these arrangements are viewed through the lens of a white middle-class child welfare or criminal justice professional, it often appears as if the mother was negligent and/or abandoned her child. Although it does seem to be true that some women in prison often abdicated their responsibility to other family members before being incarcerated, this failure only reinforces their views that they were "bad" mothers who let their children suffer. Such a view often influences feelings of depression and powerlessness in prison, and contributes to fantasies about what life will be like outside after release.

Visitation during imprisonment is problematic. Prisons are usually located at great distances from where the family lives. Still, one can find visiting rooms full in most prisons for women; the difference is that they tend to be full of mothers, sisters, and children, while the visiting rooms of prisons for men tends to be full of wives, mothers, and girlfriends. It is a truism in prison that women are rarely visited by the men in their lives; instead, visitation is primarily a way to maintain some type of contact with children (Owen, 1998: 128).

Many women do not want their children to visit them at all. This may be because they have not told their children they are in prison (the child is told the mother is "away" or in the hospital, or some other story is used to explain her absence). Another reason is that mothers feel guilty exposing their children to the trauma of the entry process, which includes metal detectors and pat-down searches. Furthermore, the distance between home and prison is often great, and the costs involved in visiting are high; mothers refuse to burden caregivers with those costs on top of those already incurred in caring for their children. Some mothers refuse visitation simply because it is too painful to say good-bye, both for her children and the woman herself (Owen, 1998: 128; also see Pollock, 1998). Baunach (1979, 32; also see Baunach 1982, 1985b) stated that fewer than half had any visits with their children during imprisonment. Bloom (2000) reported that fewer visits occur today than 10 years ago.

Women who do not receive visits from their children often maintain close contact through telephone calls: 34 percent of women in Owen and Bloom's study had telephone contact with children three to four times a week (1995a & b). Similar percentages received telephone contact in a Texas sample (Pollock et al., 1996).

Reunion with children after release is a difficult adjustment for many women and their children (McCarthy, 1980). Mothers must wrestle with their image of being "bad" mothers because of their imprisonment. Children have grown up and developed new friends, new interests and activities. Children are often resentful and angry at their mother for leaving them, and distrustful because they suspect she may leave again. Further, they have developed attachments to caregivers. During prison visits, mothers may have a difficult time adjusting to their "parent" role, either trying to be friends with the child, or "overparenting" (Kolman, 1983). Mothers often have unrealistic expectations of a "happy family reunion" (Henriques, 1996). Upon release, women experience serious problems in regaining custody, finding housing, and securing employment sufficient to support themselves and their children.

As noted earlier, mothers may have to fight the state or relatives to regain custody. Children are often in foster homes and relatively settled. State workers will resist a separation until the mother shows that she has a job and a home to care for the children. Ironically, if she has a job to afford a home, she is not in the best position to show that the children will be cared for adequately. Halfway houses typically are not designed for women and their children; thus, women who need to spend some time in a transitional facility must delay a reunion with their children. Often, this is the hardest time for women because children do not understand why their mothers cannot live with them when they are out of prison. If the woman attempts to live independently, housing poses a problem. In many cities inexpensive housing close to employment does not exist. Women are forced to live in poverty-stricken areas and in apartment complexes that are havens for drug dealers and pimps. These locations only tempt the woman to commit crimes again, if only to get enough money to get her children to a safer neighborhood.

The programs described in the following section illustrate attempts of prison administrators to alleviate the problems caused by separation. The increasing rate of imprisonment of women will necessitate continued expansion of such programs and development of others, including furlough programs, expanded visiting, and early release.

Programs for Mothers and Children

All concerned recognize the importance of improving or encouraging the relationship between the mother and the child (Muse, 1994; Mustin, 1995). Visiting is usually difficult because of the distance between the prison and where the children are living. Uncooperative or economically distressed caregivers, who do not want or cannot afford to bring children to visit, complicate the problem. The prison itself is an uncomfortable, intimidating place for children.

Some prisons, but not all, have programs that attempt to alleviate these problems. One study in 1980 found that of three federal and thirty-seven state prisons and twenty-two jails surveyed, only 60 percent had play areas for children, and only 37 percent had special visiting hours for those who could not make the regular time periods (Neto and Ranier, 1983: 125). Some states have special visiting programs. In addition to those discussed next, some prisons have conjugal or family visiting where children of certain ages are allowed to stay with the women in a special setting for a weekend or a period of days (Neto and Ranier, 1983).

Hairston (1997: 144; also see Hairston, 1991; Hairston and Lockett, 1985) found that family programs and services that helped to maintain family ties were helpful in reducing recidivism and improving order in the institution. Barriers to such programs included distance, inconvenient visitation policies, unwelcoming and discourteous staff, lack of child care, lack of overnight facilities, and surcharges on telephone calls. Programs that help women learn better parenting skills or increase and better utilize the women's visitation time with children are in the greatest demand by female inmates. In one report, women wanted more family programs and services, increased visitation, and increased support in legal and postrelease areas (Chapman, 1980: 121).

Weishet (1985) reported that 25 of 36 reporting institutions allowed weekend visits with children, and 20 of these prisons provided transportation for children of inmates. Taylor's (1982) comparison of Frontera (for women) with Chino (for men) in California showed that female inmates had more access to family visiting programs than did male inmates. Not only were there more family visiting units (apartments or trailers), but women had to wait for a shorter period of time before becoming eligible for these programs (Taylor, 1982: 164). Interestingly, today there may be fewer such programs available than there were 20 years ago.

Clement (1993) conducted a nationwide study of parenting programs and found that while most states had parenting programs, they varied widely in length and intensity, ranging from 4 to 20 weeks and from 1 to 24 hours a week. The most common modality used was STEP (Systematic Training for Effective Parenting). Boudouris (1985, 1996) found that most prisons offered parenting classes, but fewer offered any type of overnight visitation.

Johnston (1995b, 1997a & b) has provided the most detailed, comprehensive information on the effects of incarceration, as well as needed interventions. Her

Center for the Children of Incarcerated Parents in California acts as a clearing-house for information, conducts research, provides direct services to families in need, provides training and classes, and also provides training materials for inmates who desire to conduct parenting classes. Pollock (1999b) reviewed all prior surveys, and also conducted a telephone survey regarding the number and type of parenting programs. Forty states participated in this survey. Findings will be presented, where appropriate, in the following text.

Prison Nurseries Many people are surprised to learn that one can find babies in prison. In fact, prison nurseries have a long history in women's pris-ons; earlier in the century, it was not at all uncommon for women to have their babies with them in prison. Today, only a few states in the United States still have prison nurseries. Bedford Hills has the longest history; a nursery for mothers who give birth has existed at Bedford Hills since about 1900 (Boudin, 1997, 1998). There a woman who gives birth during her sentence can stay for up to a year after her baby is born.

Only two other states, Nebraska and California, have similar enabling leg-islation and operate nurseries. All other states have closed their nurseries (if they ever had them), citing concerns of security. In Florida, for instance, despite an old statute that allowed infants to be kept by inmates, prison policy prevented women from keeping infants with them in the institution until 1979 when Terry Jean Moore, sentenced to prison for twelve and one-half years for a "$5 robbery and a jailhouse mattress 'frustration fire,'" became pregnant by a male correctional officer. She demanded to keep the child with her until she was paroled five months later, and evidently in response to this case, the Florida legislature enacted a new statute that gave courts discretion to allow women to keep their infants or to require that infants be placed elsewhere. The inmate mother had to petition the court and make a case that keeping the child with her was in the best interest of the child. In 1981 a bill was passed that closed even this possibility (Mann, 1984: 231).

Rierden (1997: 49) describes the history of Niantic, Connecticut's prison nursery. In 1948, there were over 100 babies in this women's prison. Administrators ultimately decided the nursery was too costly to maintain, and they began phasing it out over the next 20 years. Heffernan (1992) explains that at Alderson, a federal facility for women, a maternity ward existed well into the 1960s. It closed during that time when there was a shift of opinion from one that valued keeping babies with their mothers to a belief that prison was "no place for babies."

Blinn (1997) describes the Massachusetts Reformatory for Women at Framingham. In 1877, the year it opened, 241 women and 35 children lived there. Mothers could keep their children up to four years. Blinn notes that even during the 1930s, national meetings concerning the care of infants in prison were held, but in the 1940s nurseries began to be phased out. Nurseries were closed because of overcrowding and cost considerations, and also because of a growing attitude that children do not belong in prison.

Today, the prison nursery at Bedford draws a huge amount of attention from the popular press. A steady stream of reporters and news professionals from the print and television media publicizes this "anomaly" of babies in prison. Even critics often come away with a belief that something good is occurring in such programs. For instance, in one newspaper report on the nursery in Nebraska, the reporter cites the cost of keeping a baby in prison ($11,000) versus in foster care ($18,000) and quotes Nebraska's prison warden, Larry Wayne, as remarking, "We view a woman's pregnancy as perhaps the best opportunity to intervene in her life at a time when she's most aware of life's great possibilities. Plus, the babies really do brighten up a prison" (Willing, 1999).[10]

Halfway Houses for Women and Children Halfway houses for women and their children provide service to women who need help in the transition from prison to the free world. (Alternatively, they can be used as a sentencing option in lieu of a prison sentence.) More states have halfway houses for mothers and children than nurseries. Pollock's (1999b) study found that 35 percent of the responding states reported having such living options for female offenders.

California, for instance, contracts with private providers for about a half dozen halfway houses for women offenders with small children. Women who meet the requirements—having no history of violence, child abuse, or neglect; was the primary caregiver of the child before imprisonment; and possessing a good prison record—may be paroled early to the halfway house setting and live with their children (under 6 years of age) and receive employment training and rehabilitative services (Bloom, 1988a). These halfway houses have been underutilized, and it is not clear why. Some argue that the requirements are too strict and that prison staff members do not publicize the opportunity. Some point out that because the woman must apply for entry after she is already in prison, the children have already been placed in alternative caregiver settings, and she may not want to uproot them again. Also, it is difficult for women to explain to older children that she can only take younger siblings to live with her. Others argue that women in prison do not want the opportunity because it is "too hard." Caring for children and being required to go to school and attend treatment programs is much harder than a prison sentence, according to this line of thinking, and many women simply are not interested.

Buccio-Notaro (1998) describes the Neil J. Houston house in Boston, a residential prerelease substance abuse treatment program for pregnant inmates. Those inmates deemed eligible are transferred from the state prison to this privately run halfway house. The program encompasses prenatal care, substance abuse treatment, family services, and follow-up. At any given time, about 15 women and their infants live at the pleasant, beautifully renovated house, close to medical facilities and city services. The women attend four group counseling sessions a week, and also have one hour a week of individual counseling. Follow-up is provided upon departure, and the private agency that runs this program reports a low rate of recidivism.

Extended Visitation Programs Some states that do not have nurseries or halfway house options do have extended visitation programs where children can spend more time with their mothers than they can during typical visitation hours, and usually in a less intimidating setting. Regular visitation in a prison is definitely not comfortable for children; entry is frightening, the wait may be very long, and there is nothing for children to do while adults talk. Children do not understand security rules regarding running or physical contact with the incarcerated parent.

Some prisons attempt to make the experience a little more friendly for children. For instance, a Sesame Street program for the children of women incarcerated at Bedford Hills provides the children a more comfortable, non-threatening place to visit. One corner of the visiting room is sectioned off, and Sesame Street characters are painted on the wall. Children's furniture and toys further enhance the goals of the program. Inmates serve as day-care aides to watch the children when the inmate mother visits with adult family members privately (Haley, 1977). Bedford also runs all-day "camps" for children during the summer and during school breaks where children can spend all day in the prison with their mother doing supervised activities.

In Kentucky, the MOLD (Mothers Offspring Life Development) program provided weekend visits and a parenting program. Women could have their children visit them in prison for an entire weekend and have open privileges across the prison grounds. Activities were also scheduled. Problems with this program included difficulties in transportation, lack of consistency in scheduling, and no continuity between parenting classes and weekends. When the female inmates were transferred to a new institution, the program was reduced to only day-long visits rather than weekend ones. In 1983, an overnight component was added, but the visit took place in isolation from the rest of the prison (Baunach, 1979: 84). A MOLD program is still in operation in Nebraska that allows weekend visits for the children (Alley, 1997; Neto and Ranier, 1983).

Other prisons also have versions of overnight or daylong visits for children. These programs may include camping (either on or off the prison grounds) (Weis, 1997). Other models, such as Girl Scout troops composed of the girls of incarcerated mothers, exist as well (Block and Potthast, 1997; Datesman and Cales, 1983; Driscoll, 1985; Moses, 1995). In Pollock's (1999b) survey, only 28 percent of responding states indicated they had overnight visitation programs, but about 75 percent had special areas for visiting children.

Parenting Classes If a state does nothing else, it typically runs parenting classes, either as part of a life skills course or separately. In Pollock's (1999b) survey, 90 percent of the responding states indicated they conducted some sort of parenting class. Some argue that these courses are either not needed and/or not effective in improving parenting skills (Johnston, 1997b). It does seem that in order to improve parenting, one must have extended contact with one's children; however, it also seems that women in prison are grateful for and benefit from educational courses concerning child development and appropriate expectations (see Showers, 1993). Such classes are most appreciated when taught by outside professionals, such as pediatricians and child psychologists. The best format is probably one that combines education and experiential learning (extended contact).

The best solution—for the mother, for the child, and for society—may be to find another correctional alternative that does not involve separation, especially for those women who are in prison for minor property and drug offenses. The economic and social costs of separation are being felt now and will continue to be experienced as these children grow up.

GENDER-RESPONSIVE PROGRAMMING

After surveying the "state of the art" in women's programming in the 1980s, Ryan (1984) offered the following suggestions for improvements in women's prisons. First, he suggested that prisons develop policies to facilitate communication and the growth of interagency agreements and cooperation among correctional agencies. Second, he urged that managers and supervisors in correctional systems with adult female offenders expand their networking activities. Third, he suggested the creation of regional and national forums for the exchange of ideas and models and the identification of resources. Fourth, he urged special issue-training programs for managers and supervisors of female offenders to address identified needs and problem areas and to develop skills, techniques, and tools for addressing these needs and problem areas (Ryan, 1984: 29; also see Ryan and Grassano, 1992).

It is safe to say that very few of his suggestions have been followed. Instead, what has occurred in the last 20 years is a strange silence regarding the tremendous increase in the number of women being sent to prison and the burgeoning number of women's prisons springing up all over the country. The new institutions are sometimes built so quickly that program needs are not even considered. The trend to treat women as men, and to run a woman's prison like all others in the system, is unmistakable and probably partly attributable to advocates' use of equal opportunity arguments in courts. As some feared (Pollock, 1990), equality for women has translated in real terms to having male standards forced upon women, and the loss of the few special programs that were designed with women's needs in mind.

One of the most ironic examples of male programming being applied to female offenders is the proliferation of boot camps for women (Chesney-Lind and Pollock, 1995). Although many women find careers in the military today, this model is obviously a male one, developed for men and later applied to a female offender population. Putting aside the general issue of effectiveness (most current studies have not found boot camps to be any more effective than traditional, program-rich institutions), the question of whether the model is appropriate for women has never been addressed in the rush to implement the "flavor of the day" punishment for offenders (Camp and Sandhu, 1995).

Critics question the whole premise of boot camps for women (Chesney-Lind and Pollock, 1995; Morash and Rucker, 1995). The boot-camp approach of "breaking down" and "building up" ego on the part of offenders seems particularly inappropriate for women who often have low self-esteem to begin with (and little false pride). Women's psychology is already such that the woman merges her identity with others; therefore, the boot-camp model of group affiliation is perhaps less appropriate than one that helps her build her own identity. The power structure, heavily laced with male authority, is often quite traumatic for women who have experienced abuse at the hands of fathers, brothers, stepfathers, and other male relatives. In fact, some studies show negative effects even for men; for instance, one study found that the hypermasculine environment was associated with lower levels of emotional support and higher levels of coercion, aggression, isolation, helplessness, stress, and conflict (Lutze and Murphy, 1999). In general, there is nothing to indicate that a boot-camp approach offers anything of value that a program-rich institution following a more nurturing family model would not offer (Marcos-Mendosa et al., 1998).

There is another approach—one that incorporates equality but also recognizes difference. A gender-specific programming approach recognizes and responds to the unique motivations, histories, needs, and realities of women in prison. The call for gender-specific programming has been made by many for a long time (Carp and Schade, 1992; Colley and Camp, 1992; DeConstanzo and Valente, 1984). The trouble is, no one seems to be listening. Covington (1998b; also see Wallace, 1995) argues that the issues that must be dealt with in a treatment program for women may or may not be those relevant to men. The issues she suggests include: the etiology of addiction, low self-esteem, race and ethnicity, gender discrimination and harassment, relationships with family and significant others, interpersonal violence, eating disorders, sexuality, parenting, grief related to losing children or other family members, work, appearance and health, isolation from support networks, and life-plan development (including child custody issues).

Austin, Bloom, and Donahue (1992) identified a series of effective strategies for working with female offenders in community settings. These strategies are multidimensional and deal with gender-specific needs. Women, for instance, respond well to empowerment models and skill building (rather than attack therapy or purely educational approaches).

Zaplin (1998b: 136–138; also see Zaplin 1998a) described a program that takes a systems approach to female offenders. Her suggestions provide psychoeducational programming (helping them think critically about dysfunctional behavior), basic education (literacy), employment readiness (addressing unemployment and underemployment), group counseling (providing catharsis and bonding), and individual counseling (for sensitive issues).

Koons et al. (1997) identified 67 effective programs for women. These programs used a comprehensive and holistic strategy, incorporated a continuum of care, utilized individualized and structured programming, and placed an emphasis on skill building. Lord (1995: 261) also noted the importance of skill building and empowerment. Her observations indicate that women in prison are "disempowered" and "disconnected" from others. A change effort gives them the opportunity to "empower" themselves—a difficult task in a prison:

> There is a need . . . to reconnect to other people and discover once again capacities for trust, autonomy, initiative, competence, identity, and intimacy. . . . The rigidity and authoritarianism of prisons by their very nature can be yet another experience of power and control as belonging to others, not the women. Prison does not allow women to experiment with their own decision making but rather reduces them to an immature state in which most decisions of consequence are made for them. (Lord, 1995: 262)

Finally, Bloom (2000) offered the following suggestions for gender-responsive programming:

- Focus on the realities of women's lives.
- Address social and cultural factors as well as therapeutic interventions.
- Provide a strength-based approach to treatment and skill building.
- Incorporate a theory of addiction, trauma, and women's psychological development.
- Provide a collaborative, multidisciplinary approach.
- Offer continuity of care.

CONCLUSION

This chapter has described prison programs for female offenders. Two statements about the current situation of women in prison may be made. First, we have incarcerated great numbers of women without the currency or commitment to provide appropriate programming for them. Second, much of the programming that exists has been "borrowed" from men's prisons. and may or may not be appropriate for women.

We should take great care to not define women solely through their roles as mothers; nor should we paint them as hapless victims of childhood abusers and manipulative men. Not all women are mothers, not all women desire to be mothers even if they have given birth to children, and not all women in prison need assistance in their role as a mother. Nor have all women been victimized or used drugs as a coping mechanism. However, the realities that have been described in this chapter do represent issues for a great number of women in prison. Further, there are distinct and important differences between women and men that need to be addressed in programming. Gender-specific programming must be more than a catch phrase used in conferences and monograph reports; it must be a commitment to not treat women "like an inmate" if that means (and it always does) treating her "like a man."

NOTES

1. 478 F. Supp. 1075 (E.D. Mich. 1979).
2. Authors note that the control group was drawn from a general sample of releasees and did not have the high-risk profile the program participants had (1999: 412).
3. Also see Viadro and Earp, 1991, for another program.
4. Also see Wellisch, 1994; Wellisch, Anglin, and Prendergast, 1993; Prendergast, Wellisch, and Anglin, 1994; and Prendergast, Wellisch, and Falkin, 1995 and 1997.
5. For other evaluations, see Mahan and Prestwood, 1993, and Welle, Falkin, and Jainchill, 1998.
6. The authors collected information on 165 community-based, 16 jail-based, and 53 prison-based programs; but this report only cited data from the community-based programs. They were either "drug-free outpatient" (77), residential (55), or day treatment (24) programs. The duration was about 30 weeks, but ranged from 1 to 105 weeks.
7. These are but a small sample of authors who have written in this area. For a more complete treatment of this subject, see Pollock, 1999b.
8. I thank Barbara Owen for emphasizing the importance of not reducing the problems and lives of women in prison to the single issue of motherhood.
9. Adoption and Safe Families Act of 1997, P.L. 105-89 (ASFA).
10. This article can also be looked at, however, as the popular press's absorption with the sexuality of imprisoned women. The reporter's main interest, it seemed, was speculating about how many babies born in prison were conceived during the term of imprisonment, and who was the father.

SUGGESTED READINGS

Harden, J., and M. Hill (eds.). 1998. *Breaking the Rules: Women in Prison and Feminist Therapy.* New York: Haworth.

Morash, M., and T. Bynum. 1995. *Findings from the National Study of Innovative and Promising Programs for Women Offenders.* Washington, D.C.: Department of Justice, National Institute of Justice.

Pollock, J. 1998. *Counseling Women in Prison.* San Francisco, CA: Sage.

Zaitzow, B. 1998. "Treatment Needs of Women in Prison." In T. Alleman and R. Gido, *Turnstile Justice: Issues in American Corrections,* p. 175. Upper Saddle River, NJ: Prentice-Hall.

Zaplin, R. 1998. *Female Offenders: Critical Perspectives and Effective Interventions.* Gaithersburg, MD: Aspen.

6

Living in Prison

I t is clear that women acutely feel the deprivations imprisonment entails, especially the loss of their children and lack of emotional support. They feel isolated and surrounded by uncaring or hostile others, and the loss of their children is cause for pervasive worry and depression. Female inmates adapt to these deprivations in a variety of ways. Many attempt to remain aloof from the prisoner subculture; they find their niches in work, their cell, and other sanctuaries. Others participate fully in the "mix," the subcultural activities involving homosexuality, drugs, and fighting (Owen, 1998). In this chapter we will first describe and reiterate some of the deprivations of prison, and then explore prisoner adaptations. The prisoner subculture, including elements of leadership, argot roles, homosexual and pseudofamily relationships, and rule-breaking, will be discussed and compared to that in prisons for men.

THE DEPRIVATIONS OF IMPRISONMENT

Researchers have long engaged in a somewhat Kafkaesque inquiry into whether male or female prisoners suffer the pains of imprisonment more deeply. For instance, Ward and Kassebaum wrote: "The impact of imprisonment is, we believe, more severe for females than for males because it is more unusual. Female inmates generally have not come up through the 'sandlots of crime,' in that they are not as likely as men to have had experience in training schools or reformatories" (1965: 161).[1]

In their study of 832 women inmates, interviewing 45 of them, Ward and Kassebaum (1965) observed that women indicated that, although prison was not physically difficult, it was emotionally stressful, both because of a fear of the unknown and because of severed ties with children. Women expressed frustration at not being able to depend on staff for help and emotional support. This frustration marks a theme pervasive throughout the literature; women evidently expect and demand more from the correctional staff, whether or not they receive it. They do not adopt the social distance and isolation that characterize the relations between male inmates and officers but rather look to staff, as well as to one another, to provide support and nurturance (Ward and Kassebaum, 1965: 162).

A more recent attempt (Harris, 1993) used measures of prison elements and compared male and female inmate responses. The themes measured were: disorientation, lack of heterosexual activity, lack of emotional support, loss of self-esteem, loss of autonomy, loss of responsibility, lack of privacy, lack of security, and lack of property (derived from Toch, 1977). Harris concluded that women did not experience "greater deprivation" than men but noted that men and women experienced the deprivations of prison differently. Women identified relationship issues, and men did not.[2]

Although both men and women obviously share similar deprivations, they are touched in a different way by the prison experience. For women, prison is most painful because it cuts off ties to family and loved ones, especially children (Jones, 1993). Sex and companionship are needs of all humans, and women cite their absence as a painful aspect of imprisonment as well. Another pain of imprisonment is the inherent and unceasing boredom of prison life. One day follows the other in pretty much an endless succession.

Another pain felt by women is forced association and lack of privacy. Women must live together with others they scorn and despise. They must share their living space against their will and must learn to coexist with others with whom they would never associate outside prison. Privacy is nonexistent, since women must shower together and may be observed even when excreting or taking care of hygiene needs. In these times of overcrowding, this deprivation is exacerbated; rooms that were built to hold two women are often holding four. Many prisons today use a dormitory style of housing, providing even less privacy for women.

In addition to the need for affiliation, women must find a way to cope with the prison environment, which is cold, inconvenient, and unaccommodating.

It is not as hostile as the prison for men, but there are dangers. Women report fears upon entry, and they learn to either isolate themselves as best they can or adapt to the prison social life. Whereas the prison for men seems to be a jungle, where the strong survive at the expense of the weak and the only option is to band together for mutual protection, the women's prison is marked by small pockets of friendship and allegiance. Although individuals must be constantly on guard against exploitation, there is less reason to fear physical harm and evidently more opportunity to create bonds of love, however transitory.

There are isolated reports of violence in women's prisons. Women have been "raped" by other women inmates with bottles and fingers. At times this is done as punishment for perceived infractions of the informal code; at other times, it seems to be done for no other reason than because the woman thought she was "better" than other prisoners and "needed to be taught a lesson." In addition to these serious but extremely rare violent incidents, women often attempt exploitation through intimidation. One female inmate, during her first day in general population, was approached by an aggressive, "tough" woman prisoner. This woman said, "Give me your ring," and upon the refusal of the newcomer, the exploiter retorted, "Give me your ring, bitch, or I'll cut your finger off!" The newcomer continued to refuse to acquiesce to the demands of the other woman and eventually was left alone, but more often the "fish" may fear the threats sufficiently to submit to exploitation.

On the other hand, much less violence is reported in the women's prison than in prisons for men. Women are also less likely to manufacture or carry weapons. The relative lack of weapons may be partly due to the fact that there are no metal shops or other industries that provide appropriate materials for weapons. Women are probably also less skilled in the manufacture of weapons because of their backgrounds and life experiences. Some women do carry weapons, but the weapons are less sophisticated than those found in prisons for men, and less lethal. During an altercation, women pick up nearby objects—chairs, brooms, irons—to use as makeshift weapons, or they fight without weapons. Violence in a women's prison usually is between two people in a personal relationship or due to perceived thefts. Thus the violence is rarely impersonal and very infrequently results in serious injury. Faith (1993a) compares the relative lack of violence in women's prisons with the stereotypes portrayed in movies wherein violent "butches" victimize innocent feminine newcomers. Screenwriters utilize the fear and pervasive violence of men's prisons, and charge this mix with sexuality. While it may be titillating and popular with audiences, this depiction is far from the reality of life in women's prisons.

Another need prisoners experience in prison is for items that are taken for granted on the outside. Prisoners develop elaborate mechanisms for preserving such small freedoms as having a cup of coffee during the evening or a sandwich at midnight. Another species of contraband, of course, is drugs. The need for drugs may be physical or psychological. Drugs may serve as a release from the frustration and boredom of a prison day or be used to forget the experiences of a lifetime.

Although much of the research reported in this chapter comes from the 1960s, 1970s, and 1980s, there is little reason to believe that these early findings are substantially outdated today. The few researchers who study prison life today reiterate some of the descriptions found in much earlier studies. For instance, a recent writer reports that toughness and individual survival are more relevant themes in men's prisons, and affective relationships are more present in women's institutions (Rolison, 1993). Owen (1998: 4–5), writing about California prisons, notes that "much of women's prison culture has changed little. Personal relationships with other prisoners, both emotionally and physically intimate, connections to family and loved ones in the free community . . . and commitments to pre-prison identities continue to shape the core of prison culture among women." However, she does note that drugs have had a tremendous impact on female offenders and prison culture.

Rierden (1997) spent 18 months interviewing in Niantic, Connecticut's prison for women. She chronicled the changes that had taken place in Niantic, from the small, "homey" prison of the first part of the 20th century, surrounded by gardens and farmland, with little social distance between officers and inmates, to a "state-of-the-art" confinement model of custody. Still, many of the issues brought out in the early studies remain the same—the importance of children, the wary nature of prison friendships, and the presence of homosexuality, among other issues. Girshick (1997) also provides us with a more current view of prison life. Her interviews also reinforce prior descriptive studies of prisons and prisoners.

ADAPTATIONS:
THE PRISONER SUBCULTURE

Individuals who are sentenced to prison must learn to adapt to the prison world: *prisonization* is the term used to describe the degree to which an individual inmate has adopted the prisoner subculture and its value system. The prisoner subculture is a subterranean culture that exists within but is distinct from the formal culture of the prison and society. It is the *sub rosa* culture of norms, values, and social roles. This system of power and interchange occurs among prisoners more or less outside the control or even knowledge of prison officials. The formal prison culture, on the other hand, is what is seen; it is the product of all the actors in the prison environment, including prison administrators, staff, and the prisoners themselves.

Elements of the Prisoner Subculture

Early researchers documented the subculture in prisons for men, describing elements of leadership, social roles, race, the role of violence, and the like (Berk, 1966; Carroll, 1974; Davidson, 1974; Hayner, 1961; Irwin, 1970; Irwin and

Cressey, 1962; Schrag, 1944, 1954, 1966; Sykes, 1958; Sykes and Messinger, 1960). At least a few studied these elements in institutions for women (e.g., Giallombardo, 1966; Hartnagel and Gillan, 1980; Heffernan, 1972; Mahan, 1984a & b; Moyer, 1984; Ward and Kassebaum, 1965; Wilson, 1980, 1986). Researchers, unfortunately, merely compared the women's institution to the descriptions of men's institutions, rather than approach the women's world without preconceptions or expectations derived from prior research.

Every institution has a somewhat unique prisoner subculture. Each subculture is molded and constrained by several variables, such as the demographic characteristics of the prisoners, the level of custody, population size, physical layout, regional location, characteristics of the city from which the prisoners are drawn, average length of sentence, and a whole range of other elements. However, there are similarities and persistent themes that prevail across institutions. We will discuss the inmate "code," argot roles, and the role of snitches in prison before moving on to a fuller discussion of the patterns of social organization found in prison.

The "Inmate Code" The "inmate code," a *Magna Carta* of prison life, was originally described by researchers studying prisons for men in the 1940s and 1950s. Interestingly, very little research has been done in the last 30 years; therefore, we do not know how different it is today from the descriptions provided to us many years ago. The major values the code has been described as endorsing are: "Don't interfere with inmate interests"; "Never rat on a con"; "Don't be nosy"; "Don't have a loose lip"; "Keep off a man's back"; "Don't put a guy on the spot"; "Be loyal to your class"; "Be cool"; "Do your own time"; and "Don't exploit inmates" (Sykes, 1958).

Female prisoners have never adhered to the code provisions in the same way as men (Hawkins, 1995). For instance, although one hears the statement that women should "do their own time," female prisoners seem to be more involved with each other and not shy about getting involved in other's business. Women's sexual involvements and latest breakups are known and discussed. Women will also become involved in an individual's confrontation with staff members, or intervene in someone's emotional crisis. Depression or suicidal tendencies sometimes have a contagious effect where one woman's pain will trigger a rash of emotional crises.

Women also do not have strong proscriptions regarding interaction with correctional officers (C.O.s). In a men's prison, inmates tend to avoid officers so as not to be labeled a "snitch." Thus, correctional officers and male inmates share very little and, except in certain settings, tend to limit interaction to formal exchanges regarding duties or needs. There is more casual and social interaction between women and C.O.s, even if it is, at times, rancorous. Some inmates believe that C.O.s should be avoided at all costs, but they have little control over other inmates' behavior.

Arguably, with changes brought about by the drug culture, a different racial mix, an altered demographic profile of offenders, and legal changes in the operation of the prison, the old system of values in men's prisons described by Sykes and others is probably quite different today. Because of differences in offender criminal background, gender differences, and different institutional features, including staff interactions and expectations, it should not be surprising that female prisoners have exhibited different values and a somewhat different inmate code from that found in prisons for men. Unfortunately, researchers have always used the male inmate code as the standard and have merely compared the women's subculture to this standard. Thus, we have had a somewhat distorted view of the inmate code for women; typically we have been told only what it is not (when it does not conform to men's). We do not have a comprehensive portrait of what it *is* because early studies merely compared the women's prison to the men's. We also do not have a comprehensive sense of what it *is* because, except for a few notable exceptions (see Owen, 1998), we have little information about what is occurring in women's prisons today.

Argot (Social) Roles Argot (social) roles describe the behavior patterns, motivation, and place of the individual in the prison culture. Not all inmates can be categorized into a social role, but some are easily recognizable. The social roles present in male institutions have been the topic of many articles and debates among researchers. Sykes's classic work (1958) specified *rats, centermen, gorillas, merchants, wolves, ball busters, real men, toughs,* and *hipsters.* Hayner (1961) described *real men, racketeers, smoothies, politicians,* and *dings.* Schrag's typology, which is perhaps the best known, included *square johns, right guys, con politicians,* and *outlaws* (1961: 12).

The *real man* was the type who populated the "Big House" of earlier days. He was an honest thief and subscribed wholeheartedly to a criminal subculture. Neither the administration nor brutal guards could break him; he would maintain control through any and all attempts to belittle or humiliate him. The *square john* was the innocent among wolves. He held middle-class values and identified more closely with the guards than with fellow inmates. Consequently, he was never trusted and often victimized. The *con politician,* because of verbal skills and intelligence, was the articulate manipulator, serving as liaison for the inmate body with the administration but ever watchful for opportunities to advance his own interests. The *outlaw* was the inmate others feared because he would use violence and force to take what he wanted, living outside the bounds of normal prison society. Finally, the *ding* was also feared, but because his violence was irrational and unpredictable. He was the inmate whose tenuous hold on sanity was destroyed by the hard edges of prison life, and he was shunned because of his unpredictable violence borne of fear and paranoia.

Apparently the social roles found in prisons for men and women were different, although there was some obvious overlap. Some roles were observed in both prisons (*squares, snitches,* and *homies*), and others were similar. For instance, Simmons (Moyer) described a type of female inmate who worked well with the administration and probably was a type of *politician* (1975: 103). She also mentioned women who used violence to get their way, and they may have represented a type of *outlaw* (Simmons, 1975: 108).

Interestingly, sometimes the same social role was explained in different terms. Giallombardo discussed the *homey* relationship found in the women's prison as one created to prevent gossipy women from spreading stories about one another on the outside. The woman befriended those who came from her neighborhood to guard against such "feminine" tendencies. Strangely, Giallombardo did not recognize that *homies* existed in men's prisons as well, and probably not merely to stem the flow of gossip (Giallombardo, 1966: 279). Giallombardo's social roles included *snitchers* (common to men's prisons), *inmate cops*, *squares* (a parallel to *square johns*), *jive bitches*, *rap buddies*, and *homies* (common to men's prisons), *boosters, pinners,* and the cluster of roles associated with homosexuality (1966: 105–123).

Real man was a term applied to old-style cons who possessed characteristics such as generosity, integrity, and stoicism in the face of provocation from guards. Giallombardo wrote that there were no corresponding *real women,* because female prisoners did not have the positive qualities associated with the role. Instead, they were described as "spiteful, deceitful and untrustworthy" (Giallombardo, 1966: 130). Heffernan (1972), however, described the *real woman,* who seemed to come fairly close to the concept of the *real man.* This inmate was described as one who was responsible, loyal, and willing to stand up for what she thought (1972: 158). Heffernan's *square, cool,* and *the life* corresponded almost identically to Irwin and Cressey's (1962) *square, thief,* and *con* subcultural roles.

These different subcultural adaptations within a prison also helped explain differential adherence to the inmate code. According to Heffernan (1972), the different normative orientations were more potent predictors of prison adaptation than length of prison sentence or other variables. They also had relevance, in the women's institution, to participation in homosexuality; those who were in *the life* subculture were involved most heavily in prison homosexuality.

These three subcultures were indicative of differential attitudes and adaptations to prison. Findings indicated that those women in *the life* were more comfortable in the prison environment. Only 22 percent of those women rejected prison, compared to 60 percent of those described as belonging to the *cool* subculture and 75 percent of those termed *square* (Heffernan, 1972: 67). Those in *the life* participated more often in the homosexual subculture and had more inmate friends. They totally immersed themselves in the prison life. This group also had the fewest contacts with the outside.

The *cool* type was described as the professional criminal. These women did their time with as little trouble as possible. They participated the least in prison programs, and they limited contacts with other prisoners. They adhered most strongly of all the groups to the inmate code. Although these results seem valid, some problems exist with Heffernan's work, including an arbitrariness in the way individuals were assigned to subcultures.[3]

Mahan (1984a) discussed several types of women inmates in her descriptions of prison life. These included the *junior C.O.s,* who were similar to Giallombardo's *inmate cops; inmates,* who were opportunistic and wanted to do easy time, and were similar to Heffernan's *cool* type; and *convicts,* who were the long termers and probably similar to *the life* type of Heffernan's research (1984a: 361). There are some differences, however, in that Mahan found that the *convicts* upheld some tenets of the inmate code, such as "Don't rat," "Don't ask for protective custody," and "Take care of your people"—values that Heffernan (1972) and Irwin and Cressey (1962) identified with the *thief* or *cool* roles.

Recent ethnographies of women's prisons have not described these social roles. Owen (1998) has offered the most complete view, and she makes little mention of argot roles or the subcultural adaptations described previously, with the exception of her description of *the mix.* In her ethnography of a California prison, this phrase describes the social world in the prison that many women tried to avoid because it represented trouble. Homosexual activity, drugs, and fighting are the elements of *the mix,* and many of her interviewees reported that they avoided going to the yard for exercise or the dining hall in order to avoid it. Owen's "mix" can be compared to Heffernan's older definition of *the life.*

Snitches A large part of the inmate code is concerned with the proscription against "ratting," or in any way conveying information about inmate activities to prison officials. The importance of the "rat" in the prisoner subculture is made clear by the number of argot terms related to the person who informs on others, or even who is seen as overly friendly with staff. The common perception is that this concern is present in both prisons for men and prisons for women, but the rule against ratting is much more heavily enforced in male prisons.

Giallombardo (1966) believed that women showed greater propensity for snitching than men; however, this was probably a misperception. "Rats" exist in both prisons, and there is no shortage of male or female prisoners willing to talk for personal reasons or for profit. The sanctions employed against "rats" are sometimes more extreme in prisons for men. In both prisons, social isolation is used against individuals, but gossip is used in women's prisons, and sometimes violence, in the form of threats or pushing and shoving sessions. Serious violence, however, is extremely rare in women's prisons, although it does occur.

Several reasons can be suggested for these differences. The stakes involved are probably not as high in prisons for women. Specifically, women do not engage in the same large-scale drug trafficking that can be found in prisons for men. Because of the money involved and the potential risk of good time lost or new charges, sanctions against inmates who expose a drug-smuggling operation or black market activities are more extreme in men's prisons. Owen (1998) reinforces some of the earlier studies of women's prisons in finding that female inmates who are believed to be snitches are avoided and shunned, but do not suffer the extreme physical sanctions that might occur in men's prisons.

Social Organization

The social organization of men's prisons is shaped primarily by gang structures and other pseudopolitical units. In many prisons for men today, gangs are very powerful and control drugs and other types of contraband. Inmates must either join a gang or risk victimization, although some male inmates successfully isolate themselves from the gang structures, and a number of others are rejected by the gangs. Inmates also create clubs in conjunction with formal prison programs. These groups are not gangs but provide safety and order through numbers and a formal hierarchy of power. Men sometimes also bond together in *homey* relationships based on where they are from. Obviously men in prison do have friendships; however, by all accounts, prison life for men is an extremely anomic existence. Men rarely get close to one another, and most ties are based on racial or political allegiance. Male inmates share a subculture with a strict hierarchy of power; those who rule and those who are ruled live in uneasy alliance, marked by frequent battles.

The social organization of a women's prison is comprised of pseudofamilies (make-believe families), friendships, and homosexual liaisons. Instead of grouping in pseudopolitical organizations such as gangs, clubs, and associations, women are more likely to group in familial units, cliques, or dyads. Their allegiances are emotional and personal; their loyalty is to a few rather than to the many.

Hart (1995) found that women in prison had higher levels of social support, meaning "close" or "meaningful" friendships with other prisoners and outsiders. A statistical relationship between social support and psychological well-being existed for women, but not for male inmates. Hart noted that social support in general seems to be gender-related; many studies show women have same-sex friendships and relatives who provide emotional support in times of stress; studies also document the importance of the role of social support for psychological well-being and recovery from illness.

In this study, social support was measured by questions that measured the degree and frequency of intimate relationships. Other measures included those that addressed depression, anxiety, self-esteem, and identity integration as measures of psychological well-being. Significant differences were found between the extent of social support indicated by female prisoners and male prisoners. Interestingly, social support did not seem to be correlated with psychological health for men, as it was for women (Hart, 1995: 79).[4]

Racial Gangs Whereas racial gangs are common in men's prisons, race is not a predominant theme in prisons for women. Although a few reports have described women banding together in racial groupings and discussing racial tensions (Mahan, 1984a & b), most studies have found that integration is the norm. For instance, one study found that although African-American women felt that job placement and other staff treatment was racially discriminatory, there was a high degree of informal racial integration among inmates. According to Kruttschnitt (1983), 55 percent of white inmates had close ties with one or more African-American women, and 75 percent of African-American women had close ties with one or more white women (1983: 583).

Current writers, for the most part, reiterate the earlier finding that racial divisions are fairly unusual in women's prisons. Although Rierden (1997: 52) reported that gang affiliation (including the Latin Queens and The Nation) is flourishing in Niantic, Connecticut, Owen (1998: 73, 151) informed us that race is "deemphasized" and not "critical" to the inmate culture. Although some of Owen's respondents reported that they felt race was a factor and there was discrimination in the way job assignments were determined, most women felt that race was not an issue. Owen saw little evidence of racial gang affiliation, and the pseudofamilies and homosexual relationships she observed often crossed racial lines.

Resource Distribution/Black Market Living in prison involves making accommodations to an institutional environment. This means developing ways of acquiring needed or desired goods, whether or not the formal organization supplies such items. Whereas men tend to operate businesslike black market systems, complete with entrepreneurs and corporate mergers, women distribute contraband and goods through family ties, small cliques, and roommate relationships.

One consistent finding of all research is that female prisoners have less variety and quantity of contraband, including drugs, than male prisoners. One possible explanation for the women's smaller black market in street drugs is that they have less ability to obtain outside drugs, fewer resources, and no organization, all of which are needed to set up a distribution system. Another explanation, as one officer spelled out, is that women get relatively smaller amounts of street drugs because of their greater success in obtaining prescribed drugs from prison officials.

> I don't see as much drunkenness, for example, among women in prison. . . . An awful lot of people will tell you that psychotropic drugs are used more and they're used probably legally perhaps because the medical staff are more prone to give out Valium, probably the same way, you know, if you went into everybody's pocketbook on this floor you'd find a lot of Valium. Doctors seem to give it to the women and it's a drug that's very easily abused. (Pollock, 1981)

No information indicates that a sophisticated black market operates in women's prisons to the extent that it can be found in institutions for men. Although women may engage in petty theft, and contraband is distributed in informal circles, the degree of organization observed in prisons for men does not seem to be present in women's institutions. Women more often tend to share legitimate and contraband goods through informal social networks, such as pseudofamilies, friendships, or roommate groups.

Many inmates prefer to avoid eating in the dining hall. Foodstuffs are purchased, received through the mail, or stolen from the institution to make private meals. Owen's (1998) respondents discussed the range of food that can be cooked using shared food and minimal equipment.

> We have some of the most screaming food go through here you would not believe. . . . I had something the other night that could have come out of a Chinese restaurant. Our whole world revolves around boiled water. (1998: 107)

Food and other products can be bought in the prison commissary. Inmates may receive money from family and friends on the outside, which is held "on account" in the commissary and from which purchases are subtracted. Those who do not have family or friends who are willing or able to send money must find other ways to get resources. Some sell services (such as doing other inmates' laundry), some "sell" boxes (that is, they receive a box in their name for another inmate who has exceeded her allowance), and others have "johns" or "tricks" on the outside that they manipulate in order to receive money (Owen, 1998: 103). Assistance may also come from others in the institution, especially for "homegirls" (women who are from the same neighborhood) who are without resources. Owen (1998: 109) discusses how some inmates receive care packages from "homegirls." These packages are also called welcome wagon packages, and include clothing, hygiene supplies, and food.

Leadership Another aspect of social organization is the existence and power of inmate leaders. In a men's prison, leaders are connected with gangs. Leaders may also arise from formal organizations in the prison, but these individuals often have no real power in the inmate subculture. Leadership in a men's institution tends to be fragmented; no universal leaders emerge, although some men may gain notoriety through violence and intimidation. Leadership is a complicated concept. In a men's prison, leadership may be shown primarily through fear and threat—the gang leader may hold his place through fear rather than respect. Another component of leadership is respect. Some male inmates may gain the respect of numbers of prisoners through the force of their personalities or their interactions with administration; these leaders, however, may not hold formal roles or be connected with a particular gang or following.

Giallombardo (1966) postulated that leaders within the women's system were to be found only within the kinship system; the male or father figure was the unquestioned leader for that family, and to some extent "he" gained status in the eyes of those outside the family by virtue of "his" position. This implies that women value qualities in a leader that parallel the traditional male role in society. One study of leadership in women's prisons found that leadership as observed in a classroom situation bore no relation to age or race, and education was a more influential factor than male or female roles (van Wormer, 1976, 1979). Other studies found that leaders tended to be young, African American, and high interactors, and they were likely to be homosexually active (Moyer, 1980; Simmons, 1975).[5]

Moyer (Simmons) described the women leaders as high interactors and young, African American, narcotics offenders with prior felony records and prison incarcerations. They were part of *the life* and were oriented toward prison life. Possessing forceful characters, they were perceived as willing and able to fight. They might have been homosexual stud broads (Simmons, 1975: 5). Moyer (1980/Simmons, 1975) defined leaders as those who stood up for others and got what they wanted. She found a relationship between interaction and leadership and a somewhat less clear relationship between homosexuality and leadership.

Van Wormer (1976) used an ethological approach to study sex role behavior in several prison classrooms. She examined the relationships between leadership and qualities such as masculinity, homosexual involvement, age, race, and dominance. The author found no significant relationship between leadership and masculinity. Leadership was related to the violence of the crime (using the Mann-Whitney test); it was also related to homosexual involvement. Van Wormer found that education was more important than masculine/feminine (M/F) factors in determining leadership, and pseudofamily involvement bore little relationship to M/F scores. No significant relationship showed up between leadership and age, race, or other variables.[6] Heffernan (1972) also discussed types of female leaders. The *real woman* was one who told people the truth regardless of consequences, never did anything spiteful, was loyal, and so on.

A recent description of a prison leader is provided by Owen (1998: 33) who met "Divine," a woman who acted as a gatekeeper in Owen's study. Because this woman was well respected and liked by other inmates, her endorsement ("cosigning") of Owen and her project ensured the cooperation of other inmates. Without such an endorsement, Owen may never have acquired the trust of her interviewees. "Divine" was a type of informal prison leader, and her leadership was based on respect and admiration. Owen also discussed "prison smarts" and the respect and reputation that comes with it. Women with "juice" were those who could get things done. Others came to them for help in navigating the unfamiliar world of the prison. Their status increased with their ability to get things done (1998: 170).

Women have been described (by correctional officers) as having difficulty organizing and cooperating with a leader: "Men are more organized than females. With the leaders they'll stand there and they'll face whatever's necessary" (Pollock, 1981). This perceived tendency of women to be resistant to organized leadership may relate to why there are fewer organized protests, fewer lawsuits, and a smaller number of formal inmate organizations in women's prisons.

More recent studies reiterate the belief that women are less likely to organize formally or follow inmate leaders; however, current explanations tend to offer a reason. Several observers have noted that women may be hesitant to oppose prison administrators because they fear being cut off from their children. Owen (1998: 73) quoted an inmate who observed that women will give up a protest or organized resistance because they are afraid of being sent to administrative segregation or losing their family visits. Other observers also have noted that women worry more about losing family visits and will not participate in formal protests because of this fear (Cook and Davies, 1999).

Homosexuality   One of the first areas that attracted researchers to women's prisons was the pervasive homosexuality that seemed to characterize most adult women's institutions. The relationships of women in prison seemed to be defined as either familial or connubial; women formed pseudofamilies, with parental and sibling roles in an extended family system, or they entered lesbian liaisons, sometimes formalized by "marriages," complete with mock ministers and marriage certificates. Less permanent relationships existed in "romantic love affairs" accompanied by love notes, hand-holding, or kissing (Leger, 1987). Often one party to a relationship plays a masculine role, with stereotypical short hair, masculine clothing, and assumed authoritativeness and dictatorial behavior. For instance, a quote from Owen's (1998: 106) recent study illustrates this: "When I shared a room with my wife, she would cook for me. But when my wife ain't living with me, I'll have to carry it outside. . . ." A prison relationship also may be one in which neither party exhibits a masculine role or any public signs of affection.

Although it is true that early researchers seemed to be interested in the homosexuality of female prisoners to the exclusion of other issues, the importance these relationships play in a prison for women demands attention. According to most research and inmate accounts, only a portion of the women who engage in homosexual relationships in prison are committed to this orientation as a lifestyle. Prison homosexuality is thus a sociological phenomenon and a subcultural adaptation to a specific situation. Except for a small group whose sexual orientation was same-sex before prison, most women are "in the life" only during their prison stay and revert back to a primarily heterosexual lifestyle upon release. In fact, what might appear as a same-sex relationship may not include a sexual component. Rather, the women involved receive the affection and attention they need in a dyad with a sexual connotation.

While sex is often a commodity for men, it is more often an expression of attachment for women. As one officer explained:

> The homosexuality that is done in the male facilities is usually masked, and there is a percentage of rapes, but I think a lot more of it is permissive, it is sold and so forth. In the female facilities it's not sold, it's not rape, it's just an agreement between two people that they're going to participate and there is a lot of participation. In this facility of 420 people or 430, I would say that maybe 50 percent of the population tends to deal in homosexual acts. (Pollock, 1981)

An inmate echoes this viewpoint:

> [A] lot of women have relationships, which is something you won't find in a men's institution. I mean, [the men] have sex, but they don't have relationships. But these women, it's more than sex to them. It's a relationship. You can get a woman who comes in off the street that ain't never been gay and is crazy about men, and she'll end up having a relationship. But it's just a substitution, I think, for lack of emotional and, you know. It's one way to try to have your needs met. (cited in Girshick, 1999: 86)

Homosexuality in men's prisons may be the result of violent assaults or coercion; older inmates (wolves) offer protection to young men (punks) for sexual favors and commissary articles. It should be noted, however, that some evidence indicates that consensual and affectionate relationships may be more prevalent in men's prisons than believed (see, for instance, Cromwell, 1999). In women's prisons, homosexuality is consensual, and the majority of females (femmes) vie for the favors of the few who have assumed the male role (butches).

Since the early 1900s, when writers first exposed this form of subculture in the women's institution, the forms of the relationships seem to have remained fairly stable. One of the first descriptions of female inmate homosexuality was written more than 80 years ago. Otis (1913) described "unnatural" relationships between white and African-American female inmates. Even today, one of the most obvious differences between men and women is that there seems to be little racial disharmony in institutions for women. Indeed, many homosexual relationships cross racial boundaries. Although homosexuality in prisons for men may also cross racial lines, it is more likely to be an expression of domination rather than the consensual liaison found in women's prisons.

Selling (1931) described four types or stages of involvement, including lesbianism, pseudohomosexuality, mother-daughter relationships, and friendship. He observed that these relationships were a substitute for the natural family group the women had been deprived of by their imprisonment. Although he observed that homosexual involvement progressed in stages, this is no doubt a misconception, since there does not seem to be any progressive nature to the women's involvement in these relationships. Women may be in either make-believe family relationships or homosexual dyads, and may even play a male role in a pseudofamily system while abstaining from sexual relationships.

Other early works described the love notes of girls in juvenile institutions involved in romantic affairs, nicknames adopted by those participating in such relationships, and level of activity (Kosofsky and Ellis, 1958; Taylor, 1968). Halleck and Herski, 1962), using self-reports, found that more than half of the females in the sample participated in some form of homosexuality. The percentage differed, however, depending on the activity. While 69 percent reported they were involved in "girl stuff," 71 percent said they had only kissed; 11 percent said they had been involved in fondling; and only 5 percent had engaged in stimulation of genitals. Nine percent predicted they would continue to be involved (Halleck and Herski, 1962: 913).

Some of these early studies were done in institutions for adolescents and some in prisons for adults, and it would be wise to differentiate between the two because some differences do seem to show up between the involvements of females at different ages. For instance, juvenile institutions seem to manifest the most active pseudofamily systems, while adults seem to be more likely to be involved in active sexual relationships. This difference may result because different needs are being met by the relationships. Whereas adult women are more likely perhaps to need and seek sexual relationships, juveniles' needs are still predominantly for love, support, and excitement. The "girl stuff" reported in juvenile institutions may meet those needs. This difference may also explain the wide range in the estimates of homosexuality. Ward and Kassebaum (1965) reported that although official records indicated only 19 percent of women were involved, more than half the staff felt that 30 to 70 percent of women were involved. Most of the inmate respondents also reported wide ranges, between 30 and 70 percent. Although the authors described homosexuality as kissing and fondling of breasts, manual and/or oral stimulation of the clitoris, and simulation of intercourse, the respondents may have had different definitions of sexual involvement (Ward and Kassebaum, 1965: 167).

Mitchell (1975) also looked at the relationship between homosexual activity and the type of institution. She used questionnaires and interviews in two prisons, one labeled a treatment institution and the other a custody institution. Mitchell found that inmates in both prisons expressed negative views of one another (1975: 27). Homosexuality was more prevalent in the treatment institution (1975: 27). Mitchell suggested that this prevalence was due to more privacy and thus more opportunity in the treatment institution. Propper (1976, 1982) compared seven juvenile institutions, three of which were cocorrectional. She used questionnaires and interviews and collected information on features of the institution, characteristics of the inmates, and the extent of homosexuality and pseudofamily involvement. She found little variability in the amount of homosexuality across the different institutions.

Interestingly, the cocorrectional institutions did not show decreased levels of pseudofamily or homosexual involvement, although fewer females took on the male role in these institutions. In cocorrectional institutions, boys were sometimes recruited to fill the male roles in the pseudofamily systems. Homosexual marriages were rare, and the most common relationships were asexual mother–daughter or sister–sister ties (Propper, 1982: 133). Her findings showed less homosexuality than other studies did; 91 percent reported no homosexual activity. Staff estimates ranged from 7 percent to 14 percent. The background of the inmate, rather than the type of institution, was more predictive of homosexual involvement. Propper found that previous histories of foster care and previous homosexuality explained 29 percent of the variance in homosexual involvement.[7]

There have been several descriptions of the role types in the homosexual subculture of the women's prison. Ward and Kassebaum (1965) discussed the *jailhouse turnout,* which represented, according to the authors, 90 percent of the women involved in homosexual activity. This individual would return to heterosexuality upon release, unlike the "true homosexual," who engaged in such affairs before her incarceration (1965: 167). The individuals who took on masculine characteristics were called *butch, stud broad,* or *drag butch.* These women may have resorted to the masculine role because of the power and privileges it brings in a women's prison, especially if they were not visibly "feminine" to begin with, either because of physical features or size (Ward and Kassebaum, 1965: 168). The *butches* traded their femininity for power. They received goods and services from the *femmes* in a parody of a traditional sexual relationship. The women who took on the masculine role controlled the relationship in much the same way that women experienced male-female relationships outside of prison.

Toigo (1962) described the *hard daddy* role found in one women's institution, which contrasted with the *mom* or *soft mama* role (1962: 9). Characteristics of toughness, belligerence, dominance, dress, and short hair identified the girls who took on the masculine role. Use of nicknames also furthered the illusion, with *hard daddies* taking on masculine variations of their given name. The role of the butch in the women's prison is interesting in its illustration of how women see men. Women evidently pattern their male personalities after the men in their lives, and tend to be dominating, aggressive, and unfaithful.

Many officers believe that the adoption of the masculine role is often a protective device designed to insulate the woman from victimization. Her masculine characteristics are indications that she is not to be exploited or attacked.

A lot of women when they come . . . they may be extremely feminine on the outside, but as a cover in order not to be picked on, they take on the masculine role, even though they have two or three kids on the outside, they have a husband and things like that. But in order not to be picked on once they come inside, they'll take on the masculine role in order to be left alone by other people. (Pollock, 1981)

Others see the adoption of the masculine role as an option after rejection.

You either gonna be a femme or you gonna be a dyke, o.k.? If you come in here and nobody is attracted to you as a femme, you gotta belong so you do a complete turnaround, you become the masculine role, you got control, you go after who you want. (Pollock, 1981)

Giallombardo (1966, 1974) described pseudofamilies and homosexuality in an adult women's institution and several juvenile institutions. At Alderson, West Virginia, she described the social roles that are part of homosexuality, including *pinners, penitentiary turnouts, lesbians, femmes, stud broads, tricks, commissary hustlers, chippies, kick partners, cherries, punks,* and *turnabouts* (Giallombardo, 1966: 277–281). These roles describe the masculine or feminine orientation of the woman (*butch, femme,* or the *turnabout* who changes roles), the commitment to a homosexual lifestyle (*lesbian* or *turnouts*), and the motivation in entering a homosexual relationship (the *commissary hustler* for goods, and the *chippie* and *kick partner* for transitory excitement and sexual gratification rather than a lasting relationship). The extent or nature of the women's involvement illustrates the needs that are being met. For some, the prison relationship is no more than an attempt to combat the boredom of prison life. For others, the relationship may be more meaningful and real than any experienced on the outside. For some, an appearance of homosexuality may mask a simple friendship. For some, the relationships may be avenues to acquire desired goods or services.

Another study (Nelson, 1974) found that African-American women were more likely to be active in the homosexual subculture. The author suggested that the African-American woman's socialization to be independent and self-sufficient predisposes her to take up the *butch* role. She also found that African-American women were more likely to have had homosexual relationships before prison. It does seem to be true that African-American women are the dominant participants in the subculture of the prison. They emerge as the leaders and as the most active proponents of the homosexual adaptation. African-American women in prison may have a similar role to African-American men in prison, in that their background and experiences give them more coping skills for prison life. They may have more experience in the institutional environment, coming from foster homes, juvenile institutions, or other state facilities. They are used to being financially independent, even though their backgrounds often exhibit chronic dysfunctional dependent relationships with men. For these reasons, African-American women more often emerge as the dominant force in an institution and shape the subculture to a great degree.

Early explanations of prison homosexuality were psychological and viewed prison homosexuality as an abnormal effect of early developmental problems. Halleck and Herski (1962), for instance, found psychoanalytic reasons for the juvenile's involvement. The authors reported that none in their study had a "mature sexual adjustment," evidently assuming heterosexuality was the only "mature" sexual orientation. Juveniles' problems may have been attributed to sexual contacts with fathers or brothers (20 percent reported such contacts) or a lack of female identification—mothers were often inadequate, and the girls' image of females was that they are weak, helpless, and vulnerable (Halleck and Herski, 1962: 914). The "masculine" partner was reported to receive vicarious gratification of her own dependency needs through unconscious identification with the dependent "feminine" partner (Halleck and Herski, 1962: 914). The unfaithfulness and flighty character of these liaisons was reported to be a coping mechanism designed to protect the girls from their fears of being abandoned (Halleck and Herski, 1962: 918). These early theories ignored the possibility of homosexuality as a rational and free choice of sexual preference. Obviously, the mental health profession has changed its approach to homosexuality, which is no longer widely believed to be an abnormal orientation. However, some sociological aspects of prison homosexuality are still important to consider.

In the women's prison, the *femme* role has the advantage of status in being attached to a "male," some affection, and some sexual gratification; but the *femme* is also required to wait on her partner, to share commissary articles, and to not become jealous if her partner decides to take on another partner. The *butch* role holds the power in the relationship. The *butch* chooses whether or not to remain monogamous; "he" also receives services and goods from the *femme*. Thus, there are many advantages to the *butch* role, even though the disadvantage is that the woman may be suppressing her own personality because she must maintain a male front at all times. The corresponding roles in a prison for men are the *wolf* and *punk* roles. The *butch* role for women has a great many more advantages to it than the *punk* role for men, which involves losing one's sexual identity but receiving no status, power, or goods and services for the loss. It is not surprising that the *butch* role is usually a consensual one, whereas the *punk* is created only by force or coercion. However, even in prisons for men, there are examples of voluntary sex role switches. *Queens* may, by charisma or the protection of powerful friends, freely take on the female role and reap rewards from a courtesan lifestyle, picking and choosing multiple partners at will. These men who act as independent females, however, are rare and must always guard against being dominated by another inmate who would use violence to ensure subordination.

Current writers continue to note the importance of same-sex relationships in women's prisons. Rierden (1997: 59), in her observations and interviews at Niantic, Connecticut, discovered that *studs* and *femmes* were still the slang names for the roles of the woman acting as male aggressor and the feminine partner in the prison. Owen (1998) also discovered that a large percentage of women engaged in same-sex relationships. One inmate explained how it happens.

> The person I met was a friend first. But in a close environment like this, it is a woman's bond. Women are very emotional and we build little families and what have you. And one thing leads to another. You know, it is not force. There is no rapes and all that shit they have in the movies. . . . It was like the girl was irresistible. . . . (Owen, 1998: 138)

Owen's (1998) interviewees described same-sex relationships in a manner similar to that found in earlier studies. Women who take on the male role (*stud broad, husband, butch,* or *little boy*) receive goods and services and are in demand. They can be recognized by their masculine nickname and by the way they wear their clothes, cut their hair, and behave. Relationships are marked by mock marriages, but are also transitory and volatile. *Box whores, canteen whores,* or *hoovers* are those women who are exploited for their commissary goods. Women who are gay explain that they stay away from *the mix* because of the promiscuity and game-playing that goes on (Owen, 1998: 146-149).

Pseudofamilies (Make-Believe Families) A different phenomenon from homosexual relationships is the pseudofamilies that exist in some prisons. These relationships may or may not involve sex. Most of the relationships are familial, including parent-child, sibling-sibling, and even extended family relationships, such as grandparents, aunts, and uncles. Each relationship is a reflection of the stereotypical one in society. "Fathers" are authoritarian and guiding; "mothers" are nurturing and comforting. Siblings fight; parents control (Foster, 1975).

Adoption of role types has something to do with personal characteristics, but roles are not necessarily demographically accurate. For instance, an older woman may more often play the mother role, but some mature younger women who are respected also may collect "daughters." The mother-daughter relationship is the most common, and some mothers may have many daughters in the institution who look to her for comfort and support. She, in turn, listens to their problems and gives advice. In larger, more elaborate family systems, a mother might have a husband who becomes a father to her daughters (but not necessarily). In some institutions, the family systems are complex, and the intergenerational ties are very complicated. Most writers who describe these social relationships point out that women may form pseudofamilies because of their need for such roles; in effect, their identity is dependent on being "mother," "sister," or other familial role (Culbertson and Fortune, 1986: 33).

Toigo found that some pseudofamilies possessed more status than others in the juvenile institution he studied (1962: 10). Staff legitimated the presence of these family systems by rewarding family leaders for controlling their inmate family members. Indeed, it seems that if the staff use the informal subculture to control inmate behavior at all, most often it is the family they utilize. For instance, a mother may be approached to keep her daughter from "cutting up," if staff guess the woman may be suicidal or depressed but do not have enough reason to put her under observation. The family leaders also may be approached and asked to calm down a consistently troublesome inmate if she is a member of a family. This parallels staff use of gang leaders to control the inmate population in a prison for men.

Commitments to such family systems differ. Whereas some women take the relationship very seriously, often the family relationships are more of a joke or a game than something influential or important in the woman's life. What may influence her commitment to the family are the other elements that make up the woman's prison life. When a women nears release or when she has maintained strong and continuing ties with her natural family, especially her children, the pull of the pseudofamily is weak. When a woman has come from a poor environment on the outside, when she is isolated from other ties, when the prison world is her only world, then often the relationships she develops there become more real than any she had on the outside. In a sense, she may be creating the type of family she wishes she had. A woman who has come from an abusive, tortured home may seek the mother she never had; the woman who is severed from her children, unable to mother, may displace her need to mother her own children by directing this maternal interest to other women in the prison.

One interesting observation about female inmates' involvement in pseudo-families and dyadic relationships is the women's attempt to create ideal relationships that probably do not represent their own experiences in real life. The inmate "mother" may be a better mother to her inmate daughters than she was to her own children before imprisonment. The inmate couple may seek a romantic bond that neither woman ever before experienced, since many in prison have had only poor and exploitative relationships with men. Indeed, because of the limitations of the prison environment and the ever-present supervision, the inmate "couple" may be, for the first time in their lives, engaging in a relationship where the bond is one of affection and romance rather than sex.

Fox (1984) found that inmate participation in pseudofamilies changed between the 1970s and the 1980s. He stated that during the 1970s a large number of youthful offenders (ages 17 to 24) were sent to Bedford Hills, and they were more often a part of pseudofamily units than were older women. The administration used the kinship systems to control these "disruptive daughters," since more than half reported involvement. Close to half also reported close personal relationships, sometimes including sex, but often only mimicking the *butch-femme* relationship (Fox, 1984: 26; also see Fox, 1982). However, in the second half of the 1970s, visiting policies and programming became more liberalized. More women became active in social programs; also, men from a nearby facility came in for recreation and, for a short time, dances. Kinship systems, once strong, began to dissipate. By late 1978, only 27 percent of women reported active membership in a kinship unit; all families had fewer than four members; and involvement in close personal relationships also declined (Fox, 1984: 32).

Today, family programs and furloughs help strengthen real family ties. Women are more politicized in that they maintain and foster ties outside the community and enjoy some attention from community interest groups. This permeability decreases dependence on prison life and deprivation; consequently, the prison family system is less necessary. However, current writers still document its existence. Owen (1998) writes that the prison family still exists, at least in the California prison where she conducted interviews.

> The family is when you come to prison, and you get close to someone, if it is a stud-broad, that's your dad or your brother—I got a lot of them here. If it's a femme, then that is your sister. Some who is just a new commitment, you try to school them into doing things right, that is your pup. But if somebody is a three-termer, and doing a lot of time like I have, then that is your dog, road dog—prison dog. (Owen, 1998: 134)

> A kid is someone you take care of and then her friend would be your "kid-in-law." Now this is my mom, even though she is younger than me and this is my girlfriend. She is Mom because she always picks me up off the ground when everybody else knocks me down and walks all over me. . . . (Owen, 1998: 135)

Owen found little evidence of racial gangs, and her interviewees reported that almost everyone was involved in some type of family relationship (Owen, 1998: 136).

Girshick (1999) and Rierden (1997) also reported the existence of pseudofamilies. Although many women did not participate in this form of social relationship, the interviewees reported its prevalence:

> I see it like maybe the reason they do that is 'cause they don't know who they [sic] father is, maybe they don't have any sisters or brothers, maybe their mother's passed away, maybe they don't have any kids and want kids, want a mother, want a father, want a brother, want a sister. I don't want none of it. It's not real, for one thing. (Girshick, 1999: 91)

Dobash, Dobash, and Gutteridge (1986) provide a cross-cultural note. They found no evidence of pseudofamilies or homosexuality in Cornton Vale in Scotland or Holloway Prison in England. The women there were socially isolated, and when asked to name friends, few named other inmates and some even named staff members. It may be that the excessive maternality and strictness of the staff at these small prisons prevented the emergence of a homosexual subculture. An alternative hypothesis is that the women came from stronger families on the outside, although this hypothesis does not seem to be supported by the women's backgrounds, which were just as fragmented as American women's. Taylor (1968), on the other hand, did find romantic liaisons between girls in an Australian Borstal; thus, these social relationships may be a cross-cultural phenomenon after all.

"The Mix"

Many women in prison choose to isolate themselves and have minimal participation in the social world of the prison, moving between school or work and
their cells, seldom venturing outside their created zones of security: "I pretty
much deal with all positive people. . . . That's a lesson that I've learned here. I
could be with this crew that gets into trouble, but you know, I shun them
now" (DeGroot, 1998: 85).

In fact, in Owen and Bloom's (1995a) study, 60 percent of women reported
spending the majority of their free time in their rooms. Girshick (1999: 83)
also said that most of the women she interviewed reported that they spent most
of their free time in their rooms where it was "safer and quieter." Others adapt
to prison by full participation in the underworld of the prison. Owen's (1998:
3) recent study described the subcultural adaptation of *the mix,* as "a continu-
ation of the behavior that led to imprisonment, a life revolving around drugs,
intense, volatile, and often destructive relationships, and non–rule abiding
behavior." She reported that some women "dip into" this world at the beginning of their prison terms but avoid it when they start to participate in programming. According to Owen, most women avoid *the mix* (1998: 8). One
difference between Heffernan (1972) and Owen (1998: 8) is that Heffernan
observed that homosexuality was a part of *the life* but Owen reported that
pseudofamilies and homosexual dyads were not a part of *the mix* and, in fact,
were sometimes the means to avoid its temptation.

It is clear that some women continue to "rip and roar" through their prison
sentence, engaging in behaviors similar to those that led them to prison in the
first place. Owen (1998) offered no demographic profile of the type of woman
who chooses *the mix* versus those who prefer to stay away from it. One gets the
impression from her interviewees, however, that the women who avoid it are
those who have become tired of a criminal lifestyle, have realized the importance of children and family, and have engaged in a journey of self-discovery that
helps them make more constructive choices in their lives. Some women
remarked that they maintain their reputation for toughness, even though they
no longer are tempted to fight: "But I still put out a reputation of hardness; that
makes [the other women] not tempt me to fight or challenge me to prove anything" (Owen, 1998: 71).

"Cutting Up," Suicide, and Self-Abuse

Women may be more prone to expressions of despair that include self-injury.
Women may attempt suicide or mutilate themselves because of emotional
problems that existed prior to imprisonment, but there is no doubt that the
deprivations of the prison also spur some women to such desperate acts.
Women may experience the deprivation of family roles more severely than
men do. They may find that the institutionalized lifestyle of the prison provides
little comfort or succor. One study in England showed an average of 1.5 incidents of self-injury each week in Holloway prison (Cookson, 1977). The
women involved tended to be younger with more previous incarcerations or

psychiatric institutionalizations, and most had committed self-injury at least once before. They had higher hostility scores, indicating the close relationship between inwardly and outwardly directed aggression. Also, self-injury tended to occur in copycat epidemics at times (Cookson, 1977: 347).

Fox (1975, 1992) also studied self-mutilation among imprisoned women. His study at Bedford Hills indicated that women were more likely than men to attempt suicide or injure themselves; in other words, women tended to turn their aggression inward, whereas men turned their aggression outward. An officer described this tendency in the following way:

> I have seen it on a number of occasions. She won't harm anybody else but she will start to destruct her own body. I've seen them have cuts from here up to their shoulders. They've had stitches in: brand new stitches were put in and they got back here from the hospital and they would sit here and pull the stitches back out again. If you look at their arms, the men don't do it as much as the women, but if you look at the females' arms, they'll sit and they'll just cut and cut and cut. They don't want to hurt anybody else and the only person that they think of hurting is themselves. (Pollock, 1981)

Suicide risk increases with depression, low self-esteem, and social isolation (Scott et al., 1982). Female inmates also identify different reasons for "cutting up" than male inmates do. Women primarily feel the loss of relationships and support in prison; men suffer from other deprivations. Women are less able to retreat into a "manly stance" and consequently feel the loss of interpersonal support more than men do. Women also are prone to release their emotion in a catharsis: 64 percent of the females sampled had this self-release theme in their responses, whereas only 13 percent of the males sampled exhibited this theme (Fox, 1975: 194). This theme involves the need to express pent-up emotions, with a resulting feeling of relief when the person "explodes."

Another explanation for "cutting up" and suicide has to do with feelings of control and a need to feel something, even if it is pain. Women's life experiences have often been traumatic, and psychological defense mechanisms create a type of disconnection from one's self and emotions. "Cutting up" is often experienced by women as a way to reconnect with their emotions, a way to make sure they are still alive (Pollock, 1998: 29–31).

COMPARING PRISONS
FOR WOMEN AND MEN

Many of the studies available on women in prison document differences in their behavior, self-concepts, or tendencies toward violence as compared with men. Women in prison may exhibit more spontaneous, emotionally based behavior. They also tend to be more open, emotional, and spontaneous in their affection and aggression. Men in prison, on the other hand, tend to be more covert and less open in their relationships as well as in their business dealings—gambling, drugs, or the black market (Pollock, 1984).

Two competing explanations for the existence of prison subcultures have been developed. The deprivation model (Sykes, 1958) explains that the deprivations of prison life, including deprivation of freedom, safety, sex, privacy, and so on, create the need for a subculture to meet the needs of the suffering prisoners. The importation model (Irwin and Cressey, 1962) explains that the characteristics of the inmates themselves create the subculture. Specifically, street gangs are brought into prison, and role types are based on previous criminal history and social class, as well as other individual variables; thus, what exists in the prison is what is brought to it from the outside.

Each of these theories could be used to explain the differences found between men's and women's prisons. For instance, the deprivation theory may be applied with the assumption that women in prison are less deprived; thus, their subculture should not be as strong or possess the elements the male subculture has developed. A variation of this hypothesis would be that since the deprivations for women are different, the subculture has developed differently to meet the needs women feel most acutely. Importation theory also may be used to explain differences. Sex roles from society are brought into prison along with criminal roles, and these roles with their contingent expectations and needs have shaped the different subcultures.

Researchers have sought to discover which of these theories has more predictive power in the commitment to a prisoner subculture in the women's prison. In an early article, Tittle (1969) looked at women and men incarcerated together in a drug treatment program. Assuming that the custodial conditions were similar for both groups, he set about to discover whether importation or deprivation factors better explained inmate organization. First, he observed differences in the two groups' subcultural adaptations to imprisonment. He noted that although the rates of homosexuality were similar, the meaning of the relationships differed. For women, homosexual activity represented affection and love; for men, it represented physical release and economic exchange. Male inmates scored higher on social cohesion and adherence to the inmate code, although the differences were not large in some areas. Women were more likely to form small groups than men. The author then held constant a number of importation features, such as criminal history, intelligence, age, and visitation contact, and found a small but apparent sex difference in the measures of social cohesion and adherence to a code. Thus, Tittle concluded that neither deprivation nor importation factors seemed as important as sex differences in explaining subcultural adaptations.

Zingraff (1980) compared 267 male inmates and 137 female inmates. He used measurements of deprivation (powerlessness) and measurements of importation (social class and involvement in criminal behavior) and examined their influence on prisonization. He found that for men, the deprivation model was a better predictor of prisonization, but for women, both models seemed to influence the prisonization (Zingraff, 1980: 284). Hartnagel and Gillan (1980), in a similar study, found that importation factors (age, prior imprisonment, and staff friends) were more influential than gender in the adoption of an inmate code.

Gender is an importation factor, since it is brought into the prison and shaped by societal forces outside the prison. Thus, even given exactly the same prison circumstances, one might expect women and men to react differently and adapt to the prison environment in a different manner. Gender differences are a controversial subject. There is no doubt, however, that socialized differences are brought into the prison and shape the subculture. For instance, women spend more time talking and worrying about their children; this concern with the outside world tends to diffuse the importance of prison life. Also, women's criminal backgrounds are different from men's. Fewer women inmates have had professional orientations to crime before their prison stay. Fewer of them have extensive criminal histories or histories of violence. Many women are amateurs at crime, and their histories reflect a lack of commitment to the criminal lifestyle. They may commit less serious crimes, such as forgery or shoplifting, and only when they need the money for drugs or because of economic pressures in their life. They may never develop techniques in the way a professional develops his or her craft, criminal or otherwise. Crime tends to be sporadic and tied to economics, drugs, or relationships with men.

A greater percentage of women are also *square johns (janes),* that is, individuals who have no criminal orientation and subscribe, for the most part, to the value system of society. Women like Jean Harris,[8] an upper-class woman who murdered her emotionally abusive lover, and battered women, who kill in passion, frustration, or fear, find themselves in prison because of their actions, yet they have no commitment to a criminal lifestyle. Although these types exist in the prison for men as well, they comprise a larger percentage in the women's prisons. There are some women who are more committed to a criminal or drug subculture on the outside; however, these types do not predominate, nor do women in prison tend to convert to such a lifestyle, as men in prison seem to do. The composition and criminality of the inmate group obviously have an impact on the subculture within a prison. Women are more fragmented and more likely to come from different backgrounds, and more of them share a fairly conventional value system; these characteristics influence the nature of the prison subculture and even its very existence. Women have some commonalities in their backgrounds as well. Many of them have had experiences of being exploited and abused. Many have struggled under an economic system that restricts their ability to care for themselves or their children. Many have come from family backgrounds of abuse, neglect, and sexual exploitation. These backgrounds shape the women and affect how they see the world and their needs.

Race is an importation factor. Interestingly, race does not seem to be the cause of animosity in the women's facility as it does in the men's facility. Although there are complaints of racism by staff and discrimination against African Americans in job assignments, and some women choose to isolate themselves from other races, there is very little evidence of violence caused by racial disharmony. Women frequently tend to develop relationships that cross racial boundaries, and certainly no predatory racial gangs are to be found in the prison for women. Because race is a predominant issue in this society, the differences between male and female inmates in this regard are intriguing. It may be that because women do not form large groups, a greater possibility exists for individual understanding and friendship rather than group stereotyping and the creation of boundaries.

The concept of prisonization means little if one does not accurately understand the subculture to which the inmate adapts. All research on prisonization, unfortunately, has relied on early descriptions of the male inmate code and value system as the subculture to which inmates are supposedly prisonized. Initially, findings indicated that women in prison possessed no "solidarity," meaning that they were unlike male inmates, who bonded together in subcultural groups. Ward and Kassebaum (1965) remarked that there was "little evidence" of social solidarity. They used a questionnaire that presented hypothetical situations such as an inmate's planned escape; the response of individual inmates as to what they would do indicated the extent to which they held subcultural values. Women evidently did not answer in the same way as male prisoners and, thus, were said to have little allegiance to a subculture. However, what the authors were measuring was the allegiance to a previously defined male subculture; whether their sample had any strong allegiance to a different, female subculture is unknown.

Solidarity with a prisoner subculture is always measured in terms common to the male inmate code, namely, adherence to such values as violence, toughness, coolness, and antiauthoritarianism. It should not be surprising, then, that many studies have failed to find these themes dominant in the institution for women. The researchers have interpreted this finding to mean that women do not bond together or do not make a subcultural adaptation to prison life. The alternative argument is that women do form a subculture in a prison, but it is a subculture that meets their particular needs. Values are those common to women in general and to prison women in particular.

An example of how researchers consistently measured female prisoners' allegiance to a male inmate code can be found in Tittle (1969), who reported that fewer women in a cocorrectional treatment center for imprisoned drug addicts subscribed to such values as "Mind your own business," "Be loyal to other [inmates]," "Be a man," and "Don't rat." These are the typical values that researchers call the inmate code or prison culture. One should have no difficulty understanding why women would be less likely to subscribe to the value "Be a man." The concept has relevance only in a men's institution, although the values in a women's institution do not necessarily conform to dominant society either.

Alpert, Noblit, and Wiorkowski (1977) used hypotheticals to measure prisonization. The hypotheticals were changed only to the extent of changing the name of the main character. Further, these hypotheticals may have been problematic even in measuring the essence of the male inmate code. The authors found that women "evidence vestiges of a traditional sex role orientation which is personal, specific, agent oriented and possibly vindictive" (Alpert et al., 1977: 32). However, since it is unclear how the authors are measuring prisonization or what prisonization is supposed to represent, this conclusion has little value.

Jensen and Jones (1976) also used male measures of prisonization with a female prisoner sample. Prisonization was defined as adopting values such as "Do not divulge information," "Do not respect staff," "Do not weaken, submit, or accept," and so on. These authors found that the career phase of female prisoners (early in the prison sentence, middle phase, or late) was related to adherence to the code. The middle phase showed the highest adherence even though it did not reach a level of significance. Age was the strongest predictor of adherence; other variables, such as visiting or number of letters received, made no difference. The author found that different types of inmates showed different patterns of adherence. For instance, misdemeanants exhibited the career phase effect whereas felons did not.

Kruttschnitt (1981) used an index of conformity to staff role expectations to measure commitment to an inmate code. In a small sample of 57 inmates, she found that female inmates failed to endorse an inmate code of ethics, yet they did not express conformity to staff expectations either. However, conformity increased during the length of the prison term—a finding directly contrary to early studies of male inmates. Unfortunately, because this measurement device only targets values from the male inmate code, again we do not know what values women did (or do) endorse.

In sum, the research in this area suffers from a lack of willingness to relinquish outdated theories regarding the inmate code.[9] There seems to be little doubt that the prison of today is different from that of Clemmer's (1940) and Syke's (1958) time. There may be a modern code of values and prescriptions of behavior, but researchers will never discover them as long as they continue to constrain inmates' beliefs to agreement or disagreement with the traditional code that characterized the "Big House." The research on female prisoners suffers the most from this single-mindedness, since women deviate the farthest from the old value system. There may indeed be a female inmate code, but it must be found by phenomenological means, by listening to women's views and values rather than attempting to measure them against an outdated and inappropriate male yardstick.

CONCLUSION

The prison is not a static environment. As crime patterns, criminals, prisons, and prison administrations change, so will the prisoner subculture. It is unfortunate that there is no tradition of research on the female subculture. The research reported in this chapter that only compares women's values and social roles to the male subculture lacks a vital component. Women in prison should be described independently of male models and definitions. The women's prison today and the subculture found there are not the same as the women's prison or female inmate's subculture of even a decade ago. For an approximation of what early prisons and prisoners were like, one must resort to biographical and journalistic information, because no tradition of academic research exists.

Women, like men, must learn to reconcile themselves to prison life. They can either do *hard time,* in which personal losses and isolation create emotional distress that continues through the period of imprisonment, or *easy time,* in which they put aside their civilian life until they can do something about it. Good time can be achieved by *doing time,* which means passing the days in prison using any activities and distractions available (Mahan, 1984b: 369). Some inmates do easier time than others because they immerse themselves in the prison culture. For them, prison becomes their life, and they fully participate in pseudofamilies and homosexual relationships that provide affection, comfort, and support. Some strong women thrive in a prison environment, as do some men. For these exploiters, the prison allows an opportunity to use their aggressiveness to get what they want with little chance of formal retaliation. Only another "tough" inmate will stand up to these women or men, since officers often have no knowledge of their trespasses. Other women remain social isolates, avoiding all but necessary contact with other inmates and leading a solitary existence among the many. For the most part, these women will be left alone, unless they verbalize or show their scorn of other inmates, in which case they may be socially or physically sanctioned.

It is unfortunate that even though greater and greater numbers of women are being sent to prison, we have so few current studies of what occurs inside. Whether most women learn to find some value there (either through relationships or prison programs), merely pass time, or emerge even more dysfunctional than when they went in is not at all clear.

NOTES

1. For a more recent review, see Paulus and Dzindolet, 1993.

2. It is questionable whether this attempt was successful in its goal to measure comparative deprivation, however, since the elements may or may not have been perceived similarly by the respondents.

3. For instance, the definition for each subcultural adaptation includes the variables employed for assignment to it, and the subcultures are not discrete. Heffernan also used many staff perceptions in assigning individuals to the subcultures and in determining the degree of homosexuality, which, arguably, is a less reliable form of identification than self-reports.

4. Hart's (1995: 73) study is interesting, but the methodology may be problematic. The sample of women was random, but the sample of men was a snowball sample of artists and jailhouse lawyers. Although the author noted the samples were similar in age, race, and marital status, she admitted they were different in criminal background and institutional environment. One wonders what other differences were introduced by the snowball sample method.

5. Researchers have learned that they must be aware of the effect of the total subculture on who is identified as a leader. For example, in a loose, atomized subculture with few ties,

those who would emerge as leaders in a questionnaire would be those identified by a cohesive group, however small. This reason was suggested to explain why young, African-American, violent inmates were identified as leaders in prisons for men, since the group Irwin (1970) characterized as the state-raised youth were likely the most cohesive force in the prison, and consequently their members showed up as leaders in questionnaires. That these individuals emerged statistically does not necessarily mean that they were status leaders for the total inmate population. This situation could be true of studies that identify certain types as leaders in female prisons as well. In this case, homosexually active leaders would likely be represented, since the homosexual subculture would likely be the strongest force at work.

6. This study suffers from methodological problems, however, in that van Wormer used sex stereotypes as the model of masculine and feminine behavior and also used staff reports to measure other items, such as homosexuality.

7. The results of this study must be viewed with caution, however, since the author mentions problems in the administration of questionnaires, including male interviewers and public interviews with staff. Also, according to the author, the institutions resembled boarding schools, and thus their characteristics are hardly a good measure of imprisonment. As mentioned earlier, one also must be careful in applying findings from juvenile institutions to adult women.

8. See Harris, 1988, for her account of life in Bedford Hills.

9. Interestingly, current authors still call for such comparisons rather than approaching the world of the women's prison without the blinders of 50-year-old research (see Alarid, 1997).

SUGGESTED READINGS

Girshick, L. 1999. *No Safe Haven: Stories of Women in Prison.* Boston: Northeastern University Press.

Harris, J. 1988. *They Always Call Us Ladies.* New York: Charles Scribner & Sons.

Owen, B. 1998. *"In the Mix": Struggle and Survival in a Women's Prison.* Albany, NY: State University of Albany Press.

Rierden, A. 1997. *The Farm: Life Inside a Women's Prison.* Amherst, MA: University of Massachusetts Press.

Watterson, K. 1996. *Women in Prison: Inside the Concrete Womb.* Boston: Northeastern University Press.

7

Legal Issues
of Incarcerated Women

The decade of the 1970s brought about many changes in courts' recognition of prisoners' legal rights. After *Holt v. Sarver,* 309 F. Supp. 362 (E.D. Ark. 1970), which challenged the conditions of the Tucker and Cummins prison farms in Arkansas and illustrated the sometimes brutal and horrifying conditions of prison, the courts were unable to continue their hands-off approach to prisoner suits. A steady stream of prisoner cases established rights in the areas of religion, censorship, discipline procedures, access to courts, and medical treatment. Basically, courts always balanced the individual inmate's particular interest against the state's interest in security, safety, and order. Sometimes, when the individual right being litigated was considered paramount and the state could demonstrate no substantial governmental interest in interfering with that right, inmates won.

For example, in early cases, courts recognized the inmate's right to practice religion in a way that did not disrupt or endanger the institution. Sometimes, when the inmate interest might arguably threaten institutional security, the state won. The view that prisoners did not "check their constitutional rights at the prison door," and that prisoners had many of the rights of free people, except those inconsistent with their status as prisoners, contrasted sharply with the earlier view that prisoners had only those rights given to them by prison administrators. More than any single element, this change in perception led to a different burden of proof and a different outcome for many of the cases decided by the Warren Court in the 1960s and 1970s (Alpert, 1980; Maschke, 1996).

Today, courts have retreated to a "deference" position, using a rational relationship test to determine whether the rule or procedure at issue violates the constitutional rights of the prisoner. In the rational relationship test, the state merely has to show a legitimate state interest (such as security) and a rational relationship between that interest and the rule or procedure in question. Using this test, the state almost always wins. The Prison Litigation Reform Act, 18 U.S.C. section 3626(a)(1)(A), has acted to reduce prisoners' litigation by putting up barriers and limiting the effect of successful lawsuits. This federal act bars injunctions unless they are narrowly drawn and use the "least intrusive" means necessary, reverses the proof requirement to the prisoner (who must prove the state has not met requirements), imposes financial penalties on frivolous lawsuits, and reduces attorneys' fees (Collins, 1998: 55). The effect has been to drastically curtail prisoner litigation. While this act, and prior court decisions blocking access to the federal courts unless administrative and state remedies have been pursued, has served to reduce the number of frivolous lawsuits, legitimate complaints of prisoners who are being treated in an unconstitutional manner probably have also been blocked.

LEGAL CHALLENGES BY WOMEN

Without exception, all the groundbreaking cases in the prisoners' rights area were brought by male inmates, including *Wolff v. McDonnell,* 418 U.S. 359 (1975), which dealt with inmates' due process rights in disciplinary hearings; *Estelle v. Gamble,* 429 U.S. 97 (1976), which established that the deliberate withholding of medical care could constitute unconstitutionally cruel and unusual punishment; and *Procunier v. Martinez,* 416 U.S. 396 (1974), which established inmates' rights to some due process protections against censorship.

Cases that have challenged the "totality of circumstances" in individual prisons or entire state systems also have involved male inmates. The conditions challenged by male prisoners in these cases are also present in prisons for women, but women have been much less likely to bring suits or seek protection from the courts.

There has been a distinct difference in the litigation patterns of men and women, with women much less likely to file lawsuits (Haft, 1974). Gabel (1982) surveyed several women's prisons to determine why women engage in less litigation than men do. She found that, although women have definite legal needs and concerns, they are less likely to have resources available to meet their needs. Administrators were found to underestimate and misinterpret women's legal needs. Women cited jail credit or good time and child custody issues as most important to them. Other issues were prison programs, appeals, and disciplinary issues. Researchers found that, although the prisons had legal services and law books, many prisoners were unaware of them or unaware of how to obtain services. The survey found that the women who were likely to utilize legal services were usually better educated and had held jobs on the outside. Communication among the inmates was also found to influence the amount of litigation. Women who served long sentences were more likely to be litigious. Finally, the amount of resources available influenced the degree to which women filed suits (Gabel, 1982: 206–207).

Aylward and Thomas (1984) compared a men's prison and a women's prison that had roughly comparable population size and inmate composition. Both institutions had law libraries and law clerks, and the authors hypothesized that because of overcrowding in the women's prison, litigation should have been prevalent; however, it was found that women were much less likely to bring suits. The study looked at summary decisions of all federal civil rights complaints filed in the Illinois Northern Division under 42 U.S.C. section 1983 between August 1977 and December 1983. Although female inmates comprised 3 percent of the population, they represented only 0.6 percent of the total cases brought to court (Aylward and Thomas, 1984: 263).

The types of cases brought by the inmates were also different. In Dwight, the women's institution, the cases tended to be about conditions and internal due process, whereas in Sheridan, the men's institution, the men also brought complaints concerning their original case and violence in the institution (1984: 264). The authors were surprised that so few suits were filed by women despite dramatic events in the prison, such as a salmonella outbreak and a sex-for-favors scandal on the part of top-level administrators (1984: 266).

Aylward and Thomas (1984) could not attribute the lower degree of legal activity of the women to a better grievance procedure, since Dwight's procedure was supposed to be less effective; nor could they attribute it to less cause for litigation at the women's institution. What they did suggest as the explanation for the women's absence of litigation was that women were "less aggressive" than men; they were more apathetic concerning attempts to try to change their environment; they had lower political consciousness; and they had no prisoner role models who were successful "jailhouse lawyers" (1984: 270). Interestingly, the women were more successful in the suits they did bring. Whereas 77 percent of the women's suits were successful, only 56 percent of the men's suits were; these statistics compared to a statewide average of 62 percent success (1984: 267) .

Fox (1984) suggested that as younger, more assertive women were incarcerated, there would be more legal action on the part of female inmates. He observed that volunteers also stimulated greater criticism and dissatisfaction over prison policies and rules because they supported the prisoners (1984: 27). In Bedford Hills Correctional Institution for Women in New York, several female activist lawyers encouraged women in the 1970s to file lawsuits. The volume of these suits increased steadily between 1972 and 1978; issues included medical care, disciplinary procedures, violation of personal privacy rights, arbitrary transfers to mental hygiene facilities, and liability for personal injuries (1984: 28). Inmates objected to older officers who treated them like children and also to newer management attempts to bring some of the order and strictness from the prisons for men into Bedford Hills. These objections also found their way into court suits (Fox, 1984: 30–32).

Wheeler et al. (1989: 93–94) compared cases of female law clerks in a women's prison to those in a men's prison. The authors found that women were more likely to need legal help for family matters. Also, female law clerks perceived their role differently than did male clerks, subscribing to more "ethics of care" themes; that is, helping others rather than love of law attracted them to the position, and they emphasized problem-solving rather than aggressiveness in winning disputes. Further, female clerks were more likely to engage in nonlegal activities (acting as paracounselors), and fewer of their cases resulted in legal actions. Requests for assistance from female inmates fell into the following categories:

Civil matters (e.g., child visitation, divorce, immigration, social security): 18.5 percent

Criminal actions (e.g., habeas corpus, speedy trial, sentence reduction, appeals): 25.1 percent

Institutional actions (e.g., injury, lost property, section 1983, grievance): 24.3 percent

Other (e.g., interstate transfer, parole rehearings, bond refund, jail credit): 32.1 percent

Although there are more women filing lawsuits today, litigation patterns still differ between men and women. Recent litigation by women has tended to concentrate in areas where they are not receiving the same opportunities as men (Smith, 1995). Some of these lawsuits, as we will see in the discussion that follows, have been successful.

CAUSES OF ACTION

In addition to the general causes of action utilized by all prisoners, women's lawsuits employ two basic sources to challenge prison conditions and treatment. The first is the equal protection clause of the Fourteenth Amendment, passed in 1868, which guarantees equal protection from state and federal laws for everyone. The difficulty of using this clause is that, so far, sex has not been ruled a "suspect class" by the Supreme Court as has race, and thus differential treatment of the sexes does not receive strict scrutiny in the determination of whether the state's action bears a rational relationship to a legitimate state purpose. However, since *Reed v. Reed,* 404 U.S. 71 (1971), courts have placed differences based on sex in a middle ground—warranting an intermediate level of evaluation. The state must show an "important" interest and a "substantial" relationship between the different treatment and the state interest. The person objecting to the differential treatment has the burden of proof to show that the law or practice was without a rational basis or was unrelated to the achievement of a valid state purpose. Thus, the state may manage to explain discriminatory or differential treatment on such grounds as women have different needs or that the state has a legitimate reason for treating women differently from men.

The second source female inmates might use in a challenge to prison conditions is the Eighth Amendment, passed in 1791, which prohibits cruel and unusual punishment. The important element of this argument is the definition of "cruel and unusual punishment" and whether the challenged condition is sufficient to meet the stringent tests the courts have established to prove unconstitutionality. The use of the Eighth Amendment has been tremendously expanded over the years. Originally used to invalidate prison practices such as whipping and other forms of physical discipline, "evolving standards of decency" now condemn other practices, such as solitary confinement for long periods of time, lack of recreation, lack of medical care, and separation from family. The particular development of this cause of action for women has been in challenges that argue certain conditions affect women differentially, so that something that might not be cruel and unusual to a man, might be to a woman.

The "totality of circumstances" test is the most recent form of the use of the Eighth Amendment in prisoner suits and has been used to invalidate entire state prison systems as unconstitutional. In this use of the Eighth Amendment, the court looks at the total environment of the prison to determine whether the living conditions violate the cruel and unusual punishment standards. Such problems as overcrowding, lack of programs, brutality, and inadequate sanitation are combined and considered as a whole. The situation still must meet the other tests of the Eighth Amendment, such as "shocking to the conscience" and "cruel and unusual."

These tests are more stringent than simple carelessness or negligence in meeting the needs of the inmate. For instance, although poor medical care may be sufficient to uphold a negligence suit against a prison doctor, a negligent finding would not be enough to meet a test for unconstitutional treatment. The lack of medical treatment must be complete and such that "deliberate indifference" was shown, leading to the conclusion that the withholding of such treatment was meant to induce unconstitutional pain and suffering. Similar stringent tests must be met to uphold a constitutional challenge for conditions or treatment.

Title VII (section 703(a)) of the Civil Rights Act of 1964, 42 U.S.C. section 2003-2(a) (1964), amended 1972, prohibits discrimination in employment on the basis of sex, and some attempts have been made to use this source to secure more equal access for female prisoners to the training and employment opportunities given to male prisoners. State constitutions may provide yet another source for suits protesting unequal treatment of female prisoners, since state constitutions often provide broader protections than does the federal Constitution. For instance, in *Inmates of Sybil Brand Institution for Women v. County of Los Angeles,* 130 Cal. App. 3d 89, 181 Cal. Rptr. 599 (1982), a California court held that the California constitution required strict scrutiny whenever a fundamental right was violated by a prison regulation. This ruling made it easier to prove unconstitutionality in the procedures and programs for women inmates. In this case, even under strict scrutiny, the court upheld the prison's regulations as advancing the state interest of security.

Causes of action may also exist under the Equal Pay Act, Americans with Disabilities Act, Religious Freedom Restoration Act, and other federal laws. Some of these may not be helpful; for instance, prisoners have been specifically cited as nonemployees for purposes of the Equal Pay Act by the Department of Labor and some state statutes (Town and Snow, 1980: 206). Another source of rights for prisoners might be Title IX, 20 U.S.C. section 1681 *et seq.,* 45 C.F.R. section 86.1 *et seq.,* the act that bars any education program that receives federal funds from discriminating on the basis of sex. In at least one case, *Jeldness v. Pearce,* 30 F.3d 110 (9th Cir. 1994), a court held that the act did apply to prisoners and required a stricter scrutiny of differential treatment than even equal protection analysis; however, such analysis still requires a finding that men and women are "similarly situated" (Collins and Collins, 1996).

Since the use of these other laws has as yet been relatively unexplored, it is unclear to what extent courts would be willing to expand their use for the purpose of challenging unequal conditions in women's prisons.

Disparate Sentencing

Some of the first targets for court challenge were the sentencing laws of several states, which mandated different sentences for female offenders. These sentencing laws were premised on the different "nature" of the female offender. She was thought to be more amenable to rehabilitation and able to benefit from an indeterminate sentence with the goal of reform, whereas the male offender was sentenced primarily for the purpose of punishment.

In the first half of the 1900s, courts were content to justify the different sentencing practices by pointing to gender differences. For instance, in *State v. Heitman,* 105 Kan. 139, 181 P. 630 (1919), the Kansas Supreme Court refused to invalidate a statute that imposed fixed sentences on men but gave women indeterminate sentences, using the rationale that the two sexes were different physically and psychologically (Rubick, 1975: 305). However, in more recent years, courts have rejected this argument and struck down differential sentencing. Another example of disparate sentencing was the "Muncy Act" in Pennsylvania, which required the sentencing judge to issue a general sentence to women convicted of offenses punishable by more than one year of imprisonment, to give a three-year sentence if the maximum permitted by law was three years or less, and to sentence the woman to the maximum allowable where the permissible term was longer than three years. The sentencing judge, therefore, had no discretion to issue less than the maximum sentence or to provide a minimum sentence with eligibility for parole, as could be done for male offenders (Bershad, 1985: 399). Because of the Muncy Act, most women were sent to the reformatory for offenses that, if committed by a man, resulted in a county jail term. In *Commonwealth v. Daniel,* 430 Pa. 642, 243 A.2d 400 (1968), the Muncy Act was overturned. The court held that there was no rational basis for distinguishing men and women in sentencing.

In *State v. Chambers,* 63 N.J. 287, 296, 307 A.2d 78, 82 (1973), the Supreme Court of New Jersey evaluated that state's disparate sentencing law and found that there were no differences between men and women "in capacity for intellectual achievement, self-perception, self-control, or the ability to change attitude and behavior, adjust to social norms and accept responsibility." Thus the law was held to be invalid (Bershad, 1985: 400). A federal district court, in *United States* ex rel. *Robinson v. York,* 281 F. Supp. 8 (D. Conn. 1968), declared the Connecticut indeterminate sentencing statute to be unconstitutional for much the same reason (Bershad, 1985: 400).

Another aspect of differential sentencing appeared in laws concerning supervision of juveniles that allowed for longer periods of jurisdiction over females, arguably because they were less mature than males, more dependent, and would benefit from continued contact with the juvenile justice system. New York's "Persons in Need of Supervision" law was struck down as unconstitutional by the New York Court of Appeals in 1972 because it permitted juvenile court jurisdiction over females, who were considered "persons in need of supervision," for two years longer than males (*Patricia A. v. City of New York,* 335 N.Y.S. 2d 33 (1972)).

Today, disparate sentencing laws no longer exist. Any attempt to reinstitute such laws would meet strong resistance from legal advocates, who could use such tools as the equal protection clause of the Fourteenth Amendment. The discretion still present in the sentencing laws, however, may create disparate treatment between men and women. Earlier chapters examined the role of "chivalry" in the system. Some evidence has indicated that women have been less likely to receive prison sentences for some crimes. In other cases, judges may actually be more harsh with a female offender. Further, some women may be sentenced more severely because they are women and pregnant. For instance, some anecdotal evidence indicates that judges might sentence a pregnant drug user to prison in order to prevent her from continuing to use drugs. Ironically, Raeder (1993a & b) and others note that gender-netural laws, such as the federal sentencing guidelines, may actually hurt women because they do not take into account special circumstances, such as single parenthood. So far, legal challenges to the use of federal guidelines and their differential impact on women with children have not been very successful. Courts today are clear that different treatment under the law is no longer allowed, but they can do little about the different realities that men and women face before and after prison.

PROGRAMMING AND MEDICAL SERVICES

Programming

Theoretically, the suits won by male inmates in the areas of medical services and program opportunities should have benefited women prisoners as well. This has not been the case, however, since the courts' decisions were often limited to conditions in specific prisons or made no reference to the women's prisons in the state (Leonard, 1983: 45). Usually women's programs are fewer in number and sex-stereotyped. Thus, whereas men may have access to programs in welding, electronics, construction, tailoring, computers, and plumbing, as well as college programs, women may have only cosmetology, child-care, keypunch, and nurse's aide programs, and often high school is the only education available to women. State prison officials offer various explanations for the paucity of programs in women's institutions: women may lack the background necessary for some technical programs; their small numbers make any program expensive; and they may not be interested in programs in some of the more lucrative but nontraditional fields. Finally, women have, on average, shorter sentences than men, making some programs impossible for them to complete (Bershad, 1985: 412).

Although courts have held that prisoners do not have a constitutional right to vocational or educational programs *per se,* the disparity in access to programs between men and women may be violative of the equal protection clause of the Fourteenth Amendment. It was not until the mid-1970s that women addressed these conditions in their own litigation efforts. Since then, many court opinions have supported women's challenges to unequal programming.

In *Barefield v. Leach,* No. 10282 (D.N.M. 1974), New Mexico was found to have failed to provide parity in vocational programming and wage-paying work within the institution. An important feature of this case was the court's definition of the equal protection standard. According to this court, the state can only justify a lack of parity in treatment or opportunities when its actions have a fair and substantial relationship to the purpose of the inmate's incarceration. When the state is guided by the inmate's gender in its determinations, the standard of review is strict in determining the rational relationship. Further, the small numbers of women and the consequent economic difficulties of providing them with vocational programs cannot justify disparate treatment. According to the court, "If the State of New Mexico is going to operate a penitentiary for women, it must operate one that measures up to constitutional standards" (*Barefield,* No. 10282, at 41). This was reminiscent of the court's views in *Holt v. Sarver,* 309 F. Supp. 362, 385 (E.D. Ark. 1970), when discussing the unsanitary and dangerous conditions in which male inmates were forced to live: "If Arkansas is going to operate a Penitentiary System, it is going to have to be a system that is countenanced by the Constitution of the United States." Interestingly, at the time of the *Barefield* case, only 36 women were incarcerated in New Mexico; two of them brought the suit (Collins, 1998: 45). In *Grosso v. Lally,* No. 4-74-447 (D. Md. 1977), a similar case, the Maryland Division of Corrections averted a trial by agreeing to a consent decree that provided for both qualitative and quantitative parity in programs, conditions, and opportunities for female inmates.

The most well-known case concerning the equal protection claim and prison programming is *Glover v. Johnson,* 478 F. Supp. 1075 (E.D. Mich. 1979), a Michigan case. At the time the suit was filed, men had access to twenty-two vocational training programs while women had access to only three. Women's programs were low-paying and sex-stereotyped. Male prisoners could earn bachelor and associate degrees, whereas women were able to take only post–high-school classes that did not lead to a degree. Men, but not women, had access to an apprenticeship program, work release, and prison industries. Women were paid lower wages than men for the same jobs. Women had no opportunity to earn incentive good time. The law library for women contained only a few outdated books. Some of the state female prisoners were housed in Kalamazoo County Jail until a new women's facility could be built, and they were held in their cells approximately 22 hours a day. Further, they were not allowed hardbound books or personal items in their cells. They lived in four- to six-person cells, sleeping on mattresses on steel slabs.

Several sources were used in the suit against Michigan. The equal protection clause of the Fourteenth Amendment was used to challenge the differences in treatment, and the First Amendment was also used to challenge some of the conditions regulating postage stamps and attendance at religious services. The Eighth Amendment was used to challenge some of the conditions at the Kalamazoo County Jail, and Title IX of the Education Amendments of 1972 was used to challenge differential access to educational opportunities (Town and Snow, 1980: 201–202).

The intermediate standard test was used in *Glover,* so that the state had to show only an important state interest and some relationship between it and the differential treatment:

> Defendants here are bound to provide women inmates with treatment and facilities that are substantially equivalent to those provided the men, i.e., equivalent in substance if not form unless their actions, though failing to do so, nonetheless bear a fair and substantial relationship to achievement of the State's correctional objectives. (478 F. Supp. at 1079)

The court was not persuaded that the state's cost argument was important enough to justify the lack of programs. The court ordered more educational courses for the women, an apprenticeship program, a work-release program, and an expanded legal training program. It also ordered the state to stop using the county jail as an overflow facility, since women there deserved the same programs as other state prisoners. Employing consent decrees and prison monitors that continued in force for almost 20 years, the court in this case continually prodded the state to improve the number and type of programs, staffing, medical services, and a range of other issues. When the state was recalcitrant, it was threatened with a $500 per day fine for noncompliance (Collins, 1998; Leonard, 1983: 48; Town and Snow, 1980: 205).

Since women constitute such a small percentage of all inmates, the state has an understandable argument in its refusal to initiate programs that are relatively expensive because of the small number of women who would participate. Some courts are sympathetic to this argument, and some are not. Recently, budgetary considerations to justify denying certain groups of prisoners access to programs have become more accepted (Collins, 1998).

Work-release programs, which allow prisoners to obtain outside employment while serving a sentence, are a valuable rehabilitative tool and beneficial to the individual inmate, yet women are often denied opportunities to participate in such programs (Krause, 1974: 1453). Work-release administrators have cited three arguments to justify exclusion: first, women are "unsuited" to work release; second, women's smaller numbers create a great deal of administrative difficulty; and third, housing for women in work release is nonexistent (Krause, 1974: 1458). Courts have not been sympathetic to such arguments and have ordered correctional systems to implement work-release programs for women. Economics and administrative convenience have been denied as valid state purposes for denying programs to any particular group of inmates if the designation is made on the basis of sex. If work-release programs are tools of rehabilitation, they should be applied equally to females and males. No support can be given for the proposition that female inmates are less in need of economic self-sufficiency than males or would benefit less from a work-release program.

In one California case, all female offenders were sent to one facility while offenders were sent to any of a number of facilities, one of which was minimum-security and offered the men access to a work-release program. The court held this practice to be violative of the California constitution and the equal protection clause of the Fourteenth Amendment (*Molar v. Gates,* 98 Cal. App. 3d 1, 159 Cal. Rptr. 239 (1979)) (Bershad, 1985: 417).

In addition to a difference in access to vocational and educational programs, women often suffer from a lack of recreational programs. Especially in county jails where women are often housed in a segregated block, incarcerated women may not receive the recreational opportunities afforded male prisoners, despite the psychological and medical benefits such physical exercise provides. In prisons, women typically are not provided the range of and equipment for recreation that males receive. State correctional officials explain these disparities by pointing to the lower participation rates of women in physical activities and cost factors. Suits challenging these deficiencies are based on the Eighth and Fourteenth amendments, as well as state constitutional protections. In many cases, courts have ruled as they have in vocational programming cases, specifically, that unless the state can prove a legitimate reason for the different treatment, parity must be achieved (Bershad, 1985: 418).

Medical Services

Lack of medical services for inmates may be unconstitutional if it is severe enough to meet the court's test of "deliberate indifference." In *Estelle v. Gamble,* 429 U.S. 97 (1976), the U.S. Supreme Court held that when medical care was deliberately withheld and when it caused needless suffering and pain, it could constitute cruel and unusual punishment, thus violating the Eighth Amendment. Most prisons for men have a full-time staff of doctors and dentists, whereas women often have to travel out of the prison for treatment. Female inmates seem to have disproportionally more medical problems than male inmates; however, medical services for women are often poor and inadequate. Women's special needs in the area of gynecological and obstetric treatment are often unmet by prison medical services. In order to highlight the disparate and poor medical treatment of women inmates, several class action suits have been brought by female inmates.

One successful class action suit brought by women at the Bedford Hills Correctional Facility in New York established that medical care at Bedford Hills was inadequate and violated the Eighth Amendment (*Todaro v. Ward,* 431 F. Supp. 1129 (S.D.N.Y. 1977), *aff'd,* 565 F.2d 48 (2d Cir. 1977)). Although the medical staff and the facilities themselves were deemed adequate, prisoners were often denied access to medical help through arbitrary procedures (Leonard, 1983: 49). Deficiencies in the availability of physicians, repeated failures to perform laboratory tests, long delays in the return of laboratory reports, a grossly inadequate system for keeping medical records, and a lack of adequate supervision of patients in the sick wing were some of the findings of the court (Bershad, 1985: 422). Also, the court found that health screenings were delayed, there was a defective chest x-ray machine, and gynecological concerns were ignored (Chapman, 1980: 158). The court noted that one woman was denied treatment for a month for an infection that could have resulted in sterility. The court acknowledged that Bedford Hills was no worse than other institutions but refused to agree that this meant its policies were constitutional (Leonard, 1983: 50). The court ordered better access, better nurse screening, prompt access to a doctor during sick call, better follow-up care, and periodic self-audits. The Second Circuit Court of Appeals affirmed the district court's decision.

Pregnancy and Prenatal Care   One major problem in health care for female prisoners is the absence of pregnancy counseling or services. The National Prison Project of the American Civil Liberties Union claims that pregnant women come under strong pressure from prison officials to abort their fetuses. In *Morales v. Turman,* 383 F. Supp. 53 (E.D. Tex. 1974), a pregnant woman testified that prison officials instructed her to take 10 unidentified pills and to exercise. Inmates warned her that this had caused other women to miscarry, but she obeyed and later aborted (Leonard, 1983: 50). The court found that pregnant women were denied access to medical care and noted that one woman who had miscarried in prison was denied medical treatment for two days (Bershad, 1985: 424; Leonard, 1983: 50).

On the other hand, at least one inmate won a suit that challenged the prison's refusal to allow her an abortion because the prison would not pay for the guards needed to bring her to the hospital during the procedure. The court agreed that the prison's refusal violated her constitutional rights (*Lett v. Withworth,* No. C-1-77-246 (S.D. Ohio 1976)). Other incidents where states refused to fund abortion on demand by pregnant women incarcerated in state prisons have also found their way into the courts. Courts have not recognized the right of incarcerated women to demand an abortion unless they can pay for it themselves (Bershad, 1985: 424). However, in *Monmouth County Correctional Institution Inmates v. Lanzaro,* 834 F.2d 326 (3d Cir. 1987), the court ruled that because of rights conferred by the Fourteenth and Eighth amendments, the jail could not require a court order before allowing a woman the opportunity to acquire an abortion from an outside medical clinic. The same result occurred in *Reproductive Health Services v. Webster,* 655 F. Supp. 1300 (W.D. Mo. 1987, settled June 23, 1987).[1] Other courts have not been as protective of the woman's right to abortion (see *Bryant v. Maffuci,* 923 F.2d 979 (2d Cir. 1991), and *Gibson v. Matthews,* 926 F.2d 732 (6th Cir. 1991).

Many prison systems have grossly inadequate facilities for treating pregnant women. Approximately eight babies were born each year in one particular Alabama prison under conditions that threatened the lives of both mother and child, since there were no facilities to deal with possible complications. Leonard (1983: 51) reported that many prisons have no facilities for giving birth, and women are transported to nearby hospitals. After giving birth, they are immediately separated from their babies and returned to the prison; sometimes they are subjected to vaginal searches despite their condition and risk of infection. Prison food, made up primarily of starches, and lack of exercise are not conducive to a safe and healthy pregnancy. Deficiencies in nutrition and lack of prenatal counseling may lead to premature births, prenatal mortality, birth defects, and mental retardation. Bershad (1985: 425) reports that many prisons provide no special diets or vitamin supplements for pregnant inmates.

The needs of female inmates in this area go beyond parity. In the areas of pregnancy services, gynecological care, treatment for sexually transmitted diseases, and complications brought on by drug use, female inmates arguably need more services than male inmates. Unfortunately, until prodded, state prisons for women often are unwilling or financially unable to provide such services.

Today, courts have become increasingly more resistant to finding states liable for deficiencies due to "deliberate indifference." In *Farmer v. Brennan,* 114 S. Ct. 1970 (1994), the Supreme Court held that to meet the test of "deliberate indifference," the plaintiff must show that the official knew and disregarded an excessive risk to inmate health or safety. It must be proven that the official knew of facts that created this situation and knew the harm that would result. This is a very difficult standard to meet, and it is likely that Eighth Amendment cases that challenge medical services after *Farmer v. Brennan* will need to rely on state constitutional protections rather than the U.S. Supreme Court.

OTHER ISSUES

The propriety of transferring female prisoners out of the state was first challenged in 1972 in *Park v. Thomson,* 356 F. Supp. 783 (D. Haw. 1976). In this case, the court found that the transfer made conditions of confinement more onerous for female prisoners and thus violated the Fourteenth and Eighth amendments (Fabian, 1980: 182). Even when a state has an institution for women, it is often farther away from her home than the prison where men might be sentenced. However, in *Pitts v. Meese,* 684 F. Supp. 303 (D.D.C. 1987), the court refused to accept an equal protection argument against the practice of sending District of Columbia female offenders to Alderson, a federal facility much farther away than the facility to which male offenders were sent. Echoing *Meachum v. Fano,* 96 S. Ct. 2532 (1976), the court said that no prisoner has a right to be in any particular prison and may be transferred within the state or out of the state according to the needs of the institution. This case and other recent cases indicate that, at least in this regard, female litigants will be unsuccessful in challenges to the practice in some states of transferring female inmates out of state.

Some cases have challenged different punishment systems for women and men. In *Canterino v. Wilson,* 546 F. Supp. 174 (W.D. Ky. 1982), female prisoners challenged a behavior modification program that was mandatory for all female prisoners and nonexistent for male prisoners. Under this system, women were restricted from the exercise of normal privileges and punished differently from men for lesser offenses. The court held that the system unconstitutionally discriminated against women. The system was based on gender and was "unrelated to any important governmental objective," thus violating the equal protection clause of the Fourteenth Amendment under the intermediate scrutiny standard (Bershad, 1985: 405). Prisoners in this case also challenged the practice whereby women were allowed only half the visiting time that men received and were limited to 15-minute phone calls while men had unlimited access to telephones during free time. The court agreed that these policies constituted unconstitutional violations of equal rights (Bershad, 1985: 407).

Although *Bounds v. Smith,* 430 U.S. 817 (1977), established the right of inmates to have meaningful access to the courts through the presence of law libraries and clerks or other devices to ensure access, the provisions made for female inmates have fallen far short of those provided to male inmates. In *Glover v. Johnson,* 478 F. Supp. 1075, 1095 (E.D. Mich. 1979), the court required

Michigan to provide a paralegal training program for female prisoners, not for reasons of parity, but because it was necessary to ensure constitutional access to the courts, since women were shown to be less skilled in research and writing legal materials (Bershad, 1985: 427). Another court held that Kentucky needed to improve the women's law library and legal programs to make them equivalent to those available to male prisoners; the rationale there was equal protection (*Canterino v. Wilson*, 546 F. Supp. 174 (W.D. Ky. 1982)).

As mentioned in Chapter 4, the small number of female prisoners makes classification problematic; thus, all types of offenders, including those with serious mental or drug problems, are housed together. The lack of classification for female offenders, resulting in forced incarceration with all types of offenders, often results in unintentional punishment (Rippon and Hassell, 1981: 457). In *Commonwealth v. Stauffer*, 214 Pa. Super. 113, 241 A.2d 718 (1969), a woman was housed in the state's prison for women even though her crime was such that a man incarcerated for the same offense would have been in a county jail. She brought suit, and the court agreed that it was unconstitutional to treat women more severely than men by incarcerating them with hardened offenders.

Chapman (1980: 157) discussed the situation where counties may have so few women that female offenders are sent to the state prison. Women are then denied programs because of where they are housed. These practices, although understandable, have been ruled unsupportable in the past. Given today's more conservative approach, however, it is unclear what latitude courts are willing to give correctional officials struggling with overcrowding and inadequate budgets.

Child Custody and Separation Issues

As mentioned earlier, surveys of male and female inmates show a consistently different pattern of litigation needs, with women much more often involved in legal issues regarding children. Inmate-mothers have generally not prevailed in their attempts to keep possession of newborns in prison. Although a few states have enabling laws for such a contingency, courts always interpret such laws as discretionary and allow prison officials to decide whether an imprisoned mother may keep her baby. More often than not, prison officials do not allow the child to remain inside prison walls for "the benefit of the child," and mothers who attempt to sue to keep custody of their baby lose (*Cardell v. Enomoto*, No. 701-094 (Cal. Sup. Ct., San Francisco Co. 1976)). Florida has repealed its statute allowing prisoner-mothers to keep their babies; New York is one of the few states that has such a law, but discretion still rests with prison officials (Schupak, 1986).

In California, the statute allowing female prisoners to keep their babies was repealed and a law allowing community placement for mothers with babies was passed in the 1980s. Community facilities require that the female inmate has a low custody grade and is near release; thus, many women do not qualify. Recently, California passed enabling legislation to build five institutions with facilities for young children. Women who are pregnant or have very young children at the time of sentencing will be sentenced directly to one of these facilities. The first has already been built in the Los Angeles area.

Another legal issue is custody. As reported in previous chapters, inmate-mothers are often the sole supports of their infant children, and while the mothers are imprisoned, the children are often cared for by the women's relatives. However, if the state takes control of the children, retaining or reestablishing custody is sometimes difficult. Although most states do not cite imprisonment in and of itself as a cause for terminating parental rights, a few states do, and others interpret imprisonment as a type of abandonment, justifying termination in that way (Bershad, 1985: 409).

The child-care agency may put tremendous pressure on the woman to put the child up for adoption. The state's orientation in these cases is to do what is best for the child, and courts will put that priority ahead of parental rights. Thus, the woman may have her parental rights terminated involuntarily solely because of her incarceration. In one case, an imprisoned woman lost her parental rights six months before release, even though the child had been in six foster homes over a period of four and one-half years. The court decided against the woman based on the fact that she was not going to be released "immediately" (*Los Angeles County Dep't of Adoptions v. Hutchinson,* No. 2 Civil 48729, unreported decision (Cal. Super. Ct. 1977)).

Another disadvantage women have in retrieving their children from the state is that the criterion to determine whether parental custody is in the best interests of the child is the parent's ability to support the child. If the woman does not receive vocational programs that enable her to support herself and her children, it becomes difficult to prove that she deserves the children upon release (Bershad, 1985: 411).

As discussed previously, the federal law that mandates states to terminate parental rights and adopt out children relatively quickly may have severe consequences for inmate-mothers. Reports are only now being provided of how many women have been affected. Poor communication between the inmate-mother and the child-care agency and lack of legal advocacy exacerbates these problems. The decisions of courts presented with a conflict between the rights of the parent and the interests of the child are mixed. Some courts will terminate parental rights quickly; others will do so only when the nature of the crime indicates that the child would be in peril if kept in the mother's custody. Inmate-mothers seek to avoid problems with custody by placing the child in the care of family members, but sometimes this is impossible. As has been noted before, child custody is one of the most important legal issues of incarcerated women and, unfortunately, the area in which they may receive the least aid.

CROSS-SEX SUPERVISION

As female correctional officers have entered men's prisons, so too have male correctional officers entered prisons for women. In fact, the ironic result of equal protection challenges by women who sought to work in prisons for men is that there are now far more men working in prisons for women. In some states, over half of the officers guarding women are men; some estimates place the average at about 70 percent.

The major case concerning female officers, *Dothard v. Rawlinson,* 433 U.S. 321 (1977), was decided in favor of the state of Alabama, which sought to prevent Diane Rawlinson from working in the state prison for men, on the grounds of legitimate state interest in protecting women from the "jungle atmosphere" of the prison. Although Alabama won this case, it was not considered much of a precedent, since the Court made it clear that it was the specific conditions of Alabama's penitentiary that influenced its decision.

Later cases pitted the equal protection (equal employment) rights of officers (either male or female) against the privacy rights of prisoners. In *Gunther v. Iowa State Men's Reformatory,* 612 F.2d 1079 (8th Cir. 1980), the privacy rights of male prisoners were noted, but the court determined that those rights could be protected by assigning female officers only to certain positions. A similar result was reached in *Harden v. Dayton Human Rehabilitation Center,* 520 F. Supp. 769 (1981).

There is no consistency in cases concerning the use of opposite-sex officers. In some cases, courts have held that "in normal circumstances," prisoners should not be viewed by an opposite-sex officer while showering or using the toilet (*Bowling v. Enomoto,* 514 F. Supp. 201 (1981)); in other cases, courts have held that women cannot be denied jobs that allow visual observation of naked inmates and performance of pat-down frisks (*Sterling v. Cupp,* 625 P.2d 123 (1981)). In *Grummet v. Rushen,* 779 F.2d 491 (9th Cir., 1985), male prisoners at San Quentin challenged the policy of female guards viewing them in the nude. The court observed that this type of viewing was not frequent and held that the male prisoners did not prove a constitutional violation.

Since promotion is based on experience in a number of settings, and promotional opportunities are limited if women are restricted to the sometimes single facility for women in the state, it was essential for women to be allowed into men's prisons to advance their careers. No such interest exists for male correctional officers who wish to work in women's institutions; however, the result of these cases has been that men can work in prisons for women, and are doing so in ever-increasing numbers.

It should be noted that men always have been in institutions for women. Even after separate institutions for women were established, male supervisors and line staff were common in institutions for women, although typically their job assignments were limited. Alpert (1980, 1984; also see Alpert and Crouch, 1991) and others described the court decisions concerning the rights of opposite-sex officers to work in prisons as using a "least restrictive means" analysis—that is, that equal employment rights "trumped" privacy rights and that the state needed to apply a "least restrictive" policy allowing female (or male) officers to work in opposite-sex prisons, but allowing policy or procedure changes to give inmates some minimal rights over bodily privacy (e.g., covering their window when they are on the toilet).

The presence of men in an institution for women, however, may raise greater privacy issues than does the presence of female officers in prisons for men. Whether sexist or not, some courts have recognized that women are socialized to have greater privacy needs than men in our society, and there are more potential dangers (sexual exploitation or assault) in having men observe women in their living units and patting down female inmates than are raised by female officers supervising men.

When male correctional officers were introduced into the living units at Bedford Hills, the women sued, alleging that the presence of male officers violated their right to privacy when supervising areas where the women should have been able to expect some bodily privacy, such as in the shower or in their cells during evening hours. Although the lower court agreed that privacy interests were at stake and restricted male officers to certain assignments that did not infringe on the women's privacy, this decision was reversed in part by the Second Circuit Court of Appeals. It was determined that arrangements could be made to allow free use of male officers and also protect the women's privacy. For instance, the court explained that the women's complaints regarding nightgowns becoming disarranged during sleep and the possibility of being observed by male officers could be solved by issuing pajamas, and shower areas could be protected by frosted glass (*Forts v. Ward,* 434 F. Supp. 946 (S.D.N.Y.), *rev'd and remanded,* 566 F.2d 849 (2d Cir. 1977), 471 F. Supp. 1095 (S.D.N.Y. 1979), *aff'd in part and rev'd in part,* 621 F.2d 1210 (2d Cir. 1980)). The state reached an agreement whereby male officers would not be placed alone in living units and would announce their presence before proceeding into the living-unit hallways.

A different result occurred in *Torres v. Wisconsin Dep't of Corrections,* 838 F.2d 944 (7th Cir. 1988), *overruled in part,* 859 F.2d 1523 (1988), where the Seventh Circuit reversed the district court's ruling favoring the equal opportunity rights of male officers. The Court of Appeals held that the state had established a "bona fide occupational qualification" based on rehabilitation and that male officers could be prohibited from working in prisons for women. The court used evidence of the high rate of sexual and physical victimization of female prisoners, and agreed with prison officials' argument that women needed an institution relatively free from men in authority. Here, the deference approach was clearly evident; the court held that excluding men was a reasonable method to accomplish a legitimate state purpose (rational relationship test). *Torres* was cited with favor by a Hawaii court that upheld the state ban on male C.O.s working in the living units at night (*Robino v. Iranon,* 145 F.3d 1109 (9th Cir. 1998)).

Cases concerning male officers supervising women in showers and other areas are not consistent. In *Thompson v. Wyandotte County,* 869 F. Supp. 893 (D. Kan. 1994), the court found that the female inmates' claims of being seen in the shower on "irregular and isolated occasions" did not violate constitutional protections, but proposed that "regular" viewing might violate privacy protections. In one particularly egregious case, the court agreed there had been privacy violations. In this case, a female prisoner was housed in a cell block with three male prisoners. Male guards viewed her showering; male prisoners sexually harassed her by making sexual advances and insinuations, harassed her while she used the toilet, and masturbated outside her cell (*Galvan v. Carothers,* 855 F. Supp. 285 (D. Alaska 1994), *aff'd,* 122 F.3d 1071, 1997 WL 542234 (9th Cir. 1997)): "The court finds that minimal standards of privacy and decency include the right not to be subject to sexual advances, to use the toilet without being observed by members of the opposite sex, and to shower without being viewed by members of the opposite sex" (855 F. Supp. at 291).

Strip Searches and Pat Downs

One of the most contentious areas of cross-sex supervision is the issue of searches (Farkas and Rand, 1997, 1999). Although prior cases have ruled that prisoners have no privacy rights and that strip searches and even body-cavity searches may be done for any reason short of harassment (see *Bell v. Wolfish,* 441 U.S. 520 (1979), and *Hudson v. Palmer,* 468 U.S. 517 (1984)), such a search by an officer of the opposite sex may present different issues.

Prisoners of both sexes have filed lawsuits objecting to being searched by a member of the opposite sex. In *Smith v. Fairman,* 678 F.2d 52 (7th Cir. 1982), *cert. denied,* 461 U.S. 907 (1983), male inmates challenged the policy allowing female guards to pat down male inmates. The court said that the Eighth Amendment was not violated; while the experience may be humiliating and degrading, it "falls short of the kind of shocking, barbarious [sic] treatment proscribed by the Eighth Amendment" (*Smith,* 678 F.2d at 53). Male inmates also were unable to persuade the court that their privacy rights were violated in other similar cases (*Johnson v. Phelan,* 69 F.3d 144 (7th Cir. 1995), *cert. denied, Johnson v. Sheahan,* 117 S. Ct. 506 (1996), and *Somers v. Thurman,* 109 F.3d 614 (9th Cir.), *cert. denied,* 118 S. Ct. 143 (1997).

The issue facing some courts, however, is whether the situation of male C.O.s patting down female inmates presents different privacy concerns. Female inmates complain that male C.O.s use the opportunity of a pat down to "grope genitals," "masturbate," and make "sexual advances" (*Feming* et. al. *v. Gourd,* 98 CIV 8022, unpublished opinion (U.S. Dist. Ct., Southern Dist. of New York 1997)). Zupan (1992a) noted that in 21 percent of the states she surveyed, male officers conducted pat downs routinely; in 21 percent of the states, males conducted these searches with restrictions (i.e., another officer present); and in 29 percent of the states, men could conduct such searches only in emergency situations. In other states, male officers may assist in strip searches as well. When challenged, courts seem to allow great deference to state authorities, especially if "emergency" situations can be alleged. For instance, in *Lee v. Downs,* 641 F.2d 1117 (1981), the court held that male officers' supervision of a strip search by a female nurse did not violate the prisoner's rights because "the additional harm to be inflicted did not warrant the delay . . . that would have been required to assemble an all female crew." It is unclear what emergency could possibly exist in a prison whereby an inmate could not be held long enough for a female staff member to arrive.

The most-cited case concerning opposite-sex searches occurred in the state of Washington—*Jordan v. Gardner,* 986 F.2d 1521 (9th Cir. 1993) (*en banc*).

A prison policy that allowed male officers to pat down female inmates was instituted despite the objections of prison staff, who argued that many prisoners had been sexually abused by men and that such searches would be psychologically traumatic. On the first day of implementation, one inmate with a history of sexual abuse "had to have her fingers pried loose from bars she had grabbed during the search, and she vomited after returning to her cell block" (*Jordan,* 986 F.2d at 1523). Prisoners filed suit, arguing that such searches were a violation of their Eighth Amendment rights. The Ninth Circuit agreed that the pat downs could be traumatic to those who had been sexually victimized:

> During the cross-gender clothed body search, the male guard stands next to the female inmate and thoroughly runs his hand over her clothed body starting with her neck and working down to her feet. According to the prison training manual, a guard is to "[u]se a flat hand and pushing motion across the [inmate's] crotch area." The guard must "[p]ush inward and upward when searching the crotch and upper thighs of the inmate." All seams in the leg and the crotch area are to be "squeez[ed] and knead[ed]." Using the back of the hand, the guard also is to search the breast area in a sweeping motion, so that the breasts will be "flattened." Superintendent Vail estimated that a typical search lasts forty-five seconds to one minute. A training film, viewed by the court, gave the impression that a thorough search would last several minutes. (*Jordan,* 986 at 1523)

The court recognized that because of their histories of victimization, female prisoners were more likely to be psychologically harmed by cross-sex searches, and ruled that such a policy was cruel and unusual. The idea that women may experience a situation differently from men is extremely important for Eighth Amendment analysis:

> If one accepts the basic assumptions that the cognitive perceptions of men and women sometimes differ and recognizes the fact that the experience of incarceration is different for men and women, the importance of building gender into the standard for the objective part of the test for cruel and unusual punishment in conditions of confinement becomes clear. . . . Without building into the standard the perceptions of both men and women, the standard is tailored for when a man perceives the conditions of confinement such as cross-gender searches have become cruel, without regard to when a woman perceives that the treatment has crossed the line. (Krim, 1995: 105)

Jordan was rejected as a persuasive precedent by a different court that held there was not a sufficient showing of stress and that even if there had been, because there were not enough female C.O.s to conduct all security searches, it was acceptable for the state to allow male C.O.s to continue to conduct pat downs (*Carl v. Angelone,* 883 F. Supp. 1433 (D. Nev. 1995)).

Some argue that courts are practicing reverse discrimination by protecting women's privacy rights over men's. For instance, Jurado (1999) argues that all

inmates "are entitled to an expectation of bodily integrity" and is "disheart-
ened" by some courts' willingness to attach greater protections to strip searches
of women by men. She argues that such a protection derives from sex stereotypes. However, such a position ignores the realities of prison. Prisoners have
no "bodily integrity," nor power, nor much ability to protest searches that cross
the line. There is enough history and current examples to show that when men
are given the power to grope women, at least some will abuse that power. The
dangers of sexual exploitation, harassment, and assault are simply much greater
when men guard women than when women guard men.

Chesney-Lind (1997) and others discuss several cases across the nation
where women have been sexually assaulted by male officers. Chesney-Lind
notes a case in New York that involved officers videotaping strip searches of
women for later viewing. Henriques and Gilbert (2000) also discuss the growing problem of sexual abuse and assault in prisons. They report, for instance,
that in 1995, there were 135,000 rapes of female inmates (2000: 256). One
inmate, after accusing an officer of rape, was transferred from a minimum-
security prison to a maximum-security institution, was beaten and harassed by
guards, and ultimately jumped from a second-story window (2000: 258). The
authors also describe the case of a federal facility in Dublin, California, where
women were being held in the solitary confinement unit of a men's prison.
These women, who were serving time for nonviolent crimes, were the victims
of a prostitution ring whereby prison guards took money from inmates in
return for access to the women.

Several states (i.e., California, Georgia, and Washington, D.C.) have
reached out-of-court settlements over cases of sexual harassment and assault.
Other states are passing laws that criminalize any sexual contact, consensual or
not, between officers and inmates. It seems clear that with increasing numbers
of men guarding women, these cases will not go away. This issue will be discussed more fully in the next chapter.

PARITY VERSUS DIFFERENT NEEDS

In the 1990 edition of this book, this author argued that legal challenges by
women employing an equal protection argument may be problematic because
if the courts applied parity, women might lose some of the special advantages
they had. As Ardeti (1973) pointed out, the sexual segregation of our prisons
leads to some advantages as well as disadvantages for the female inmates.
Although women usually have fewer programs and vocational programming
for them is often sex-stereotyped, they have enjoyed more privacy in separate
rooms rather than dormitories (Ardeti, 1973: 1238, 1242). They also have
received more protection from staff because of better ratios of officers to
inmates (Ardeti, 1973: 1240). Advocates must steer carefully between Scylla
and Charybdis in attacking unequal treatment without sacrificing the mandate
to meet the special needs of female inmates (see Herbert, 1985).

Women who are inmates are not men. Some needs of women are identical to those of men; thus, women deserve and must receive parity in opportunity. Such needs include vocational and educational opportunities, sanitation, correspondence, legal access, and other services necessary in an institutional environment. Some women's needs are different from those of men. They have greater and different medical needs: women need gynecological and obstetric services, and they may need to have more dollars per person spent on their medical services than is spent on those for male inmates because of physical differences between the two sexes. In this area, parity would not be sufficient, and it is necessary to recognize the need for "unequal" treatment. In other areas, the arguments are not as clear. Should women receive different sentencing, such as community placement, because of childbirth, or would that be "unequal treatment" without a rational basis? Should greater privacy rights of women be recognized, so that they are protected from opposite-sex officers? Should women enjoy greater access to children through visiting and child-care programs, or is that a violation of men's equal protection rights? These questions continue to be addressed by this nation's court system. The issue is always equal protection/parity versus special needs.

If parity demands equal protection, might it be that correctional departments, already faced with huge problems and court orders requiring expenditures that legislatures are not funding, cannot improve women's prisons without cuts in men's prisons? A conceivable solution would be, then, a decline in services for all, as long as the level of services was equal between men and women. This prediction, made in the first edition of this book, has, to some extent, occurred. There has been a cookie-cutter approach to programming for men's and women's prisons, but with a minimal level of service for all. Women's prisons have been "brought into line" with the other prisons in the state, often under the guise of "parity." Once again, we see that equal treatment under the law does not necessarily mean fair treatment.

Is Parity Dead?

Ironically, it may be that legal analysts are arguing a dead issue. At least some observers note a shift in court cases and believe that courts have more recently retreated into a "deference" model that allows states to use economics or other arguments to justify different treatment of the sexes. Collins (1998: 43–44)[2] argues that parity has been abandoned, citing as evidence recent court decisions that have evaluated different treatment using a more forgiving standard (the rational relationship test); the Prison Litigation Reform Act, which constricts the power of federal courts to utilize consent decrees and removes financial incentives for lawyers to take cases; and the Supreme Court's increasingly conservative trend regarding prisoner rights cases.

Collins (1998) notes that from the first parity case (*Barefield v. Leach*) in 1974, to today, the trend has swung from utilizing a parity argument and an intermediate standard to judge the state's argument as to why it was treating men and women differently, to a much less accommodating approach. The most extreme example of a parity approach can be found in *McCoy v. Nevada Dep't of Prisons,* 776 F. Supp. 521 (D. Nev. 1991). In this case, the court evaluated small details such as the number of ice machines and items available in the commissary. Where differences existed, they could be justified only if the gender-disparate treatment served important governmental objectives and the means employed were substantially related to the achievement of those objectives.

However, no great number of parity cases followed. While some cases were filed in several states, courts and state corrections departments usually worked out consent decrees. The few cases that have reached higher appeals courts have not been decided in favor of female inmates (Collins, 1998: 48). Courts that refuse to use an intermediate scrutiny standard (which requires an important and substantial interest before the state can employ differential treatment) do so for one of two reasons. First, there is precedent that requires an intermediate standard be used only when there is a case of direct discrimination; in cases where a facially neutral rule or law affects the sexes differently, the rational relationship test must be used (Collins, 1998: 49, citing *Personnel Administrator v. Feeney,* 442 U.S. 256 (1979)). The second reason courts refuse to use the intermediate standard is when they find that the sexes are not "similarly situated." If two groups are not "similarly situated," the state does not have to justify different treatment. (See *Klinger v. Department of Corrections,* 31 F.3d 727 (8th Cir. 1994), *cert. denied,* 115 S. Ct. 1177 (1995).)

In other cases, it is not clear what argument the court uses in its decision. In *Pargo v. Elliot,* 894 F. Supp. 1243 (W.D. Iowa), *aff'd,* 69 F.3d 280 (8th Cir. 1995), female prisoners in Iowa pursued a parity claim. They lost. The court said that a simple comparison between the programs for men and women was not appropriate and that a number of variables needed to be taken into account, including population size (which was explicitly rejected in prior cases), security level, types of crimes, length of sentence, and "other special characteristics."

In *Women Prisoners of the District of Columbia Dep't of Corrections v. District of Columbia,* 877 F. Supp. 634 (D.D.C. 1994), *rev'd in part,* 93 F.3d 910 (D.C. Cir. 1996), legal advocates for female prisoners were careful to show that the women's institution was comparable to the men's in terms of custody level, sentence structure, and purpose of incarceration before they proved that program opportunities were less adequate for the women. The lower court ordered broad relief, but was overturned by the circuit court. The court held that the men and women were not "similarly situated," noting the size of population and offering the possibility that the men were in for different crimes. Further, the holding indicated that a "comparison of programs approach" would not be entertained because prison administrators should be given "deference" to choose programs. The court did uphold the lower courts' ruling that educational and vocational programs must be equal or similar, and it did find that showing deliberate indifference to female inmates who were being sexually harassed and assaulted by male staff members was violative of the Eighth Amendment (Collins, 1998: 55).

CONCLUSION

In this chapter we have seen the difficulties of balancing equal treatment with special needs. This issue is not unique to prisons. Williams (1983) and many feminists writing in jurisprudence ponder the difficulties of equality versus justice, given the special positions of women and men, and the deeply held cultural beliefs about the role of each sex. From the time period in which women were civilly dead and a mere appendage to their husbands, to emerging rights with the married women's property laws in the mid-19th century, to the removal of sex-based differences in the 1970s in such areas as military benefits, social security, welfare, workers' compensation programs, alimony, and probate, the law has not worked well in determining or protecting the rights of women. Ironically, the equal protection challenges that often are successful are those in which men argue against some favorable treatment that women are supposed to be receiving. We have seen that equal protection cases filed by female C.O.s who desired promotional opportunities resulted in large numbers of male C.O.s working in prisons for women. Litigation challenging fewer educational and vocational programs and opportunities (such as work release) for women may have led to the trend of women's prisons adapting to male standards and procedures in the name of "parity." If Collins (1998) is correct that "parity" is dead, it means that courts have moved back to a deference test, where prisoners' rights and opportunities are contingent on prison officials' budgets and "expertise." What impact this may have on programming and services in women's prisons remains to be seen.

NOTES

1. These cases, and others, are cited in Barry, 1996.

2. Also see Collins and Collins, 1996.

SUGGESTED READINGS

Barry, E. 1991. "Jail Litigation Concerning Women Prisoners." *The Prison Journal* LXXI: 44–50.

Barry, E. 1996. "Women Prisoners and Health Care." In K. Moss (ed.), *Man-made Medicine,* pp. 250–272. Durham, NC: Duke University Press.

Collins, W. 1998. "Equal Protection and Women's Prisons: Is the Parity Era Over?" In J. Morton (ed.), *Complex Challenges, Collaborative Solutions: Programming for Adult and Juvenile Female Offenders,* pp. 43–61. Lanham, MD: American Correctional Association.

Collins, W., and A. Collins. 1996. *Women in Jail: Legal Issues.* Washington, D.C.: National Institute of Corrections.

8

Working in Prison:
Staff and Administration

P art of the uniqueness of women's prisons may be due to the correctional officers found there. At the women's institution, as at any "total institution," a chasm stretches between the staff and residents who live within the walls.[1] The relationship between these two groups is part of the nature of the total institution. As Goffman (1961) wrote:

> Each group tends to conceive of members of the other in terms of narrow hostile stereotypes, staff often seeing inmates as bitter, secretive, and

untrustworthy, while inmates often see staff as condescending, high-handed and mean. Staff tends to feel superior and righteous; inmates tend, in some ways at least, to feel inferior, weak, blameworthy and guilty. Social mobility between the two strata is grossly restricted; social distance is typically great and often prescribed; even talk across the boundaries may be conducted in a special tone of voice. The restrictions on contact presumably help to maintain the antagonistic stereotypes. In any case, two different social and cultural worlds develop, tending to jog along beside each other, with points of official contact but little mutual penetration. (Goffman, quoted in Glaser, 1964: 114)

Indeed, that is an apt description of any prison. Officers stereotype inmates as worthless and evil; inmates stereotype officers as lazy and ignorant. The lack of meaningful communication between the two groups makes the job harder for the officer and life more difficult for the inmate. The social distance between the groups makes casual mistreatment possible: officers may use their power to withhold necessities or humiliate inmates forced to ask for needed items. Note how Jean Harris, a firsthand observer, describes the predicament of being under the power of a correctional officer:

One must have experienced prison as an inmate to know into what kind of hands this power of destruction has been placed. The young c.o. who is presently pregnant with her third illegitimate baby . . . the woman who goaded me daily to get me to hit her so she could scream "assault" and have me put in solitary, the male c.o.'s who impregnate inmates, the female c.o. who gets so stoned on duty I have seen her struggle to unlock a door while pushing the key into the door two feet above where the lock was. Any one of these and many more like them could walk into my cell as I sit here and tear up the pictures of my sons and the manuscript I am writing and anything else that strikes their fancy. (Harris, 1988: 238)

The relationship between male inmates and officers has been documented by Sykes (1958), Carroll (1974), Jacobs (1977), Crouch (1980), Crouch and Marquart (1980), Irwin (1980), Johnson and Price (1981), and Owen (1985, 1988), among others. However, the women's prison is different from the men's prison in many ways. For example, the relationship between officers and inmates is characterized by less social distance and greater informal communication. Many descriptions of women's prisons note the maternalistic relationship that exists between officers and inmates (sometimes this relationship is described positively, sometimes negatively).

As previously noted, separate institutions for female offenders originally were created as places where female role models could influence their charges without the brutalizing and corrupting presence of men. This original premise led to female staff, who were socialized to approach their role differently from male officers in parallel positions. Moreover, most of the women in early institutions did not come from a military background, as did many of the male officers, but rather from social work and teaching backgrounds. They had no experience in custody control and approached their charges as they would a dependent client, child, or student. Consequently, the early histories reported staff and female inmates working together hand in hand to build new buildings or plant in the fields. Many of those attracted to corrections work were educated in women's colleges or possessed an almost religious fervor to change the lives of female offenders for the better.

As is true of all innovations in corrections, gradually the great experiment in women's reformatories slipped off track. The educated and zealous female reformers who had started the movement lost interest or became exhausted from their efforts, and they were replaced by those who saw corrections as a job rather than a vocation. Partly because qualified women were so rare and partly because administrators never really believed women could handle the responsibility of management, men stepped in to take control of the early institutions, and women were relegated to lower positions of authority. Over time, the women's institution in any particular state correctional system became last on the priority list for funds and other considerations. Female correctional officers did not have the same pay grade as men, nor was a position in a female facility considered comparable to a similar position in a men's facility. Women who worked in corrections as correctional officers did so for very pragmatic reasons rather than the idealistic motivations of their forerunners. The female correctional officer, until recently, was very different from the male correctional officer in how she was treated, in her reasons for entering corrections, and to a very large degree, in her opportunities for career advancement.

In the last several decades correctional staff have become less sex-segregated. That is, female officers can be found in prisons for men and male officers work in prisons for women. Although the legal challenges by female correctional officers who fought to be allowed into prisons for men began in the 1960s, the integration was slow and sporadic. By the mid-1980s we started to see evaluations of female officers in prisons and jails (see Peterson, 1982; Zimmer, 1986, 1989; Zupan, 1986, 1992b). These evaluations compared male and female officers on various indices of performance—including academy training, discipline ticket writing, and ability to respond appropriately to hypothetical situations posed to them. Evaluations also conducted surveys of male officers and male inmates rating the female officers' performance. Findings indicated that, overall, they were grudgingly accepted by inmates and younger male officers and that there was a belief they might be more effective than male officers in some areas ("talking to" inmates), but in other areas, both inmates and officers distrusted their effectiveness (stopping fights, subduing an inmate). While some believed they created a dangerous situation and were an unnecessary distraction, others believed they "normalized" the prison and male inmates behaved better because of the presence of female officers.

The flip side of equal employment has been that male officers must also have an equal opportunity to work in women's prisons. A woman might desire to work in a men's facility because it is closer to home, she has an easier time supervising men (see Pollock, 1986), or she wants to be promoted and must work in a range of custody levels and types of facilities before being considered for promotion. The first two reasons may explain why men desire to work in a women's prison, but not the last—working in a women's prison does not usually assist in promotion. Men also point out that they feel safer in a prison for women; no doubt that is a consideration. Interestingly, contrary to the situation with female officers in prisons for men, evidently it has occurred to no one to test men's effectiveness in prisons for women, to survey whether female officers think men can do the job as well as female officers, or to evaluate men's performance in academy training areas that are relevant to prisons for women.

In some state systems, men now outnumber women as correctional officers in women's prisons, yet their effectiveness has not been evaluated or even questioned. Recently numerous incidences of sexual assault and harassment of female inmates have drawn attention to the presence of men in prisons for women. There have been a steady stream of allegations, investigations, indictments, and convictions over sexual abuse and exploitation. This issue will be addressed in a later section.

FEMALE CORRECTIONAL OFFICERS

In the past, female workers were believed to have different habits, motivations, skills, and worth than men. Despite recent advances, women are still clustered in "female occupations," such as nursing, social work, and education—fields that emphasize nurturant skills and traditional, "feminine" attributes. Most women work in nonmanual, white-collar occupations, as do most men, but men are also distributed across other categories. A much larger percentage of women than men are in clerical and manual, blue-collar positions (Baker, 1987: 172). Fields with large numbers of women are observed to be more centralized, with less autonomy for the individual worker. This tendency supposedly resulted from the psychological characteristics of female workers, including a greater deference to authority, greater need for approval and association, guilt about expressing aggressiveness, and less opposition to centralization because of less commitment to the job and less concern with decision making (Marrett, 1972).

More recent research disputes these assumptions. Much of the current literature either finds no differences or explains the differences as resulting from differential job demands or other factors (Baker, 1987: 183; Nieva and Gutek, 1981: 85). Further, women were believed to have personal characteristics (compliance, submissiveness, emotionality) that made them unsuitable for leadership or supervisory positions (Nieva and Gutek, 1981). These supposedly feminine traits also created the perception that women were unsuitable for work with offenders, except for juveniles and female offenders.

Whether women in leadership roles perform differently from men is not clear. Results of research are mixed. Some studies report that women emphasize "human" factors, while men emphasize "task" factors. Other research, however, can find no differences between the two groups. Older studies indicate that the nurturant role of women may be carried with them into the workplace. For instance, female supervisors have been perceived as performing more supportive functions than men in a similar position (Bayes and Newton, 1978; Lipman-Blumen and Tickmayer, 1975). Even when women and men have the same occupation, women may bring more nurturing qualities to the job. For instance, female teachers may engage in more personal relationships with their students, female social workers and counselors may emphasize the importance of the relationship over achievement goals, and female managers may use a more personal style of supervision. However, studies that rate women's and men's leadership find negligible differences on certain objective measures (Nieva and Gutek, 1981: 86). One might conclude that women may emphasize a less task-directed and more personal style of supervision when they have the flexibility to do so, but when the environment demands a certain style of supervision—for instance, the military, where some studies finding no differences were performed—women follow the pattern in which they have been trained.

Perceptions and expectations of workers regarding female supervisors are also different. Whereas women are rated more negatively for direct approaches and authoritarian, unemotional styles of supervision, they are rated less negatively than men for using an emotional style of supervision (Nieva and Gutek, 1981: 87–88). These findings indicate that, despite work pattern changes and the employment of the majority of women outside the home in modern society, sex roles are hard to change. Women can still be found in certain occupations (probably more from self-selection than discrimination today); they also may bring different characteristics to an occupation or adapt themselves to it in a different way. Women who entered corrections not only inherited the legacy of early reformatory ideals, but also were influenced by their socialization and predilections for how they saw and responded to others. Research in corrections has found that the female correctional officer performs her role differently from male C.O.s in some ways. As a result, the prison for women, when it is staffed primarily by women, is different from the men's prison.

Matrons

As already noted, most early women's prisons were built so that female staff could guide and advise female inmates in a setting away from the influence of men. This separation from men was felt to be important because female offenders were perceived to have experienced only negative male-female relationships, either having been exploited by men or having manipulated men to their own advantage. Before the emergence of this concept of the fallen or misguided woman, female offenders were thought of as worse than male offenders and as irredeemable. They were guarded by men in separate wings or buildings in men's facilities and subjected to various forms of mistreatment and sexual exploitation. Parisi (1984) notes, for instance, that women were isolated in a separate wing in Auburn Prison in 1825, but no matrons were hired until 1832. Even then, the managers and administrators were men until the women were moved to Bedford Hills and other separate facilities for women in New York.

The rise of the reformatory movement opened new avenues of employment for educated women and provided them with opportunities to use their newfound skills and experience independent careers. Some of the early administrators were influenced by religious motives as well as altruistic ones. Few of the early administrators were feminists *per se;* that is, they did not necessarily support equal rights for women but rather believed women had a special and exalted place in society, as the bearers of children and keepers of the home. Because of the importance of the woman's role, it was necessary to guide the female offenders back to an ideal of womanhood (Rafter, 1985).

Lekkerkerker (1931), in her review of women's prisons in the early 1900s, found that almost all who came in contact with female offenders in women's prisons were female, even the physicians. The sole exceptions were sometimes dentists and the farmers who supervised the fields. Some states had laws specifying that the officers be women, and several states had laws requiring that a woman be hired as the superintendent (Lekkerkerker, 1931: 272). These early female administrators initiated many reforms in institutional corrections that are still with us today. The presence of libraries, music programs, recreation, formal education, and other reforms were initiated by female administrators. Because of the lower security risk presented by female offenders, women's prisons were the locale for many forms of innovative programming. For instance, some early institutions had very little in the way of security. Women were not placed behind bars and stone walls, since they were not considered dangerous. Some programs placed women in the community as house servants, in a kind of early work-release program. Female administrators often had the luxury of starting from scratch, since women's prisons were built with no models to pattern themselves after, thus allowing the administrator to create her own conception of an ideal prison.

The line staff in these early reformatories may have had some education, but many took their positions for purely pragmatic reasons. The reformatories offered bed and board as well as a small salary, an attractive aspect of the job for those who had to support themselves. The women sacrificed a great deal of freedom and privacy for this privilege, however, and were watched almost as closely as the inmates in their private lives and personal habits.

Lekkerkerker (1931) described the life of the matron in early institutions. Matrons were usually paid no more than domestics except in a few institutions and the federal system, although the salaries of those who worked in institutions for white women were much higher than those who worked in institutions housing African-American women (1931: 278). The shifts were long and there were few days off. For instance, Lekkerkerker reports that in Iowa, female staff had half a day off every third Sunday and one to three weeks of vacation a year, depending on length of service. In Ohio, matrons worked 12-hour shifts and received two days off each month. Massachusetts, perhaps the most lenient state, allowed a day and a half off each week and three weeks of vacation (Lekkerkerker, 1931: 279). Officers were prohibited from cooking for themselves and had to take their meals in a common dining room; they were not allowed visitors and had nowhere to go during free time because of the isolated location of the institution. Cottage matrons lived with the inmates. Even when officers did not live in the inmate quarters, staff housing was not much better than that provided for inmates, and in some cases it was the same as inmate housing.

Despite these drawbacks, institutional corrections was one of the few fields in which educated women could work. Lekkerkerker (1931) described the importance of good matrons as essential for the institution:

> There is a real place in the reformatory for "matrons" in the good sense of the word, women of great refinement and intelligent social workers, who know not only to create a fine home atmosphere, but who above all have the confidence of their charges and know how to help them in re-adjusting their personalities. Viewed in this light, the work of the cottage matrons should be considered a "key-position" only to be trusted to the best. Unfortunately, rather the opposite meaning seems to prevail in many institutions, if one considers the low salaries of the matrons and the position these officers occupy. (1931: 265)

> The type of person who could handle this important function was very special. Generally, reformatory officers should be physically and mentally healthy, well-balanced, even-tempered, socially mature women, with steady moral standards and a cheerful disposition. . . . The officers should undoubtedly be women who know life and the world at large, and who have what may be called a convincing personality; the woman who feels her own life as a failure or who is emotionally repressed usually has small success with delinquent women who instinctively sense her weaknesses and have only contempt for her. It is especially important that the offi-cers have a wholesome and objective understanding of and attitude towards sex, for they will often have to deal with sexual problems, and it is almost entirely through the attitudes and reactions of the officers that the inmates have to gain a correct interpretation of sexual questions which many of them so badly need. (Lekkerkerker, 1931: 273)

Lekkerkerker (1931) observed that the matron, who was responsible for all aspects of the inmate's supervision, was being replaced by specialists in educa-tion and counseling. This change was accompanied by instructions to the matron staff prohibiting them from becoming involved in the personal lives of the inmates (1931: 262). Obviously, the increasing professionalization of coun-seling staff during this period changed the role of the female matron. The author bemoaned the specialization and the way it deprived the matron of the more important features of her role; she was relegated to mere supervision by this time and was not expected to know or influence the female offenders she supervised.

The other problem with decreasing the responsibilities of the matron was that educated and ambitious women no longer were interested in the position. As other avenues of employment opened up for women, especially in educa-tion and social work, it was no doubt more difficult to attract them to corrections.

Consequently, the matron role grew to be less important as a role model for female inmates and instead became more custodial. Women were attracted to the matron job increasingly for purely financial and pragmatic reasons.

The history of women's reformatories implies that the early institutions were havens of enlightenment and good staff care. This depiction is probably not accurate. For every educated and enlightened administrator or matron, many more saw their function in a harsher light. Although brutality has never been as prevalent in institutions for women, certain practices, such as cold baths and isolation, were just as painful as practices found in prisons for men. A few staff in any custodial institution succumb to the temptation to abuse their position. Women, unfortunately, are no better than men in this regard; female staff are just as capable of using their positions to unnecessarily taunt and humiliate the inmates under their control. Outright abuses, however, are rarely documented. The more insidious tendency of the female staff in women's prisons is to maternalize their relationship with inmates, treating them in a manner that does not recognize their adulthood. This tendency still holds true today.

Female Officers Today

Women who work in corrections today are very different from their forerunners in the reformatory era or even in the early 1900s. Women seek correctional positions because of job security and the salary, which, in some states, is hard to match in any other unskilled position. Some women hope for a career in corrections, and these women seek more education and pursue advancement through diverse work assignments and affiliation with professional organizations. Many women, however, like many men, view the work as "just a job," and one with substantial drawbacks, especially for women with children (Chapman, 1983).

A 1979 survey reported that only 29.3 percent of correctional workers were women; moreover, these women were overrepresented in clerical and support functions, and only 41 percent of them had contact with prisoners. Many of these women worked in institutions for women and juveniles. Women, on average, were younger and had less experience than male correctional officers, and their salary levels were lower. Parisi (1984) reported that in 1966, only 10 female institutions were headed by women. Strickland reported in 1976 that of the 30 facilities for women in existence, only 3 were headed by men (1976: 139). Crawford reported that by the late 1980s, 56 percent of the facilities for women were headed by women (1988a: 12).

Women in corrections seem to be less likely than men to list corrections as a career goal; they more often chose it because of financial reasons or because the job was close to home. They seem to have lower career aspirations than men, lower job satisfaction, and less positive attitudes toward employee relations (Chapman, 1983). Jurik and Halemba (1984) found that women had different reasons than men for going into corrections; women often had an interest in human service work, while men were more likely to cite job security, salary, and fringe benefits. (Whether these differences still exist today is debatable.)

Because a correctional institution is somewhat like a paramilitary organization, female staff members may feel uncomfortable operating within it. The nature of a bureaucracy leaves little room for flexibility and personality; thus, women may have a hard time adjusting to the constraints of such an occupation, whereas men may have experienced similar situations. Women in corrections usually have children to support—in fact, that is often why they work as correctional officers in the first place, since it provides a steady source of income to someone likely to be unskilled and without a college degree. Correctional work, however, is peculiarly unsuited to the working mother. The shifts are long, and overtime, even involuntary overtime, is not uncommon. There is often no chance to leave work during an emergency, and sometimes it is very difficult for family or child-care workers to reach the officer-mother at work.

Institutions are often far away from urban centers, and women either live in the small towns where the institutions are located or commute long distances. Often women come from the rural area that surrounds the prison, in which case they have very little in common with the primarily urban inmate population. Female correctional officers may come from a corrections family; that is, they may have fathers, brothers, or husbands who also work in corrections. Although working in corrections as a family allows the family to share problems and discuss their work, facilities for men and women often differ in regard to rule enforcement and other practices.

When the woman has no family involved in corrections, she is often forced to explain and defend her reasons for entering such a profession. Lurid movies that portray women's institutions as hotbeds of lesbian activity accompanied by guard brutality fuel the imagination of friends and relatives. When African-American women from urban areas enter correctional work, they face unique problems. Often they come from the same neighborhoods as the women they supervise; they may even know people in common with the prisoners. The female correctional officers are viewed as "cops," and many inmates are openly hostile to what they see as betrayal on the part of the officers.

Although most states have academies now that train correctional officers before placing them in facilities, little training is provided to prepare the female officer for the facility for women. The academies are largely geared for male officers who will be transferred to prisons for men. Consequently, all the rules, procedures, and problems discussed relate to facilities for males. If women's institutions are mentioned, it is often in a comparative manner, indicating the "peculiarities" of women's prisons. Typically, state correctional systems have moved from an approach that isolates and differentiates the women's institution to an approach that alleges that all inmates and all prisons are the same in terms of rules, supplies, assignments, and other factors. This latter approach is no more helpful than the benign neglect that previously characterized the central office's attention to facilities for women; women's prisons are unique environments that have supervision issues distinct from those for men.

Female Officers in Men's Prisons

In the 1980s and 1990s, female C.O.s began to work in prisons for men. A study in the early 1980s found that most correctional institutions had female staff; in fact, an average of 8.4 percent of the staff in surveyed facilities were women. However, these women typically had restricted assignments, such as in the administration building or in the visiting room where they were employed to search female visitors (Parisi, 1984: 95).

In *Dothard v. Rawlinson,* 433 U.S. 321 (1977), Diane Rawlinson challenged Alabama's rules that kept her from working in the men's penitentiary. In this case, the U.S. Supreme Court overturned the use of height and weight restrictions unless the state could show how they were related to the job; but it did uphold the state's argument that, because of the violence and conditions of the Alabama state prison, it would be dangerous to allow women to work there. However, *Dothard* was a narrow ruling, applying only to Alabama's prison, and many states interpreted the dictum in the case as supportive of women's right to work in men's prisons (Jacobs, 1979). Title VII of the Civil Rights Act forbids sex discrimination at all levels of employment except when sex is a bona fide occupational qualification. Since states have been unable to show that height and weight restrictions or sex itself influences what is necessary to be an effective correctional officer, the number of women in men's prisons has increased substantially.

The hesitancy in allowing women to work in facilities for men was the same as the resistance met by women who entered the police force as patrol officers in the early 1970s. Basically, the traits that have been considered "feminine" in our society are inconsistent with the tasks of correctional and law enforcement personnel. Women's control has tended to be emotional and affectional in this society, not derived from the use of fear or intimidation. Since it is difficult to imagine any emotional ties between inmates and staff, the general consensus was that women would be unable to control male inmates; also, their peculiarly "feminine" traits, such as seductiveness, fearfulness, and weakness, would make them a danger to themselves and to colleagues. "Male" traits such as emotional detachment, assertiveness, and aggressiveness are considered more suited to the prison environment (Coles, 1980). It was felt that not only would women be poor officers, but their presence also would entice male inmates to sexual assault or acts of homosexuality. Like female police officers, women in corrections have had to struggle against strong resistance.

Other similarities between police officers and correctional officers exist. In both fields, women have been present for a long time, but only recently have their positions been equal to those of men. In law enforcement, women were placed in juvenile departments and as matrons in local jails beginning in the late 1800s. Women in corrections were relegated to institutions for women and juveniles. In both areas, the placement of women was due to the perceived role of women in society and the unique contributions women could make in working with those special groups of offenders. However, when women

became tired of being limited to narrow career ladders and restricted assignments and recognized that these restrictions also meant lower salaries, they
sought court help in breaking employment barriers based on sex.

Women in law enforcement and in corrections encountered a great deal of
resistance on the part of their male colleagues. Although education and age had
some influence on the receptivity of males to the entry of females, ordinarily a
great deal of sexual harassment and scapegoating went on. While female police
officers reported being made the target of sexual jokes and innuendos, and being
prevented—sometimes physically—from engaging in physical altercations with
suspects, female correctional officers reported much the same experiences when
they entered the prisons for men. Female correctional officers still report having male officers proposition them in front of male inmates and having supervisors threaten them with poor assignments or termination to gain their sexual
acquiescence. While those working in the field today cannot imagine the hostility and harassment that the women of 20 years ago faced, there is still a degree
of suspicion and resentment directed to female officers in both fields.

Women who adapt to correctional work and law enforcement by adopting
male behavior patterns in voice and manner experience a fair degree of stress
in other parts of their lives. Women report that it is hard to be authoritarian at
work and go home to be "mommy." Relationships with male colleagues are
often difficult in that a balance always has to be struck between being friendly
and being thought of as sexually available—being "one of the boys" or designated as the fraternity whore. Arguably, there is less role dysfunction for female
C.O.s who work in institutions for women. The feminization of the institution
guarantees that female officers need not adapt themselves to a role that emphasizes "machismo," as does the police officer role and the role of officers in prisons for men. With the increasing number of men in women's prisons, however,
it will be interesting to see whether the women's institution, and the female
officer who works there, will adopt styles of supervision more common in
men's prisons.

Evaluations of Performance Findings from evaluations of women in both
law enforcement and corrections have been generally positive. Studies that
evaluated female police officers found some differences in the way women
patrolled. They were said to patrol "less aggressively," meaning they made fewer
arrests and had fewer altercations with citizens. They also had more "good
arrests" and fewer complaints. Some weak areas included shooting firearms and
driving skills, but in most areas of evaluation, such as number of sick days, calls
for help, use of backups, or departmental ratings, the men and women were
rated as substantially the same (Block and Anderson, 1974; Martin, 1980).

Evaluations of female correctional officers in prisons for men or in cocorrectional institutions indicate that women may not get assigned to certain
posts where administrators feel security might be risked. However, they are perceived as competent in giving first aid, cooling down angry inmates, and dealing with verbally abusive inmates. They are perceived as less competent in
handling physical altercations. Most correctional officers surveyed got along

equally well with both sexes, but men were less likely to rate female officers as excellent or good. This study found that inmates reacted to the presence of women by improving their appearance and language and behaving more politely toward the female officers. Three out of four male officers and 80 percent of the inmates gave female officers favorable ratings (Kissel and Seidel, 1980).

Martin (1980) found that one problem of female police officers that probably applies to female correctional officers as well was that they lacked the anticipatory socialization men brought to the work. They had less experience with aggression in organized sports and less experience with teamwork or authority; they had to learn these patterns of behavior. They needed to develop an authoritative tone and learn new facial expressions that indicated authority rather than subservience. They had to restrain themselves from smiling as much as is natural for a woman socialized in this society. They needed to learn to use more direct language to convey instructions, rather than requesting or suggesting what they wanted. All of these "deficiencies" were due to the socialized role of women in this society, and the "masculine" characteristics of the law enforcement and corrections job.

Most of the research in this area supports the notion that female officers can and do perform their role quite adequately in men's prisons despite the problems associated in entering a previously all-male bastion of employment (Bowersox, 1981; Coles, 1980; Crouch, 1985; Nicolai, 1981). The two most cited studies in this area are those by Zupan (1986, 1992b) and Zimmer (1986, 1989). Jurik and Halemba (1984; also see Jurik, 1985a & b, 1988) found that while there were no differences between men and women in "work adjustment" measures or job satisfaction, women did experience higher levels of job stress. These researchers also noted that women tended to prefer more structure while men preferred more discretion in the performance of their job. Another finding was that women showed no "greater sensitivity" to inmate needs.

Zupan (1992b) noted that the percentage of female C.O.s assigned to prisons for men varied between states—in Alabama, 85 percent of all female officers worked in male prisons, but in North Carolina, less than 1 percent of the state's female C.O.s worked in prisons for men. Reviewing the literature available on female C.O.s working in prisons for men, including her own 1986 study, Zupan concluded that no significant differences had been found in performance measures. Still, in the 1990s, women continued to face tokenism, differential treatment by supervisors, and opposition by male coworkers.

Zimmer (1986) found that women desired to work as correctional officers in prisons for men because of the financial benefits and/or lack of alternative job opportunities. These women had quite conservative (traditional) sex role beliefs. Zimmer found that female officers in prisons for men tended to exhibit different adaptations to their jobs: the institutional role (these women followed rules and acted like male officers); the modified role (they allowed men to protect them and utilized sex roles for job "favors"); and the inventive role (they managed to balance their femininity and the demands of the job).

Zimmer (1989) pointed out that legal action put women into institutions, but differential assignments kept them as tokens. Zimmer concluded that women continued to face sexual harassment, teasing, shunning, verbal opposition, and discriminatory treatment. This might have been partly because they routinely received differential job assignments that limited contact with inmates and promotional opportunities. She concluded that administrators needed to assign equally and make it perfectly clear that harassment would not be tolerated (1989: 67). Whether this has occurred since Zimmer's study in the late 1980s is questionable.

More recent reviews of female officers' performances have continued to find generally that women perform equally to men (Wright and Saylor, 1991). Lawrence and Mahan (1998) reviewed prior studies and conducted a survey study of their own in Minnesota. They obtained 162 useable responses from correctional officers, with a little over half of the respondents (53 percent) being men. More female respondents than male respondents thought women were accepted by male officers, and more women believed that inmates accepted women. As with older studies, these researchers found that age was a factor in men's beliefs regarding hiring women (with older men less supportive). It was clear that women were still not wholly accepted as correctional officers. For instance, 61 percent of men but only 32 percent of women thought women were in more danger. Most men did not believe women were as effective in controlling physical altercations. Fewer men than women believed women performed adequately in all roles, although the differences were sometimes small. For instance, in performing supervisory tasks, 88 percent of men but 99 percent of women thought women performed adequately; other tasks surveyed included report writing (84 percent of men compared to 99 percent of women), sufficient force (40 percent of men compared to 89 percent of women), and controlling fights (44 percent of men compared to 96 percent of women) (1998: 80). Thus, after 20 years of women working in prisons for men, there has not been much change in male officers' perceptions regarding women's effectiveness in certain areas of supervision (see Lovrich and Stohr, 1993; also see Pogrebin and Poole, 1997). Note that these evaluations are ratings by other officers, not objective indices of women's performance. Determining whether women are truly less effective in controlling fights or using sufficient force would require different research methods.

MEN GUARDING WOMEN

When women began to work in prisons for men, it was inevitable that male officers would increase their numbers in prisons for women. In fact, the existence of cocorrectional facilities and men guarding women means that we have now come full circle to the time before the first reformatory for women was built. Unfortunately, it appears this means that many female inmates now have to fear the same type of sexual exploitation and assault that women in the 1800s suffered.

The legal challenges to male officers working in prisons for women were discussed in Chapter 7. In this chapter, we will revisit the issue with an emphasis on the management and interactional issues present when men guard women. Issues that are discussed include the reasons for the increase, the effect that larger numbers of male officers have on supervision in the women's prison, and the problem of sexual abuse and harassment by male officers of female inmates.

Increasing Numbers

Crawford reported that in 1988, about 35 percent of the correctional officers in women's prisons were men (1988b: 13); today, the figure is much higher. Nesbitt (1992) reported that in 1992, almost half (46 percent) of staff in women's prisons were men. The most current statistics indicate that the average percentage of men in women's facilities is about 41 percent (Human Rights Watch, 1996: 51). Zupan (1992a: 200) found that certain states were much higher; for instance, while there were no male officers in two states (Arkansas and Delaware), in Colorado, 81 percent of officers in a women's prison were men. Many states had over 50 percent: New York, 72 percent; Michigan, 67 percent; California and Oklahoma, 63 percent. Forty-three states allowed men to supervise living units; eight did not. Owen (1998: 165) reported that at the California Institution where she conducted research, about 70 percent of the staff were men.

This is an amazing change from prior decades when women's facilities were staffed primarily by women. It is not clear why so many men have ended up in prisons for women while the numbers of women in men's prisons have remained quite small. Probably one reason is that corrections is not an occupation of choice for large numbers of women. Corrections departments fill staff positions in prisons for women with men because, quite simply, more men than women are applying for the jobs.

As discussed in the last chapter, the increased numbers of men in women's institutions have meant that sometimes men observe women showering and using the toilet, and they may conduct pat downs and even strip searches. Zupan (1992a: 302) found that less than half of the facilities employing male officers made physical changes (e.g., shower doors) to protect women's privacy; however, a little over half made policy changes (e.g., revised dress code, special training, or having a same-sex officer on the unit at all times). She found that 13 states allowed pat searches; 15 allowed them with some restrictions; 18 allowed them only in emergencies; and 16 did not allow pat searches by male officers at all. Five states allowed strip searches by male officers; 29 states allowed them in an emergency; and 28 states disallowed strip searches by men completely (1992a: 303–304).

The arguments in favor of men in women's prisons is that they "normalize" the environment and that women behave better and have better hygiene (Zupan, 1992a: 304). Interestingly, these are the same arguments used to support the presence of women in men's prisons. The female inmates that Owen

(1998) talked to said they felt "safer" around male officers and that "it is more natural to take orders from a man" (1998: 165). They also admitted that men were easier to manipulate with tears and flattery.

Zupan (1992a) provides one of the few studies that surveyed inmate perceptions regarding the presence of male officers. She interviewed 113 inmates in one prison. Overall, the majority of inmates were positive toward male officers; in fact, they indicated they preferred to be supervised by male officers because they believed male officers treated them more fairly, more respectfully, and more honestly than did female officers: "Men are dominant and women are used to being told what to do by men and they do it. Women [officers] tell them what to do and inmates buck it" (1992a: 304). Zupan also found that female inmates felt more comfortable discussing personal problems with female officers and disagreed strongly with male officers doing pat searches or strip searches (1992a: 307). Female inmates indicated that male officers were more respected, made "better" officers, were more likely to overlook minor rule infractions, and were more easily "conned," while female officers were more likely to get into verbal arguments, show favoritism, and use physical force. Inmates indicated that both male and female officers were equally likely to help inmates with problems. About 20 percent of the women believed men worked there to get sex or because they felt safer there than in the men's prison (1992a: 307).

Masculinizing the Women's Prison

The larger number of male officers and the increasing practice of transferring officers back and forth between facilities for men and women means there is greater pressure to make prisons for women more "normal"—meaning more like prisons for men. More stringent security measures and more formalized interactions between inmates and C.O.s are two developments that have occurred. Women's institutions, because of their small size, have, in the past, enjoyed the luxury of often being run in a manner more personal than efficient. Although there were procedures and rules, the top administrators were relatively accessible, and there was less of a hierarchy.

Female officers often prefer to work with male inmates, but male officers in the past have not expressed a preference for supervising female inmates. Men find it difficult to interact with female inmates; they are troubled by the possibility of rape charges, and they find it difficult to disassociate their culturally induced attitudes toward women from their security role.

> I know how to handle [men]. . . . Now with females, all my life I've been brought up to protect them and respect them, so when you have to use force, it's difficult. (Pollock, 1981)

In Pollock's (1986) study, the few men who did prefer to work with female inmates felt that way because of the greater degree of safety, the possibility of "reaching" the inmate because she was more expressive, and the more "light-hearted" nature of the institution (Pollock, 1986).

Sexual Abuse and Harassment

The most troubling aspect of the increasing numbers of men in prisons for women is the continuing and consistent stream of allegations, investigations, indictments, and convictions over sexual assault and sexual harassment of female inmates by male officers. Researchers and articles have noted reports of sexual abuses in a number of states (see Baro, 1997; Cook, 1993; Curriden, 1993). A report by Human Rights Watch (1996) provided details of sexual abuse in California, Washington D.C., Georgia, Illinois, Michigan, and New York.

Amnesty International (1999: 38) published a condemnatory report concerning this issue. This report included excerpts from findings of the U.S. Justice Department after an investigation of sexual abuse in Michigan:

> Nearly every inmate we interviewed reported various sexually aggressive acts of guards. A number of women reported that officers routinely "corner" women in their cells or on their work details in the kitchen or laundry room and press their bodies against them, mocking sexual intercourse. Women described incidents where guards exposed their genitals while making sexually suggestive remarks. (reported in Amnesty International, 1999: 38)

The Department of Justice investigation also found that officers routinely watched women shower and that they squeezed their breasts, buttocks, and genital areas during pat down searches in a way unwarranted by legitimate security needs. Michigan disputes the Department of Justice findings, and legal action is ongoing at this time. However, Michigan is not alone. The Amnesty International (1999) report chronicled a long list of incidents.

- The U.S. Justice Department also investigated the Julia Tutwiler prison in 1994.

- In Arizona, more than 60 people have been disciplined or dismissed for sexual relations with inmates since 1992.

- Amnesty International has received reports of sexual harassment at Valley State Prison in California.

- Inmates won a lawsuit against the Federal Bureau of Prisons for sexual abuse against them at Pleasanton, California (in this case, guards took money from male inmates to be allowed to enter women's cells at night and sexually assault them).

- In Florida, a former guard was sentenced to prison in 1998 for raping a female inmate.

- A Florida inmate hung herself after writing letters to a judge, detailing sexual harassment.

- Guards have been disciplined, fired, and indicted for sexual abuse in Idaho, Illinois, Maryland, Massachusetts, New Hampshire, New York, Ohio, Texas, Virginia, Washington, Washington D.C., West Virginia, and Wyoming.

A cursory review of newspapers and magazines also reveals examples of this problem:

- "Coercing Sex Behind Bars" (Meyer, 1992)
- "Caldwell Jailers Accused of Sex with an Inmate" (Gee, 2000)
- "Texas Rangers Investigating Rockwell Jail" (Bensman and Mosier, 2000)
- "Jailers Indicted on Sex Charges" (Quin, 1999)
- "Sex Scandal Erupts at Women's Prison" (Dayton, 1991)
- "Georgia Indictments Charge Abuse of Female Inmates" (Watson, 1992)
- "Sex Abuse Charges Rock Women's Prison" (Sewenely, 1993)

This is not a new issue. Hanson (1983: 669) noted that one of the issues of the *Forts v. Ward* case in New York was sexual abuse, and part of the court record included the rape indictment against one officer and the guilty plea of official misconduct from another male officer. Mann (1984) discussed this problem and offered the following quotation from another researcher:

> In my interviews with more than 50 women serving time in southern jails or work-release programs, inmate after inmate repeated virtually the same stories of what happened to them, or to the woman in the next cell: the oral sex through bars; the constant intrusion of male trustees who slither in and out of the women's cells as unrestricted as the rats and roaches; the threats of "you do, or else. . . ." (Sims, reported in Mann, 1984: 245)

The problem seems to be becoming more prevalent with the larger number of male officers in women's prisons. For instance, in Austin, Texas, 11 former guards and a case manager at a state jail run by Wackenhut Corporation were indicted on criminal sex charges, and 12 others were charged with sexual assault and improper sexual activity (felonies) or misdemeanor sexual harassment against 16 female inmates, with the events evidently occurring between May 1997 and August 1999. This incident led to the state removing all female inmates and sending them to the state-run women's prison in Gatesville, Texas, and taking the management contract away from Wackenhut Corporation (Gee, 2000; Quin, 1999).

Not long after this occurred, two male officers in a nearby county were dismissed for having sexual relations with female inmates (Gee, 2000). The allegations were that county jail officers gave drugs and alcohol to female inmates in exchange for sex. The Texas Rangers were called in to investigate this pattern of activity that evidently had been going on for two years (Bensman and Mosier, 2000).

States have now begun to pass laws that make it a felony to have sexual relations with an inmate; 36 states have such laws. Thirteen states make the sexual relationship a crime even if it was consensual, while three make it a crime for the inmate as well (Amnesty International, 1999: 49). In New York, a dozen state guards have been charged under the law since its inception in 1996—nine were convicted, two charges were dismissed, and one is pending (Kuo, 2000). Other states are in the process of considering such statutes (Ginsberg, 1999).

In many situations, state officials refuse to admit there is a problem, despite widespread allegations and even proven incidents. For instance, the Virginia Department of Corrections concluded there were no "patterns of sexual assault, harassment or fraternization" at the Fluvanna Correctional Center for Women, even though 13 prison employees had been fired or resigned because of violating prison rules and 5 others were disciplined. Even though the report concluded there was no pattern of abuse, it recommended video surveillance and rotation of guards (Ginsberg, 1999).

Amnesty International (1999: 47) pointed out that under international law, the rape of a prisoner by correctional staff is considered to be an act of torture, and international standards specify same-sex guards for body searches and supervision of shower areas. In effect, the United States is one of the worst violators of international standards regarding the treatment of female prisoners. Amnesty International recommended that men should be removed from women's prisons entirely and women should be guarded only by female officers (1999: 61).

In some states, incidents have led to considering the option recommended by Amnesty International—that is, removing men from women's prisons. In New York, the Department of Corrections is considering removing men from the living quarters of women because of issues of privacy and potential abuse (Kuo, 2000). In Westchester County, New York, the arrest of four guards prompted county officials to remove male guards from women's quarters (Kuo, 2000).

Michigan was considering a same-sex policy (dropped in 1985) because of the allegations of sexual abuse in women's prisons described earlier. The officers' union was against such a move because it "limited opportunities" and predicted that if the Department of Corrections were to go through with the policy, there would be a wave of lawsuits by C.O.s. An attorney for female inmates pointed out that because there were over 24 confirmed incidents of sexual contact between staffers and inmates in four years, the state had a fairly good argument as to why such a policy was necessary (Heinlein, 1999).

The defense of some officers is that the relationship was consensual or that the woman "seduced" the officer. Obviously these relationships do not all follow a pattern of a sexually predatory male and a hapless female victim. In fact, inmates themselves recognize that some amount of sexual attraction is inevitable when you have men in women's prisons.

> As far as the male officers, a lot of the women around here are flirtatious. Now, if they see you undressed, they're going to look. They're men. They can write you up, but a lot of them don't. They give you a verbal warning. 'Cause they like to look. . . . If an officer just pays attention to one of the women, she'll think he likes her. We got an officer in our cottage now. He's just a gentleman. He don't mean no harm. He's not out to hit on the girls. But just the way he talks, women think he be coming on to them. But he's an all right man. (Wojda and Rowe, 1997: 27)

It must be recognized, however, that there can be no real voluntary consent given by a female inmate because of the differential power relationship between an officer and inmate. There is always the implicit or explicit threat to use the officer's authority to make trouble for the female inmate. Women fear retaliation if they report harassment, and if they do report it, they have difficulty making people believe them instead of the officer. Further, women in prison have often had extremely dysfunctional relationships with men, for example, they may have been sexually abused as children by father figures; men in positions of authority who desire sex from them may be forcing them to relive childhood abuse trauma (Veysey, DeCou, and Prescott, 1998). In some cases, women have been socialized their whole life to bargain with their sexuality; thus, a sexual relationship with a male officer continues a life-long pattern of sexual exploitation.

OFFICER SUBCULTURE

Research illustrates the unique subculture of the correctional officer. As with police officers, the working hours, stigmatization, and frequent isolation of the job create a certain solidarity among officers. This solidarity is marked by reticence with outsiders and protection of members. Correctional officers who break rules are sometimes protected by their fellow officers in the same way that police officers are protected by the "blue shield of secrecy." In recent years, again similarly to police officers, this solidarity has been broken down by the integration of minority and female officers who neither come from the same backgrounds nor are as receptive to the same values as officers in years past. The homogeneity of the workplace gives way to heterogeneity, and officer solidarity is broken down and replaced by more formal and bureaucratic methods of dealing with daily events.

In the correctional officer force, minorities and women have broken the ranks of the white, rural guard subculture, and the result has been similar to what has occurred in police forces. Also, civil suits and possible individual liability or perjury charges have resulted in more C.O.s coming forward with evidence of correctional officer misdeeds. It is safe to say that today the correctional officer subculture is a much different one from that of earlier years. There is greater professionalization, greater bureaucratization, and less solidarity. In the women's prison, the officer subculture never reached the degree of intensity observed in prisons for men. The reasons for this are unclear. It may be that there was less homogeneity in the female officer population, or that the less severe nature of the institution did not create a need for a strong subculture. It is also possible that there was a subculture so different from the male subculture as to be unrecognizable.

One can use the deprivation and importation theories to explain officer subcultures as well as inmate subcultures. Deprivation theory would suggest that because staff members in a women's prison are not faced with the same degree of danger and isolation, they have less need to create an insulating subculture to protect themselves from these stressors. Thus, the subculture is more permeable; less stereotyping and physical brutality occur because the same degree of anxiety and stress is not present to engender them. The importation theory would indicate that because female staff members (women having been the majority in prisons for women), like female prisoners, are very concerned with children and family, they are able to find common ground as a basis for communicating. Obviously female officers and inmates are interested in other things besides children, but this bond seems to be very pervasive and bridges the gap between the two groups in some ways. However, it would be unrealistic to view the women's prison as a place where officers and inmates happily share baby stories all day long. The backgrounds of officers and inmates usually are very different. Officers are often judgmental about the inmate's lifestyle, especially as it has affected her children, and these issues may serve to separate rather than draw the two groups together.

Today, with all officers attending a central training academy, transfers between the facilities, and union activity, there is less of an institution-based subculture and more of a state identity among C.O.s. Officers may share similar interests, regardless of the institution at which they are housed, if they aspire to managerial positions and attend national conferences or are involved in higher education. Female officers who have worked in facilities for men before being transferred to a prison for women may have more in common with the male officers who have worked in the same facility than with the female officers who have not.

INTERACTIONS WITH INMATES

The bottom line of supervision in any prison is that much of the officer's power is illusory. Although the threat of officially sanctioned violence is ever present, on a day-to-day basis, the officer must depend on the force of his or her personality to motivate the inmates to perform required behaviors. The officer must make inmates perform tasks they would probably prefer not to do. The C.O. is responsible to see that inmates leave the housing unit and arrive where they are supposed to, keep the buildings and grounds clean, follow rules, and avoid hurting themselves or others. How a C.O. manages this supervision is influenced by his or her personality. An officer's day may be either relatively pleasant or extremely difficult, depending on the inmates he or she supervises.

Female correctional officers who have supervised both sexes often prefer to work with male inmates because they are "more respectful" and do not demand the time and energy of the C.O. in the same way that female inmates are perceived as needing (Pollock, 1986). More than 10 years after Pollock's (1986) study, Owen also found that most staff preferred working with men (1998: 165). Officers complain that female inmates argue and refuse orders and that they are verbally abusive and expressive in their frustration and anger. In other words, female inmates are described as acting like children. On the other hand, female inmates complain that officers (especially female officers) treat them like children by calling them "girls" and scolding or patronizing them concerning dress, behavior, language, cleanliness, and other trivial issues in a heavy-handed, "maternal" way.

The history and tradition in women's institutions has been to "correct" rather than simply "punish." Even fairly recent accounts reinforce the concept that female staff members are meant to be role models and help the female inmates develop a more appropriate feminine identity. Eyman (1971), for instance, wrote that the purpose of female staff was to satisfy the emotional needs of the female inmates, so that inmates would not need to turn to pseudo-families to meet their needs. She also wrote that male administrators could serve as father figures who could not be manipulated, thus helping the women to develop more positive relationships with the opposite sex (Eyman, 1971: 139).

The perception of the female inmate as needing more emotional support and guidance in establishing her femininity is widespread in the literature—certainly through the 1970s. This view of female inmates very often creates an environment where they are treated as children; they are called "girls" or "ladies," and the tone is often that used to discipline teenagers, or somewhat dense and naughty adults. Older officers are especially likely to use this approach with inmates, regardless of the age or experience of the inmate. Fox (1984; also see Fox, 1982: 213) explains that often the supervision style whereby female officers treat the inmates as errant children is cause for frustration on the part of the female inmates.

> For a 33 year old woman to have another woman tell her that she is misbehaving, it's funny to me, it's funny! I have a child who is 15 years old and I wouldn't tell him that he is misbehaving. He'd look at me like I was crazy. To be 33 and have somebody tell you that you're acting like a little child, and that means that you're going to be punished. It's funny. (Fox, 1984: 23)

A slightly different issue is raised when officers do not treat inmates with respect. This is a fairly consistent theme of both men and women in prison. Girshick (1999) heard from women who complained of lack of respect from officers:

> We know we are incarcerated. We're already tried and sentenced. No need to do it over again. They tell you you should act like adults and then talk to you like you're two. (1999:78)

> And I don't care if I'm an inmate or not, I'm still a human being. I'm a woman just like they are. Yeah, I may have committed a crime, but I'm paying for it. I've been paying for it almost a decade of my life. You don't have to talk to me like I'm a dog, 'cause I'm not. (1999: 94)

Younger officers may not be able to carry off the maternal role and instead resort to either jocular friendships or a bureaucratic role, where the officer expects the inmate to do what is asked because "she says so."

Female inmates may take more liberties with officers; the truism is that although officers will rarely be seriously hurt by female inmates, women have a greater ability to make the officers' lives difficult. In the following anecdote, Jean Harris (1988) describes why many officers do not enjoy working with female inmates.

> There is a woman currently on my corridor in lock for a month. There are three young, white males on duty from 7:00 A.M. to 3:00 P.M. She calls for their services by yelling, "One a you dumb motherfuckin' honkie assholes . . ." One always comes running to provide what she demands. "I'm the king," she yells. "We doin' it my way." (Harris, 1988: 126)

Owen (1998: 116) also provides inmates' commentaries regarding other inmates' treatment of officers. Note these inmates astutely conclude that treating officers badly usually results in negative consequences for the inmates in the end.

> Sometimes these women start cussing at the police. . . . They don't think that yelling at the police like that is going to make it much harder for them back here? When they need a roll of toilet paper, the police will take their time to bring it to them.

> To get respect in here, you have to give them respect. And some officers are pretty good about that. . . . If you be nice to them and don't give them no hassle and talk to them with respect, they are pretty good about talking to you with respect.

For the most part, Owen's (1998) respondents recognized officers were only doing their job and concluded that most officers were "o.k.," but not all.

> There is a lot of them who are just plain assholes because they take their badge out of control, you have a couple of those. (1998: 162–163)

Owen's (1998) respondents also offered the observation that C.O.s instigated some racial strife, and more minority women than white inmates perceived C.O.s as prejudiced. Some women reported extreme incidences of racism.

> They are mean. . . . They will tell you to get up on the wall and be rough with you and kick open your legs with their knees. . . . They said, "You fucking nigger, I ought to body slam you." I looked at him like he was crazy. The black officers don't like it, but they . . . back each other up. (1998: 157)

Even though there is less violence and danger in the institution for women, a few female offenders in any prison are known as violent troublemakers. Most female offenders pose a danger only when they are angry at another inmate. Then, in their emotional outburst, they may unintentionally injure an officer attempting to break up the fight. Female correctional officers in facilities for women may be less forceful in handling violent incidents, partly because of anticipatory socialization, partly because of lack of training, and partly because of the infrequency with which they are called upon to perform physically. Female officers may experience a degree of fear when dealing with these violent women, and they often cover their fear by overreacting to threats or calling in male officers to handle the threatening female offenders.

Many prisons now have a cadre of trained male and female officers to intervene in disturbances. These "goon squads" are feared and hated by female as well as male inmates. The display of reactionary force is all the more dramatic in its impersonality. Indeed, the special uniforms and appearance of the team are akin to an invading army. Some observe that this "innovation" may be necessary in an institution for males but is perhaps unnecessary and ill-adapted to institutions for women.[2]

Jean Harris (1988) provides a critical summary of the officer and inmate in a women's prison.

> In this prison, c.o.'s harass the inmates, and the inmates harass the c.o.'s. I've seen a c.o. work laboriously for two hours writing charge sheets for women who didn't jump fast enough for him. Having finished the job he chose, unwisely, to go to the bathroom. As soon as he closed the bathroom door a woman tiptoed to the bubble, grabbed the charge sheets, tore them and flushed them down the nearest toilet. The confused c.o. spent the next two hours looking for them. It's boarding school stuff played with Keystone Cops. (1988: 233)

Gender Differences in Styles of Supervision

When women entered prisons for men, many observers noted that they performed the officer role differently from men. Certainly the style of supervision and general atmosphere in a women's prison seemed to be quite different from men's prisons. Whether these differences in a women's prison occurred because of the female inmates or because of female officers, or some combination of the two factors, is an interesting question. There is some research that attempts to address it, but it is a complicated topic and existing research seems inconsistent (Pollock, 1995).

Most observations of women working in prisons for men have emphasized the differences women bring to the officer role. The manner of supervision seems to be different, along with the relationship with the inmate. Crouch and Marquart (1980) have characterized the male officer as cynical and authoritarian. Often the male officer feels obliged to give orders using demanding tones and obscenities. The relationship between male officers and male inmates may, at times, reach a level of acceptance and respect, especially in isolated settings such as work assignments or in special niches, but these relationships are tenuous at best, and they are often fragmented and shattered when reality brings home the gulf between the two groups of men and polarizes each group, as when a lockdown or beating takes place. It must be noted that some writers describe much closer ties between men, even reaching the point where names such as "kid" and "dad" describe parental relationships between officers and inmates; but these accounts are rare (Webb and Morris, 1980).

Female officers are much more likely to use emotional tools to supervise their inmates, and are even more likely to do so when working with juveniles or adult women. The control from an emotional attachment is often more powerful than the fear that may be employed in facilities for men, but it comes at a cost. Toigo (1962) explains that sometimes the staff person is also caught in the pull of emotional ties, and reduced social distance and emotional attachment blur the lines of authority.

While differences in supervision styles seem to be noted by both male and female officers in prisons for men, the "feminine" style of supervision is even more noted by observers in women's prisons, and especially by male officers who transfer to them. For instance, observers have noted that in the past, many situations that would call for force in a men's facility were handled by negotiation and persuasion in the facility for women. Female officers were much more likely to argue with female offenders or explain rules to them; they were much more likely to coax a recalcitrant inmate from a cell than to call for backup and the use of force.

It may be that the differences between male and female inmates force officers to behave differently.

> The female inmates come over and they always want a little bit more than what's there, you know, if you say you can't have this or this, they'll argue about it. They take up more time because you listen to them, you don't have to. You could say "you can't have it and that's all there is to it" and throw them out the door, but it is very hard to do because you know you prevent a lot of problems if you take the time to talk to them, even if it's just to explain. You know, the rule is changed and they usually then accept it, but they have to argue it all the time. (Pollock, 1981)

Interestingly, Owen (1998) obtained, in her more recent study, a similar comment from a staff person. It seems that, at least in this area, female inmates (or perceptions of them) have not changed much over the years.

> The men take answers at face value. When you tell them "no," they go away, but the women want to discuss their particular problem in great detail. When staff are trained at a male institution, they do not know how to deal with it. Women take more time and some staff are not prepared for that. (Owen, 1998: 73)

The personal style of supervision that seems to characterize the women's institution means that the female C.O. may interact with inmates with more sensitivity and attachment. For instance, one observer noted the differences between men and women in one facility that housed both sexes: "On the women's division, there was not the denial of feelings and callousness observed on the men's division of the same institution" (Ackerman, 1972: 365). The reduced social distance may allow for productive bonds to form between female officers and inmates. On the other hand, some observers believe that the interactions between inmates and officers are superficial at best. Inmates do not share real problems with officers and may use a friendly relationship to manipulate the officer.

> Relationships with officers were described as a "game" where you communicated with them just enough to avoid being put on report for ignoring them. At the same time, unpredictability and lack of confidentiality meant that there was little trust and a large element of fear in staff/adult relationships. A commonly expressed feeling was that officers did not regard them as individuals, but treated them as one of a (sometimes subhuman) herd. (Dobash et al., 1986: 189)

A Feminine Style of Supervision? Research on female officers and observations of officers have indicated that female officers perform their supervision functions in a slightly different way from men. Their style has been characterized as using less authoritarian methods to obtain control and as one that encourages more interaction with inmates (Pollock, 1986). Others have called it a "softer" role or "more communicative" (Lawrence and Mahan, 1998). Typically officers and practitioners themselves note these differences (see Belknap, 1991).

After some reports of a possible "feminine" style of supervision were published, a number of survey research projects attempted to quantify differences between male and female officers and concluded that the officers were the "same" in their treatment of inmates. Jurik (1985a & b), Jurik and Halemba (1984), and Zupan (1986) found that there were no differences in "attitudes" toward inmates, and that women C.O.s were no more sensitive to the needs of inmates than their male counterparts.

Jenne and Kersting (1996) used hypotheticals to test whether men and women would handle incidents differently. Contrary to the proposition that women had a "softer" approach, they found women sometimes handled incidents more aggressively than did men. Officers of both genders were given 16 critical incidents and asked to respond. Few gender differences in the use of aggression were presented; and when there were differences, it was the women who were more aggressive. The authors attributed this to the need for women to prove themselves. Interestingly, consistent with previous findings, female officers in the study perceived themselves to be less aggressive than men.

Farkas's 1999 study also used hypotheticals with a sample of 22 female and 57 male officers. Although they were similar in age, the women were more educated, and the men had just over a year more experience in corrections. Responses to the hypothetical situations were coded into: rule enforcement, human service action, use of physical force, and indirect intervention (1999: 33). The hypotheticals involved minor rule infractions, major rule infractions, observing an officer involved in a verbal altercation with an inmate, and a physical altercation between two inmates. Farkas, like others, found that both male and female respondents believed men and women performed the role differently, with women being less authoritative—male officers described female officers as lacking in confidence and too friendly with inmates, while women said they had a human service approach and solved problems by talking with the inmates. Women also perceived themselves as following rules more often than men (to not appear as a pushover and because they were scrutinized more closely than male officers).

Despite these perceptions, the officers' responses to the hypotheticals supported Jenne and Kersting's (1996) findings that women were more likely to take a formal, aggressive approach, and it was male officers who were more likely to talk or reason with inmates. Male officers also were more likely to come to the aid of another officer, while women indicated they would "stand by" and monitor the situation.

So what is one to make of these contrary findings? Are officers and other observers simply wrong in their perception that female officers supervise differently than male officers? It is doubtful that those who are closest to the situation can be completely wrong about what they see and experience. Farkas (1999) warned that her study was exploratory and that level of custody, race, and other factors might make her findings less generalizable. There may be other reasons, however, that explain why these studies are not consistent with perceptual realities.

Hypotheticals place officers in unrealistic situations where there is no background or buildup to the incident. All the hypotheticals involved inmates challenging officer authority. Yet in real life, it may be that challenges to authority are experienced differentially by male and female officers. Perhaps, women do not encounter threats to authority as often, and therefore, when such threats do occur, they mean something different, that is, that the inmate is not amenable to reason. Hypotheticals cannot capture the day-to-day interactions between officers and inmates that build a relationship and influence how each treats the other. More research is necessary before we can completely discount the long-standing and consistent perceptions of the officers themselves.

Other studies also have looked at differences between supervision styles of men and women. Stohr, Lovrich, and Mays (1997) studied officers in all-women jails and found that women did not prefer service-type training over security training (which would be expected if they possessed a more "personal" style of supervision). In fact, both men and women showed preference for service type of training (communication skills, etc.). Leiber (2000) conducted a study on probation officers' views toward punishment and generally supported findings indicating that women are more nurturing and men more authoritarian; however, it was also found that religious orientation interacted with gender and changed beliefs regarding punishment (fundamentalist women were more punitive).

MANAGEMENT ISSUES
IN A WOMEN'S PRISON

Although there are similarities between managing prisons for women and men, there are differences as well. Serious violence, drug use, and gang activity are not as prevalent in women's institutions, but there are other problems with a female population. Medical issues, including the number of HIV/AIDS cases, demand time and resources, as does the general "expressiveness" of women—that is, women may require more crisis intervention. The problems presented by the female inmate's continuing concern and custody issues regarding children affect the management of a women's prison. Also, the special issues presented when male officers are introduced to the facility concern administrators of women's institutions.

Violence

Although some evidence indicates they may be responsible for more minor rule-breaking,[3] women are much less likely to engage in large-scale riots. In Crawford's (1988b) study, 82.6 percent of the facilities reported that they had experienced no major disturbances, fires, riots, or demonstrations for the previous five years (1988b: 16). Only a few examples of collective disturbances have been documented at women's prisons. For instance, a 1971 riot occurred at Tennessee's State Prison for Women. In the four hours it lasted, 30 of the nearly 100 women incarcerated there overcame the guards who were bringing them back from an evening meal. One officer ran, leaving the other to face the inmates. She was taken hostage, and the women demanded certain changes, most having to do with unreasonable rules and "racist" staff who treated the women "like animals." The women involved were transferred to a maximum-security section of the Central State Hospital a few days after the incident.

In 1971, women in Alderson, a federal facility, rioted in support of the male prisoners who were rioting at Attica. The women's riot lasted four days and required extreme force to quell (Mann, 1984: 210). A 1973 riot in Georgia forced the warden to use a 10-man riot team, which took control over the rioting women (Baunach and Murton, 1973: 8). Various incidents have occurred at Bedford Hills over the years. In one fairly serious incident in the early 1980s, the women in segregation overpowered the guards, took them hostage, and armed themselves with boiling water and other makeshift weapons. In other incidents, the male correctional officers from a nearby prison for men had to be called in to take control. Despite these examples, very few prison administrators take these disruptions seriously. The fear of a takeover in a women's prison is not a major issue. Consequently, some say that the women's complaints are not taken as seriously as those of male inmates.

Adapting to a Male Standard

Administrators of women's prisons are now receiving greater numbers of officers and supervisors who have worked in prisons for men. Although a certain amount of diversity is healthy, what also occurs when there is a mix of trained staff is tension because of a feeling that things are done "better" in the other institution. In corrections for women, "better" usually means how things were done in the prison for men. Fleisher et al. (1997) surveyed inmates and staff at two new federal facilities for women and found that strife existed between staff who came from facilities for men and those who had histories of working in facilities for women.

Those staff coming from men's prisons saw security concerns in practices that were quite common in women's prisons, such as family day programs (where there were relaxed rules of visitation). Staff trained in men's facilities instituted what were perceived as overly strict rules, and excessive searches and shakedowns. Since most of these staff were men, there was continuing tension and conflict between female inmates and male staff. Female inmates indicated they preferred female C.O.s because of privacy concerns and because female C.O.s "understood them better" (Fleisher et al., 1997: 32).

Observers note that officers who work in facilities for women need to have special training. First, the dislike that officers express toward female offenders ("I'd rather work with 50 men than 5 women") needs to be addressed, and the stigma removed from being assigned to a women's institution (Rasche, 2000). Second, there needs to be "gender-specific training," that is, training that informs the officers of the issues he or she needs to be aware of when working with women. For instance, Cranford and Williams (1998) explain that staff need to be aware that women will talk to them more and that the women are not necessarily trying to manipulate the staff; that social relationships are important to women; that there are inappropriate touching or communication patterns; and that women are not "worse"—they are different.

CONCLUSION

Any prison is made up not only of inmates but also of officers. The nature of the institution for women is influenced in large part by the female correctional staff employed there. Female officers' different style of supervision and different interactional patterns with the inmates have, in the past, made the women's prison in some ways a better place and in other ways a more confining place to be. Although female correctional officers have been described as having more personal relationships with inmates and greater sensitivity to women's problems and concerns, officers also have been prone to maternalize their role and treat the inmates like children. Today, this supervision style may be less apparent because of more uniform training practices, greater numbers of male officers in women's prisons, and the greater bureaucratization of corrections in general.

Finally, one must remember that even in women's institutions, which are relatively small as prisons go, there are literally hundreds upon hundreds of correctional officers, all of whom touch the inmates' lives in some way. Some are professional; some are not. Some are cruel; some are kind. Some should never be allowed to have control over others; others touch inmates' lives in very positive ways. A few generalizations may be made, but in the end, each officer is an individual—as is each inmate.

NOTES

1. A "total institution" is a place described by Goffman (1961) as one where the boundaries of work, play, and sleep are eliminated. Examples include the military, mental hospitals, boarding schools, and the like.

2. The next chapter discusses an incident at the Kingston Prison for Women in Ontario, Canada, in which a special "extraction team," composed of men from the men's prison, was used to extract and strip women in segregation. The video of the procedure ended up on television, and the resulting shock and public outrage led to a special inquiry and commission that made recommendations regarding building smaller "women-centered" correctional facilities.

3. Note, however, that there is some dispute about whether these figures may measure disciplinary practices and behavioral expectations of officers rather than actual behaviors of inmates (see McClellan, 1994a & b).

SUGGESTED READINGS

Henriques, Z., and E. Gilbert. 2000. "Sexual Abuse and Sexual Assault of Women in Prison." In R. Muraskin, *It's a Crime: Women and Justice,* 2d ed., pp. 253–268. Upper Saddle River, NJ: Prentice-Hall.

Jurik, N. 1985. "An Officer and a Lady: Organizational Barriers to Women Working as Correctional Officers in Men's Prisons." *Social Problems* 32: 375–388.

Jurik, N. 1988. "Striking a Balance: Female Correctional Officers, Gender Role Stereotypes, and Male Prisons." *Sociological Inquiry* 58, 3: 291–305.

Jurik, N., and G. Halemba. 1984. "Gender, Working Conditions and the Job Satisfaction of Women in a Nontraditional Occupation: Female Correctional Officers in Men's Prisons." *The Sociological Quarterly* 25: 551–566.

Zupan, L. 1986. "Gender-Related Differences in Correctional Officers' Perceptions and Attitudes." *Journal of Criminal Justice* 14: 349–361.

Zupan, L. 1992. "Men Guarding Women: An Analysis of the Employment of Male Correctional Officers in Prisons for Women." *Journal of Criminal Justice* 20: 297–309.

Zupan, L. 1992. "The Progress of Women Correctional Officers in All-Male Prisons." In I. Moyer (ed.), *The Changing Roles of Women in the Criminal Justice System,* 2d ed., pp. 323–343. Prospect Heights, IL: Waveland Press.

9

Women Incarcerated: Jails and Prisons Around the World

Much of the literature that has been reviewed to this point applies equally well to women incarcerated in jails and even to women incarcerated in other countries around the world. In fact, some of the studies discussed earlier were done with jail inmates or officers in jails. However, there are differences, depending on whether women are in prison or jail and on the country in which they are incarcerated; we will explore some of these differences briefly in this chapter.

JAIL INMATES

Women in jail experience many of the same fears and deprivations that women in prison do, as well as some that are unique to the jail experience (Weisheit and Parsons, 1986). Jail is the first experience of incarceration; thus, it is more traumatic. Child-care is unsettled, the woman may be experiencing withdrawal from drugs, and the separation from family and children is recent and still extremely painful. Jails are typically in urban locations so there is very little space available; consequently, women may have fewer programs and almost no outdoor opportunities (often jail recreation "yards" are the roof). Because of their small numbers, women typically are housed in a wing or unit of a jail for men, although there are a few women-only jails in the United States (see Stohr, Lovrich, and Mays, 1997).

Growing Numbers

In 1983, women comprised about 7.1 percent of the total jail population; in 1985, 8 percent; in 1989, 9.5 percent; and in 1996 they increased to over 10 percent (Harlow, 1998; Veysey, 1998). In 1998, males constituted 89 percent of the jail inmate population. The adult female jail population has grown 7 percent annually since 1990, compared to an annual 4.5 percent increase for males (BJS, 1999a; Beck and Mumola, 1999).

Characteristics of Women in Jail

Men and women in jails are similar in age and race/ethnicity. Their median age is 28. Slightly less than 40 percent are African American, 16 percent are Hispanic, and 3 percent are categorized as "other." A greater number of women than men in jail have been married. More women than men have completed high school (Veysey, 1998).

A national survey of jail inmates in 1989 found that two-thirds had children under 18 and half of these children were living with grandparents; 40 percent had grown up in a single-parent household (an additional 17 percent grew up with neither parent); 4 in 10 had family members who had served time in jail or prison; and 44 percent reported physical or sexual abuse (BJS, 1992; Snell, 1992).

In their 1992 study, Singer et al. (1995) presented the characteristics of a small sample ($n = 201$). In this sample:

- 72 percent were African-American.
- 64 percent had not completed high school.
- 85 percent were not married.
- 73 percent had children under 18.
- Half had no legal custody of any of their children.
- The majority of children were being cared for by grandparents.
- 13 percent were pregnant.
- Over half had received drug treatment.
- Half were incarcerated for prostitution.
- 64 percent of women were categorized as clinically distressed.

- 61 percent reported regular cocaine use.
- 55 percent were dual diagnosed (drug and psychological problems).
- 75 percent had been threatened with physical violence in prior year.
- 69 percent had actually been victimized.
- 68 percent reported forced sexual activity.
- 48 percent reported sexual victimization as a child.
- 40 percent reported they had no one to help them deal with traumatic life events.

The authors concluded that what female jail inmates needed upon release was housing, drug counseling, mental health counseling, financial aid, alcohol counseling, education and training, medical care, family support, food, help getting children back, child-care, and parenting classes (Singer et al., 1995).

Rice, Smith, and Janzen (1999) also conducted a small study of 100 women in a large urban county jail (Salt Lake City). Most of the women were incarcerated for drugs or property crimes related to drugs. The sample did not reflect a disproportional percentage of minority women, but all other demographics reflected the national profile—about half were incarcerated for drug crimes or crimes related to drug use; the average length of stay was 42 days; half had been on probation or parole status; there were high rates of drug abuse and use; drug use started early in life (13 was the average age), a large percentage of women had mental health needs; and about 38 percent reported physical abuse, 39 percent reported sexual abuse as a child, but a much higher percentage reported adult victimization.

Women are more likely than men in jail to be diagnosed with mental illnesses (18.5 percent versus 8.9 percent). The most frequent diagnosis is clinical depression (13.7 percent of women versus 3.4 percent of men). About a quarter (22.3 percent) of women in jail are diagnosed with posttraumatic stress disorder (PTSD). Further, a dual diagnosis (both mental illness and drug addiction) is very common (Veysey, 1998: 371).

As with women in prisons, female jail inmates are most likely to be drug abusers. Reporting on 1989 figures, a Bureau of Justice Statistics (1992) report indicated that more than half had used drugs in the month prior to their jail incarceration; 40 percent used drugs daily. Cocaine or crack was the most frequently used drug (about 39 percent had used cocaine or crack in month before arrest). About a quarter of the women committed crime to buy drugs. About 20 percent of the women were under the influence of alcohol at the time of the offense (Snell, 1992).

Crimes A smaller number of women than men have committed violent crimes; and a greater percentage of women than men are in jail for drug crimes (34 percent versus 22 percent) (Veysey, 1998). In one Bureau of Justice Statistics (1998) report, it was noted that 28 percent of men were in jail for violent offenses, while only 15 percent of women were. Further, 32 percent of women were in for property offenses, 27 percent for drug offenses, 25 percent for public order offenses, and the remainder for "other" (BJS, 1998; Harlow, 1998).

Issues and Concerns

As mentioned earlier, because of their small numbers, women in jail probably receive even less programming and opportunities for activity, especially physical activity, than women in prison (Koons et al., 1997: 513; also see Connolly, 1983). Amnesty International (1999), in their report on incarcerated women in this country, noted that outdoor recreation was problematic for women in jails. They cited several jails across the country where women had either no or very little time for outdoor recreation; this was sometimes in violation of court orders and certainly in violation of national and international correctional standards.

As with prisons, there is very seldom an attempt to use a gender-specific classification system for women. Consequently, it may be that women are overclassified and housed in higher security settings than necessary. Farr (2000a: 5), for instance, reviews other studies that show that jails overwhelmingly use a single classification system for men and women. The system used for male inmates has not been validated for females. In fact, little is known of risk factors (escape, violence, suicide) for women because no one has conducted any risk assessment research on a female jail sample.

Medical and psychological services for women in jail are, in many jurisdictions, inadequate. One national survey reported that less than half of female inmates received a physical examination upon entry (BJS, 1998; Harlow, 1998). Often medical changes in services come about through court action; for instance, litigation over the Santa Rita County jail resulted in the county being required to fund a $21 million contract for health care providers that included substance abuse treatment for pregnant inmates, prenatal laboratory services, mental health services, nutrition services, social services for single parents, child-care, family planning, and coping (Veysey, 1998).

Singer et al. (1995: 103) noted that between one-third to two-thirds of entering women needed psychological services. Another study indicated that 64 percent of female jail detainees had signs of depression (Rice, Smith, and Janzen, 1999). In fact, all studies of female jail detainees report that they are more likely than male detainees to be diagnosed with mental health problems (Teplin, Abrams, and McClelland, 1996; Veysey, 1998). Mood-altering drugs are prescribed two to three times as often for women in jails as for men (about 21 percent in one study had been prescribed a mood-altering drug for a psychological problem) (Singer et al., 1995: 103). At the Sybil Brand Institute in Los Angeles County, there was one psychiatrist for over 415 women; 300 of the women were on psychotropic medication (Amnesty International, 1999: 82).

A portion of the mental health problems of women in jails is probably related to prior victimization. As reported previously, at least as many, if not more, women in jail report childhood and adult sexual and physical victimization as women in prison. In a 1996 profile of jail inmates, 37 percent of women (compared to 6 percent of men) reported sexual abuse before jail admission; 27 percent of women (compared to 3 percent of men) reported rape; more women (37 percent) than men (12 percent) reported sexual or physical abuse as children; and women also reported more victimization as adults (27 percent compared to 2 percent of men) (BJS, 1998; Harlow, 1998). In another, smaller sample, 64 percent had mental health problems, 83 percent had substance abuse problems, and 8 percent had been sexually abused (Singer et al., 1995). While there is obviously underreporting of victimization by men, especially sexual victimization, there is probably a certain amount of underreporting by women as well. It seems clear that, similarly to prison inmates, there is a difference in the likelihood of prior victimization between male and female jail inmates.

Veysey (1998) provides a clear argument that the characteristics of the jail, combined with women's background of victimization, act to retraumatize the offender. She notes that about a quarter (22.3 percent) of female jail detainees are diagnosed with PTSD. Symptoms include hypervigilance, startle reflex, phobias, auditory and visual flashbacks to incidents of abuse, and uncontrollable anger or rage (1998: 372). The presence of male officers, strip searches, and an environment characterized by loss of control are elements of the jail that may increase stress and anxiety:

> Uniforms, male officers, lack of privacy, loud noises, a sense of lack of control, fear based on lack of information, and darkness all may increase the stress level and vulnerability of women with histories of physical and sexual abuse. (Veysey, 1998: 51)

Veysey (1998) notes that this situation not only impacts the women, but also results in increased institutional costs, including increased health costs, physical injury, and greater use of medications. She suggests that there are certain procedural and resource distribution changes that can be made to help reduce women's stress levels, for example, making an effort to give more information to offenders during booking as to what is happening, screening for vulnerable women, crisis and de-escalation intervention counseling, the use of female staff, training of all staff to understand women's issues, a respite from administrative segregation if necessary, architectural changes to improve privacy, reducing contact between female detainees and male detainees in the facility, specialized staff, and providing community referrals (1998: 53).

Several studies indicate that female jail detainees may not receive adequate programs or services. Gray, Mays, and Stohr (1995) surveyed women's jails in 1992, with a sample of 566 inmates. They visited five (of 18) jails that housed exclusively women. Their findings indicated that programming was inadequate, although jails that housed only women met their needs better than those jails where women were housed with men. Drug and alcohol programming was offered most often, but it was still inadequate to meet demand. Inmates placed educational and vocational training as their top need, yet programs were nonexistent, had waiting lists, and/or were sex-stereotyped. Medical services were consistently inadequate. Singer et al. (1995)

noted similar findings. Female offenders in a jail said that housing and counseling were their areas of greatest need.

Schafer and Dellinger (1999: 77) have provided one of the few studies comparing male and female jailed parents awaiting trial or serving county sentences. Using the 1983 and 1989 results of the National Jail Survey, conducted by the U.S. Census Bureau for the Bureau of Justice Statistics, they found that mothers were more likely than fathers to have minor children and to have been living with them at the time of arrest. The authors concluded that incarceration poses more problems for inmate mothers than fathers.

One study discussed how the "new generation" jail affects women. In this study, Jackson and Stearns (1995) concluded that women did not seem to do as well in the "new generation" jail as in the jail based on traditional architectural style. New generation facilities are podular designs with individual rooms. Most research suggested that inmates responded better to this physical environment and management style. The authors looked at both men and women in one new generation jail in Sonoma County, California. They conducted a pretest before and a posttest six months after the move, using a jail inventory scale measuring inmate concerns like privacy and safety. Women represented about 15 percent of the total sample. Results indicated that men improved their attitude, but women became increasingly dissatisfied with the podular design. There were declines in social stimulation, emotional feedback, activity levels, and an increase in physical anxiety. Other concerns, like privacy and safety, showed no gender differences. Although the results were unclear, there were some indications that direct supervision reduced women's relationships with each other and, thus, increased their anxiety. Also, the authors noted that the new jail resulted in equalizing rules between the men's and women's units, and this affected women differentially. In effect, the informality of old jail gave way to more structure, more rules, and fewer activities for women.

Arguably, female jail inmates have more problems than their male counterparts but fewer services available to them. They are more likely to have drug and alcohol problems, medical needs, mental health needs, and experience stress due to the characteristics of incarceration. They are more likely to have major problems related to child-care (e.g., finding child placement, experiencing stress due to separation). In some jails, women are housed in proximity to male offenders who sexually harass them. There also have been numerous reports across the country of male jail staff sexually harassing and even assaulting female jail inmates (see Chapters 7 and 8). Women in jails are similar to men in prisons in their problems—drug abuse, single parenthood, history of victimization—but have fewer services available to them. Some indications are that recent innovations result in more negative than positive effects for women. What seems obvious is that very few jurisdictions make the effort to think about any special needs or differences that characterize female jail populations from male populations.

PRISONS FOR WOMEN
ACROSS THE WORLD

A few general comments can be made about women's institutions in other countries. First, the incarceration rate for women is much lower in other countries, so the numbers of women imprisoned are extremely small compared to the population in the United States. For instance, the female prison population in certain states such as Texas or California is larger than the female prison population of entire countries. While many elements of women's prisons are the same whether one is in the United States, Great Britain, or other countries, there are differences. For instance, it is much more common in other countries to have mother-baby units in women's prisons. It is also more common to have "open" prisons, institutions where inmates may work outside the prison during the day and return at night to serve their sentence. On the other hand, it is also more common for jails and prisons to be merged in other countries, so that unconvicted and convicted women live in the same facility.

Great Britain

A few books have been published that describe women's prisons in Great Britain (Dobash et al., 1986; Smith, 1962). The history and current conditions of British female prisoners appear very similar to those of their sisters in the United States. Women prisoners in Great Britain are also disproportionately women of color and poor, are incarcerated mostly for property crimes, and comprise a very small portion (3 to 4 percent) of the total incarcerated population (Dobash et al., 1986: 2). These women were housed in eight "closed" and three "open" institutions for adult women in England and Wales and one prison in Scotland (Dobash et al., 1986: 4).

Like the United States, Great Britain has experienced a tremendous increase in the number of women incarcerated in the last 20 years. O'Dwyer et al. (1987) reported that British women were held in six closed and three open facilities, two youth custody centers, and three remand centers.[1] The combined daily population in 1987 was roughly 1,600 (O'Dwyer et al., 1987: 177). Carlen (1999: 124) reported that in 1997, 2,680 women were imprisoned in Great Britain, comprising about 4 percent of the total incarcerated population; 16 percent of these women were foreign nationals. In 1998, the number of women imprisoned stood at the highest level since 1905 (about 3,000). It was reported that 70 percent posed no security risk and should not be held in closed prisons (Gentleman, 1998: 8). It appears that, as in the United States, a large percentage of women in prison in Great Britain are there because of drugs. Carlen (1999: 124) reported that about a third of all prisoners were there for drug offenses.

We have a few enlightening descriptions of how women prisoners fare in Great Britain. These studies point to international differences in the treatment of prisoners. Mawby (1982) explained that British prisons may hold more petty and first-time offenders than prisons for women in the United States. He described the difference between open prisons and closed prisons, the latter being more similar to American prisons. Dobash, Dobash, and Gutteridge (1986), writing of women offenders in Great Britain, also emphasized the petty, economic nature of women's crime. They indicated that one reason for women's incarceration is that they cannot pay the fines assessed against them, unlike men who commit the same type of crimes and receive no imprisonment (1986: 93).

Carlen (1983) studied Cornton Vale, a women's prison in Scotland in the 1980s. She pointed out that it was rare for women to be incarcerated; if they were, their sentences were likely to be fairly short, 115 days on average (1983: 13). Carlen described Cornton Vale as a well-kept place composed of cottages and lined with "trim paths" and flower gardens. The rooms were brightly furnished and were "light and airy in summer" (1983: 14). She further explained, however, that within the walls, females were disciplined by being socially isolated from one another. This practice created a situation where women were dependent on their keepers for everything, including affection. Training tended to be solely in the "domestic arts," reinforcing the idea that the women had violated social rather than legal norms—and, indeed, very few were in prison for more than petty crimes. One-third were committed for property crimes without violence, and one-third were there for public order crimes (breach of the peace). Half of those involved the failure to pay a fine (1983: 115). Carlen proposed that the women who ended up in prison were there because of their failures as mothers, rather than for criminality *per se*. If a woman showed herself to be the caregiver to children, she would escape imprisonment, almost regardless of what offense she had committed. On the other hand, a woman who had no children, or who had not taken care of her children, was considered no great loss to society, and thus found herself in prison (1983: 68).

The "family life" artificially created at Cornton Vale was said to be a substitute and training for the family life that these women had been deprived of or had deprived their children of and that they needed to learn. Carlen (1983) explained that since some of the women ran away from home or husband in order to escape this type of family life, it was ironic that they were forced to submit to it in prison. She further proposed that it was hypocritical to promote a family atmosphere when women were punished for helping one another or for getting involved with one another's problems. In fact, the division of the blocks into small family units was primarily useful as a discipline device, since it further increased women's isolation and dependency (1983: 73).

At Cornton Vale, the women led a much more structured and strict life than at any American prison. All letters were censored, there were no phone calls, and visiting was rare. The women got little time to socialize with one another, and all conversations were monitored. Carlen (1983), like many American researchers who discussed American prisons, described how the institution for women encouraged them to be childlike, and in response, many of the women acted in immature ways. Suggested explanations for the apparent immaturity of female inmates included the following: some officers believed that all women were essentially childlike; the hierarchical organization created the childishness; or disciplinary and security measures were "actually designed" to induce feelings of infantile dependency in the prisoners (1983: 109).

Dobash, Dobash, and Gutteridge (1986) also described Cornton Vale and other British prisons. They provided a historical account as well as more current descriptions of women's prisons that indicate that British women are treated similarly to American women. During the rehabilitative era (1960s and 1970s), women's prisons in England were reformed, and a medical approach to corrections was adopted. It was much more common to explain female criminality through resort to medical and psychiatric terminology than male criminality; and the "treatment model" was used more often in women's institutions than in men's prisons (1986: 126). Adherence to a treatment ethic was probably more superficial than real, however, since the authors suggested that social work staff pressured women to be pleasant and ladylike, rather than engage in any real attempt to deal with personal problems. Useful vocational programs were less apparent than domestic and maintenance work (1986: 144).

The authors went on to explain that women had fewer outlets for physical recreation or social programs. Women tended to be involved in individual pursuits such as sewing or handicrafts and, to a lesser extent, education. Dobash, Dobash, and Gutteridge (1986) also described female correctional officers in Scotland as being not too different from female C.O.s in the United States. The female officers were attracted to the job as an alternative to what they considered boring clerical jobs. Some came to corrections from the military; some entered corrections as a practical solution to a problem (they needed a place to live and one was provided). The authors reported that female officers in Scotland received the same training as the male officers received (1986: 189). Similar to female officers in the United States, Scottish female officers were closer to female inmates than male officers were to male inmates. This did not mean, however, that there was an excessive degree of trust between the two groups.

A journalist/activist has recently offered a comprehensive account of the issues surrounding women's prisons in Great Britain (Devlin, 1998). It appears that not much has changed since the earlier descriptions by Carlen (1983) and Dobash et al. (1986). In Devlin's (1998) book, there are consistent and clear parallels to the problems and issues of incarcerated women in Great Britain and the United States. Some of the issues that are covered in Devlin's book include:

- Poverty is endemic among prisoners.
- Many female inmates are addicts in need of treatment.
- Drug smuggling in women's prisons is the cause of violence when drugs are forcibly removed from the smuggler.
- Mandatory drug testing influences women to switch from cannabis to heroin or crack which is excreted from the body quicker.

- Frequent strip searches degrade women.
- Suicides are more common because of overcrowding and reduction in therapeutic programs.
- Psychotropic medication is being prescribed routinely.
- Shackling is still routine even for seriously ill women in the hospital.
- Women of color allege that racism is pervasive.
- Male officers feel at risk of sexual assault charges.
- There are fewer education and training programs for women than for men.

One of the more intriguing elements of the British penal system is the presence of mother-baby units. There are four mother-baby units, comprising 68 beds. In Holloway, babies may remain with their mother up to 9 months, and at the other facilities, babies up to 18 months may stay with their imprisoned mother (Carlen, 1999).

Carlen (1999) describes how, similarly to American women, British women are preoccupied with family issues. In fact, because of the greater proximity of prisons to where prisoners live, it is even more likely that the imprisoned woman will continue to "mother" from behind prison walls. For instance, an officer's description of one inmate indicates this reality:

> [An inmate] used to ring home every morning to make sure everyone was up, to make sure the kids were dressed, to make sure they'd had their breakfast and to make sure they'd gone to school. (Carlen, 1999: 129)

Thus, in Britain, perhaps even more so than in the United States, mothers in prison continue to mother.

Canada

Canada opened the first separate prison for women in 1880 under the reformatory model in Toronto. Until recently Canadian women serving terms of over two years have been housed in Kingston Prison for women in Kingston, Ontario. Women serving shorter terms have been housed in provincial prisons. The prison for women in Kingston has been the subject of critical inquiries and reports almost since 1835 when women were first housed there in part of the penitentiary for men (Berzins and Cooper, 1982). The prison was turned over to women in 1934 (Faith, 1999). Various investigative reports and commissions have recommended housing women in smaller, regional facilities since 1913 (Berzins and Cooper, 1982: 402). *Creating Choices* (1990) was a document created by a research and policy group after surveying the needs of Canadian women and what systems existed in other countries. The report recommended a series of small prisons, including one with a healing lodge. Before the decision-making process was complete, however, another event occurred that moved women inmates squarely into the public eye.

In 1994, a male special response team was deployed to conduct cell extractions of a number of women in segregation. These women had been involved in an assault on officers and continued to act out in segregation, including setting fires and threatening guards. The special response team—all men—employed the same procedures they used for male inmates. Heavily armored and helmeted, they entered the cell of each woman in force. They held the women down on the floor and cut off their clothes, then removed them from their cells shackled and naked (except for small paper gowns that did not cover the whole body), while the cells were stripped. During this time, the women were visible to all parties, including male maintenance workers. The women were then put back into their empty cells with the small paper gown and body chains and left there until the next afternoon. The video that was taken of the cell extractions ended up on national television, creating a huge outcry of public dismay and shock that resulted in a commission and an inquiry into the incident and, in a more general sense, an investigation of what should be done with female offenders (Arbour, 1996).

Finally, the Canadian government built and opened several new, smaller women's prisons geographically dispersed throughout the country. Today, women comprise about 2.5 percent of the federal prisoner population. This translated in 1997 to 357 women (Faith, 1999: 99). In 1997, the Elizabeth Fry Society issued a "report card" over Canada's treatment of female prisoners—the grade was an "F." Criticisms included the fact that the smaller women's prisons ended up being built with more security features and less gender-specific programming than what was planned. The facilities—at Truro, Edmonton, Kitchener, Joliette, Vancouver, and Maple Creek—turned out to be mini-prisons rather than "women-centered" institutions rich in resources (Faith, 1999).

One of the new prisons included a "healing lodge" for Aboriginal women—Okimaw Ohci Healing Lodge. This facility houses only 30 women, and the healing lodge is reserved specifically for Aboriginal women. Green (1998: 159–161) describes the planning of the facility, which included a series of meetings with Aboriginal leaders, who also meet regularly to monitor the program and provide support. The architecture followed the cottage plan for privacy and to create a feeling of community, and an emphasis was placed on nature (with windows and an attempt to orient the buildings to the outside). Evidently problems have emerged; the main issue seems to be that because of classification procedures, Native American women are being excluded from the lodge, even though it was built specifically for them. Some accuse the managers of the facility of straying from the original concepts (Faith, 1999).

Shaw (1991, 1992) and others (e.g., Adelberg and Currie, 1987, 1993) discuss how Canadian offenders face somewhat unique issues. First, the enormous size of the country virtually ensures that they will be spending their sentence far away from family and friends. The indigenous population is overrepresented in the prison population and their cultural traditions are particularly inconsistent with incarcerative punishments. The most interesting phenomenon, however, compared to America, is how incredibly few prisoners are in the Canadian system. The federal population still numbers in the hundreds, whereas in the United States, the national female prison population is over 90,000!

Other Countries

As with all countries, women form a small percentage of the total incarcerated population in Australia. Before the late 1980s, government reports on the state of prisons either neglected women entirely or devoted only a few pages to their issues. The history of female offenders in Australia is related to the transportation system, the system whereby criminals were sent from England to serve their sentences in Australia. Some of these criminals were women. Ostensibly sent to work as domestic laborers on large ranches, evidence indicates they were, in effect, prostituted to service male landowners and reward male convict workers. Institutions that housed women were built in the early 1900s, and, similarly to the United States, the reformatory ideal was applied to the women's institution; however, the first separate institution for women was not built until 1956 (Brown, Kramer, and Quinn, 1988: 281). This prison housed 51 women and closed in 1996 when a new, private prison (built and managed by the Corrections Corporation of America, or CCA) was opened (George, 1999).

In Australia, Aboriginal women are much more likely to be incarcerated than white women (as are Aboriginal men, who, in the late 1980s, were incarcerated at 372 times the rate of white women) (Brown, Kramer, and Quinn, 1988: 283). Similarly to the United States, incarcerated women are likely to be from the lower classes and to have significant alcohol and/or drug problems.

The rate of imprisonment for women has been increasing, although at a more modest rate than that of the United States (Brown, Kramer, and Quinn, 1988: 285). It is said that the security controls over women in prison are more extreme than those for men, the stereotypical role of women in society is reinforced by prison rules and expectations, and distance makes visitation with family difficult if not impossible. There were mother and baby units in the Australian prison for women until the 1980s. During that decade, a series of fires and disruptions caused some women to be transferred to the men's prison, and rules and procedures were tightened considerably (George, 1999: 192).

As elsewhere, there is controversy over whether more prisons for women should be built to ease overcrowding and provide facilities for better programming or whether building more prisons will lead to more women being needlessly incarcerated (Brown, Kramer, and Quinn, 1988: 295). George (1999) is highly critical of the new private prison for women, pointing out that promises regarding all-day visitation in the units have not been kept, and the private prison does not allow access to the media or researchers. In fact, she describes a strange application of Australia's trade secrets law that permits CCA to keep almost all information private, including such things as number of program slots and the number of violent incidents (1999: 199).

The history and current conditions of incarcerated women in New Zealand are not too different from those of Australian inmates. Women comprised up to 20 percent of New Zealand's prison population during the late 1800s and early 1900s. As in most countries, the Aboriginal population is overrepresented. In the case of New Zealand, it is the Maoris who comprise almost two-fifths of the prison population, but are only 12 percent of the total population. Women in New Zealand's prisons face the same issues as Canadian and Australian prisoners—loss of children and difficulty in maintaining contact with family members because of distances. Although there is enabling legislation to allow mothers to keep their babies in prison, it does not happen in practice. Most women are involved in "personal development" programming, rather than vocational programs (Morris and Kingi, 1999).

CONCLUSION

While the cross-cultural comparisons offered here have been abbreviated, it is clear that women across the world share the same issues as women incarcerated in prisons and jails in the United States. Women may be "inmates first," but they do not abdicate their roles as women, which often include being a mother, with all the attendant responsibilities and worries. Some countries accept and encourage that role more than other countries (Henriques, 1981; Kauffman, 1997). The United States falls far behind other countries in this area, ignoring this reality and having prison policies that make it difficult for female inmates to maintain family bonds. Women have gained a degree of economic and social equality in the United States as compared to some other countries in the world; the cost has been, evidently, that some women pay with a harsh sentencing policy that incarcerates quickly and revokes parole even more quickly, and that offers little hope for changing one's life while in prison.

The world looks with disfavor on many aspects of the incarceration of women in the United States. The sheer number of incarcerated women is far out of sync with the rest of the world; the practice of separating mothers and babies runs against the practices and belief systems of many other countries; and there is a growing condemnation of the widespread problem of sexual abuse of female prisoners by male officers as the problem makes headlines around the world.

NOTE

1. It is unclear why the discrepancy exists between O'Dwyer et al.'s figures and those of Dobash et al. cited in the previous paragraph.

SUGGESTED READINGS

Carlen, P. 1990. *Alternatives to Incarceration.* Philadelphia: Open University Press.

Carlen, P. 1994. "Why Study Women's Imprisonment? Or Anyone Else's?" *British Journal of Criminology* 34: 131–140.

Carlen, P. 1999. "Women's Imprisonment in England." In S. Cook and S. Davies, *Harsh Punishment: International Experiences of Women's Imprisonment,* pp. 123–141. Boston: Northeastern Press.

Cook, S., and S. Davies. 1999. *Harsh Punishment: International Experiences of Women's Imprisonment.* Boston: Northeastern Press.

10

Conclusions
and Future Directions

LEGACIES OF THE PAST

Women and men are different; so, too, are women and men in prison. In this book, we have seen how the history, rationale, and philosophy of women's institutions developed differently from those for men. The women's institution was created to protect female inmates from the abuses that occurred when they were housed with and supervised by men. The goal of women's institutions was to teach the woman inmate to behave "more like a lady." What it meant to be a lady during the late 1800s, however, was distinctly different from the life experience of most female inmates, then and now.

In the past, women were expected to become domestic and demure and to learn the gentle arts of sewing, cooking, housekeeping, and child rearing. It was hoped that the criminal woman, after becoming more refined, would be able to attract a husband who would keep her out of crime. The reality for

these women, however, was poverty. They typically escaped from their own
family early by marriage, running away, or being kicked out after an illegitimate pregnancy. They lived by prostitution and petty crime, at times exploit-
ing men, but more often being exploited by them. Their lives were often
marred by sexual and physical abuse. In the same manner that they themselves
had been victimized, they often passed abuse down to their children by
neglecting and abandoning them, either to get money or to squeeze some
pleasure from their bleak lives by "carousing."

Even during the time when wayward women were placed in reformatories, the majority of minority women and many older women who were considered irredeemable were housed in institutions that did not profess much
treatment of any kind. There the women continued to be used for their labor
and their sex—too weak to be true criminals, too deviant to be worthy of consideration. Today, there is still a disproportionate number of minority women
in prison. As is true of men's institutions, the most obvious fact when one
enters a women's prison is that it is largely an institution run by whites to
house minorities, for the most part, African Americans. Today one sees that in
some more urban prisons, it is increasingly an institution where African
Americans guard other African Americans.

Women in the correctional field have always been an afterthought—an
addendum to a world almost completely male. Women have suffered the fate
of all minority groups. Their needs have been ignored or misunderstood, and
they have been relegated to restricted roles and functions, for instance, sewing
and washing for the entire prison system or being sexually exploited by male
correctional officials. Because of disinterest, institutions for women remained
remarkably unchanged through the decades, whereas there was a great deal of
activity in the prisons for men. During the 1950s, 1960s, and 1970s, prisons
for men were under enormous pressure to change, in terms of treatment and
vocational programs and general living conditions. The pressure came from the
courts but also from scrutiny by the academic community and the public.

On the other hand, during this time period, very little litigation occurred
over conditions in women's prisons, and researchers showed very little interest
in them. Consequently, well into the 1960s the same psychiatric and biological explanations for female crime and behaviors in prison were being used that
had been current 100 years earlier. Only in the 1970s did interest develop in
the female offender and the women's prison. During the 1980s, there was
more activity and interest, including litigation that addressed the sex stereotyping and inadequate prison programming and treatment. Nontraditional
programs were developed, and there was more interest in providing a greater
range and depth of programming.

During the 1990s, the efforts to improve programming and provide
resources to help women help themselves upon release were derailed by the
explosion in numbers of inmates. Administrators found themselves housing
women in gymnasiums and education buildings because building could not
proceed fast enough; programming was a distinct second priority. The harden-
ing of public opinion toward all offenders, and especially drug offenders, has

impacted women tremendously. Federal sentencing guidelines and determinate sentencing structures in some states have meant that some women are going to prison who would not have been incarcerated even 20 years ago. The shift in the courts' approaches back to a "deference" model, which allows great latitude to prison administrators in determining what rights prisoners should have, has meant that, once in prison, female inmates (and male inmates) have little recourse. Further, women may continue to suffer greater deprivations because of imprisonment. They are usually housed further away from their home; they are often separated from young children and must arrange for alternative child custody arrangements; they face a greater risk of having their parental rights terminated; and they probably have greater social and mental health needs that remain unmet.

COMPARING PRISONS
FOR WOMEN AND MEN

An objective picture of the prison world is impossible. One can try to mesh the perceptions of officers and staff, prisoners, and outsiders to arrive at some stitched-together "truth." Our perceptions of the women's prison are inevitably shaped by our stereotypes of women. Women are always compared to men because prison is such a male world. For instance, women are said to be harder to supervise because they act like children, but they are also more likely to be treated like children. When a female inmate is told to comb her hair or clean her room or is otherwise spoken to in a manner that ignores the fact that she is an adult, she may respond with an obscenity or refusal that seems to the observer irrational and petulant. She does so as a defense against the infantilization, but the behavior is taken as proof that inmates really do act like children, and thus the cycle is perpetuated.

In the same manner, inmates resent being dependent on officers for the most minute details of daily living. It is difficult for an adult to ask for toilet paper, and so inmates mask the dependency by ordering and demanding that officers meet their needs immediately. Often such orders are accompanied by obscenities, to indicate that the inmate despises the need to ask and despises the officer for having the power to refuse. Because officers resent this type of treatment by inmates, they may use the little bit of power they have to retaliate. Inmates may find that request slips do not get processed; inmate belongings get lost; visitors are made to wait because their names do not appear on the visiting list; and sanitary napkins are rationed to one a day. These petty tyrannies only reinforce the perception of inmates that officers are all sadists, and again the cycle is perpetuated.

The unique subculture of female inmates has been of great interest to researchers and continues to be intriguing in its relative absence of violence, racism, or a black market. No doubt the result of the socialization of women in society and their needs for affiliation and support, the pseudofamilies and dyad relationships in prison often provide women with greater support and love than they have ever received on the outside. Women report that these relationships help make prison bearable. Yet prison officials typically discourage such connections among women, and some states deny visitation from friends who have been released. It is true that some relationships in prison are exploitive, but it is unfortunate that beneficial prison relationships are not more widely recognized as productive and rehabilitative.

One interesting example of how men and women created a different social organization even given a similar setting was presented by Scharf and Hickey's (1981) "just community" experiment. The authors created a therapeutic community in a women's prison, using the concepts of participation and commitment to increase the moral development of the residents. They had an opportunity to create a similar model in a men's prison and were able to observe differences between the two groups. The women tended to govern using emotional, personal decision making, whereas men were more political. The daily meetings of the women were marked by feelings; men tended to be concerned with tensions and conflicts, frequently exhibiting an adversarial front toward the staff. The female inmates tended to be oriented toward a greater sense of community than the men; they were observed to support one another emotionally. In the male unit, there existed a political consciousness strikingly absent among the women; men challenged the justification of the program and pushed the limits of their power. The authors termed the women's unit communitarian and the men's political (Scharf and Hickey, 1981).

The rich subcultural studies of the 1960s through the 1970s have not been replicated (with a few notable exceptions). Thus, we have no clear sense of what is occurring in the women's prison today. What we do know indicates that the differences observed 20 and 30 years ago remain remarkably unchanged. Women and men continue to create different worlds in the prison, with the women's world less marked by violence and racism; instead, the more prevalent themes of children, family, and a greater enthusiasm for programs are present in prisons for women.

PARITY VERSUS DIFFERENCE

As discussed in Chapter 7, parity was a goal of legal advocates and activists who observed that women in prison did not receive the same opportunities as men in prison. Some courts accepted this argument and attempted to force prison officials to equalize programming opportunities. The prevalent effect of a parity approach, however, has been that women's prisons are now supposed to be managed like men's prisons—with similar procedures, policies, and practices.

Although it is useful to compare prisons for men and women on such criteria as number of programs, staff-inmate ratios, and rules and privileges, it is also important to remember that to aspire to the standard of a prison for men is, first of all, not a very high standard and, second, may be an inapplicable standard. Some programs may be more appropriate in a facility for men. For instance, women show a definite disinterest in many types of recreational pro-grams. There is no reason to assume they would take advantage of all the pro-grams offered in institutions for men, but they might be interested in different programs. Few courts have mandated such a mechanical approach to parity, but it must be noted that a rigid parity approach would not necessarily allow for meeting the unique needs of female offenders.

The pressure for parity has been seen in an attempt to equalize vocational programs in prison; however, it seems more appropriate, given the lower secu-rity risk women pose and their lower rates of recidivism, to push for work-release and community programs for women. While women may benefit from nontraditional programming, it appears that not many are interested in such occupations. Thus, often a state spends a great deal of money to train women and then the skills are not used upon release. Parity in medical services would almost certainly mean women would not receive needed services because every indication is that their needs are different and greater than men's in this area. Prison administrators must realize that women need prenatal care throughout their pregnancies. This kind of care is even more important for women who have used drugs and have other health problems. The services women's prisons provide in this area are woefully inadequate and must be improved, not only for the sake of the female inmate but also for the unborn child. Legal programs are relatively underutilized in women's prisons, yet women's legal needs are extreme. Women need legal assistance in custody issues and other civil matters and seem less prepared and in need of greater assistance than men in this regard.

As discussed in Chapter 7, it may be that because of a growing inhospitable stance toward prisoners' rights suits, parity is a dead issue anyway. It seems that the most recent decisions regarding programming for women utilize a defer-ence standard that allows prison officials to decide what types of and how many programs should exist, given the small numbers of women (in relation to men) who are served.

GENDER-SPECIFIC PROGRAMMING

There is now a solid literature base in the concept of a feminist jurisprudence and "woman-centered" corrections. Feminist jurisprudence made it clear that the male perspective has always been the "universal" point of view (Daly and Chesney-Lind, 1988; Hannah-Moffat, 1994; Harris, 1987; Howe, 1990; Lahey, 1985; Rafter, 1989; West, 1988). In order for a woman's voice to be heard, one must first recognize that there is a different perspective.

A Different Voice

Daly (1989a), and many others, discuss the influence of Carol Gilligan (1982). Gilligan's work has been enormously influential in psychology, sociology, and law, despite some critics (see Daly, 1989a: 3). Gilligan argues that women may have a different perspective on morality, valuing intimacy and relationships more than rule-making, objectivity, and "justice" (at least justice as understood in the Western legal tradition). Gilligan firmly places the essence of morality for women in relationships. Women's greater sensitivity to the needs of others also lies in her attachment to others: "Since masculinity is defined through separation while femininity is defined through attachment, male gender identity is threatened by intimacy while female gender identity is threatened by separation" (Gilligan, 1982: 8).

Gilligan's work is often combined with that of Noddings (1989) who also postulates that women derive their identity, their morality, and their ability to "connect" through their attachment to others: "Direct contact with the helpless and needy stimulates care, and centuries of such experience may well have induced in females a predisposition for caring" (Gilligan, 1982: 127). Whether these differences arise from socialization or are partially biological is irrelevant to the end result, which is that women view the world differently and make decisions based on their greater attachment to others.

Heidensohn (1986) and Daly (1989a) offer the dichotomy of Portia and Persephone as illustrations of gender differences in perceptions of justice. The "male" version of justice emphasizes fairness, equal treatment, and rationality (Heidensohn's Portia model), while the "female" version of justice (Heidensohn's Persephone model) emphasizes needs, motives, and relationships. When one employs the male model of justice, the ideal is fair treatment; however, as Heidensohn points out, equal treatment may not be fair because the social reality is that women may have different economic needs, may have been victimized, and may be in a different position from male defendants.

Heidensohn (1986) asks what a justice model might look like based on the feminine "caring" perspective. She points out that the juvenile justice system is supposedly just such a model. Daly (1989a) points out that the corrections system, ideally at least, should reflect the Persephone model, since it concentrates on the offender; sentencing does and should take into account relationships and contextual elements that are important in the ethics of care.

These approaches can be seen at different times in history. The Persephone model can be attached to the indeterminate sentencing reform movement of the Progressive era, while the move back to a "just deserts" model, including determinate sentencing, in the 1980s is obviously more consistent with the Portia model. The justice approach has been applied to female offenders as well in more equal sentencing and in the trend toward equalization in programming and prison conditions.

Wheeler et al. (1989) uses these concepts more specifically in an application to corrections and prisons. She describes the parity approach as a Portia model of male justice (while the "difference" approach would be the Persephone model). In her analysis of one women's prison and female jailhouse lawyers, she concluded that parity is not a desirable goal for women, given their different needs.

Women-Wise Penology

Applied to corrections, the Portia model of justice would treat women equally, but would not take into account women's reality, that is, social inequalities, narrow stereotypes, and unequal distribution of power (Heidensohn, 1986: 290). Thus, Heidensohn suggests small hostels or houses with good community links and support as places of correction for women. These alternatives to prison would meet women's special needs and motivations to crime, which often are related to family pressures.

Carlen (1989, 1990) argues that what is needed instead of equality is a "women-wise penology." This penology would take into account realities of women's lives without stereotyping and punishing women who do not fit the ideal (good mother) role. Further, it would be an approach that does not oppress them in ways already occurring (by treating them as children, making them dependent). The penology she proposes would include using community options for women, emphasizing and encouraging the woman's role as mother and family member but also helping her to become self-sufficient (also see Pollock, 1998).

Gender-Specific Programming

The catch phrase in women's corrections today is "gender-specific" programming. One hesitates to connect this concept with the earlier concepts of Carlen and others, because while the women-wise penology concept empowers offenders, this latest concept is more like definitions by professionals who identify the needs of offenders and dictate the programs they should be receiving. Still, the attempt to identify female offenders' needs is laudable and necessary, and any voice that points out women are not men in corrections is one that needs to be heard.

For instance, Conley (1998: 2) presents a summary of the differences between male and female offenders:

- Women have different health needs.
- Women are three times as likely to report physical or sexual abuse.
- Women are more likely to have been caretakers of their children, and their children are much less likely to be with the other parent during the incarceration.
- Women are more likely to be first offenders and have less of a criminal record, they are less likely to be incarcerated for violent crime, and their violence follows different patterns (they are more likely to have killed a relative or intimate).
- Women and men differ in their patterns of drug use and drug-related crime (women are heavier abusers).

Given these differences, certain programming needs can be identified. Morton (1998: 12–15) provides a list of components for a model of effective programming for female offenders:

- Incarceration should be the last option to be considered in sanctioning women offenders.
- Supervision and programming must provide parity with male programs but be women-centered.
- Programs and services should be individualized and based on the needs and circumstances of each woman.
- Programs and supervision must be humane.
- Services and programs must reflect the biological characteristics of women as well as the impact of gender and acculturation in our society.
- Agency policies, programs, and practices should be gender-sensitive.
- Staff and other service providers who work with female offenders should be selected carefully and given gender-specific training to enable them to effectively supervise their clients.
- Supervision, programming, and management of female offenders should receive ongoing monitoring and periodic evaluation to ensure that these areas are accomplishing the goals they were designed to addresss.

Innovative programs are those that meet women's individual needs (women are both different from men and different from each other). Morash and Bynum (1995: 75), for instance, after reviewing a large number of programs in women's prisons, conclude that innovative programs share the following elements:

- Well-trained and dedicated staff
- Women-only programming
- Program materials focused on skills development and meeting women's particular needs
- Willingness to tailor approaches to meet individual needs
- Treatment with appropriate controls
- Use of peer support and development of peer networks
- Formal recognition of participant achievement
- Options for women who fail

Several authors note that prison is experienced differently by men and women; and in relation to the issues discussed earlier, it seems to be a particularly unlikely place for women to experience real growth. Although women are relatively safe in prison, and may create some support networks through pseudofamilies or other relationships, prison is a place where women are completely dependent on authority figures and have few opportunities to exercise responsibility. Velimesis (1981: 133) notes that:

> Under the prison system, dependence on authority figures is maximized, and opportunities to learn and exercise responsible personal decision making are minimized. Many women are in prison because of excessive dependence on others, and for them this type of administration does

nothing to counter thinking and behavior patterns that are personally destructive and that, in many cases, result in a return to prison.

The important point here is that while women in prison chafe at dependency, as do men in prison, it is more natural for them to accept dependency (especially on men). When some women say it is more "natural" for them to take orders from a man, they are merely putting words to their socialization and adherence to traditional sex roles. However, if they are ever to become emotionally strong and productive members of society, they need to learn independence. This is difficult to do in a traditional prison.

Unfortunately, it seems as if the trend in women's prisons is increasingly to make them more like traditional prisons, that is, prisons for men. New buildings are large, with obvious perimeter security, and designed under an institutional model (central mess-hall and dormitories or multiple-person cells). Every writer discussed here has pointed to the need for smaller facilities, in the community, where women can take responsibility for family roles and learn to live on their own. There are examples of these facilities; Huntington House (for homeless women) and Hopper House (an alternative to jail or prison) are managed by the Women's Prison Association, an organization that also provides housing, case management, housing and employment referral, parent training, and support groups to female offenders (Conley, 1998).

CONCLUSION

Currently, we have enormous numbers of women living in prison. True, their numbers are still minuscule compared to the numbers of men in prison, but since their numbers are now approaching 100,000, it can no longer be said that this is a negligible population. It is important to note that this increase is probably due more to sentencing practices than to a substantial change in criminal patterns of women. Evidence indicates that women are more likely to engage in property and drug crimes, but their violent crime rates remain essentially the same as in those time periods when they comprised a much smaller proportion of the prison population. We must ask ourselves whether prison is truly necessary for many female drug or property criminals (a question that can be applied to male inmates as well).

Historically, courts have shown a tendency to use imprisonment as a last resort for women. Their dependent marital status, the presence of dependent children, and other factors seemed to affect the likelihood of a prison sentence. For women who fit the societal roles of wife and mother, courts were more willing to use alternative means of sentencing. No evidence indicates that these alternative sentencing measures resulted in more crime. Women did not violate probation in larger numbers than men. In fact, by all accounts, recidivism has been lower for women, whatever the sentence. In some states, before a prison was built, alternative sentencing practices were even more apparent.

Only women who committed murder and other very serious crimes were incarcerated, because the state had to utilize county jails or contract with another state to house female offenders. Those states that chose not to imprison many women did not experience a crime wave among the female population because of the reticence to imprison.

Despite this history, almost all states are now incarcerating greater and greater numbers of women. Every state that builds a new prison for women fills it within a year or so. States that had only a couple of dozen women prisoners before a prison was built have suddenly had a couple of hundred once a prison was available. States that managed with one small prison from the early 1900s until recently have found that once they built two or three prisons, they filled those prisons and needed to go back to the legislature to ask for money to build more. As cells for women have increased in number, the women deemed as needing institutionalization have also increased in number. The old truism that you never close a prison certainly is true for women's prisons.

This development is unfortunate and probably unnecessary. For the most part, women commit minor property crimes. Their imprisonment destroys a family unit and subjects their children to extreme dislocation and anxiety. Many women never regain a maternal relationship with children who are left with others to care for them; sometimes the mother loses the children entirely when the state takes custody. The fact of imprisonment, and the separation it entails, necessitates the family programs found in some prisons. A prison can never provide a program, however, that makes up for the fact that the mother is separated from the child—sometimes for months, sometimes for years. This separation may have cyclical implications, since there is evidence that children are prone to delinquency and crime when their mother is in prison.

Some women in prison are there because the state was unable to protect them from abusive husbands. These battered women have been doubly victimized—first, by having to endure the abuse in a marriage because society does not provide economic or legal solutions to battering; and second, because when such a woman kills her husband as a desperate act of self-defense, society feels justified in punishing her for "taking the law into her own hands."

Some women in prison are committed to criminal lifestyles. For these women, crime is a job, and they have extensive criminal histories. The professional female criminal seems to be a rarity, and most do not profess such an orientation. There has been very little research on career criminals among female offenders, however, so it is unclear what types of female career criminals exist, and the nature of their activities and motivations has not been explored. It is clear that women are not becoming more violent; their numbers in robbery and other violent crimes continue to remain stable or decrease. Women continue to commit such crimes as shoplifting, forgery, check fraud, larceny, and to a lesser extent burglary.

Increasing numbers of women are becoming involved in drug violations and other crimes due to drug use. This trend will probably continue, and jails and prisons will have to deal with the medical problems of addicted women—problems that will be more acute if the women are pregnant. Drugs will probably continue to have an effect on the numbers and types of crimes women commit, and treatment programs must adapt accordingly. Although treatment programs exist in most prisons, the numbers of women that must be accommodated continue to grow.

In fact, all programs in women's prisons will need to be expanded if the trend of sentencing more and more women to prison continues. Women, if they must be imprisoned, should not waste the time spent there. Adequate vocational programs are needed to prepare them to take care of themselves and their children without resort to drugs or other types of crime. Vocational programs in the clerical areas are well received by women, but prisons should continue to expand their offerings in nontraditional areas, such as the skilled trades. As long as society continues to undervalue "women's work," such as the clerical and service trades, women inmates are not well served by training programs designed to place them in such occupations. Computers, carpentry, mechanical training, and other programs prepare women for occupations that pay almost double what they might make as a secretary or cafeteria worker.

There will continue to be cross-sex supervision; thus, the problems that arise when male officers supervise female inmates must be addressed. The provisions made for male officers working in living units for women need to be evaluated and changed if necessary. Suggestions have included architectural designs to provide some amount of privacy, such as frosted glass in the shower and curtains in front of toilets. Some prisons use such designs, along with other alternatives. The most important factor, however, is people. If training and supervision cannot prevent occurrences of problems, then states should reconsider the practice of cross-sex supervision. At least some courts have recognized a sex as a bona fide occupational qualification, given the women's victimization history and the increasing evidence of sexual abuse by male officers. It is incredibly ironic that women today are faced with sexual abuse by male guards—the very reason separate women's reformatories were created in the 1800s!

Training in correctional academies should recognize that women's institutions are part of the corrections system and should address the special training needs of officers destined for such facilities. The trend now seems to be to get women's institutions "in line" with the rest of the system, which means treating women "like inmates." If this means to treat them like adults, that is a step forward. It is more likely, however, that it means treating them like men in prison, which means that women may lose the more personal nature of staff-inmate interaction typically found in women's institutions. For instance, staff are trained to treat all inmates alike. Although such treatment is helpful in that it reduces favoritism and encourages fairness, all inmates are not alike. In fact, some women, as well as men, at times literally scream to be recognized for their individuality by "cutting up," fighting, or mistreating officers and inmates with loud and abusive behavior. It is more beneficial to inmates, but perhaps more stressful for officers, to recognize each inmate as an individual with unique needs and motivations. For example, it takes more skill to recognize that one woman is sincere in her need to see a counselor, while another is merely manipulating the system to avoid work or boredom. It takes skill to recognize when a woman is suffering from acute depression and needs to be put under observation. It takes skill to recognize that the rude and abusive behavior of some women is a reaction to the fact of imprisonment and not to be taken personally.

One cannot put more demands on the correctional officer staff without some provisions for greater rewards. Professionalization has been the theme for the last decade, but this trend needs encouragement. For instance, all correctional officers should be rewarded and assisted if they desire higher education or membership and attendance at national or regional professional conferences. Actually, two trends are developing among correctional staff today; the first is professionalization, which tends to emphasize education and enforced standards of conduct, and the second is unionization, which emphasizes material rewards and security concerns. Both of these movements are important for correctional staff, but unionization may be more shortsighted, in that ordinarily demands center on wage increases rather than job enrichment. As long as the role of correctional officer is one that demands or expects no intelligence or skill, there will be people in these positions who display none. Their lack of skill undercuts the performance of those who aspire to do more than count inmates and turn keys and frustrates attempts to enlarge the role. At this time, people who do aspire to a larger role are typically leaving the correctional officer position as soon as they acquire the necessary qualifications for other positions. This result is unfortunate, and some attempts should be made to keep these individuals in the positions that require the most contact with inmates.

Improvements should continue in women's prisons, but efforts should also be made to greatly expand the alternatives to prison for women. The number of halfway-house beds for women is drastically disproportional to the number available for men. This disproportionality seems to stem from a belief that women have a place to go after release, either with family or back to a husband. Unfortunately, many women do not have such a place to go, and women are in great need of a transition from prison to the outside. The offender needs time to get herself settled into a position where she can afford to take her children back. Sometimes, however, because of custody problems, she must take responsibility for her children immediately; this is rarely a good alternative, since women may need time to reestablish ties and certainly need time to build up some economic reserves.

The greatest need of female offenders is for correctional alternatives that recognize the presence of children in their lives. For instance, halfway houses that would accept women and children would be a vast improvement over what is currently available. A few facilities scattered across the country house female offenders and their children, but they are the exception. A halfway house centered around women's needs and the needs of their children would provide parenting classes and day-care. Day-care would give the woman the security of knowing her children were safe while she was at work. The children could benefit from programs that would address their special problems—namely, the anxiety of reuniting with a mother who might have been absent for a long time, perhaps even for the lifetime of a young child. Birth control should be encouraged. Some female offenders started having children very early and continue to have children without regard to who will care for them. These child-mothers never had a childhood of their own; they are criticized for being bad mothers when, in fact, they are simply too young to take on the responsibilities of motherhood.

Rather than large facilities, halfway houses should be homes, small enough to blend in with the neighborhood and not stigmatize the women and children who live within them. Because women are typically not feared, as male criminals are, the problems of community acceptance should be less severe. Women can provide support for one another in their attempts to lead a life free from drugs, crime, and negative associations with men. Perhaps there should even be a range of custody grades; the lowest-security homes would not need staff but could operate as group homes, providing three or four women and their children with a house to live in and resident day-care until they were able to afford to live on their own.

These facilities could also be used for women instead of a prison term. In fact, any attempts to keep women in the community instead of prison should be welcomed, as long as accompanying measures go toward preventing the factors that cause women to commit crime. Placement in a residential community setting allows control but does not destroy beneficial family ties, especially if the woman is able to keep her children with her. Correctional professionals may be able to help provide a setting where she can learn to be a good mother if she was not before, to stay off drugs if she could not on her own, and to support herself without resort to criminality. Most women will continue to seek relationships with men, but in a setting where self-discovery is possible, women may help one another break the pattern of disastrous relationships with abusive, drug-addicted, or criminal men. Some women must learn to be more independent from men; others need to learn to be less fearful and suspicious of them; and still others need to learn to be less exploitive of men. Not all women are victims; some do the victimizing.

Corrections should punish wrongdoing. Many people hear the terms *resources* and *needs* in relation to offenders and are disgusted. They argue that law-abiding people have "needs" and require "resources," too, but no one is interested in them, and that offenders should have thought about the deprivations in prison before they committed the crime. These are valid concerns; however, it is not only for offenders' benefit that we need to provide them with the tools to change their lives—it is for our benefit as well. As described previously, women in prison often have come from the worst childhoods imaginable. They simply may not have the individual skills necessary to live a productive, law-abiding life, because no one ever taught them how. If the lessons come when they are 30 rather than 13, then at least they have the rest of their lives to make use of them. Further, one assumes that those who object to resources being provided to female offenders do not think that the offenders' innocent, young children deserve to be punished as well. Yet, these children are punished by the woman's imprisonment, and they also will be punished if she continues in a dysfunctional lifestyle upon her release. While we do not mean to reduce the realities of women's lives to only their role as mothers, it cannot be overstated that women's imprisonment also affects the lives of close to a half million children in this country. Many women in prison could serve their sentence in minimum-security or reduced-liberty settings; many desire to change. Although we cannot force an individual to change, we can certainly help them to do so by providing the necessary environment and resources. Do women's prisons today facilitate productive or destructive changes in the lives of the women who are incarcerated within them? The answer to that question affects us all.

SUGGESTED READINGS

Daly, K. 1989. "Criminal Justice Ideologies and Practices in Different Voices: Some Feminist Questions about Justice." *International Journal of the Sociology of Law* 17: 1–18.

Gilligan, C. 1982. *In a Different Voice: Psychological Theory and Women's Development.* Cambridge, MA: Harvard University Press.

References

Ackerman, P. 1972. "A Staff Group in a Women's Prison." *International Journal of Group Psychotherapy* 23: 364–373.

Acoca, L. 1998. "Defusing the Time Bomb: Understanding and Meeting the Growing Health Care Needs of Incarcerated Women in America." *Crime and Delinquency* 44, 1 (January): 49–69.

Acoca, L., and J. Austin. 1996. *The Hidden Crisis: Women in Prison*. San Francisco: National Council on Crime and Delinquency.

Adams, H. 1914. *Women and Crime*. London: T. Warner Laurie.

Adelberg, E., and C. Currie. 1987. *Too Few to Count: Canadian Women in Conflict with the Law*. Vancouver, BC: Press Gang Publishers.

Adelberg, E., and C. Currie. 1993. *In Conflict with the Law: Women and the Canadian Justice System*. Vancouver, BC: Press Gang Publishers.

Adler, F. 1975. *Sisters in Crime: The Rise of the New Female Criminal*. New York: McGraw-Hill.

Alarid, L. 1997. "Female Inmate Subcultures." In J. Marquart and J. Sorensen, *Correctional Contexts: Contemporary and Classical Readings*, pp. 134–152. Los Angeles: Roxbury.

Alley, M. 1997. "The Mother Offspring Life Development Program." In *Maternal Ties: A Selection of Programs for Female Offenders*," pp. 151–159. Lanham, MD: American Correctional Association.

Alpert, G. P. 1980. *Legal Rights of Prisoners*. Newbury Park, CA: Sage.

Alpert, G. 1984. "The Needs of the Judiciary and Misapplications of Social Research." *Criminology* 22, 3: 441–456.

Alpert, G., and B. Crouch. 1991. "Cross-Gender Supervision, Personal Privacy, and Institutional Security." *Criminal Justice and Behavior* 18: 304–317.

Alpert, G. P., G. Noblit, and J. Wiorkowski. 1977. "Comparative Look at Prisonization: Sex and Prison Culture." *Quarterly Journal of Corrections* 1, 3: 29–34.

American Correctional Association. 1990. *The Female Offender: What Does the Future Hold?* Washington, D.C.: St. Mary's Press.

American Correctional Association. 1993. *Female Offenders: Meeting the Needs of a Neglected Population*. Baltimore, MD: United Book Press.

Amnesty International. 1999 (March). *"Not Part of My Sentence": Violations of the Human Rights of Women in Custody*. London: Amnesty International.

Anglin, M., and Y. Hser. 1987. "Addicted Women and Crime." *Criminology* 25, 2: 359–394.

Arbour, L. 1996. *Commission Inquiry into Certain Events at the Prison for Women in Kingston*. Toronto, Canada: Public Works and Government Services.

Ardeti, R. 1973. "The Sexual Segregation of American Prisons." *Yale Law Journal* 82, 6: 1229–1273.

Arnold, R. 1994. "Black Women in Prison: The Price of Resistance." In M. Zinn and B. Dill (eds.), *Women of Color in U.S. Society*. Philadelphia: Temple University Press.

Asseo, L. 1999 (November 18). "Women, Families Feeling Effects of U.S. Drug War." *Austin American Statesman*, p. A20.

Austin, J., B. Bloom, and T. Donahue. 1992. *Female Offenders in the Community: An Analysis of Innovative Strategies and Programs*. San Francisco: National Council on Crime and Delinquency.

Aylward, A., and J. Thomas. 1984. "Quiescence in Women's Prisons Litigation: Some Exploratory Issues." *Justice Quarterly* 1, 2: 253–276.

Baker, D. 1999. "A Descriptive Profile and Socio-Historical Analysis of Female Executions in the United States:

1632–1997." *Women and Criminal Justice* 10, 3: 57–95.

Baker, M., ed. 1987. *Sex Differences in Human Performance.* New York: Wiley.

Baro, A. 1997. "Spheres of Consent: An Analysis of the Sexual Abuse and Sexual Exploitation of Women Incarcerated in the State of Hawaii." *Women and Criminal Justice* 8, 3: 61–84.

Barry, E. 1989. "Pregnant Prisoners." *Harvard Women's Law Journal* 12: 189–205.

Barry, E. 1991. "Jail Litigation Concerning Women Prisoners." *The Prison Journal* LXXI: 44–50.

Barry, E. 1996. "Women Prisoners and Health Care." In K. Moss, ed., *Man-made Medicine,* pp. 250–272. Durham, NC: Duke University Press.

Baunach, P. 1977. "Women Offenders: A Commentary—Current Conceptions on Women in Crime." *Quarterly Journal of Corrections* 1, 4: 14–18.

Baunach, P. 1979. "Mothering Behind Prison Walls." Paper presented at American Society of Criminology Conference, Philadelphia, PA.

Baunach, P. 1982. "You Can't Be a Mother and Be in Prison . . . Can You? Impacts of the Mother-Child Separation." In B. Price and N. Sokoloff, eds., *The Criminal Justice System and Women,* pp. 155–170. New York: Clark and Boardman.

Baunach, P. 1985a. "Critical Problems of Women in Prison." In I. Moyer, ed., *The Changing Roles of Women in the Criminal Justice System,* pp. 95–110. Prospect Heights, IL: Waveland.

Baunach, P. 1985b. *Mothers in Prison.* New Brunswick, N.J.: Transaction Books.

Baunach, P., and T. Murton. 1973. "Women in Prison, an Awakening Minority." *Crime and Corrections* 1: 4–12.

Bayes, M., and P. Newton. 1978. "Women in Authority: A Socio-Psychological Analysis." *Journal of Applied Behavioral Science* 14, 1: 7–28.

Beck, A. 1995. *Bureau of Justice Statistics Bulletin: Profile of Jail Inmates, 1989.* Washington, D.C.: U.S. Department of Justice.

Beck, A., and C. Mumola. 1999. *Bulletin: Prisoners in 1998.* Washington, D.C.: U.S. Department of Justice, Bureau of Justice Statistics. (Also cited as BJS.)

Beckerman, A. 1989. "Incarcerated Mothers and Their Children in Foster Care."

Children and Youth Services Review 11, 2: 175–183.

Beckerman, A. 1994. "Mothers in Prison: Meeting the Prerequisite Conditions for Permanency Planning." *Social Work* 39: 9–14.

Bedell, P. 1997. *Resilient Women: Risk and Protective Factors in the Lives of Female Offenders.* Master's thesis; Vermont College of Norwich University, Northfield, VT.

Belknap, J. 1991. "Women in Conflict: An Analysis of Women Correctional Officers." *Women and Criminal Justice* 2: 89–115.

Belknap, J. 1996. "Access to Programs and Health Care for Incarcerated Women." *Federal Probation* 60: 34–39.

Belknap, J. 1996/2000. *The Invisible Woman: Gender, Crime and Justice.* Belmont, CA: Wadsworth.

Bell, D. 1999. (October 13). "Prisons Study Reassigning Guards: Alleged Sex Abuse May Prompt Action." *Detroit Free Press,* http://www.freep.com/news/mich/qpris13.htm.

Bensman, T., and J. Mosier. 2000 (February 24). "Texas Rangers Investigating Rockwall Jail." *Dallas Morning News,* http://dallasnews.com/metro/39546_ROCKWALL24.html.

Berk, B. 1966. "Organizational Goals and Inmate Organization." *American Journal of Sociology* 71 (March): 522–534.

Bernat, F. 1995. "Opening the Dialogue: Women's Culture and the Criminal Justice System." *Women and Criminal Justice* 7, 1: 1–8.

Bershad, L. 1985. "Discriminatory Treatment of the Female Offender in the Criminal Justice System." *Boston College Law Review* 26, 2: 389–438.

Berzins, L., and S. Cooper. 1982. "The Political Economy of Correctional Planning for Women: The Case of the Bankrupt Bureaucracy." *Canadian Journal of Criminology* 24, 4: 399–416.

Biron, L, S. Brochu, and L. Desjardins. 1995. "The Issue of Drugs and Crime Among a Sample of Incarcerated Women." *Deviant Behavior* 16: 25–43.

Blinn, C. 1997. *Maternal Ties: A Selection of Programs for Female Offenders.* Lanham, MD: American Correctional Association.

Block, K., and M. Potthast. 1997 (March). "Living Apart and Getting Together: Inmate Mothers and Enhanced Visitation through Girl Scouts." Paper presented at

Academy of Criminal Justice Sciences meeting, Nashville, TN.

Block, P., and D. Anderson. 1974. *Policewomen on Patrol.* Washington, D.C.: Police Foundation.

Bloom, B. 1988a. "Mothers in Prison: A Neglected Population." *Nurturing Today* 10, 1: 11, 32.

Bloom, B. 1988b. "Women Behind Bars: A Forgotten Population." Paper presented at the 1988 Academy of Criminal Justice Sciences Conference, San Francisco, CA.

Bloom, B. 1993. "Incarcerated Mothers and Their Children: Maintaining Family Ties." In American Correctional Association, eds., *Female Offenders: Meeting Needs of a Neglected Population,* pp. 60–68. Laurel, MD: American Correctional Association.

Bloom, B. 1995. "Imprisoned Mothers." In K. Gabel and D. Johnston, eds., *Children of Incarcerated Parents.* New York: Lexington Books.

Bloom, B. 2000 (August). "Gender Responsive Programs and Services." Presentation at American Correctional Association meeting, San Antonio, TX.

Bloom, B., and M. Chesney-Lind. 2000. "Women in Prison: Vengeful Equity." In R. Muraskin, *It's a Crime: Women and Justice,* 2d ed., pp. 183–204. Upper Saddle River, NJ: Prentice-Hall.

Bloom, B., M. Chesney-Lind, and B. Owen. 1994. *Women in California Prisons: Hidden Victims of the War on Drugs.* San Francisco: Center on Juvenile and Criminal Justice.

Bloom, B., R. Immarigeon, and B. Owen, eds. 1995. "Women in Prisons and Jails. Special Issue." *Prison Journal: An International Forum on Incarceration and Alternative Sanctions* 75, 2.

Bloom, B., and D. Steinhart. 1993. *Why Punish the Children? A Reappraisal of the Children of Incarcerated Mothers in America.* San Francisco: National Council on Crime and Delinquency.

Blount, W., T. Danner, M. Vega, and I. Silverman. 1991. "The Influence of Substance Use Among Adult Female Inmates." *The Journal of Drug Issues* 21, 2: 449–467.

Blount, W., J. Kuhns, and I. Silverman. 1993. "Intimate Abuse Within an Incarcerated Female Population: Rates, Levels, Criminality, A Continuum, and Some Lessons About Self-Identification." In C. Culliver, ed., *Female Criminality: The State of the Art,* pp. 413–462. New York: Garland.

Boudin, K. 1997. "The Nation's Oldest Complete Prison Program." In C. Blinn, *Maternal Ties: A Selection of Programs for Female Offenders,"* pp. 55–87. Lanham, MD: American Correctional Association.

Boudin, K. 1998. "Lessons from a Mother's Program in Prison: A Psychosocial Approach Supports Women and Their Children." *Women and Therapy* 21: 103–125.

Boudouris, J. 1985. *Prisons and Kids.* Laurel, MD: American Correctional Association.

Boudouris, J. 1996. *Parents in Prison: Addressing the Needs of Families.* Lanham, MD: American Correctional Association.

Bowersox, M. 1981. "Women in Corrections: Competence, Competition, and the Social Responsibility Norm." *Criminal Justice and Behavior* 8, 4: 491–499.

Bowker, L. 1979. *Women, Crime and the Criminal Justice System.* Lexington, MA: Lexington Books.

Bowker, L. 1980. *Prison Victimization.* New York: Elsevier Press.

Bowker, L. 1981. "The Institutional Determinants of International Female Crime." *International Journal of Comparative and Applied Criminal Justice* 5, 1: 11–28.

Box, S., and C. Hale. 1983. "Liberation and Female Criminality in England and Wales." *British Journal of Criminology* 23, 1: 35.

Brennan, T. 1998. "Institutional Classification of Females: Problems and Some Proposals for Reform." In R. Zaplin, ed., *Female Offenders: Critical Perspectives and Effective Interventions.* Gaithersburg, MD: Aspen.

Brewer, V., J. Marquart, J. Mullings, and B. Crouch. 1998. "AIDS-Related Risk Behavior Among Female Prisoners with Histories of Mental Impairment." *Prison Journal* 78: 101–119.

Brown, D., H. Kramer, and M. Quinn. 1988. "Women in Prison: Task Force Reform." In M. Findlay and R. Hogg, *Understanding Crime and Criminal Justice,* pp. 273–308. Melbourne, Australia: Law Book Company, Limited.

Browne, A. 1987. *When Battered Women Kill.* New York: Free Press.

Buccio–Notaro, P. 1998. "An Innovative Solution: The Neil J. Houston House." In J. Morton, ed., *Complex Challenges, Collaborative Solutions: Programming for Adult and Juvenile Female Offenders,* pp. 141–151.

Lanham, MD: American Correctional Association.

Bureau of Justice Statistics (BJS). 1989. *Prisoners in 1988*. Washington, D.C.: U.S. Department of Justice.

Bureau of Justice Statistics (BJS). 1991. *Women in Prison (Bulletin)*. Washington, D.C.: U.S. Department of Justice. (May be cited as Greenfield, L., and S. Minor-Harper.)

Bureau of Justice Statistics (BJS). 1992. *Women in Jail: 1989. Special Report*. Washington, D.C.: U.S. Department of Justice. (May be cited as Snell, T.)

Bureau of Justice Statistics (BJS). 1994a. *Domestic Violence: Violence Between Intimates. Special Report*. Washington, DC: U.S. Department of Justice.

Bureau of Justice Statistics (BJS). 1994b. *Special Report: Women in Prison*. Washington, D.C.: U.S. Department of Justice. (May be cited as Snell, T.)

Bureau of Justice Statistics (BJS). 1994c. *Survey of State Prison Inmates, 1991: Women in Prison*. Washington, D.C.: U.S. Department of Justice Statistics.

Bureau of Justice Statistics (BJS). 1995. *Correctional Populations in the United States. 1992*. Washington, DC: U.S. Department of Justice. (May be cited as Snell, T.)

Bureau of Justice Statistics (BJS). 1997a. *Correctional Populations in the U.S.* Washington D.C.: U.S. Department of Justice.

Bureau of Justice Statistics (BJS). 1997b. *Prisoners in 1997*. Washington, D.C.: U. S. Department of Justice. (May be cited as Gilliard, D., and A. Beck.)

Bureau of Justice Statistics (BJS). 1998. *Profile of Jail Inmates 1996. Special Report*. Washington, D.C.: U.S. Department of Justice. (May be cited as Harlow, C.)

Bureau of Justice Statistics (BJS). 1999a. *Prisoners in 1998*. Washington, D.C.: U.S. Department of Justice. (May be cited as Beck, A., and C. Mumola.)

Bureau of Justice Statistics(BJS). 1999b. *Selected Findings: Prior Abuse Reported by Inmates and Probationers*. Washington D.C.: U.S. Department of Justice. (May be cited as: Harlow, C.)

Bureau of Justice Statistics (BJS). 1999c. *Special Report: Women Offenders*. Washington, D.C.: U.S. Department of Justice. (May be cited as Greenfield, L., and T. Snell.)

Burke, P., and L. Adams. 1991. *Classification of Women Offenders in State Correctional Facilities: A Handbook for Practitioners.* Washington, D.C.: National Institute of Corrections.

Burkhardt, K. 1973. *Women in Prison*. Garden City, NJ: Doubleday.

Bush-Baskette, S. 1995. "The War on Drugs as a War Against Black Women." In S. Miller, *Crime Control and Women,* pp. 113–121. Thousand Oaks, CA: Sage.

Camp, C., and G. Camp. 1997. *The Corrections Yearbook*. South Salem, NY: Criminal Justice Institute.

Camp, D., and H. Sandhu. 1995. *Evaluation of Female Offender Regimented Treatment Program (FORT) (Final Report)*. Oklahoma City: Oklahoma State University, Department of Sociology.

Campbell, C., D. Mackenzie, and J. Robinson. 1987. "Female Offenders: Criminal Behavior and Gender-Role Identity." *Psychological Reports* 60: 867–873.

Carlen, P. 1983. *Women's Imprisonment: A Study in Social Control*. London: Routledge & Kegan Paul.

Carlen, P. (ed.). 1985. *Criminal Women*. Cambridge, England: Polity Press.

Carlen, P. 1988. *Women, Crime and Poverty*. Philadelphia: Open University Press.

Carlen, P. 1989. "Feminist Jurisprudence—Or Women-Wise Penology?" *Probation Journal* 36, 3: 110–114.

Carlen, P. 1990. *Alternatives to Incarceration*. Philadelphia: Open University Press.

Carlen, P. 1994. "Why Study Women's Imprisonment? Or Anyone Else's?" *British Journal of Criminology* 34: 131–140.

Carlen, P. 1999. "Women's Imprisonment in England." In S. Cook and S. Davies, *Harsh Punishment: International Experiences of Women's Imprisonment,* pp. 123–141. Boston: Northeastern University Press.

Carp, S., and L. Schade. 1992. "Tailoring Facility Programming to Suit Female Offender Needs." *Corrections Today* 54, 6: 152–159.

Carroll, L. 1974. *Hacks, Blacks and Cons*. Lexington, MA: Lexington Press.

Catalino, A. 1972. "Boys and Girls in a Co-Educational Training School Are Different, Aren't They?" *Canadian Journal of Criminology and Corrections* 14: 120–131.

Catan, L. 1992. "Infants with Mothers in Prison." In R. Shaw, ed., *Prisoners' Children: What Are the Issues?,* pp. 26–42. New York: Routledge.

Chandler, E. 1973. *Women in Prison*. New York: Bobbs-Merrill.

Chapman, J. 1980. *Economic Realities and Female Crime*. Lexington, MA: Lexington Books.

Chapman, J. 1983. *Women Employed in Corrections*. Washington, D.C.: National Institute of Justice.

Charles, M. 1981. "The Performance and Socialization of Female Recruits in the Michigan State Police Training Academy." *Journal of Police Science and Administration 9*, 2: 209–223.

Chesney–Lind, M. 1982. "Guilty by Reason of Sex: Young Women and the Juvenile Justice System." In B. Price and N. Sokoloff, *The Criminal Justice System and Women,* pp. 77–105. New York: Clark Boardman.

Chesney-Lind, M. 1988. "Girls in Jail." *Crime and Delinquency* 34, 2: 150–168.

Chesney-Lind, M. 1991. "Patriarchy, Prisons and Jails: A Critical Look at Trends in Women's Incarceration." *The Prison Journal* 71, 1: 51–67.

Chesney-Lind, M. 1995. "Rethinking Women's Imprisonment: A Critical Examination of Trends in Female Incarceration." In B. Price and N. Sokoloff, eds., *The Criminal Justice System and Women, Offenders, Victims, and Workers,* 2d ed., pp. 105–117. New York: McGraw-Hill.

Chesney-Lind, M. 1997. *The Female Offender: Girls, Women and Crime*. Thousand Oaks, CA: Sage.

Chesney-Lind, M. 1998. "The Forgotten Offender: Women in Prison: From Partial Justice to Vengeful Equity." *Corrections Today* (December): 66–73.

Chesney-Lind, M., and J. Pollock. 1995. "Women's Prisons: Equality with a Vengeance." In A. Merlo and J. Pollock, eds., *Women, Law and Social Control,* pp. 155–175. Boston: Allyn and Bacon.

Chesney-Lind, M., and N. Rodriquez. 1983. "Women Under Lock and Key: A View from the Inside." *The Prison Journal* 63, 2: 47–65.

Chesney-Lind, M., and R. Sheldon. 1998. *Girls, Delinquency, and Juvenile Justice*. Belmont, CA: West/Wadsworth.

Chigwada-Bailey, R. 1997. *Black Women's Experiences of Criminal Justice*. Winchester, England: Waterside Press.

Clark, J. 1995. "The Impact of the Prison Environment on Mothers." *Prison Journal* 75, 3: 306–329.

Clement, M. 1993. "Parenting in Prisons: A National Survey of Programs for Incarcerated Women." *Journal of Offender Rehabilitation* 19, 1/2: 89–100.

Clemmer, D. 1940. *The Prison Community*. New York: Holt, Rinehart & Winston.

Climent, C. E., A. Rollins, and C. J. Batinelli. 1977. "Epidemiological Studies of Female Prisoners." *Journal of Nervous and Mental Disease* 164, 1: 25–29.

Cochrane, R. 1971. "The Structure of Value Systems in Male and Female Prisoners." *British Journal of Criminology* 11: 73–79.

Coles, F. 1980. "Women in Corrections: Issues and Concerns." In A. Cohn and B. Ward, *Improving Management in Criminal Justice,* pp. 105–115. Newbury Park, CA: Sage.

Colley, E., and A. Camp. 1992. "Creating Programs for Women Inmates." *Corrections Today*. (April): 208–209.

Collins, W. 1998. "Equal Protection and Women's Prisons: Is the Parity Era Over?" in J. Morton, ed., *Complex Challenges, Collaborative Solutions: Programming for Adult and Juvenile Female Offenders,* pp. 43–61. Lanham, MD: American Correctional Association.

Collins, W., and A. Collins. 1996. *Women in Jail: Legal Issues*. Washington, D.C.: National Institute of Corrections.

Conley, C. 1998. *The Women's Prison Association: Supporting Women Offenders and Their Families (Program Focus)*. Washington, D.C.: National Institute of Justice.

Connolly, J. 1983. "Women in County Jails: An Invisible Gender in an Ill Defined Institution." *Prison Journal* 63: 99–115.

Cook, R. 1993 (June 24). "Prison Guard Acquitted on All Counts." *Atlanta Journal,* p. C1.

Cook, S., and S. Davies. 1999. *Harsh Punishment: International Experiences of Women's Imprisonment*. Boston: Northeastern University Press.

Cookson, H. M. 1977. "Survey of Self-Injury in a Closed Prison for Women." *British Journal of Criminology* 17, 4: 332–347.

Coontz, P. 1983. "Women Under Sentence of Death: The Social Organization of Waiting to Die." *The Prison Journal* 63, 2: 88–98.

Cotton-Oldenburg, N., B. Jordan, S. Martin, and L. Kupper. 1999. "Women Inmates' Risky Sex Behaviors: Are They Related?" *The Journal of Drug and Alcohol Abuse* 25, 1: 129–150.

Covington, J. 1985. "Gender Differences in Criminality Among Heroin Users." *Journal of Research in Crime and Delinquency,* 22: 329–354.

Covington, S. 1998a. "The Relational Theory of Women's Psychological Development: Implications for the Criminal Justice System." In R. Zaplin, ed., *Female Crime and Delinquency: Critical Perspectives and Effective Interventions.* Gaithersburg, MD: Aspen.

Covington, S. 1998b. "Women in Prison: Approaches in the Treatment of Our Most Invisible Population." In J. Harden and M. Hill, *Breaking the Rules: Prison and Feminist Therapy,* pp. 141–155. New York: Harrington Park Press Books.

Cowie, J., J. Cowie, and E. Slater. 1968. *Delinquency in Girls.* Cambridge, MA: Humanities Press.

Cranford, S., and R. Williams. 1998. "Critical Issues in Managing Female Offenders." *Corrections Today* 60: 130–134.

Crawford, J. 1988a. *Tabulation of a Nationwide Survey of Female Offenders.* College Park, MD: American Correctional Association.

Crawford, J. 1988b. *Tabulation of a Nationwide Survey of State Correctional Facilities for Adult and Juvenile Female Offenders.* College Park, MD: American Correctional Association.

Creating Choices: The Report of the Task Force on Federally Sentenced Women. 1990 (April). Toronto, Ottawa, Canada: Correctional Services of Canada.

Crites, L. 1976. *The Female Offender.* Lexington, MA: Lexington Books.

Cromwell, P., ed. 1999. *In Their Own Words: Criminals on Crime.* Los Angeles: Roxbury.

Crouch, B. 1980. *The Keepers: Prison Guards and Contemporary Corrections.* Springfield, IL: Charles C. Thomas.

Crouch, B. 1985. "Pandora's Box: Women Guards in Men's Prisons." *Journal of Criminal Justice* 13: 535–548.

Crouch, B., and J. Marquart. 1980. "On Becoming a Prison Guard." In B. Crouch, ed., *The Keepers: Prison Guards and Contemporary Corrections,* pp. 65–111. Springfield, Ill.: Charles C. Thomas.

Culbertson, R., and E. Fortune. 1986. "Incarcerated Women: Self Concept and Argot Roles." *Journal of Offender Counseling, Services and Rehabilitation* 10, 3: 25–49.

Cullen, F. 1979. "Sex and Delinquency: A Partial Test of the Masculinity Hypothesis." *Criminology* 17, 3: 301–311.

Curriden, M. 1993 (September 20). "Prison Scandal in Georgia: Guards Traded Favors for Sex." *National Law Journal,* p. 8.

Dalton, K. 1964. *The Premenstrual Syndrome.* Springfield, IL: Charles C. Thomas.

Daly, K. 1989a. "Criminal Justice Ideologies and Practices in Different Voices: Some Feminist Questions about Justice." *International Journal of the Sociology of Law* 17: 1–18.

Daly, K. 1989b. "Gender and Varieties of White-Collar Crime." *Criminology* 27, 4: 769–791.

Daly, K. 1989c. "Neither Conflict Nor Labeling Nor Paternalism Will Suffice: Intersections of Race, Ethnicity, Gender, and Family in Criminal Court Decisions." *Crime and Delinquency* 35: 136–159.

Daly, K. 1994. *Gender, Crime and Punishment.* New Haven, CT: Yale University Press.

Daly, K., and M. Chesney-Lind. 1988. "Feminism and Criminology." *Justice Quarterly* 5, 4: 497–535.

Danner, M. 1998. "Three Strikes and It's Women Who Are Out: The Hidden Consequences for Women of Criminal Justice Policy Reforms." In S. Miller, *Crime Control and Women,* pp. 1–11. Thousand Oaks, CA: Sage.

Datesman, S., and G. Cales. 1983. " 'I'm Still the Same Mommy': Maintaining the Mother/Child Relationship in Prison." *The Prison Journal* 63, 2: 142–154.

Davidson, T. 1974. *Chicano Prisoners: The Key to San Quentin.* New York: Holt, Rinehart & Winston.

Dayton, K. 1991 (March 14). "Sex Scandal Erupts at Women's Prison." *Honolulu Advertiser,* p. A1.

DeConstanzo, E., and H. Scholes. 1988. "Women Behind Bars: Their Numbers Increase." *Corrections Today* 50, 3: 104–108.

DeCostanzo, E., and J. Valente. 1984. "Designing a Corrections Continuum for Female Offenders: One State's Experience." *The Prison Journal* 64, 1: 120–128.

DeGroot, G. 1998. "A Day in the Life: Four Women Share Their Stories of Life Behind Bars." *Corrections Today* (December): 82–86.

Devlin, A. 1998. *Invisible Women: What's Wrong with Women's Prisons?* Winchester, England: Waterside Press.

Dobash, R., R. Dobash, and S. Gutteridge. 1986. *The Imprisonment of Women.* New York: Basil Blackwell.

Dressel, P., and S. Barnhill. 1994. "Reframing Gerontological Thought and Practice: The Case of Grandmothers with Daughters in Prison." *The Gerontologist* 34, 5: 685–691.

Driscoll, D. 1985. "Mother's Day Once a Month." *Corrections Today* (August): 18–24.

Dugdale, R. 1895. *The Jukes: A Study in Crime, Pauperism, Disease and Heredity.* New York: Putnam.

Eaton, M. 1993. *Women After Prison.* Philadelphia: Milton Keynes (Open University Press).

Ellis, D. P., and P. Austin. 1971. "Menstruation and Aggressive Behavior in a Correctional Center for Women." *Journal of Criminal Law, Criminology and Police Science* 62, 3: 388–395.

Enos, S. 1998. "Managing Motherhood in Prison: The Impact of Race and Ethnicity on Child Placements." In J. Harden and M. Hill, eds., *Breaking the Rules: Women in Prison and Feminist Therapy*, pp. 57–73. New York: Haworth Press.

Epp, J. 1996. "Exploring Health Care Needs of Adult Female Offenders." *Corrections Today,* 96–97, 105, 121.

Erez, E. 1988. "The Myth of the New Female Offender: Some Evidence from Attitudes Toward Law and Justice." *Journal of Criminal Justice* 16: 499–509.

Ewing, C. 1987. *Battered Women Who Kill.* Lexington, MA: Lexington Books.

Eyman, J. 1971. *Prisons for Women: A Practical Guide for Administration Problems.* Springfield, IL: Charles C. Thomas.

Fabian, S. 1980. "Women Prisoners: Challenge of the Future." In G. Alpert, ed., *Legal Rights of Prisoners,* pp. 129–171. Newbury Park, CA: Sage.

Faily, A., and G. A. Roundtree. 1979. "Study of Aggression and Rule Violations in a Female Prison Population." *Journal of Offender Counseling, Services and Rehabilitation* 4, 1: 81–87.

Faily, A., G. A. Roundtree, and R. K. Miller. 1980. "Study of the Maintenance of Discipline with Regard to Rule Infractions at the Louisiana Correctional Institute for Women." *Corrective and Social Psychiatry and Journal of Behavior Technology Methods and Therapy* 26, 4: 151–155.

Faith, K. 1993a. "Media, Myths and Masculinization: Images of Women in Prison." In E. Adelberg and C. Currie, *In Conflict with the Law: Women and the Canadian Justice System,* pp. 174–211. Vancouver, BC: Press Gang Publishers.

Faith, K. 1993b. *Unruly Women: The Politics of Confinement and Resistance.* Vancouver, BC: Press Gang Publishers.

Faith, K. 1999. "Transformative Justice v. Reentrenched Correctionalism." In S. Cook and S. Davies, *Harsh Punishment: International Experiences of Women's Imprisonment,* pp. 92–122. Boston: Northeastern Press.

Faiver, K., and D. Rieger. 1998. "Women's Health Issues." In K. Faiver, ed., *Health Care Management in Correction,* pp. 133–141. Lanham, MD: American Correctional Association.

Farkas, M. 1999. "Inmate Supervisory Style: Does Gender Make a Difference?" *Women and Criminal Justice* 10, 4: 25–47.

Farkas, M., and K. Rand. 1997. "Female Correctional Officers and Prisoner Privacy." *Marquette Law Review* 80: 995–1030.

Farkas, M., and K. Rand. 1999. "Sex Matters: A Gender-Specific Standard for Cross-Gender Searches of Inmates." *Women and Criminal Justice* 10, 3: 31–57.

Farr, K. 2000a. "Classification for Female Inmates: Moving Forward." *Crime and Delinquency* 46, 1: 3–17.

Farr, K. 2000b. "Defeminizing and Dehumanizing Female Murderers: Depictions of Lesbians on Death Row." *Women and Criminal Justice* 11, 1: 49–66.

Farrell, A. 2000. "Women, Crime and Drugs: Testing the Effect of Therapeutic Communities." *Women and Criminal Justice,* 11, 1: 21–49.

Farrington, D., and A. Morris. 1983. "Sex, Sentencing and Reconvictions." *British Journal of Criminology* 23, 3: 229.

Feinman, C. 1983. "An Historical Overview of the Treatment of Incarcerated Women: Myths and Realities of Rehabilitation." *The Prison Journal* 63, 2: 12–26.

Feinman, C. 1986. *Women in the Criminal Justice System.* New York: Praeger.

Fernald, M., M. Hayes, and A. Dawley. 1920. *A Study of Women Delinquents in New York State.* New York: Century.

Fishbein, D. 1992. "The Psychobiology of Female Aggression." *Criminal Justice and Behavior* 19: 99–126.

Fishbein, D. 2000. "Sexual Preference, Crime and Punishment." *Women and Criminal Justice* 11, 2: 67–84.

Fleisher, M., R. Rison, and D. Helman. 1997. "Female Inmates: A Growing Constituency in the Federal Bureau of

Prisons." *Corrections Management Quarterly* 1, 4: 28–35.

Fletcher, B., L. Shaver, and D. Moon. 1993. *Women Prisoners: A Forgotten Population.* Westport, CT: Praeger.

Flowers, R. B. 1987. *Women and Criminality: The Woman as Victim, Offender and Practitioner.* Westport, CT: Greenwood Press.

Flynn, E. 1963. *The Alderson Story: My Life as a Political Prisoner.* New York: International Publishers.

Fogel, C. 1991. "Health Problems and Needs of Incarcerated Women." *Journal of Prison and Jail Health* 10, 1: 43–57.

Fogel, C. 1993. "Hard Time: The Stressful Nature of Incarceration for Women." *Issues in Mental Health Nursing* 14: 367–377.

Fogel, C. 1995. "Pregnant Prisoners: Impact of Incarceration on Health and Health Care." *Journal of Correctional Health Care* 2: 169–190.

Fogel, C., and S. Martin. 1992. "The Mental Health of Incarcerated Women." *Western Journal of Nursing Research* 14, 1: 30–40.

Foster, T. 1975. "Make-Believe Families: A Response of Women and Girls to the Deprivations of Imprisonment." *International Journal of Criminology and Penology* 3: 71–78.

Fox, J. 1975. "Women in Crisis." In H. Toch, *Men in Crisis*, pp. 181–205. Chicago: Aldine-Atherton.

Fox, J. 1982. "Women in Prison: A Case Study in the Social Reality of Stress." In R. Johnson and H. Toch, eds., *The Pains of Imprisonment*, pp. 205–220. Prospect Heights, IL: Waveland Press.

Fox, J. 1984. "Women's Prison Policy, Prisoner Activism, and the Impact of the Contemporary Feminist Movement: A Case Study." *The Prison Journal* 64, 1: 15–36.

Fox, J. 1992 (original copyright 1975). "Women in Crisis." In H. Toch, *Mosiac of Despair: Human Breakdown in Prison,* pp. 227–252. Washington, D.C.: American Psychological Association.

Freedman, E. 1974. "Their Sister's Keepers: A Historical Perspective of Female Correctional Institutions in the U.S." *Feminist Studies* 2: 77–95.

Freedman, E. 1981. *Their Sister's Keepers: Women's Prison Reforms in America, 1830–1930.* Ann Arbor, MI: University of Michigan Press.

Fritsch, T., and J. Burkhead. 1982. "Behavioral Reactions of Children to Parental Absence Due to Imprisonment." *Family Relations* 30, 1: 83–88.

Fuller, L. 1993. "Visitors to Women's Prisons in California: An Exploratory Study." *Federal Probation* 57, 4: 41–47.

Gabel, K. 1982. *Legal Issues of Female Inmates.* Northampton, MA: Smith College, School for Social Work.

Gabel, K., and D. Johnston. 1995. *Children of Incarcerated Parents.* New York: Lexington Books.

Gaudin, J. 1984. "Social Work Roles and Tasks with Incarcerated Mothers." *Social Casework* 53: 279–285.

Gee, R. 2000 (January 28). "Caldwell Jailers Accused of Sex with an Inmate." *Austin American Statesman,* p. B6.

Gendreau, P. 1996. "The Principles of Effective Intervention with Offenders." In A. T. Harland, ed., *Choosing Correctional Options That Work.* Thousand Oaks, CA: Sage.

Gentleman, A. 1998 (March 25). "Too Many Women in U.K. Prisons." *The Guardian,* A8.

George, A. 1999. "The New Prison Culture." In S. Cook and S. Davies, *Harsh Punishment: International Experiences of Women's Imprisonment,* pp. 189–210. Boston: Northeastern University Press.

Gerrietts, J. 2000 (January 13). "Girls Detail Day of Score's Death." *Argus Leader News.com,* http://www.argusleader.com/news/Thursdayfeature.shtml.

Giallombardo, R. 1966. *Society of Women: A Study of a Women's Prison.* New York: Wiley.

Gilfus, M. 1988. *Seasoned by Violence/Tempered by Law: A Qualitative Study of Women and Crime.* Unpublished doctoral dissertation, Brandeis University, Waltham, MA.

Gilfus, M. 1992. "From Victims to Survivors to Offenders: Women's Routes of Entry and Immersion into Street Crime." *Women and Criminal Justice* 4, 1: 63–88.

Gilliard, D., and A. Beck. 1997. *Prisoners in 1997.* Washington D.C.: U.S. Department of Justice, Bureau of Justice Statistics.

Gilligan, C. 1982. *In a Different Voice: Psychological Theory and Women's Development.* Cambridge, MA: Harvard University Press.

Ginsberg, S. 1999 (December 23). "Va. Investigation Finds No Pattern of Abuse at Women's Prison." *Washington Post.com,* http://www/washingtonpost.com/wp-srv/Wplate/1999-12/23/2181-122399-idx.html.

Giordana, P., and S. Cernkovich. 1979. "On Complicating the Relationship Between

Liberation and Delinquency." *Social Problems* 26, 4: 467–481.

Girshick, L. 1999. *No Safe Haven: Stories of Women in Prison.* Boston: Northeastern University Press.

Glaser, D. 1964. *The Effectiveness of a Prison and Parole System.* Indianapolis, IN: Bobbs-Merrill.

Glick, R., and V. Neto. 1977. *National Study of Women's Correctional Programs.* Washington, D.C.: U.S. Government Printing Office.

Glueck, S., and E. Glueck. 1934. *Five Hundred Delinquent Women.* New York: Knopf.

Goetting, A., and R. Howsen. 1983. "Women in Prison: A Profile." *The Prison Journal* 63, 2: 27–46.

Goffman, E. 1961. "On the Characteristics of Total Institutions: The Inmate World." In D. Cressey, ed., *The Prison: Studies in Institutional Organization and Change.* New York: Holt, Rinehart and Winston.

Government Accounting Office (GAO). 1979. *Who Are the Women in Prison and What Are the Problems Confronting Them?* Washington, D.C.: U.S. Government Printing Office.

Government Accounting Office (GAO). 2000. "Government Accounting Office Report Gives an Overview of Women in U.S. Prisons." *Women, Girls and Criminal Justice* 1, 3: 1, 41–42.

Gray, T., L. Mays, and M. Stohr. 1995. "Inmate Needs and Programming in Exclusively Women's Jails." *Prison Journal* 75: 186–203.

Green, N. 1998. Correctional Service of Canada—The Federally Sentenced Women's Initiative: Okimaw Ohci Healing Lodge." In J. Morton, ed., *Complex Challenges, Collaborative Solutions: Programming for Adult and Juvenile Female Offenders,* pp. 159–167. Lanham, MD: American Correctional Association.

Greenfield, L., and S. Minor–Harper. 1991. *Special Report: Women In Prison.* Washington, D.C.: U.S. Department of Justice, Bureau of Justice Statistics.

Greenfield, L., and T. Snell. 1999. *Special Report: Women Offenders.* Washington, D.C.: U.S. Department of Justice, Bureau of Justice Statistics.

Haft, M. 1974. "Women in Prison: Discriminatory Practices and Some Legal Solutions." *Clearinghouse Review* 8: 1–6.

Hahn, N. 1979. "Too Dumb to Know Better: Cacogenic Family Studies and the Criminology of Women." Paper presented at American Society of Criminology meeting, Philadelphia, PA.

Hairston, C. 1988. "Family Ties During Imprisonment: Do They Influence Future Criminal Activity?" *Federal Probation* 52, 1: 48–52.

Hairston, C. 1991. "Family Ties During Imprisonment: Important to Whom and for What?" *Journal of Sociology and Welfare* 18, 1: 87–104.

Hairston, C. 1997. "Family Programs in State Prisons." In C. McNeece and A. Roberts, eds., *Policy and Practice in the Justice System,* pp. 143–159. Chicago: Nelson-Hall.

Hairston, H., and D. Lockett. 1985. "Parents in Prison: A Child Abuse and Neglect Prevention Strategy." *Child Abuse and Neglect* 9: 471–477.

Haley, K. 1977. "Mothers Behind Bars: A Look at the Parental Rights of Incarcerated Women." *New England Journal of Prison Law* 4, 1: 141–155.

Halleck, S., and M. Herski. 1962. "Homosexual Behavior in a Correctional Institution for Adolescent Girls." *American Journal of Orthopsychiatry* 32: 911–917.

Hannah-Moffat, K. 1991. "Creating Choices or Repeating History: Canadian Female Offenders and Correctional Reform." *Social Justice* 13, 2: 184–203.

Hannah-Moffat, K. 1994. "Feminine Fortresses: Woman-Centered Prisons?" *The Prison Journal* 75, 2: 135–164.

Hannum, T. E., F. H. Borgen, and R. M. Anderson. 1978. "Self-Concept Changes Associated with Incarceration in Female Prisoners." *Criminal Justice and Behavior* 5, 3: 271–279.

Hannum, T. E., and R. E. Warman. 1964. "The MMPI Characteristics of Incarcerated Females." *Journal of Research in Crime and Delinquency* 1: 119–125.

Hanson, L. 1983. "Women Prisoners: Freedom from Sexual Harassment—A Constitutional Analysis." *Golden Gate University Law Review* 13: 667–696.

Harden, J., and M. Hill, eds. 1998. *Breaking the Rules: Women in Prison and Feminist Therapy.* New York: Haworth.

Harlow, C. 1998. *Profile of Jail Inmates 1996. Special Report.* Washington, D.C.: U.S. Department of Justice, Bureau of Justice Statistics.

Harlow, C. 1999. *Selected Findings: Prior Abuse Reported by Inmates and Probationers.*

Washington D.C.: U.S. Department of Justice, Bureau of Justice Statistics.

Harris, J. 1988. *They Always Call Us Ladies.* New York: Charles Scribner & Sons.

Harris, J. 1993. "Comparison of Stressors Among Female v. Male Inmates." *Journal of Offender Rehabilitation* 19, 1/2: 43–56.

Harris, M. 1987. "Moving Into the New Millenium: Toward a Feminist Vision of Justice." *The Prison Journal* 67: 27–38.

Hart, C. 1995. "Gender Differences in Social Support Among Inmates." *Women and Criminal Justice* 6, 2: 67–88.

Hartnagel, T., and M. Gillan. 1980. "Female Prisoners and the Inmate Code." *Pacific Sociological Review* 23, 1: 85–104.

Hawkes, M. 1998. "Edna Mahan: Sustaining the Reformatory Tradition." *Women and Criminal Justice* 9, 3: 1–23.

Hawkins, G. 1976. *The Prison: Policy and Practice.* Chicago: University of Chicago Press.

Hawkins, R. 1995. "Inmate Adjustments in Women's Prisons." In K. Haas and G. Alpert, *The Dilemmas of Corrections: Contemporary Readings,* pp. 103–123. Prospect Heights, IL: Waveland Press.

Hayner, N. 1961. "Characteristics of Five Offender Types." *American Sociological Review* 26: 97–98.

Healy, W., and A. Bronner. 1926. *Delinquents and Their Children: Their Making and Unmaking.* New York: Macmillan.

Heffernan, E. 1992. "The Alderson Years." *Federal Prisons Journal* 3 (Spring); 20–26.

Heffernan, R. 1972. *Making It in Prison: The Square, the Cool and the Life.* New York: Wiley.

Heidensohn, F. 1985. *Women and Crime: The Life of the Female Offender.* New York: New York University Press.

Heidensohn, F. 1986. "Models of Justice: Portia or Persephone? Some Thoughts on Equality, Fairness and Gender in the Field of Criminal Justice." *International Journal of the Sociology of Law* 14: 287–298.

Heinlein, G. 1999 (October 14). "State May Revert to Old Same-Sex Prison Guard Rule." *Detroit News.com,* http://www.detnews.com/1999/metro/9910/14/10140143.htm.

Heney, J., and C. Kristiansen. 1998. "An Analysis of the Impact of Prison on Women Survivors of Childhood Sexual Abuse." In J. Harden and M. Hill, *Breaking the Rules: Women in Prison and Feminist Therapy,* pp. 29–44. New York: Haworth Press.

Henriques, Z. 1981. "The Human Rights of Incarcerated Mothers and Their Children." *International Child Welfare Review* 49: 18–27.

Henriques, Z. 1982. *Imprisoned Mothers and Their Children: A Descriptive and Analytical Study.* Washington, D.C.: University Press of America.

Henriques, Z. 1996. "Imprisoned Mothers and Their Children: Separation-Reunion Syndrome." *Women and Criminal Justice* 8, 1: 77–95.

Henriques, Z., and E. Gilbert. 2000. "Sexual Abuse and Sexual Assault of Women in Prison." In R. Muraskin, *It's a Crime: Women and Justice,* 2d ed., pp. 253–268. Upper Saddle River, NJ: Prentice-Hall.

Herbert, R. 1985. "Women's Prisons: An Equal Protection Evaluation." *Yale Law Journal* 94, 5: 1182–1206.

Hill, G., and E. Crawford. 1990. "Women, Race and Crime." *Criminology* 28, 4: 601–623.

Hirsch, A. 2000. "The Impact of Welfare Reform on Women with Drug Convictions in Pennsylvania: A Case Study." *Women, Girls and Criminal Justice* 1, 3: 1–2, 45.

Hoffman, P. B. 1982. "Females, Recidivism and Salient Factor Score: A Research Note." *Criminal Justice and Behavior* 9, 1: 121–125.

Hoffman-Bustamante, D. 1973. "The Nature of Female Criminality." *Issues in Criminology* 8, 2: 117–123.

Howe, A. 1990. "Prologue to a History of Women's Imprisonment: In Search of a Feminist Perspective." *Social Justice* 17, 2: 5–33.

Huling, T. 1991 (March 4). "Breaking the Silence." (Internal Report). New York: Correctional Association of New York.

Huling, T. 1995. "Women Drug Couriers." *Criminal Justice* 9, 4: 14–20.

Human Rights Watch Women's Project. 1996. *All Too Familiar: Sexual Abuse in U.S. State Prisons.* New York: Human Rights Watch.

Hungerford, G., 1993. "The Children of Incarcerated Mothers: An Exploratory Study of Children, Caretakers and Inmate Mothers in Ohio." Ph.D. dissertation, Ohio State University, Columbus, OH.

Hunter, S. 1984. "Issues and Challenges Facing Women's Prisons in the 1980s." *The Prison Journal* 64, 1: 129–135.

Immarigeon, R. 1994. "When Parents Are Sent to Prison." *National Prison Project Journal* 9, 4/5: 14–16.

Immarigeon, R. 1997. "Gender-Specific Programming for Female Offenders." *Community Corrections Report on Law and Corrections Practice* 4, 5: 65–80.

Inciardi, J., ed. 1993. "Drug Use and Crime Among Two Cohorts of Women Narcotics Users: An Empirical Assessment." *Journal of Drug Issues,* 16: 1–105.

Inciardi, J. 1996 (June). *A Corrections-Based Continuum of Effective Drug Abuse Treatment. NIJ Research Preview.* Washington, D.C.: U.S. Department of Justice.

Inciardi, J., D. Lockwood, and A. Pottieger. 1993. *Women and Crack Cocaine.* New York: Macmillan.

Irwin, J. 1970. *The Felon.* Englewood Cliffs, NJ: Prentice-Hall.

Irwin, J. 1980. *Prisons in Turmoil.* Boston: Little, Brown.

Irwin, J., and D. Cressey. 1962. "Thieves, Convicts and Inmate Culture." *Social Problems* 10: 142–155.

Jackson, P., and C. Stearns. 1995. "Gender Issues in the New Generation Jail." *Prison Journal* 75, 2: 203–221.

Jacobs, J. 1977. *Statesville: The Penitentiary in Mass Society.* Chicago: University of Chicago Press.

Jacobs, J. 1979. "The Sexual Segregation of the Prison's Guard Force: A Few Comments on *Dothard v. Rawlinson.*" *University of Toledo Law Review* 10: 389–418.

Jenne, D., and R. Kersting. 1996. "Aggression and Women Correctional Officers in Male Prisons." *Prison Journal* 76, 4: 442–460.

Jensen, G., and D. Jones. 1976. "Perspectives on Inmate Culture: A Study of Women's Prison." *Social Forces* 54, 3: 45–56.

Johnson, R. 1987/1999. *Hard Time.* Belmont, CA: Wadsworth.

Johnson, R., and S. Price. 1981. "The Complete Correctional Officer." *Criminal Justice and Behavior* 8, 3: 343–373.

Johnston, D. 1995a. "Child Custody Issues of Women Prisoners: A Preliminary Report from the Chicas Project." *The Prison Journal* 75, 2: 222–239.

Johnston, D. 1995b. "Effects of Parental Incarceration." In K. Gabel and D. Johnston, *Children of Incarcerated Parents,* pp. 259–263. New York: Lexington Books.

Johnston, D. 1995c. "Intervention." In K. Gabel and D. Johnston, *Children of Incarcerated Parents,* pp. 199–232. New York: Lexington Books.

Johnston, D. 1995d. "Parent–Child Visitation in the Jail or Prison." In K. Gabel and D.

Johnston, *Children of Incarcerated Parents,* pp. 135–143. New York: Lexington Books.

Johnston, D. 1997a. "The Center for Children of Incarcerated Parents," In C. Blinn, *Maternal Ties: A Selection of Programs for Female Offenders,"* pp. 15–25. Lanham, MD: American Correctional Association.

Johnston, D. 1997b. "Developing Services for Incarcerated Mothers." In C. Blinn, *Maternal Ties: A Selection of Programs for Female Offenders,"* pp. 1–9. Lanham, MD: American Correctional Association.

Jones, M., and B. Sims. 1997. "Recidivism of Offenders Released from Prison in North Carolina: A Gender Comparison." *Prison Journal* 77, 3: 335–348.

Jones, R. 1993. "Coping with Separation: Adaptive Responses of Women Prisoners." *Women and Criminal Justice* 5, 1: 71–97.

Jurado, R. 1999. "The Essence of Her Womanhood: Defining the Privacy Rights of Women Prisoners and the Employment Rights of Women Guards." *American University Journal of Gender, Social Policy and the Law* 7, 1: 1–53.

Jurik, N. 1983. 'The Economics of Female Recidivism." *Criminology* 21, 4: 3–12.

Jurik, N. 1985a. "Individual and Organizational Determinants of Correctional Officer Attitudes Toward Inmates." *Criminology* 23, 3: 523–539.

Jurik, N. 1985b. "An Officer and a Lady: Organizational Barriers to Women Working as Correctional Officers in Men's Prisons." *Social Problems* 32: 375–388.

Jurik, N. 1988. "Striking a Balance: Female Correctional Officers, Gender Role Stereotypes, and Male Prisons." *Sociological Inquiry* 58, 3: 291–305.

Jurik, N., and G. Halemba. 1984. "Gender, Working Conditions and the Job Satisfaction of Women in a Nontraditional Occupation: Female Correctional Officers in Men's Prisons." *The Sociological Quarterly* 25: 551–566.

Kauffman, K. 1997. "A Cross–national Perspective on Residential Programs for Incarcerated Mothers and Their Children." In C. Blinn, *Maternal Ties: A Selection of Programs for Female Offenders,"* pp. 159–167. Lanham, MD: American Correctional Association.

Kay, B. 1969. "Value Orientations as Reflected in Expressed Attitudes Are Associated with Ascribed Social Sex Roles." *Canadian Journal of Corrections* 11, 3: 193–197.

Kellor, F. 1900a. "Criminal Sociology: Criminality Among Women." *Arena* 23: 516–524.

Kellor, F. 1900b. "Psychological and Environmental Study of Women Criminals." *The American Journal of Sociology* 5: 527–543.

Kempfner, C. 1995. "Post-Traumatic Stress Reactions in Children of Imprisoned Mothers." In K. Gabel and D. Johnston, eds., *Children of Incarcerated Parents,* pp. 89–100. New York: Lexington Books.

Kendall, K. 1993. *Program Evaluation of Therapeutic Services at the Prison for Women.* Ottawa: Correctional Service of Canada.

Kendall, K. 1994a. "Creating Real Choices: A Program Evaluation of Therapeutic Services at the Prison for Women." *Forum on Corrections Research* 6, 1: 19–21.

Kendall, K. 1994b. "Therapy Behind Prison Walls: A Contradiction in Terms?" *Prison Service Journal* 96: 2–11.

Kestenbaum, S. E. 1977. "Women's Liberation for Female Offenders." *Social Casework* 58, 2: 77–83.

Kiser, G. 1991. "Female Inmates and Their Families." *Federal Probation* (September): 56–63.

Kissel, P., and J. Seidel. 1980. *The Management and Impact of Female Corrections Officers at Jail Facilities Housing Male Inmates.* Boulder, CO: National Institute of Corrections.

Klein, D. 1973. "The Etiology of Female Crime: A Review of the Literature." *Issues in Criminology* 8: 3–29.

Koban, L. A. 1983. "Parents in Prison: A Comparative Analysis of the Effects of Incarceration on the Families of Men and Women." *Research in Law, Deviance and Social Control* 5, 2: 171–183.

Kolman, A. 1983. "Support and Control Patterns of Inmate Mothers." *The Prison Journal* 63, 2: 155–116.

Koons, B., J. Burrow, M. Morash, and T. Bynum. 1997. "Expert and Offender Perceptions of Program Elements Linked to Successful Outcomes for Incarcerated Women." *Crime and Delinquency* 43, 4: 512–532.

Kosofsky, S., and A. Ellis. 1958. "Illegal Communications Among Institutionalized Female Delinquents." *Journal of Social Psychiatry* 48: 155–160.

Krause, K. 1974. "Denial of Work Release Programs to Women: A Violation of Equal Protection." *Southern California Law Review* 47: 1453–1490.

Krim, L. 1995. "A Reasonable Woman's Version of Cruel and Unusual Punishment: Cross-Gender, Clothed Body Searches of Women Prisoners." *UCLA Women's Law Journal* 6: 85–121.

Kruttschnitt, C. 1981. "Prison Codes, Inmate Solidarity and Women: A Re-examination." In M. Warren, ed., *Comparing Male and Female Offenders,* pp. 123–141. Beverly Hills, CA: Sage.

Kruttschnitt, C. 1982. "Women, Crime and Dependency." *Criminology* 19, 4: 495–513.

Kruttschnitt, C. 1983. "Race Relations and the Female Inmate." *Crime and Delinquency* 29, 4: 577–592.

Kruttschnitt, C., and M. Dornfield. 1993. "Exposure to Family Violence: A Partial Explanation for Initial and Subsequent Levels of Delinquency." *Criminal Behavior and Mental Health* 3: 61–75.

Kruttschnitt, C., and D. Green. 1984. "The Sex Sanctioning Issue: Is It History?" *American Sociology Review* 49: 541–551.

Kuo, A. 2000 (January 31). "Plan to Ban Male Guards Sparks Debate." *Albany Times Union,* http://www.timesunion.com/AspStories/story.asp?storyKey=26925&category=Y.

Lahey, K. 1985. ". . . Until Women Themselves Have Told All That They Have to Tell . . ." *Osgood Hall Law Journal* 23, 3: 519–541.

Larson, J., and J. Nelson. 1984. "Women, Friendship, and Adaptation to Prison." *Journal of Criminal Justice* 12, 5: 601–615.

Lawrence, R., and S. Mahan. 1998. "Women Corrections Officers in Men's Prisons: Acceptance and Perceived Job Performance." *Women and Criminal Justice* 9, 3: 63–87.

Leger, R. 1987. "Lesbianism Among Women Prisoners: Participants and Non-Participants." *Criminal Justice and Behavior* 14: 463–479.

Leiber, M. 2000. "Gender, Religion, and Correctional Orientations Among a Sample of Juvenile Justice Personnel." *Women and Criminal Justice* 11, 2: 15–41.

Lekkerkerker, E. 1931. *Reformatories for Women in the U.S.* Gronigen, Netherlands: J. B. Wolters.

Leonard, E. 1982. *Women, Crime and Society.* New York: Longman.

Leonard, E. 1983. "Judicial Decisions and Prison Reform: The Impact of Litigation on Women Prisoners." *Social Problems* 31, 1: 45–58.

Lindquist, C. 1980. "Prison Discipline and the Female Offender." *Journal of Offender Counseling, Services and Rehabilitation* 4, 4: 305–319.

Lipman–Blumen, J., and A. Tickmayer. 1975. "Sex Roles in Transition: A Ten Year Perspective." *Annual Review of Sociology* 1: 297–337.

Lombroso, C., and W. Ferrero. 1920/1894. *The Female Offender.* New York: Appleton.

Lord, E. 1995. "A Prison Superintendent's Perspective on Women in Prison." *Prison Journal* 75, 2: 257–269.

Lovrich, N., and M. Stohr. 1993. "Gender and Jail Work: Correctional Policy Implications of Perceptual Diversity in the Work Force." *Policy Studies Review* 12, 1–2: 66–84.

Lujan, C. 1995. "Women Warriors: American Indian Women, Crime, and Alcohol." *Women and Criminal Justice* 7, 1: 9–33.

Lutze, F., and D. Murphy. 1999. "Ultra-masculine Prison Environments and Inmates' Adjustment: It's Time to Move Beyond the 'Boys Will Be Boys' Paradigm." *Justice Quarterly* 16, 4: 709–733.

Mahan, S. 1984a. "Imposition of Despair: An Ethnography of Women in Prison." *Journal of Crime and Justice* 7: 101–129.

Mahan, S. 1984b. "Imposition of Despair: An Ethnography of Women in Prison." *Justice Quarterly* 1, 30: 357–385.

Mahan, S., and D. Prestwood. 1993. "A Radical Analysis of a Treatment Program for Cocaine-Abusing Mothers." In C. Culliver, ed., *Female Criminality: The State of the Art*, pp. 503–515. New York: Garland.

Mandaraka-Sheppard, A. 1986a. *The Dynamics of Aggression in Women's Prisons in England.* London, England: Gower.

Mandaraka-Sheppard, A. 1986b. "The Dynamics of Aggression in Women's Prisons in England." *The Howard Journal of Criminal Justice* 25, 4: 317–319.

Mann, C. 1984. *Female Crime and Delinquency.* Birmingham, AL: University of Alabama Press.

Mann, C. 1988. "Getting Even? Women Who Kill in Domestic Encounters." *Justice Quarterly* 5, 1: 33–53.

Mann, C. 1993. "Sister Against Sister: Female Intrasexual Homicide. In C. Culliver, ed., *Female Criminality: The State of the Art*, pp. 195–225. New York: Garland.

Marcos-Mendosa, S., J. Klein-Saffon, and F. Lutze. 1998. "A Feminist Examination of Boot Camps: Prison Programs for Women." In J. Harden and J. Hill, eds., *Breaking the Rules: Women in Prison and Feminist Therapy*, pp. 173–185. New York: Haworth Press.

Marrett, G. 1972. "Centralization in Female Organizations: Reassessing the Evidence." *Social Problems* 19: 221–226.

Martin, M. 1997. "Connected Mothers: A Follow-Up Study of Incarcerated Women and Their Children." *Women and Criminal Justice* 8, 4:1–23.

Martin, S. 1980. *Breaking and Entering: Policewomen on Patrol.* Washington, D.C.: Police Foundation.

Maschke, K. 1996. "Gender in the Prison Setting: The Privacy-Equal Employment Dilemma." *Women and Criminal Justice* 7, 2: 23–42.

Mauer, M., C. Potler, and R. Wolf. 2000. "The Impact of the Drug War on Women: A Comparative Analysis in Three States." *Women, Girls and Criminal Justice* 1, 2: 21–22, 30–31.

Mawby, R. 1982. "Women in Prison: A British Study." *Crime and Delinquency* 28, 1: 24–39.

McCarthy, B. 1980. "Inmate Mothers: The Process of Separation and Reintegration." *Journal of Offender Counseling, Services and Rehabilitation* 13: 5–13.

McClellan, D. 1994a. "Disparity in the Discipline of Male and Female Inmates in Texas Prisons." *Women and Criminal Justice* 5, 2: 71–97.

McClellan, D. 1994b. "Women in Texas Prisons: A Test Case for Feminist and Critical Criminology." Paper presented at American Society of Criminology meeting, Miami, FL.

McDonald, D., and J. Grossman. 1981. *Analysis of Low Return Among Female Offenders.* Albany, NY: Department of Correctional Services.

McGowan, B., and K. Blumenthal. 1976. "Children of Women Prisoners: A Forgotten Minority." In L. Crites, ed., *The Female Offender*, pp. 121–135. Lexington, MA: D. C. Heath.

McGowan, B., and K. Blumenthal. 1978. *Why Punish the Children? A Study of Children of Women Prisoners.* Hackensack, NJ: National Council on Crime and Delinquency.

McKerracher, D. W., D. R. K. Street, and L. S. Segal. 1966. "A Comparison of the Behavior Problems Presented by Male and

Female Subnormal Offenders." *British Journal of Psychiatry* 112: 891–899.

Merlo, A., and J. Pollock, eds. 1995. *Women, Law and Social Control*. Boston: Allyn and Bacon.

Meyer, M. 1992 (November 9). "Coercing Sex Behind Bars." *Newsweek*, pp. 23–25, 76–77.

Miller, E. 1986. *Street Woman*. Philadelphia: Temple University Press.

Miller, S., ed. 1998. *Crime Control and Women*. Newbury Park, CA: Sage.

Mitchell, A. 1975. *Informal Inmate Social Structure in Prisons for Women: A Comparative Study*. San Francisco: R & E Research Associates.

Morash, M., and T. Bynum. 1995. *Findings from the National Study of Innovative and Promising Programs for Women Offenders*. Washington D.C.: Department of Justice, National Institute of Justice.

Morash, M., R. Haarr, and L. Rucker. 1994. "A Comparison of Programming for Women and Men in U.S. Prisons in the 1980s." *Crime and Delinquency* 40, 2: 197–221.

Morash, M., and L. Rucker. 1995. "A Critical Look at the Idea of Boot Camps as a Correctional Reform." In S. Miller, *Crime Control and Women*, pp. 32–46. Thousand Oaks, CA: Sage.

Morgan, E. 1999. "The Violence of Women's Imprisonment," In S. Cook and S. Davies, eds., *Harsh Punishment: International Experiences of Women's Imprisonment*, pp. 32–46. Boston: Northeastern University Press.

Morgan, E. 2000. "Women on Death Row." In R. Muraskin, ed., *It's a Crime: Women and Justice*, pp. 269–283. Upper Saddle River, NJ: Prentice-Hall.

Morris, A. 1987. *Women, Crime and Criminal Justice*. London: Basil Blackwell.

Morris, A., and V. Kingi. 1999. "Addressing Women's Needs or Empty Rhetoric? An Examination of New Zealand's Policy for Women in Prison." In S. Cook and S. Davies, eds., *Harsh Punishment: International Experiences of Women's Imprisonment*, pp. 142–159. Boston: Northeastern University Press.

Morris, A., and C. Wilkinson. 1995. "Responding to Female Prisoners' Needs." *Prison Journal* 75: 295–306.

Morris, A., C. Wilkinson, A. Tisi, J. Woodrow, and A. Rockley. 1995. *Managing the Needs of Female Offenders. Report from the Center*

for the Study of Public Order. Leicester, UK: University of Leicester.

Morton, J. 1998. *Complex Challenges, Collaborative Solutions: Programming for Adult and Juvenile Female Offenders*. Lanham, MD: American Correctional Association.

Moses, M. 1995. *Keeping Incarcerated Mothers and Their Daughters Together: Girl Scouts Behind Bars*. (National Institute of Justice Program Focus). Washington, D.C.: Government Printing Office.

Moss, K. (ed.). *Man-made Medicine*. Durham, NC: Duke University Press.

Moyer, I. 1980. "Leadership in a Women's Prison." *Journal of Criminal Justice* 8, 4: 233–242.

Moyer, I. 1984. "Deceptions and Realities of Life in Women's Prisons." *The Prison Journal* 64, 1: 45–56.

Mullings, J., J. Marquart, and V. Brewer. 2000. "Assessing the Relationship Between Child Sexual Abuse and Marginal Living Conditions on HIV/AIDS-Related Risk Behavior Among Women Prisoners." *Child Abuse and Neglect* 24, 5: 677–688.

Muraskin, R. 2000. *It's a Crime: Women and Justice*, 2d ed. Upper Saddle River, NJ: Prentice-Hall.

Muse, D. 1994. "Parenting from Prison." *Mothering* 72 (Fall): 99–105.

Mustin, J. 1995. "Parenting Programs for Prisoners." *Family and Corrections Network Report* 5: 1–2.

Naffine, N. 1987. *Female Crime: The Construction of Women in Criminology*. Sydney, Australia: Allen & Unwin.

Naffine, N. 1996. *Feminism and Criminology*. Philadelphia: Temple University Press.

Negy, C., D. Woods, and R. Carlson. 1997. "The Relationship Between Female Inmates' Coping and Adjustment in a Minimum Security Prison." *Criminal Justice and Behavior* 24, 2: 224–233.

Nelson, C. 1974. *A Study of Homosexuality Among Women Inmates at Two State Prisons*. Ph.D. dissertation, Temple University, Philadelphia, PA.

Nesbitt, C. 1992. "The Female Offender: Overview of Facility Planning and Design Issues and Considerations." *Corrections Compendium* 17, 8: 4–20.

Neto, V., and L. Ranier. 1983. "Mother and Wife Locked Up: A Day with the Family." *The Prison Journal* 63, 2: 124–141.

Nicolai, S. 1981. "The Upward Mobility of Women in Corrections." In R. Ross,

Prison Guard / Correctional Officer. Toronto, Canada: Butterworth.

Nieva, V., and B. Gutek. 1981. *Women and Work: A Psychological Perspective.* New York: Praeger.

Noddings, N. 1989. *Women and Evil.* Berkeley, CA: University of California Press.

Norz, F. 1989. "Prenatal and Postnatal Rights of Incarcerated Mothers." *Columbia Human Rights Law Review* 20: 555–573.

O'Dwyer, J., et al. 1987. "Women's Imprisonment in England, Wales and Scotland: Recurring Issues." In P. Carlen and A. Worral, *Gender, Crime and Justice,* pp. 176–190. Philadelphia: Open University Press.

Oregon Department of Corrections. 1993. *Childhood Abuse and the Female Inmate: A Study of Teenage History of Women in Oregon Prisons.* Salem, OR: Oregon Department of Corrections, Information Services Division.

O'Shea, K. 1999. *Women and the Death Penalty in the United States, 1900–1998.* Westport, CT: Praeger.

Otis, M. 1913. "A Perversion Not Commonly Noted." *Journal of Abnormal Pyschology* 8: 113–116.

Owen, B. 1985. "Race and Gender Relations Among Prison Workers." *Crime and Delinquency* 31: 147–159.

Owen, B. 1988. *The Reproduction of Social Control: A Study of Prison Workers at San Quentin.* Westport, CT: Praeger.

Owen, B. 1998. *"In the Mix": Struggle and Survival in a Women's Prison.* Albany, NY: State University of Albany Press.

Owen, B., and B. Bloom. 1995a. *Profiling the Needs of California's Female Prisoners: A Needs Assessment.* Washington, D.C.: National Institute of Corrections.

Owen, B., and B. Bloom. 1995b. "Profiling Women Prisoners: Findings from National Surveys and a California Sample." *The Prison Journal* 75, 2: 165–185.

Palmer, T. 1995. "Programmatic and Non-programmatic Aspects of Successful Intervention: New Directions for Research." *Crime and Delinquency* 41: 100–131.

Panton, J. 1974. "Personality Differences Between Male and Female Prison Inmates Measured by the MMPI." *Criminal Justice and Behavior* 1, 4: 332–339.

Parisi, N. 1984. "The Female C.O.: Her Progress Toward and Prospects for Equality." *The Prison Journal* 64, 1: 92–109.

Paulus, P., and M. Dzindolet. 1993. "Reaction of Male and Female Inmates to Prison Confinement: Further Evidence of a Two–Component Model." *Criminal Justice and Behavior* 2, 2: 149–166.

Peterson, C. 1982. "Doing Time with the Boys: An Analysis of Women Correctional Officers in All-Male Facilities." In B. Price and N. Sokoloff, eds., *The Criminal Justice System and Women,* pp. 437–460. New York: Clark Boardman.

Pettiway, L. 1987. "Participation in Crime Partnerships by Female Drug Users." *Criminology* 25: 741–766.

Poe-Yamagata, E., and J. Butts. 1996. *Female Offenders in the Juvenile Justice System.* Pittsburgh, PA: National Center for Juvenile Justice.

Pogrebin, M., and E. Poole. 1997. "The Sexualized Work Environment: A Look at Women Jail Officers." *The Prison Journal* 77: 41–47.

Pollak, O. 1950. *The Criminality of Women.* Philadelphia: University of Pennsylvania Press.

Pollock, J. 1978. "Early Theories of Female Criminality." In L. Bowker, *Women, Crime and the Criminal Justice System,* pp. 25–50. Lexington, MA: Lexington Books.

Pollock, J. 1981. From interviews conducted with correctional officers.

Pollock, J. 1984. "'Women Will Be Women': Correctional Officers' Perceptions of the Emotionality of Women Inmates." *The Prison Journal* 64, 1: 84–91.

Pollock, J. 1986. *Sex and Supervision: Guarding Male and Female Inmates.* New York: Greenwood Press.

Pollock, J. 1995. "Women in Corrections: Custody and the 'Caring Ethic.'" In A. Merlo and J. Pollock, eds., *Women, Law and Social Control,* pp. 97–116. Boston: Allyn and Bacon.

Pollock, J., ed., 1997. *Prisons: Today and Tomorrow.* Philadelphia: Aspen.

Pollock, J. 1998. *Counseling Women in Prison.* San Francisco: Sage.

Pollock, J. 1999a. *Criminal Women.* Cincinnati, OH: Anderson.

Pollock, J. 1999b. *A National Survey of Parenting Programs in Women's Prisons.* Unpublished monograph available from the author.

Pollock, J., S. Williams, and S. Schroeder. 1996. *The Needs of Texas Women Prisoners—Final Report.* Unpublished report.

Pollock-Byrne, J. 1990. *Women, Prison and Crime.* Monterey, CA: Brooks/Cole.

Pollock-Byrne, J. 1992. "Women in Prison: Why Are Their Numbers Increasing?" In P. Benekos and A. Merlo, eds., *Corrections: Dilemmas and Directions,* pp. 79–95. Cincinnati, OH: Anderson.

Prendergast, M., J. Wellisch, and M. Anglin. 1994. *Drug-Abusing Women Offenders: Results of a National Survey. NIJ: Research in Brief.* Washington, D.C.: U.S. Department of Justice.

Prendergast, M., J. Wellisch, and G. Falkin. 1995. "Assessment of and Services for Substance-Abusing Women Offenders in Community and Correctional Settings." *Prison Journal* 75, 2: 240–256.

Prendergast, M., J. Wellisch, and G. Falkin. 1997. "Assessment of and Services for Substance-Abusing Women Offenders in Community and Correctional Settings." In J. Marquart and J. Sorensen, *Correctional Contexts: Contemporary and Classical Readings,* pp. 318–327. Los Angeles: Roxbury.

Price, B., and N. Sokoloff. 1982. *The Criminal Justice System and Women.* New York: Clark Boardman.

Propper, A. 1976. *Importation and Deprivation Perspectives on Homosexuality in Correctional Institutions: An Empirical Test of Their Relative Efficacy.* Ph.D. dissertation, University of Michigan, Ann Arbor, MI.

Propper, A. 1981. *Prison Homosexuality: Myth and Reality.* Lexington, MA: D.C. Heath.

Propper, A. 1982. "Make-Believe Families and Homosexuality Among Imprisoned Girls." *Criminology* 20, 1: 127–139.

Quin, L. 1999 (December 16). "Jailers Indicted on Sex Charges." *Austin American Statesman,* p. A1, 6.

Raeder, M., 1993a. "Gender Issues in the Federal Sentencing Guidelines." *Journal of Criminal Justice* 8, 3: 20–35.

Raeder, M. 1993b. "Gender and Sentencing: Single Moms, Battered Women and Other Sex-Based Anomalies in the Gender Free World of Federal Sentencing Guidelines." *Pepperdine Law Review* 20, 3: 905–990.

Rafter, N. 1983. "Prison for Women, 1790–1980." In M. Tonry and N. Morris, eds., *Crime and Justice: An Annual Review of Research* (Vol. 5), pp. 129–182. Chicago: University of Chicago Press.

Rafter, N. 1985. *Partial Justice: State Prisons and Their Inmates, 1800–1935.* Boston: Northeastern University Press.

Rafter, N. 1989. "Gender and Justice: The Equal Protection Issue." In Goodstein and

MacKenzie, eds., *The American Prison: Issues in Research and Policy.* New York: Plenum.

Rafter, N. 1990. *Partial Justice: Women, Prisons, and Social Control.* New Brunswick, NJ: Transaction Books.

Rafter, N. 1992. "Equality or Indifference." *Federal Prisons Journal* 3: 16–18.

Rasche, C. 1975. "The Female Offender as an Object of Criminological Research." In A. Brodsky, ed., *The Female Offender,* pp. 9–28. Newbury Park, CA: Sage.

Rasche, C. 2000. "The Dislike of Female Offenders Among Correctional Officers: Need for Specialized Training." In R. Muraskin, *It's a Crime: Women and Justice,* 2d ed., pp. 237–252. Upper Saddle River, NJ: Prentice-Hall.

Reed, B. 1987. "Developing Women–Sensitive Drug Dependence Treatment Services: Why So Difficult?" *Journal of Psychoactive Drugs* 19, 2: 151–164.

Resnick, J. 1982. "Women's Prisons and Men's Prisons: Should Prisoners Be Classified by Their Sex?" *Policy Studies Review* 2, 2: 246–252.

Resnick, J. 1987. The Limits of Parity in Prison." *National Prison Project Journal* 13: 26–28.

Resnick, J., and N. Shaw. 1980. "Prisoners of Their Sex: Health Problems of Incarcerated Women." In I. Robbins, ed., *Prisoners Rights Sourcebook: Theory, Litigation and Practice,* pp. 399–416. New York: Prentice-Hall.

Rice, A., L. Smith, and F. Janzen. 1999. "Women Inmates, Drug Abuse, and the Salt Lake County Jail." *American Jails* 13 (July/August): 43–47.

Richie, B. 1996. *Compelled to Crime: The Gender Entrapment of Battered Black Women.* New York: Routledge.

Rierden, A. 1997. *The Farm: Life Inside a Women's Prison.* Amherst, MA: University of Massachusetts Press.

Ring, W. 1999 (September 22). "State Considering Sending Female Inmates Out of State." *Boston Globe.com,* http://www.boston.com/dailyne...ion/St_considering_sending_female_inmates_out_ofwysiwyg.

Rippon, M., and R. A. Hassell. 1981. "Women, Prison and the Eighth Amendment." *North Carolina Central Law Journal* 12, 2: 434–460.

Rolison, G. 1993. "Toward an Integrated Theory of Female Criminality and Incarceration." In B. Fletcher, L. Shaver, and D. Moon, eds., *Women Prisoners: A Forgotton Population,* pp. 135–146. Westport, CT: Praeger.

Rosen, L. 1998. "Long–Term Effects of Childhood Maltreatment History on Gender-Related Personality Characteristics." *Journal of Child and Adolescent Behavior* 22, 3: 197–212.

Rosenbaum, J. 1989. "Family Dysfunction and Female Delinquency." *Crime and Delinquency,* 35, 1: 31–44.

Rosenbaum, J. 1993. "The Female Delinquent: Another Look at the Family's Influence on Female Offending." In R. Muraskin and T. Alleman, eds., *It's a Crime: Women and Justice,* pp. 399–416. New York: Prentice-Hall.

Rosenbaum, M. 1981. *Women on Heroin.* New Brunswick, NJ: Rutgers University Press.

Ross, P., and J. Lawrence. 1998a. "Health Care for Women Offenders." *Corrections Today* 60, 7: 122–129.

Ross, P., and J. Lawrence. 1998b. "Health Care for Women Offenders." In T. Alleman and R. Gido, *Turnstile Justice: Issues in American Corrections,* pp. 176–191. Upper Saddle River, NJ: Prentice-Hall.

Ross, R., and A. Fabiano. 1986. *Female Offenders: Correctional Afterthoughts.* Jefferson, NC: McFarland.

Roundtree, G., B. Mohan, and L. Mahaffey. 1980. "Determinants of Female Aggression: A Study of a Prison Population." *International Journal of Offender Therapy and Comparative Criminology* 24, 3: 260–269.

Rubick, R. B. 1975. "The Sexually Integrated Prison: A Legal and Policy Evaluation." *American Journal of Criminal Law* 3, 3: 301–330.

Ryan, T. 1984. *Adult Female Offenders and Institutional Programs: A State of the Art Analysis.* Washington, D.C.: National Institute of Corrections.

Ryan, T., and J. Grassano. 1992. "Taking a Progressive Approach to Treating Female Offenders." *Corrections Today.* (August): 184–186.

Ryan, T., and K. McCabe. 1997. "A Comparative Analysis of Adult Female Offenders." *Corrections Today* 59, 4: 28–30.

Santana, A. 2000 (February 1). "Female Prison Ranks Double: Citing Study, Norton Plans Bills to Improve Conditions." *Washington Post.com,* http://washington-post.com/wp–srv/Wplate/2000–02/01/11 31–020100–idx.html.

Sargent, E., S. Marcos-Mendosa, and C. Ho Yu. 1993. "Abuse and the Woman Prisoner." In B. Fletcher, L. Shaver, and D. Moon, eds., *Women Prisoners: A Forgotten Population,* pp. 55–73. Westport, CT: Praeger.

Schafer, N., and A. Dellinger. 1999. "Jailed Parents: An Assessment." *Women and Criminal Justice* 10, 4: 73–91.

Scharf, P., and J. Hickey. 1981. "Ideology and Correctional Intervention: The Creation of a Just Prison Community." In P. Kratcoski, ed., *Correctional Counseling and Treatment,* pp. 409–422. Monterey, CA: Duxbury.

Schrag, C. 1944. *Social Types in a Prison Community.* Unpublished M.A. thesis, Department of Sociology, University of Washington, Seattle, WA.

Schrag, C. 1954. "Leadership Among Prison Inmates." *American Sociological Review* 19: 37–56.

Schrag, C. 1966. "A Preliminary Criminal Typology." *Pacific Sociological Review* 4: 11–39.

Schupak, J. 1986. "Women and Children First: An Examination of the Unique Needs of Women in Prison." *Golden Gate University Law Review* 16: 455–474.

Schweber, C. 1984. "Beauty Marks and Blemishes: The Coed Prison as a Microcosm of Integrated Society." *The Prison Journal* 64, 1: 3–15.

Scott, N., T. Hannum, and S. Gilchrist. 1982. "Assessment of Depression Among Incarcerated Females." *Journal of Personality Assessment* 46, 4: 372–379.

Selksky, D. 1980. *Assaults on Correctional Employees.* Albany, NY: Department of Correctional Services,.

Selling, L. 1931. "The Pseudo-family." *American Journal of Sociology* 37: 247–253.

Sewenely, A. 1993 (January 6). "Sex Abuse Charges Rock Women's Prison." *Detroit News,* p. B1.

Shaffer, E., C. Pettigrew, C. Gary, D. Blouin, and P. Edwards. 1983. "Multivariate Classification of Female Offender MMPI Profiles." *Journal of Crime and Justice* 6: 57–65.

Shaw, M. 1991. *Paying the Price. Federally Sentenced Women in Context.* Ottawa: Correctional Service of Canada.

Shaw, M. 1992. "Issues of Power and Control: Women in Prison and Their Defenders." *British Journal of Criminology* 32, 3: 438–452.

Shaw, M. 1993. "Reforming Federal Women's Imprisonment." In E. Adelberg and C. Curred, eds., *In Conflict with the Law: Women and the Canadian Justice System,* pp. 50–75. Vancouver, BC: Press Gang Publishers.

Showers, J. 1993. "Assessing and Remedying Parenting Knowledge Among Women Inmates." *Journal of Offender Rehabilitation* 20: 35–45.

Simmons, I. (Moyer). 1975. *Interaction and Leadership Among Female Prisoners.* Ph.D. dissertation, University of Missouri, Columbia, MO.

Simon, R. 1975. *Women and Crime.* Lexington, MA: Lexington Books.

Simon, R., and J. Landis. 1991. *The Crimes Women Commit and the Punishment They Receive.* Lexington, MA: Lexington Press.

Simpson, S. 1989. "Feminist Theory, Crime and Justice." *Criminology* 27, 4: 605–631.

Sims, A. 1992. "Women's Prisons: Their Social and Cultural Environment." *Federal Prisons Journal* 3, 1: 44–48.

Singer, M., J. Bussey, S. Li-Yu, and L. Lunghofer. 1995. "The Psychosocial Issues of Women Serving Time in Jail." *Social Work* 40, 1: 103–113.

Smart, C. 1976. *Women, Crime and Criminology: A Feminist Critique.* London: Routledge.

Smart, C. 1979. "The New Female Criminal: Reality or Myth?" *British Journal of Criminology* 19, 1: 50–57.

Smart, C. 1989. *Feminism and the Power of Law.* London: Routledge.

Smart, C. 1995. *Law, Crime and Sexuality.* London: Sage.

Smith, A. 1962. *Women in Prison: A Study in Penal Methods.* London: Stevens.

Smith, B. 1995. *A Vision Beyond Survival: A Resource Guide for Incarcerated Women.* Washington D.C.: National Women's Law Center.

Smith, B., and N. Waring. 1991. "The AIDS Epidemic: Impact on Women Prisoners in Massachusetts—An Assessment with Recommendations." *Women and Criminal Justice* 2, 2 : 117–43.

Smith, D., and R. Paternoster. 1987. "The Gender Gap in Theories of Deviance: Issues and Evidence." *Journal of Research in Crime and Delinquency* 24: 140–172.

Smith, D., and C. Visher. 1980. "Sex and Involvement in Deviance/Crime: A Quantitative Review of the Empirical Literature." *American Sociological Review* 45: 691–701.

Smykla, J., and J. Williams. 1996. "Co-Corrections in the United States of America, 1970–1999: Two Decades of Disadvantages for Women Prisoners." *Women and Criminal Justice* 8, 1: 61–76.

Snell, T. 1992. *Women in Jail: 1989. Special Report.* Washington, DC: U.S. Department of Justice, Bureau of Justice Statistics.

Snell T. 1994. *Women in Prison: Survey of State Prison Inmates, 1991. Special Report.* Washington D.C.: U.S. Department of Justice, Bureau of Justice Statistics.

Snell, T. 1995. *Correctional Populations in the United States. 1992.* Washington, DC: U.S. Department of Justice, Bureau of Justice Statistics.

Sommers, I., and D. Baskin. 1992. "Sex, Race, Age and Violent Offending." *Violence and Victims* 7, 3: 191–201.

South, S., and S. Messner. 1986. "The Sex Ratio and Women's Involvement in Crime: A Cross-National Analysis." *The Sociological Quarterly* 28, 2: 171–188.

Spaulding, E. 1923. *An Experimental Study of Psychopathic Delinquent Women.* New York: Rand McNally.

Stanton, A. 1980. *When Mothers Go to Jail.* Lexington, MA: Lexington Books.

Steffensmeier, D. 1980. "Assessing the Impact of the Women's Movement on Sex–Based Differences in the Handling of Adult Criminal Defendants." *Crime and Delinquency* 26: 344–357.

Steffensmeier, D. 1983. "Sex Differences in the Patterns of Adult Crime: 1965–1977." *Social Forces* 58, 4: 1080–1109.

Steffensmeier, D., J. Kramer, and C. Streifel. 1993. "Gender and Imprisonment Decisions." *Criminology* 31, 3: 411–445.

Steffensmeier, D., and R. Steffensmeier. 1980. "Trends in Female Delinquency." *Criminology* 18: 62–85.

Stohr, M., N. Lovrich, and G. L. Mays. 1997. "Service v. Security Focus in Training Assessments: Testing Gender Differences Among Women's Jail Correctional Officers." *Woman and Criminal Justice* 9, 1: 65–85

Strickland, K. 1976. *Correctional Institutions for Women in the U.S.* Lexington, MA: Lexington Books.

Sultan, F., and G. Long. 1988. "Treatment of the Sexually/Physically Abused Female Inmate: Evaluation of an Intensive Short–Term Intervention Program." *Journal of Offender Counseling, Services and Rehabilitation* 12, 1: 131–143.

Sultan, F., G. Long, S. Kefer, D. Schrum, J. Selby, and L. Calhoun. 1984. "The Female Offender's Adjustment to Prison Life: A Comparison of Psychodidactic and Traditional Supportive Approaches to Treatment." *Journal of Offender Counseling, Services and Rehabilitation* 9, 1: 49–56.

Sykes, G. 1958. *The Society of Captives.* Princeton, NJ: Princeton University Press.

Sykes, G., and S. Messinger. 1960. "The Inmate Social System." In R. Cloward, ed., *Theoretical Studies in the Social Organization of the Prison,* pp. 5–19. New York: Social Science Research Council.

Szockyi, E. 1989. "Working in a Man's World: Women Correctional Officers in an Institution for Men." *Canadian Journal of Criminology* 31: 319–327.

Tappan, P. 1947. *Delinquent Girls in Court.* New York: Columbia University Press.

Taylor, B. 1982. *Sexual Inequities Behind Bars.* Ph.D. dissertation, Claremont Graduate School, Claremont, CA.

Taylor, C. 1968. "A Search Among Borstal Girls for the Psychological and Special Significance of Their Tatoos." *British Journal of Criminology* 8: 170–185.

Taylor, C. 1993. *Girls, Gangs and Drugs.* East Lansing, MI: Michigan State University Press.

Teplin, L., K. Abrams, and G. McClelland. 1996. "Prevalence of Psychiatric Disorders Among Incarcerated Women." *Archives of General Psychiatry* 53, 2: 505–512.

Thomas, W. I. 1937. *The Unadjusted Girl.* Boston: Little, Brown.

Tittle, C. 1969. "Inmate Organization: Sex Differentiation and Influence of Criminal Subcultures." *American Sociological Review* 34: 492–505.

Tittle, C. 1973. "Institutional Living and Self Esteem." *Social Problems* 20, 4: 65–77.

Tjaden, P., and C. Tjaden. 1981. "Differential Treatment of the Female Felon: Myth or Reality?" In M. Warren, ed., *Comparing Male and Female Offenders,* pp. 73–89. Newbury Park, CA: Sage.

Toch, H. 1975. *Men in Crisis.* Chicago: Aldine-Atherton.

Toch, H. 1977. *Living in Prison.* New York: Free Press.

Toigo, R. 1962. "Illegitimate and Legitimate Cultures in a Training School for Girls." *Rip Van Winkle Clinic Proceedings* 13: 3–29.

Town, R., and C. Snow. 1980. "Women: The Forgotten Prisoners: *Glover versus Johnson.*"

In G. Alpert, *Legal Rights of Prisoners,* pp. 195–216. Newbury Park, CA: Sage.

Uniform Crime Reports, 1988. Washington D.C.: Federal Bureau of Investigation.

Uniform Crime Reports, 1995. Washington D.C.: Federal Bureau of Investigation.

Uniform Crime Reports, 1998. Washington D.C.: Federal Bureau of Investigation.

Uniform Crime Reports, 1999. Washington D.C.: Federal Bureau of Investigation.

van de Warker, E. 1875/1876. "The Relations of Women to Crime." *Popular Science Monthly* 8: 1–16.

Van Ochten, M. 1993. "Legal Issues and the Female Offender." In American Correctional Association, ed., *Female Offenders: Meeting the Needs of a Neglected Population,* pp. 31–36. Laurel, MD: American Correctional Association.

van Wormer, K. 1976. *Sex Role Behavior in a Women's Prison: An Ethological Analysis.* San Francisco: R & E Research Associates.

van Wormer, K. 1979. "Study of Leadership Roles in an Alabama Prison for Women." *Human Relations* 32, 9: 793–801.

van Wormer, K. 1987. "Female Prison Families: How Are They Dysfunctional?" *International Journal of Comparative and Applied Criminal Justice* 11: 263–271.

Vedder, C., and D. Somerville. 1970. *The Delinquent Girl.* Springfield, IL: Charles C. Thomas.

Velimesis, M. L. 1981. "Sex Roles and Mental Health of Women in Prison." *Professional Psychology* 12, 1: 128–135.

Veysey, B. 1998. "Specific Needs of Women Diagnosed with Mental Illnesses in U.S. Jails." In B. Levin, A. Blanch, and A. Jennings, eds., *Women's Mental Health Sources: A Public Health Perspective,* pp. 368–389. Thousand Oaks, CA: Sage.

Veysey, B., K. DeCou, and L. Prescott. 1998. "Effective Management of Female Jail Detainees with Histories of Physical and Sexual Abuse." *American Jails* 12 (May/June): 50–54.

Viadro, C. I., and J. Earp. 1991. "AIDS Education and Incarcerated Women: A Neglected Opportunity." *Women and Health* 17: 105–117.

Vigilante, K., M. Flynn, P. Afflect, J. Stunkle, N. Merriman, T. Flanigand, A. Mitty, and J. Rich. 1999. "Reduction in Recidivism of Incarcerated Women Through Primary Care, Peer Counseling and Discharge Planning." *Journal of Women's Health* 8, 3: 409–415.

Wallace, B. 1995. "Women and Minorities in Treatment." In A. Washton, ed., *Psychotherapy and Substance Abuse,* pp. 470–491. New York: Guilford.

Ward, D., and G. Kassebaum. 1965. *Women's Prison: Sex and Social Structure.* Chicago: Aldine-Atherton.

Watson, T. 1992 (November 16). "Georgia Indictments Charge Abuse of Female Inmates." *USA Today,* p. A3.

Watterson, K. 1973. *Women in Prison: Inside the Concrete Womb.* New York: Doubleday.

Watterson, K. 1996. *Women in Prison: Inside the Concrete Womb.* Boston: Northeastern University Press.

Webb, G., and D. Morris. 1980. "Prison Guard Conceptions." In B. Crouch, ed., *The Keepers: Prison Guards and Contemporary Corrections,* pp. 160–174. Springfield, IL: Charles C. Thomas.

Weidensall, J. 1916. *The Mentality of the Criminal Woman.* Baltimore: Warwick and York.

Weis, R. 1997. "Camp Dismas." In C. Blinn, *Maternal Ties: A Selection of Programs for Female Offenders,"* pp. 141–151. Lanham, MD: American Correctional Association.

Weisheit, R. 1984. "Women and Crime: Issues and Perspectives." *Sex Roles* 11, 7/8: 567–580.

Weisheit, R. 1985. "Trends in Programs for Female Offenders: The Use of Private Agencies as Service Providers." *International Journal of Offender Therapy and Comparative Criminology* 29, 1: 35–42.

Weisheit, R., and S. Mahan. 1988. *Women, Crime, and Criminal Justice.* Cincinnati, OH: Anderson.

Weisheit, R., and L. Parsons. 1986. "Problems Facing Women in Local Jails." In D. Kalinich and J. Klofas, eds., *Sneaking Inmates Down the Alley,* pp. 101–114. Springfield, IL: Charles C. Thomas.

Welch, M. 1997. "Regulating the Reproduction and Morality of Women: The Social Control of Body and Soul." *Women and Criminal Justice* 9, 1: 17–38.

Welle, D., and G. Falkin. 2000. "The Everyday Policing of Women with Romantic Codefendants: An Ethnographic Perspective." *Women and Criminal Justice* 11, 2: 45–65.

Welle, D., G. Falkin, and N. Jainchill. 1998. "Current Approaches to Drug Treatment for Women Offenders: Project WORTH."

Journal of Substance Abuse Treatment 15, 2: 151–163.

Wellisch, J., M. Anglin, and M. Prendergast. 1993. "Treatment Strategies for Drug Abusing Women Offenders." In J. Inciardi, ed., *Drug Treatment and Criminal Justice.* Newbury Park, CA: Sage.

Wellisch, J., M. Prendergast, and M. Anglin. 1994. *Bureau of Justice Statistics Report: Drug Abusing Women Offenders: Results of a National Survey.* Washington D.C.: U.S. Department of Justice.

Wellisch, J., M. Prendergast, and M. Anglin. 1996. "Needs Assessment and Services for Drug-Abusing Women Offenders: Results from a National Survey of Community-Based Treatment Programs." *Women and Criminal Justice* 8, 1: 27–60.

West, R. 1988. "Jurisprudence and Gender." *The University of Chicago Law Review* 55, 1: 1–72.

Wheeler, P., R. Trammell, J. Thomas, and J. Findlay. 1989. "Persephone Chained: Parity or Equality in Women's Prisons?" *The Prison Journal* 69, 1: 88–102.

Widom, C. 1979. "Female Offenders: Three Assumptions About Self–Esteem, Sex-Role Identity and Feminism." *Criminal Justice and Behavior* 6, 4: 365–382.

Widom, C. 1989. "Child Abuse, Neglect, and Violent Criminal Behavior." *Criminology* 27, 2: 251–366.

Widom, Spatz C. 1996. "Childhood Sexual Abuse and Criminal Consequences." *Society* 33, 4: 47–53.

Wilbanks, W. 1986. "Are Female Felons Treated More Leniently by the Criminal Justice System?" *Justice Quarterly* 3, 4: 517–529.

Williams, W. 1983. "The Equality Crisis: Some Reflections on Culture, Courts, and Feminism." *Women's Rights Law Reporter* 7, 3: 175–200.

Willing, R. 1999 (April 21). "Babies Behind Bars: Coddling Cons or Aiding Them?" *USA Today,* pp. 15A–16A.

Wilson, N. K. 1980. "Styles of Doing Time in a Coed Prison." In J. Smykla, *Co-Corrections,* pp. 160–165. New York: Human Services Press.

Wilson, T. 1986. "Gender Differences in the Inmate Code." *Canadian Journal of Criminology* 28, 4: 397–405.

Wojda, R., and J. Rowe. 1997. *Women Behind Bars.* Lanham, MD: American Correctional Association.

Wooldredge, J., and K. Masters. 1993. "Confronting Problems Faced by Pregnant Inmates in State Prisons." *Crime and Delinquency* 39, 2: 195–203.

Worrall, A. 1990. *Offending Women*. London: Routledge.

Wright, K., and W. Saylor. 1991. "Male and Female Employees' Perceptions of Prison Work: Is There a Difference?" *Justice Quarterly* 8, 4: 505–524.

Yang, S. 1990. "The Unique Treatment Needs of Female Substance Abusers in Correctional Institutions: The Obligation of the Criminal Justice System to Provide Parity." *Medicine and Law* 9: 1018–1027.

Zaitzow, B. 1998. "Treatment Needs of Women in Prison." In T. Alleman and R. Gido, *Turnstile Justice: Issues in American Corrections*, p. 175. Upper Saddle River, NJ: Prentice-Hall.

Zalba, A. 1964. *Women Prisoners and Their Families*. Los Angeles: Delmar Press.

Zang, N., M. Morash, G. Paul, and R. Cherry. 1998. "Life Skills Programming for Women Offenders, Michigan Department of Corrections." In J. Morton, ed., *Complex Challenges, Collaborative Solutions: Programming for Adult and Juvenile Female Offenders*, pp. 173–187. Lanham, MD: American Correctional Association.

Zaplin, R. 1998a. *Female Offenders: Critical Perspectives and Effective Interventions*. Gaithersburg, MD: Aspen.

Zaplin, R. 1998b. "A Systems Approach to the Design and Implementation of a Day Program for Women Offenders." In J. Morton, ed., *Complex Challenges, Collaborative Solutions: Programming for Adult and Juvenile Female Offenders*, pp. 129–141. Lanham, MD: American Correctional Association.

Zedner, L. 1991. *Women, Crime and Custody in Victorian England*. Oxford: Clarendon Press.

Zimmer, L. 1986. *Women Guarding Men*. Chicago: University of Chicago Press.

Zimmer, L. 1989. "Solving Women's Employment Problems in Corrections: Shifting the Burden to Administrators." *Women and Criminal Justice* 1, 1: 55–79.

Zingraff, M. 1980. "Inmate Assimilation: A Comparison of Male and Female Delinquents." *Criminal Justice and Behavior* 7, 3: 275–292.

Zupan, L. 1986. "Gender–Related Differences in Correctional Officers' Perceptions and Attitudes." *Journal of Criminal Justice* 14: 349–361.

Zupan, L. 1992a. "Men Guarding Women: An Analysis of the Employment of Male Correctional Officers in Prisons for Women." *Journal of Criminal Justice* 20: 297–309.

Zupan, L. 1992b. "The Progress of Women Correctional Officers in All–Male Prisons." In I. Moyer, ed., *The Changing Roles of Women in the Criminal Justice System*, 2d ed., pp. 323–343. Prospect Heights, IL: Waveland Press.

TABLE OF CASES

Name Index

Subject Index